Instructor's Resource Manual for

THE AMERICAN PROMISE

SECOND COMPACT EDITION

SARAH E. GARDNER
Mercer University

Bedford/St. Martin's   Boston ◆ New York

For information, write: Bedford/St. Martin's, 75 Arlington Street, Boston MA 02116
(617-399-4000)

ISBN: 0-312-40548-0

PREFACE

This manual draws upon my experiences teaching with the first edition of *The American Promise*. Intended to help make your American survey course as successful as possible, it offers chapter-by-chapter suggestions and resources for teaching with *The American Promise*, Second Compact Edition. The manual includes the following features to help you make the most of your course.

Features

An outline of each chapter in the form of thematic questions offers a quick overview of the chapter's contents for easy reference and acts as a starting point for class discussions.

Three detailed lecture strategies for each chapter provide flexible approaches to teaching the chapter's major themes and events. Each suggests ways to use the textbook's images, boxed features, and maps to illustrate or reinforce points in the narrative and to provoke discussion. (Please note that all of the maps and many of the images referenced in these lectures are provided as transparencies or on CD-ROM for classroom use.) Each strategy also includes suggestions for incorporating selections from *Reading the American Past: Selected Historical Documents*, Second Edition, an inexpensive primary-source reader that works very well with *The American Promise*. (Please note that the chapter numbering in *The American Promise*, Second Compact Edition, is one ahead of the chapter numbering in *Reading the American Past*, Second Edition. For example, documents that relate to the content of Chapter 2 in *The American Promise*, Second Compact Edition, are found in Chapter 1 of *Reading the American Past*, Second Edition.)

"Anticipating Student Reactions" discusses common misunderstandings that new students of American history bring to class and addresses topics that students frequently find difficult to grasp. It points to ways in which instructors can debunk misconceptions, complicate generalizations, clarify topics, and, in general, incite students into active thinking about history.

"Using the Bedford Series in History and Culture and the Historians at Work Series" offers ideas for complementing the text with in-depth reading on topics treated in Bedford/St. Martin's highly regarded primary-source series. Suggestions are updated to include recently published titles. Overviews of selected volumes from these series are provided with notes on how they fit into the survey course. Wherever appropriate, titles in Bedford's Cultural Editions series from Bedford's literature list are also noted. For further guidance in using the series books, *Using the Bedford Series in History and Culture in the U.S. History Survey*, Second Edition, at <www.bedfordstmartins.com/usingseries>, a short online guide by Scott Hovey (Boston University), gives practical suggestions for teaching in the U.S. survey classroom with more than sixty volumes from the Bedford Series in History and Culture and the Historians at Work series.

"Lecture Supplements and Classroom Activities" offer suggestions for classroom activities that will engage students, such as debates and simulations based on important topics in the text. A subsection on **Historical Contingencies** is designed to stretch students' historical imagination and impress on them the conditional nature of history, unseating the notion that history moves forward as a predetermined sequence of events. Another subsection offers suggestions for **Using Multimedia Sources in the Classroom** such as documentaries and Hollywood films. A new subsection on **Using the Internet** includes advice on relevant Internet sources for the classroom and out-of-class assignments.

Ten to fifteen multiple-choice questions — with an answer key — make it easy to generate informal quizzes, oral or written. In addition to testing students' comprehension of the narrative and chronology, questions address the chapter's boxed features, a map, an illustration, or a selection from *Reading the American Past: Selected Historical Documents,* Second Edition. Several outline maps, identical to those in the text but with place names omitted, are provided with suggested identification questions. These maps can be photocopied to hand out for pop quizzes.

"Proposing More," a brief bibliography for instructors who want to emphasize recent scholarship, provides a list of relevant secondary readings on chapter topics.

Essay Questions that cover content from several chapters allow instructors to test students' ability to integrate material and think analytically.

Discussing **The American Promise:** *A Survival Guide for First-Time Teaching Assistants,* by Michael A. Bellesiles (Emory University), appears at the back of this manual. This unique resource supplements the instructors' materials with concrete advice on teaching with *The American Promise,* Second Compact Edition; working with professors; overcoming problems with students; running discussion sections; designing assignments; grading tests and papers; relating dissertation work to classroom teaching; overcoming common problems; and more.

Sample Syllabi, which appear in Appendix II of this manual, offer suggestions for structuring survey courses using *The American Promise,* Second Compact Edition, and supplemental Bedford/St. Martin's texts. Syllabi are included for quarter schools, semester schools, and for the one-semester survey.

Also Available with **The American Promise,** *Second Compact Edition*

This manual serves as the keystone to the comprehensive collection of ancillaries available for *The American Promise,* Second Compact Edition. These ancillaries provide an integrated support system for veteran teachers, first-time TAs, and instructors who lecture to large classes. Suggestions for incorporating many of the ancillaries can be found throughout this manual.

For Instructors

Online Instructor's Resource Manual at <www.bedfordstmartins.com/roarkcompact>. The Online Instructor's Resource Manual combines all of the advantages of the print Instructor's Resource Manual along with links for Using the Internet exercises, annotated Web links for each chapter, PowerPoint slides for lectures, syllabus hosting, and the ability to track student work.

Computerized Test Bank CD-ROM for Windows or Macintosh. This thoroughly revised test bank by Valerie Hinton (Richland College) and Norman C. McLeod (Dixie State College) provides easy-to-use software to create and administer tests on paper or over a network. Instructors can generate exams and quizzes from the print test bank or write their own. A grade-management function helps keep track of student progress. It includes for each chapter in the text fifty multiple-choice questions, ten short-answer questions, four essay questions (all ranked as easy, medium, or difficult); an exercise in which students match important terms with definitions or examples; a chronology exercise; and a multipart map exercise. Answers for objective questions are provided. Also included are twenty-eight black outline map quizzes.

Map Transparencies. Full-color transparencies of full-size maps from both the full and compact editions of *The American Promise* help instructors present the materials and teach students important map-reading skills.

Instructor Resources CD-ROM. This new CD-ROM offers all the maps and figures and numerous illustrations from the text in Microsoft PowerPoint-ready files designed to enhance class presentations.

Using the Bedford Series in the U.S. History Survey at <www.bedfordstmartins.com/usingseries>. This short guide by Scott Hovey (Boston University) gives practical suggestions for using more than sixty volumes from the Bedford Series in History and Culture and the Historians at Work Series with a core text in the survey classroom. The guide not only supplies links between the text and the supplements but also provides ideas for starting discussions focused on a single primary-source volume.

Map Central at <www.bedfordstmartins.com/mapcentral>. Bedford/St. Martin's is proud to announce Map Central, a database of more than 450 maps that appear in *The American Promise* and its other history survey texts. Designed to help instructors create more effective lecture presentations, Map Central is easily searchable by specific chapter or by keyword. Maps are in full color and downloadable for use in PowerPoint or other presentation software.

Videos. Available to all adopters of the text are segments drawn from the award-winning telecourse "Shaping America," developed and distributed by the LeCroy Center for Educational Telecommunications, Dallas County Community College District. Bedford/St. Martin's is proud to announce that *The American Promise: To 1877,* Second Edition, has been selected for use in this distinguished long-distance learning program.

e-Content for Online Learning. e-Content for Online Learning helps instructors using *The American Promise,* Second Compact Edition, develop custom Web sites with WebCT, Blackboard, and other course-building systems.

For Students

***Reading the American Past: Selected Historical Documents,* Second Edition.** This highly regarded primary-source collection, edited by Michael Johnson (Johns Hopkins University), one of the authors of *The American Promise,* complements the textbook by offering 4 or 5 documents for each chapter. The new edition provides a host of compelling features while retaining its low cost and brevity: a rich selection of over 125 documents (one-quarter of them new to this edition), balancing accounts by well-known figures with the voices of ordinary people; a wide array of sources that vividly illustrate the diversity of materials with which historians work; and user-friendly editorial apparatus such as chapter introductions, headnotes, questions, and an Introduction for Students on the goals and methods of source analysis.

Online Study Guide at <www.bedfordstmartins .com/roarkcompact>. For each chapter, our free Online Study Guide offers an initial multiple-choice test that allows students to assess their comprehension of the material and a Recommended Study Plan that suggests specific exercises on the subject areas students still need to master. Two follow-up multiple-choice tests per chapter help students judge their command of the material. Additional exercises encourage students to think about chapter themes as well as

help them develop skills of analysis. Password-protected reports for instructors allow them to monitor students' activity easily.

The Bedford Series in History and Culture. Over fifty American titles in this highly praised series combine first-rate scholarship, historical narrative, and important primary documents for undergraduate courses. Each book is brief, inexpensive, and focused on a specific topic or period. Package discounts are available.

Historians at Work Series. Brief enough for a single assignment yet substantive enough to provoke thoughtful discussion, each volume in this series combines the best thinking about an important historical issue with helpful learning aids. Selections by distinguished historians, each with a differing perspective, provide a unique structure within which to examine a single question. With headnotes and questions to guide their reading and the complete original footnotes, students are able to engage in discussion that captures the intellectual excitement of historical research and interpretation. Package discounts are available.

Links Library at <www.bedfordstmartins.com/ historylinks>. Links Library is a searchable database of more than 350 carefully reviewed and annotated U.S. and Western history links by historical topic area and textbook chapter.

Acknowledgments

Working on this project has fostered a new sense of creativity in my pedagogical approach and renewed my enthusiasm for teaching survey courses. I have tried to offer innovative and relevant suggestions to spark students' interest in (dare I say passion for) American history. Brianna Germain, my editor at Bedford/St. Martin's, has made my work on this instructor's manual a pleasure. Her helpful suggestions and well-founded criticisms have surely strengthened this volume. I would also like to thank Elizabeth Welch, Senior Development Editor, for convincing me to take on this project. The production staff and the authors of the textbook have saved me from embarrassing factual errors and awkward phrasings and have turned a sheaf of papers into a handsome volume. For that, and much more, I thank them.

— Sarah E. Gardner
Macon, Georgia

CONTENTS

BEFORE THE WRITTEN RECORD

ANCIENT AMERICA TO 1492

1

Outlining Chapters: Thematic Questions

I. What commonalities do the disciplines of archaeology and history share? In what ways do they differ? What can archaeologists tell us about ancient America? What can't they tell us?

II. What developments allowed for ancient Asian migration to the Western Hemisphere? Who were the first Americans?
A. What were the origins of ancient Asian migration to the Western Hemisphere?
B. How did Paleo-Indians live, and how did environmental changes and crises engender changes in their way of life?

III. When was the era of the Archaic hunters and gatherers, and what distinguishes them from Paleo-Indians?
A. In what ways did the Great Plains bison hunters form a link between the cultures of the Paleo-Indians?
B. How did the diversity of environments affect the peoples living in the Great Basin area?
C. How did the plentiful resources of the Pacific Coast permit a large and dense population to thrive without agriculture?
D. How did the Eastern Woodland peoples live, and how did the introduction of agriculture and pottery affect their lives?

IV. How and why did the Archaic cultures make the transition from being nomadic hunter-gatherers to being cultures that increasingly relied on agriculture and permanent settlements?
A. Why did southwestern cultures adopt corn, and how did the establishment of corn-based agriculture affect their societies? How do archaeologists and anthropologists characterize the southwestern cultures?
B. What do the mounds and chiefdoms of the Eastern Woodland and Mississippian cultures reveal about the people that built them?

V. On the eve of Columbus's arrival, what were the primary major Native American cultures in North America? What similarities united these diverse American cultures?

VI. How extensive and powerful was the Mexican (Aztec) empire? How was Mexican society structured?

Teaching with The American Promise, *Second Compact Edition:* Lecture Strategies

LECTURE 1

An Introduction to the Discipline of History

Because archaeological and anthropological evidence inform much of this chapter, you may want to take the time in this first lecture to introduce to your students the discipline of history, explore why it is worth the effort of study, and discuss how it differs from other disciplines. History is generally document-based; archaeology focuses on recovering and interpreting artifacts; historical anthropology frequently uses narratives to understand social arrangements of past civilizations. You can use the creation stories "The Woman Who Fell from the Sky" and the account from Genesis (both in the documents reader) to start a discussion of how legends can reflect a culture's interpretation of its past and what type of information can be gleaned from such legends. To examine differences between archaeology and anthropology, compare the creation narratives with the story of George McJunkin's discovery of the Folsom Bone Pit, described in the chapter's opening vignette. To show the differences between history and archaeology, point out that the story of the Bone Pit's discovery is history, whereas the use of the artifacts found in the pit to discern information about the past is archaeology. Use the chapter's photos of artifacts alongside the documents (in the documents reader) to explore the ways in which scholars reconstruct the past through material culture, legends, and narratives written about similar events in later years. End by asking students if they see limits to history as a discipline. Do preliterate societies have histories?

LECTURE 2

The Peopling of Prehistoric America and the Diversity of North American Culture

The first part of this lecture should focus on the geography of immigration. Using the maps in the text, show how the land bridge between Asian Siberia and American Alaska, referred to as Beringia, allowed small bands of hunters to migrate to the Western Hemisphere. Demonstrate that a single small group, reproducing, could have populated the Americas in a single millennium while following herds of mammoth, which had never previously encountered human predators. You may also want to cover the physical geography and topography of the Western Hemisphere at this point. Explore the extent of glaciation during the Wisconsin period and the shifts in the ecological balance once this period ended. Confront the misconceptions of the "noble savage" when discussing the extinction of the mammoths. You may also want to bring into perspective the short span of recorded history compared with the length of time that humans have populated the Western Hemisphere.

You might want to continue this lecture by asking students to identify prevalent stereotypes of Native Americans and confronting the myth of the Plains Indian culture as the prototypical indigenous culture. Use this exercise to move to a discussion of the development of cultural diversity based on food sources. The extinction of the mammoths 11,000 years ago forced humans to scavenge for whatever type of food existed in their general vicinity. These food sources reflect the availability of water and the general climate and location of the area. Discuss each of the cultural regions presented in the textbook: how the people lived, how populous they were, and how they evolved. Note the transition of a culture from strictly hunting to hunting and gathering to the inclusion of migratory or sedentary agriculture. Have students discuss whether the notion of "progress" is applicable to early Native American societies. Here, you may want to confront the common misconception that these cultures were "less civilized," or the people less intelligent, than those of today. Use the image (found in many movies) of a prehistoric person plucked from his or her time and place and forced to deal with modern American society. Ask your students how they think they would fare if removed from the culture in which they are embedded. Then ask them to define the word *civilized*. Apply some of their standards to North American cultures of the Archaic period. Be sure to mention the Mississippian and Anasazi cultures, and ask whether they meet the criteria established by the class. (You may want to direct students to the spot map "Major Mississippian Mounds, A.D. 800–1500," to help them think about this question.)

Anticipating Student Reactions: Common Misconceptions and Difficult Topics

1. Dinosaurs and Humans Coexisted

No matter how informed your class may be, some students may have the impression, strongly developed by Hollywood, that humans and dinosaurs coexisted. The best time to dispel this fallacy is as soon as you start to discuss the first Americans as mammoth hunters. Mammoths were large and are now extinct, but here their similarity to dinosaurs ends. Mammoths were mammals, just like the other large animals of this geological era.

2. The Lack of Civilization in the Ancient World

Students frequently equate "old" with backward and undeveloped. It is important to point out not only the great diversity of Native American cultures that developed during the Archaic period but also the high degree of sophistication attained by some of these cultures. While some of the hunter-gatherer cultures, such as those of the Pacific Coast, demonstrated the social stratification indicative of a well-developed society, those cultures that made the transition to sedentary agriculture to support large populations — for instance, the Mississippian and Southwestern cultures — had to create sophisticated social systems to maintain themselves.

3. The Noble Savage — From Rousseau to James Fenimore Cooper

Western writers have portrayed Native Americans' behavior as unrealistically exalted and noble. The modern version of this myth tends to feature Native American cultures as ecologically sound or nonviolent. Point out that this myth reflects implicit (and invites explicit) comparison with, reaction against, or apology for European behavior on coming to the Americas. When presenting the transition from the Paleo-Indian era, be sure to point out that scholars suspect overhunting to have played a major role in the extinction of their primary food source (the mammoth). You may also want to suggest that violent death and intertribal warfare for hunting-and-gathering territory played a role in reducing Native American life expectancy.

4. The Plains Indian as the Prototypical Native American

Most of your students will be aware that movies offer fictional representations, fraught with factual errors. Nonetheless, your students may have internalized the oft-repeated Hollywood depiction of Native Americans as people with tepees who chase buffalo from horseback. An emphasis on the diversity of cultures in North America will best dispel this error. Specifically, you may want to remind students that the ancient horses that had once existed in the Western Hemisphere were extinct. Native Americans were not reintroduced to horses until Europeans brought them in the late fifteenth century.

Lecture Supplements and Classroom Activities

Using Multimedia Sources in the Classroom

You might consider showing Episode 1, "Seeking the First Americans," from the *Odyssey I* series, produced and distributed by PBS. This first episode follows archaeologists from Alaska to Texas as they search for clues to the identity of the earliest inhabitants of North America.

Historical Contingencies

Have students imagine, "What if ancient Asian migration to the Western Hemisphere had not occurred?" Would the land have existed in some sort of "pristine" condition until the arrival of Europeans in the fifteenth century? How might the Western Hemisphere have evolved? What might the Europeans have found when they arrived in the New World?

Classroom Activities

To impress on your students that meaning is contingent, have them consider the photographs of various artifacts presented in the first chapter (you might want to use the images found on the Instructor's Resources CD) and offer their interpretations of the significance of those artifacts. Remind them that scholars often disagree on the meaning of these artifacts, and so, as the textbook notes, much of what is written about ancient America is open to debate. This discussion should suggest to students that the study of history is more than the mere recitation of facts. Facts have meaning, and meaning is always contentious.

You might have students consider the long history of ancient America. Have them map on a time line the persistence of the Paleo-Indians — during the period of the Archaic hunters and gatherers. Students should be sure that they mark when corn cultivation began in Central America and in the American Southwest, when Woodlands burial mounds appeared, and when the Anasazi first began to build cliff dwellings and pueblos. Have them then mark the time that has elapsed since the arrival of Columbus. The length of the time line before the arrival of Columbus should impress on them the long scope of ancient America.

Using the Internet

Students interested in learning more about Mexican cultures can turn to a Web site managed by the Richard Stockton College of New Jersey. The Global History Consortium makes available a "virtual research institute" for Central and South America. Direct your students to <http://loki.stockton.edu/~gilmorew/consorti/index.html>.

ASSESSING RESULTS
Multiple-Choice Questions

1. Prior to George McJunkin's discovery of the Folsom Bone Pit, scientists believed Native Americans inhabited the New World for
   a. 3,000–4,000 years.
   b. 5,000–10,000 years.
   c. 10,000–20,000 years.
   d. over 25,000 years.

2. What convinced skeptics that Native Americans inhabited the Western Hemisphere more than 10,000 years ago?
   a. anthropological interpretations of Native American origin stories
   b. carbon dating of fossilized human feces from caves in Utah
   c. the detection of a spearhead stuck in the bones of a giant bison discovered near Folsom, New Mexico
   d. the geological discovery of the melting of the Wisconsin glaciers

3. How do scientists believe the earliest peoples came to the Western Hemisphere?
   a. Polynesian adventurers sailed to the coast of Peru on rafts made of balsa wood.
   b. Ancient sailors floated across the Bering Strait seeking trade and commerce.

c. Hunters from Asia walked over a land connection nearly 1,000 miles wide.
   d. Farmers rode their horses through the tundra seeking better climates for their crops.

4. The era of Paleo-Indians ended because
   a. climatic changes helped cause the extinction of large mammals they hunted.
   b. diseases ravaged a society without natural immunities.
   c. migration over large distances ended their common culture.
   d. a new wave of settlers forced them to leave their traditional lands.

5. What Native American cultural group built canoes?
   a. Northwest peoples
   b. Iroquoian peoples
   c. Arctic peoples
   d. buffalo-hunting peoples

6. What ultimately caused the failure of the Mexican empire?
   a. Its social structure, with priests at the top, left the empire incapable of dealing with military emergencies.
   b. Its reliance on human sacrifice reduced the number of young men it could force into its armies to fight invaders.
   c. Its insistence on payment of gold for tribute caused the economic collapse of its subject tribes.
   d. Its failure to create among its subjects a belief that Mexican domination was, at some level, legitimate and equitable caused resentment and feelings of oppression, a fact Spanish conquerors eventually discovered.

7. According to the Seneca origin narrative, reprinted in the documents reader, human beings arrived on earth after
   a. the daughter of the chief of heaven fell through a hole in the sky.
   b. the West Wind impregnated the god Othagwenda, who gave birth to a human.
   c. the god Djuskaha fashioned a human from the rocks on earth.
   d. Djuskaha killed his demigod brother, Othagwenda, and from his remains sprung a human.

8. When Europeans first encountered Native Americans,
   a. Native Americans had just started writing.
   b. Native Americans in different regions had nothing in common.

c. Native Americans in different regions had adapted to the natural environment in their region.

d. Native Americans had just begun practicing metallurgy.

9. Identify the correct sequence of historical events and artifacts.

a. Folsom points, bows and arrows, Clovis points

b. sedentary agriculture, hunters and gatherers, mound building

c. Pangaea, land bridge, Clovis points, glacial melting, agriculture

d. bows and arrows, corn cultivation in Central America, burial mounds, Clovis points

10. Identify the following on Map 1.2, "Native North American Cultures."

a. Poverty Point

b. Hopewell

c. Adena

d. Folsom

e. Anasazi

Proposing More: Additional Readings

James W. Hatch et al., "Hopewell Obsidian Studies: Behavioral Implications of Recent Sourcing and Dating Research," *American Antiquity* 55, no. 3 (1990): 461–79.

Calvin D. Howard, "The Clovis Point: Characteristics and Type Distinction," *Plains Anthropologist* 35, no. 129 (1990): 255–62.

Robert C. Mainfort Jr., "Adena Chiefdoms? Evidence from the Wright Mound," *Midcontinental Journal of Archaeology* 14, no. 2 (1989): 164–78.

Dean J. Saitta, "Power, Labor, and the Dynamics of Change in Chacoan Political Economy," *American Antiquity* 62, no. 1 (1997): 7–26.

Gregory Waselkov, "Prehistoric Agriculture in the Mississippi Valley," *Agricultural History* 51, no. 3 (1977): 513–19.

Answer Key to Multiple-Choice Questions: 1-a, 2-c, 3-c, 4-a, 5-b, 6-d, 7-a, 8-c, 9-c

2 EUROPEANS AND THE NEW WORLD

1492–1600

*O*utlining Chapters: Thematic Questions

I. What compelled Europeans to explore regions outside their own continent?
   A. Why was European trade largely confined to the Mediterranean during the twelfth through the fifteenth centuries? What demographic and technological changes set the stage for the Age of Exploration?
   B. How did the Portuguese initiate European exploration beyond the Mediterranean Sea to Africa, Asia, and the Americas?

II. How did Christopher Columbus precipitate a geographic revolution?
   A. What theories informed Columbus's thinking about the geography? How successful did Columbus's ventures prove to be for Spain?
   B. How did Europeans come to realize that America was not part of Asia?
   C. What was traded in the Columbian exchange? What were the costs and benefits, to both Indians and Europeans, of this exchange?

III. How did Spain create its empire in the Caribbean and in Central and South America?
   A. How did Hernán Cortés conquer the twenty-five-million-person Mexican (Aztec) empire with only six hundred soldiers?
   B. How did Cortés's success in Mexico spur further European exploration in the New World? How successful were these ventures?
   C. How did Spain govern its American territories, and how did the Spanish empire set a precedent for later North American colonies?
   D. What were the costs to Indian cultures and populations of Spanish conquest and colonization?
   E. What compelled Spain to establish colonies in Florida and New Mexico, and how successful were these colonies?

IV. How did Spain's New World colonies aid its political ambitions in Europe?
   A. What were Martin Luther's criticisms of the Catholic Church, and how did Spain's kings respond to them?
   B How did confiscated American riches contribute to the state of warfare in Europe and the deterioration of the lifestyle of ordinary Spaniards in the sixteenth century?
   C. What example did Spain's colonies set for other European nations' attempts to establish colonies in the New World?

Teaching with The American Promise, *Second Compact Edition: Lecture Strategies*

LECTURE 1

The Transition of Spain from the Periphery to the Center of European Politics

This first lecture could illustrate the interaction of social, political, cultural, and religious elements in the Old World that influenced Spanish colonization of the New World. Specifically, you could map out the peripheral status that the Iberian Peninsula held in Europe during the early-modern period, noting the rise of commercial exploration in Portugal and of a veteran soldier class in Spain. Yet within twenty-five years of discovery of the New World, the Spanish king won election as emperor of the Holy Roman Empire and funneled the massive wealth expropriated from the Americas into military and political campaigns in Europe to fend off further incursions by Muslim Turks and to root out the heresy of Martin Luther's Protestant Reformation. The wealth of the empire ironically led to the financial ruin of Spain, as inflation and taxation destroyed the value of local wealth, and as increasingly ambitious political maneuvering ultimately moved wealth into the hands of northern European merchants to finance the empire's costly wars. Be sure to illustrate that Spain's experience influenced other Western European nations at the periphery (principally France and England), to attempt to imitate that country's colonial empire. Draw your students' attention to Map 2.2 "New Spain in the Sixteenth Century," to demonstrate both the fervency with which Spain explored the New World and activities of the "latecomers" in the Americas.

LECTURE 2

The Authoritarian Native American Civilizations

Use this lecture to show the limits of Meso-American culture and society. Caribbean island societies were either not large enough or not centralized enough to resist domination by European invaders. The larger civilizations on mainland America, however, could have resisted had they been organized to do so. Both the Mexican (Aztec) and Incan emperors ruled with a heavy hand, and neither culture was much loved by those it controlled. The rulers of the Mexica captured surrounding groups to obtain tribute and human sacrifices, once sacrificing twenty thousand captives in a single day. The Incas of Peru, likewise, were unwelcome rulers who moved entire populations of their conquered neighbors into disparate, far-flung communities so that they could not unite and rebel. Counterbalance a discussion of the administrative and cultural achievements of these Native American empires with the human price they exacted on their subjugated peoples and the resentment such oppression engendered.

LECTURE 3

The Fruits of Empire

A third lecture could investigate the alterations of the New World as a result of the ongoing encounter with Spain. First, examine the legalism of Spanish society by exploring the *Requerimiento,* covered in the *Documenting the American Promise* feature. The justification for the conquests and the actual ways in which they were carried out expose the cavalier nature of Spain's colonizers. Second, explore the legal instruments of forced labor: the *encomienda* and the *repartimiento.* Third, discuss the effects of conquest on the indigenous peoples and the failure of dissent within Spanish society to alleviate those hardships. The exchange of diseases, livestock, and technology permanently altered the modes of living in the New World with rapid depopulation and the introduction of livestock farming. The mixture of pagan and Christian beliefs in the New World resulted from the incomplete spiritual conquest of America. The elimination of native populations on the Caribbean islands owing to brutal labor combined with exposure to alien diseases resulted in the introduction of African labor into American agriculture and mining and influenced all successive waves of European immigration. A stratified social hierarchy limited future economic growth as Spanish America defined itself racially to extract maximum booty for the coffers of the crown at the expense of the people of the Americas.

Anticipating Student Reactions: Common Misconceptions and Difficult Topics

1. The Flat Earth

Sailors of late-medieval/early-modern Europe did not believe the earth was flat, contrary to what many students may have learned in grade school. You may want to introduce this topic as you explain Columbus's efforts and failures to obtain financial backing for his westward exploration. Have students consider the relatively easy observations by which fifteenth-century sailors would have realized the earth was spherical by asking them how many have ever seen a sailboat go over the horizon. The sail disappears last, which indicates to the observer that the boat is traveling on something rounded or spherical. Columbus's financial backers were not concerned with the earth's shape but with the size of the earth and the estimated distance to Asia.

2. Guns Gave Spain a Technological Edge over the Native Americans

While the conquistadors did indeed have and use guns during their conquests of the New World, guns played a minor role at best. The gunpowder-operated weapons used during this age were neither accurate nor easy to manipulate. Mounted on supporting rods because of their weight, these weapons required that more than one person operate them, and bullets rarely hit their targets. They were more effective for the noise and smoke they made than for the enemy they killed or wounded. More important tactically was the presence of horses and war mastiffs, dogs bred and trained to kill people under battlefield conditions. Native Americans had never seen this type of warfare. The Spaniards' iron and steel armor and weaponry gave them a slight technological edge but were more important psychologically in advancing the idea that the Spanish represented powerful gods or were gods themselves. In the long run, the few Spanish who came to the New World as military conquerors achieved their ends as much through diplomacy as through warfare. They made alliances with the oppressed peoples subjugated to the authority of the controlling civilization, be it Mexican, Mayan, or Incan. In the longer run, diseases brought by the Spanish weakened the will of many to resist and killed many who would have resisted.

3. The Black Legend

La Leyenda Negra, "the Black Legend," of early-modern European history contends that Spain's conquests and empire building in the New World were solely episodes of barbarism, greed, exploitation, and human cruelty. As the textbook makes clear, there is more than a grain of truth to this interpretation of Spain's Century of Gold. But the legend itself is based on British nationalist propaganda attempting to explain why Spanish claims in the New World should be disregarded as contrary to international law and human morality. Spanish reformers attempting to force the crown to alleviate the suffering of Native Americans wrote the texts used in the propaganda, their own efforts at reform disproving the legend's claim that all Spanish were cruel and evil. The legend needs clarification: Spain was no worse than any other imperial European power of that age, and in the New World it created a version, but not an exact copy, of Spanish culture. Ask students to evaluate the excerpts in the documents reader. Why were Spanish friars collecting stories of Native American culture and history? What sort of respect did the priests have during the spiritual conquest for the local culture?

Using the Bedford Series in History and Culture and the Historians at Work Series: Suggestions

To encourage students to think about the establishment of a Spanish empire in the New World from the points of view of both the Spanish and the indigenous peoples, consider assigning *Victors and Vanquished: Spanish and Nahua Views of the Conquest of Mexico*, edited by Stuart B. Schwartz. To facilitate discussion of the factors that motivated Europeans to journey to the New World, you might consider assigning *Envisioning America: English Plans for the Colonization of North America, 1560–1640*, edited by Peter C. Mancall. This volume, which also works well in conjunction with Chapter 3, contains promotional literature designed to "sell" the establishment of British colonies in North America.

Lecture Supplements and Classroom Activities

Using Multimedia Sources in the Classroom

When discussing the Incan empire, consider showing Episode 3, "The Incas," of the *Odyssey I* documentary series, produced and distributed by PBS. This episode examines the sixteenth-century Incan empire through the work of three archaeologists. *Lost Kingdoms of the Maya,* available through the National Geographic Society, examines the ancient Mayan civilization of Central America. When discussing the arrival of Columbus, show *The Columbian Exchange* or *Columbus's World,* both available through Films for the Humanities. Finally, you might show *The New Found Land,* distributed by Zenger Films, which covers the reasons for the European migration to America.

You might also use clips of Hollywood films to address the nature of the changing legacy of Columbus's voyage. Films include *Christopher Columbus* (1985), starring Gabriel Byrne, and *1492: Conquest of Paradise* (1992), starring Gerard Depardieu and directed by Ridley Scott.

Historical Contingencies

Have students imagine alternatives to the conquistador mode of interaction with the Native Americans. Could peaceful exchange have been possible? What directions might the course of history have taken had a more peaceful interaction ensued?

Classroom Activities

Have your students discuss and debate the viability of the justifications for conquest. Be sure to incorporate the *Documenting the American Promise* feature here, which outlines the ways in which Spain developed an official justification of the conquest. Ask your students to identify the reasons Europeans gave for subjugating the native peoples of North and Central America. Did they have any legitimate reasons? Did Europeans register any doubts about their practice? If not, and if they had a few legitimate reasons for conquest, why do we find it so much easier today to condemn the conquest than Europeans in the sixteenth century did? Why is our perspective so different from theirs?

Using the Internet

You may want to direct your students to relevant Web sites. The site for the Library of Congress's "1492: An Ongoing Voyage" at <http://www.loc.gov/exhibits/1492> describes both pre- and postcontact America. The online exhibit includes images of twenty-two objects culled from over three hundred in the original exhibit; the objects represent six sections: "What Came to Be Called 'America,'" "The Mediterranean World," "Christopher Columbus: Man and Myth," "Inventing America," "Europe Claims America," and "Epilogue."

The site for the University of Virginia's "Exploring the West from Monticello: A Perspective in Maps from Columbus to Lewis and Clark" at <http://www.lib.virginia.edu/exhibits/lewis_clark/home.html> might also prove instructive. Tell students to click on "Novus Orbis: Images of the New World, 1507–1669" from the home page.

ASSESSING RESULTS
Multiple-Choice Questions

1. The *encomenderos* were the
    a. offspring of Spanish men and women living in the New World.
    b. missionaries sent to convert the Indians to Christianity.
    c. warriors given the powers of feudal lords over the indigenous peoples of Central America, commanding their labor while supposedly granting them protection.
    d. bureaucrats sent to gather the crown's fifth of the booty for taxes.

2. After the Spanish conquest of Mexico, the group with the highest social status was the
    a. *mestizos.*
    b. Indians.
    c. *creoles.*
    d. *peninsulares.*

3. The Treaty of Tordesillas of 1494
    a. established a boundary 1,100 miles west of the Canary Islands to define the spheres of Spanish and Portuguese possessions in the New World.
    b. prohibited the Portuguese from any territorial claim in the New World.
    c. established for the Spanish king legal claim to all the precious metals in the New World.
    d. prohibited Indian slavery in the New World.

4. The *repartimiento*
    a. justified the conquest and subjugation of the natives of the New World.

b. reformed the *encomienda* system by limiting the labor an *encomendero* could command from his Indians to forty-five days per year per adult male.

c. prevented the Portuguese from infringing on the territorial claims of the Spanish in the New World.

d. promoted the conversion of indigenous peoples to Christianity.

5. From the viewpoint of Spain, the single most important economic activity in New Spain after 1540 was
   a. gold mining.
   b. copper mining.
   c. silver mining.
   d. nickel mining.

6. The Columbian exchange was
   a. the gift of enslaved Taino Indians to the Spanish king and queen.
   b. the interchange of items common in Europe but rare or nonexistent in the Americas for items common in the Americas but rare or nonexistent in Europe.
   c. a commercial center in Spain named for the "discoverer" of America.
   d. the European method of taking native leaders captive to gain power.

7. African slavery was introduced to the New World by the
   a. Portuguese.
   b. Spanish.
   c. Dutch.
   d. English.

8. What position do the documents in the *Documenting the American Promise* feature support?
   a. The position that the Indians were well informed of what was expected of them, so they deserved the treatment they received.
   b. The position that no one cared about the Indians.
   c. The position that the Spaniards were unfairly authoritative and harsh with the Indians.
   d. The position that the Indians were dangerous.

9. What encouraged Western Europeans to take the risks of exploring outside of Europe?
   a. the westward displacement of peoples as Asiatic tribes invaded Eastern Europe
   b. the capture of Jerusalem by Muslims
   c. the Protestant Reformation started by Martin Luther
   d. the unstable society caused by rapid depopulation owing to the plague

10. Excerpted in the *Documenting the American Promise* feature, the *Requerimiento*, devised by King Ferdinand's advisers,
    a. lambasted the conquistadors for displaying "pride, . . . lust, . . . anger, . . . [and] sloth" in the New World.
    b. ordered the execution of all Spanish critics of royal policy in the New World.
    c. proclaimed to the Indians that failure to welcome Spanish conquest and all its blessings would result in death and that "the deaths and losses which shall accrue from this are your fault, and not that of their highnesses, or ours, or of these soldiers who come with us."
    d. instructed the conquistadors to tolerate the Indians' efforts to blend Christianity with their native religions.

11. The search for other Mexicos in the New World
    a. led the Spaniards to conclude that the inhabitants of present-day Florida, the Southwest and Great Plains of North America, and California had much wealth to loot and exploit.
    b. succeeded for the Spanish only with Francisco Pizarro's conquest of the Incan empire in Peru.
    c. failed to convince the Spaniards that enormous territories stretched northward in the New World.
    d. led to the establishment of numerous permanent Spanish settlements in much of present-day Central and North America.

12. Spain's example in the New World
    a. encouraged both France and England to venture overseas because great wealth could be found there.
    b. convinced no European powers that an empire in the Americas could make a major contribution to a nation's power and prestige in Europe.
    c. frightened other European powers from contesting Spain's dominance in Europe and the Americas.
    d. provided France and England with a model for settlements in North America that would be permanently sustainable.

13. Identify the correct sequence of historical events and figures.
    a. de Soto, Cabot, Balboa, Cortés
    b. Treaty of Tordesillas, Cape Verde, *repartimiento*, Protestant Reformation

   c. Cape of Good Hope, Cape Verde, Magellan, establishment of St. Augustine
   d. Columbus, Cortés, Pizarro, Frobisher

14. Identify the following on Map 2.3, New Spain in the Sixteenth Century"
   a. Treaty of Tordesillas boundary
   b. the Mexica empire at the time of conquest
   c. the Inca empire at the time of conquest
   d. St. Augustine
   e. Spanish conquests

PROPOSING MORE: Additional Readings

James Axtell, "The Moral Dimensions of 1492," *Historian* 56, no. 1 (1993): 17–28.

Mario D. Fenyo, "Columbus and All That: 'Discovery' and 'Expansion' in American Textbooks," *Perspectives: American Historical Association Newsletter* 14, no. 9 (1986): 14–16.

Francisco Guerra, "The European-American Exchange," *History and Philosophy of the Life Sciences* 115, no. 3 (1993): 313–27.

Wilbur R. Jacobs, "Columbus, Indians, and the Black Legend Hocus Pocus," *American Indian Culture and Research Journal* 17, no. 2 (1933): 175–87.

Ralph E. Vigil, "Bartolome De Las Casas, Judge Alonso de Zorita and the Franciscans: A Collaborative Effort for the Spiritual Conquest of the Borderlands," *Americas* 38, no. 1 (1981): 45–57.

Answer Key to Multiple-Choice Questions: 1-c, 2-d, 3-a, 4-b, 5-c, 6-b, 7-b, 8-d, 9-d, 10-c, 11-b, 12-a, 13-d

3 THE SOUTHERN COLONIES IN THE SEVENTEENTH CENTURY

1601–1700

*O*utlining Chapters: Thematic Questions

I. Why did England colonize the New World, and why did it choose to use a joint stock company as its agent?
   A. What were the various threats to the survival of early Jamestown?
   B. Why did Powhatan allow the English colony of Virginia to survive? Why did the colony fail to become self-supporting during its first fifteen years? What happened in 1622 that changed the relations between the Native Americans and the Jamestown colonists?
   C. Why did Virginia become a royal colony in 1624, and how did that event affect the institutions of the colony?

II. How did the introduction of tobacco into the Chesapeake region affect the Virginia colony?
   A. Why were colonists willing to grow tobacco when they had been reluctant to grow food crops?
   B. What factors prompted the development of a servant labor system in the Virginia colony? What was life like for indentured servants, and why did they come to the new colony? What legal restraints did masters impose on servants? Why did masters and servants tolerate this contentious arrangement?

III. How did Chesapeake society evolve within the tobacco political economy? What inequalities developed?
   A. How did the tobacco economy influence the patterns of settlement in the Chesapeake? What factors contributed to a lack of religious zeal in the Chesapeake? Why was Maryland founded, and how much did it differ from Virginia? What three developments altered the relative "frontier equality" of Chesapeake society after 1650?
   B. How did political structures and institutions amplify growing class divisions within Chesapeake society? What is mercantilism, and how did the English king profit from the tobacco trade?
   C. What was Bacon's Rebellion? How did it start, who were its supporters, what did the opposing sides represent, and what were its consequences?

IV. How did the British develop a slave labor society in the southern colonies of the North American mainland?
   A. Why was Barbados considered the jewel of the British West Indies? How extensive was slave labor in sugar production in the West Indies by 1700? Where did the slaves come from, and how did they live?
   B. What relation did Carolina have with the British West Indian colony of Barbados?
   C. How did a slave society develop in the Chesapeake between 1670 and 1700, and how did it differ from that of the West Indies? How did the slave labor system polarize Chesapeake society?

Teaching with The American Promise, *Second Compact Edition: Lecture Strategies*

LECTURE 1

The Process of British Colonization

In this first lecture you may want to stress the expectations the British held about colonization. Have your students consider the "promises" of colonization. Relate the ways in which those expectations led to the pattern that characterized most of the early British colonies. Explain that each colony obtained a charter from the king, recruited colonists, established a beachhead settlement, and forced the indigenous peoples to aid in their initial survival and later to relinquish land that the colonists desired. Then, referring back to Chapter 2, compare the process of English colonization with that of the Spanish in Central and South America. Neither group of colonizers included farmers in its initial wave, but both included soldiers and adventurers to aid in the conquest of new lands. Both groups used alliances with the natives to their advantage, and both could have been easily exterminated by the numerically superior local peoples. Unlike the Spanish, who were largely motivated by religion, the English colonists who settled in the south of the North American mainland and Caribbean were motivated chiefly by profit. The king was not directly involved in the initial risks of colonization in either the British or the Spanish empire. Compare colonization via joint stock companies with the use of the *encomienda* in

New Spain. Prepare your students for discussions (in later chapters) about American ideas regarding corporations by examining what it meant to put together a joint stock company. Finally, point out that unlike New Spain, where the traditions of agricultural production for domestic consumption already existed under the centralized Incan and Mexican empires conquered by the Spaniards, the English colonies in North America languished until they were able to develop successful export-oriented staple agriculture. The Caribbean colonies grew sugar, the Chesapeake grew tobacco, and Carolina grew rice. Describe the process of finding and exploiting a successful agricultural strategy.

LECTURE 2

From Servitude to Slavery in the Chesapeake

You can start this lecture by exploring the conditions of the tobacco boom that made servitude so widespread in the Chesapeake. Then describe the process of becoming an indentured servant, making clear that servitude was normal at that time. Show the brutality of the system and define the mortality rates for servants through the 1650s. Finally, talk about the shift to slave labor. There had been Africans in Virginia since 1619, but not all Africans were imported as slaves. A slave-for-life was more costly than a servant-for-a-period-of-years. Moreover, no one expected a servant to survive the term of contract. The cost of a slave was therefore an unnecessary expense. With the drop in mortality rates in the 1640s, slavery became more cost-effective. The Virginia authorities finally set laws defining slavery in 1660: Children of female slaves followed the matriarchal line into slavery, in contrast to the English tradition of inheritance following the male lineage. But African slaves were not imported in great numbers until the 1680s. Bacon's Rebellion partly explains the shift. Here, you will want the class to discuss Nathaniel Bacon's "Declaration" (in the documents reader). Other factors also help explain the shift. Demographic changes in England reduced the number of jobless seeking indenture as a desperate last chance. Also, the rise of other colonial destinations, without the Chesapeake's reputation for brutality, drew potential servants away from the Chesapeake. Make the point that indentured servitude continued to provide laborers in America until the American Revolution. In the South, however, a society based on slavery came into existence by 1700, with portions of the southern colonies having a larger slave population than free population.

LECTURE 3
Chesapeake and Carolina Societies Compared

Virginia and South Carolina were, and continue to be, very different places. Use a comparison of the two to discuss the racial composition and class origins of each colony. Although indentured servitude did exist in South Carolina, slavery, from the outset, became the major system of labor in the colony. Carolina was the only colony established by settlers from another colony rather than by settlers directly from Britain, and its social institutions reflected that origin. Like Barbados, the Caribbean island from which most of Carolina's colonists came, Carolina had a majority black population, often working in large groups on plantations isolated from the white masters, who resided in town. Virginia had a white majority; large plantations were much less predominant, and most masters worked beside their few slaves. Use the inventory of the yeoman planter's tobacco farm (in the documents reader) to discuss what a typical household might contain in the Chesapeake and compare it with the discussion of the settlement of Charleston in Carolina. The slave population in the Caribbean was not self-sustaining because of high mortality rates. It therefore depended on continuous imports from Africa. The Carolina slave population followed this pattern until the 1760s. Declining slave mortality rates in the Chesapeake allowed that population to reproduce itself by the 1720s. Among whites, Virginia did not create a self-replicating elite until the 1660s, when lesser nobles bought established plantations for their younger sons. Until that time, everyone was affected by high mortality rates. An elite was formed in Carolina from the beginning, with younger brothers and sons of Barbadian planters migrating to Carolina and establishing Barbadian culture there. For this lecture, have students refer to Map 3.1, "The Chesapeake Colonies in the Seventeenth Century," and Map 3.2, "The West Indies and Carolina in the Seventeenth Century."

Anticipating Student Reactions: Common Misconceptions and Difficult Topics

1. *The Earliest Immigrants Had the Best Chance of Obtaining Wealth and Position*

It is generally true that the first arrivals in a new colony somewhat arbitrarily decided on the rules of political participation and the protection of property. And they usually made these rules to their own advantage, and to subsequent colonists' detriment, to guarantee and perpetuate their status as the political and economic elite of the colony. But these general rules were tempered by two conditions in the Chesapeake and in other British colonies. First, not everyone was equal on arrival; some had greater wealth, distinction of ancestry, or simply better connections. Thus, some had better access to the decision-making process than others. Second, the death rate eliminated many influential families who helped make the initial rules. In Virginia, the grandees against whom Nathaniel Bacon railed became established not during the tobacco boom of the 1620s, when massive profits were possible and the first rules for consolidation of wealth were laid out, but in the 1660s, after two generations of entrepreneurial Virginians had died. With chances of survival increasing in the colonies after the 1640s, minor nobility in England started sending younger sons to purchase established plantations and buy their way into an existing system that guaranteed their establishment as the economic and political elite of the colony. Participants in Bacon's Rebellion were not only members of the lower classes fighting exploitation by the elite but also displaced middling planters who saw this recently imported elite as a challenge to their chances for social mobility. (Have students read the Bacon's Rebellion selection in the documents reader when discussing this topic.)

2. *Servitude Was an Abnormal Condition*

You may need to explain to students that servitude was a normal part of early-modern European and, by extension, early American society. It was common for men, women, and even children to be bound out for a period of time. It is important, however, to make clear that the seven-year indenture of the Chesapeake servants was abnormal within this social system of servitude. Such an indenture was similar to the apprenticing of orphans — lengthy periods of servitude with no legal requirements for the master to provide more than basic needs during the period of indenture. Also abnormal was the servant's lack of voice in choosing a master. The condition often approached that of slaves. Even "freedom dues" could be evaded by clever masters who offered or forced servants to take their freedom a few months early in exchange for renouncing the little food and clothing owed them at the end of their service. So, while servitude was commonplace in seventeenth-century society, the indentured servitude of the Chesapeake was unusually harsh. You can use the primary sources in the documents reader to give students an idea of what life was like for indentured servants. Have them read the yeoman planter's tobacco farm inventory (in the documents reader) to explore the household goods provided for servants in a typical setting. Also, look at the depositions of the "thieving servants" to discuss ways that servants resisted the brutal system of indentured labor and the punishment they expected when they were caught. Finally, students may be surprised to learn that these servants were usually their age or younger. The average age of Chesapeake servants was sixteen. In fact, most colonists were under the age of thirty, and in the "killing years" of Virginia's first decade, most were under twenty. Help students identify with colonists of every social class, but emphasize that servants made up the majority of colonists.

3. Native Americans Retreated and Disappeared in the Face of English Superiority

Indians were everywhere in British North America. Some groups were forced to retreat when the English arrived. Others were completely wiped out in the systematic warfare envisioned by Nathaniel Bacon. But many others, "the protected and Darling Indians" mentioned by Bacon, were treaty Indians who paid tribute to the governor in exchange for being left in peace. Hence, many Indians lived directly among the newly freed servants who were in direct competition with them for the limited lands available. Colonial authorities were not opposed to the eventual assimilation of the Indians, unlike African slaves. Finally, make the point that colonial authorities profited from the Indians' continued presence through payment of tribute and through monopolies on trade with them. The

Indians did not really retreat abruptly; they were subjected over time to disease, genocide, and assimilation.

Using the Bedford Series in History and Culture and the Historians at Work Series: Suggestions

When discussing European and especially English views of colonization and the New World, consider assigning *Envisioning America: English Plans for the Colonization of North America, 1560–1640*, edited by Peter C. Mancall. To expose students to the Indian perspective during this period, you might have them read documents from *The World Turned Upside Down: Indian Voices from Early America*, edited by Colin G. Calloway. When discussing the origins of American slavery, you might wish to assign *How Did American Slavery Begin?*, edited by Edward Countryman. You may also want to consider assigning *Oroonoko; or, The Royal Slave*, by Aphra Behn, edited by Catherine Gallagher.

Lecture Supplements and Classroom Activities

Using Multimedia Sources in the Classroom

When discussing the transformation of servant to slave labor in the British colonies, you can use the first episode of the PBS series *Africans in America*, "The Terrible Transformation," which covers the institutionalization of slavery in America.

Historical Contingencies

When discussing the early settlement of Jamestown, have your students consider, "What if English farmers had colonized Virginia?" What would have been the possible ramifications for colonial–Native American relations if the colonists had not depended on Powhatan's confederation for survival? Would the colonists have resorted to African slavery if they had built an economy based on food crops rather than cash crops? Here, bring in the *Promise of Technology* feature, "Corn, the 'Life-Giver,'" to have students think about the ways in which corn could have transformed the British colony. Would corn have been enough to sustain the colony?

Classroom Activities

When discussing the institutionalization of slavery in the British colonies, have your students consider the degree to which the colonists were motivated by economics and the degree to which they were motivated by racism. You may want to use *How Did American Slavery Begin?*, edited by Edward Countryman, a volume in the Bedford/St. Martin's Historians at Work series. Was slavery a manifestation of the colonists' racism? Or did the colonists become racist after they enslaved Africans? Although most historians now concur that modified versions of both positions are valid, students can benefit from working through the arguments and evidence themselves.

Using the Internet

Point out relevant Web sites to your students. The Alfa-Informatica project at <http://odur.let.rug.nl/alfa> makes available online a number of primary documents relating to the southern colonies in the seventeenth century. From the home page, click on "Projects," then click on "The American Revolution HTML-project," then "Documents," then "1601–1650" or "1651–1700." Students will find here various documents, including Virginia Charters, the Ordinance and Constitution for the Virginia Company in England, and Governor Berkeley's response to Bacon's Rebellion.

You may also want to direct them to the site for the University of Virginia's "Exploring the West from Monticello: A Perspective in Maps from Columbus to Lewis and Clark at <http://www.lib.virginia.edu/exhibits/lewis_clark/home.html>. Tell students to click on "Novus Orbis: Images of the New World, 1507–1669" from the home page.

A map of Virginia in 1612 is available from the Bodleian Library of Oxford University at <http://www.bodley.ox.ac.uk/guides/maps/virginia.gif>.

ASSESSING RESULTS
Multiple-Choice Questions

1. Powhatan
   a. introduced tobacco as an export crop in Virginia.
   b. systematically tried to slaughter all the English settlers he could find, which resulted in Carolina becoming a royal colony.
   c. aided the Jamestown settlement to the point of saving the colony.
   d. aided the settlement of the "Lost Colony" at Roanoke by acting as an interpreter and teaching the colonists how to plant corn.

2. What led to the high mortality rate in the first decade of the Virginia Colony?
   a. starvation and bear attacks
   b. accidents and severe weather
   c. Indian attacks and starvation
   d. disease and starvation

3. Why did indentured servants become important to Chesapeake society?
   a. Tobacco was a labor-intensive crop; the more servants one obtained, the more tobacco one could plant.
   b. Rice was a labor-intensive crop; the more servants one obtained, the more rice one could plant.
   c. African slaves were not available in the Chesapeake until the 1700s.
   d. Because women rarely inhabited the English colonies, hiring a female indentured servant was the only way a young man could find a woman to court.

4. How did the Navigation Act of 1660 affect the king?
   a. The king received two pounds sterling per hogshead for English ships carrying tobacco from Virginia to any port outside England.
   b. The king received 2 percent of the value of every shipment, regardless of its destination.
   c. The king received two pence for every pound of tobacco exported, regardless of the price received by the planters.
   d. The king received two pounds sterling per hogshead for non-English ships carrying tobacco from Virginia to England.

5. South Carolina was originally colonized by
   a. indentured servants.
   b. Catholics.
   c. Barbadians.
   d. Scots-Irish yeomen.

6. How did the slave society of the Chesapeake differ from that of the West Indies?
   a. Slaves of the Chesapeake frequently outnumbered the whites, while those in the West Indies rarely outnumbered the whites.
   b. Masters in the Chesapeake usually controlled more than one hundred slaves on each plantation, while those in the West Indies had very few and usually worked alongside their slaves.

c. Slaves of the Chesapeake were watched more closely than slaves in the West Indies.

d. Masters in the Chesapeake usually purchased their slaves from ships coming directly from Africa, while those in the West Indies obtained seasoned slaves from the Chesapeake.

7. What do the authors mean by "the technology of corn"?
   a. This is a phrase that, in the seventeenth century, meant "farming."
   b. This is a phrase that refers to plows.
   c. The knowledge gained and used to grow, harvest, prepare, and eat corn.
   d. The knowledge and information colonists learned and then passed on to the Algonquian Indians.

8. According to Map 3.2, "The West Indies and Carolina in the Seventeenth Century," how far south did the Carolina border extend?
   a. almost to Florida, at the approximate border of modern Georgia and Florida
   b. deep into Florida, south of St. Augustine
   c. on the western bank of the Savannah River, just barely into modern Georgia
   d. only along the coastal islands of Georgia to just north of St. Augustine, then back up to the Savannah River, where the western boundary ran along the middle of the river

9. According to Nathaniel Bacon's declaration in the documents reader, why had the grandees of the colony, including the governor, conspired to allow the Indians to attack the western planters?
   a. Having a monopoly on trade with the Indians, the grandees would lose money if they held the protected Indians accountable for the attacks on western planters.
   b. The grandees held the western planters in contempt because they believed the western men had risen in wealth very quickly by selling guns to the Indians.
   c. The grandees, having a monopoly on the trade in servants, wanted to use the Indians to reenslave the western planters who had just recently finished their servitude.
   d. The grandees, having a monopoly in the slave trade, wanted to eliminate obstacles

to enlarging the plantation system and wished to replace the small holdings of the western planters with large plantations such as those of the tidewater region.

10. Locate the following places on Map 3.1, "The Chesapeake Colonies in the Seventeenth Century."
    a. Jamestown
    b. Chesapeake Bay
    c. areas settled by 1650
    d. areas settled by 1700

11. Identify the correct sequence of historical events and figures.
    a. tobacco planted in Virginia, Virginia Company founded, Bacon's Rebellion, Maryland founded
    b. Navigation Act, Jamestown founded, Virginia becomes a royal colony, Powhatan dies
    c. Bacon's Rebellion, first Africans arrive in Virginia, Carolina founded, Maryland founded
    d. Virginia Company founded, Jamestown founded, Carolina founded, Bacon's Rebellion

PROPOSING MORE: Additional Readings

Warren M. Billings, "Sir William Berkeley and the Diversification of the Virginia Economy," *Virginia Magazine of History and Biography* 104, no. 4 (1996): 433–54.

David Brion Davis, "Constructing Race: A Reflection," *William and Mary Quarterly* 54, no. 1 (1997): 7–18.

Jack P. Greene, "Interpretive Frameworks: The Quest for Intellectual Order in Early American History," *William and Mary Quarterly* 48 (1991): 515–30.

Allan Kulikoff, "The Colonial Chesapeake: Seedbed of Antebellum Southern Culture," *Journal of Southern History* 45, no. 4 (1979): 513–41.

Bradley J. Nicholson, "Legal Borrowing and the Origins of Slave Law in the British Colonies," *American Journal of Legal History* 38, no. 1 (1994): 38–51.

Martin H. Quitt, "Trade and Accumulation at Jamestown, 1607–1609: The Limits of Understanding," *William and Mary Quarterly* 52, no. 2 (1995): 227–58.

Answer Key to Multiple-Choice Questions: 1-c, 2-d, 3-a, 4-c, 5-c, 6-c, 7-c, 8-b, 9-a, 11-d

4 THE NORTHERN COLONIES IN THE SEVENTEENTH CENTURY

1601–1700

Outlining Chapters: Thematic Questions

I. How did England become a Protestant nation, and who were the Puritans?

II. How did Puritans come to dominate New England society?
   A. Who founded the Plymouth colony? Why was it self-governing? How successful was its expansion?
   B. How did the Massachusetts Bay colony come into existence, and how did it differ from other joint-stock colonies? What evidence exists to suggest that the Massachusetts colonists were more religious than most? What were the social origins of the colonists, and how did they differ from colonists in the Chesapeake? How successful was the colony in attracting immigrants during its first decade?

III. How did Puritanism influence the development of New England?
   A. What were the central tenets of New England Puritanism, and what effect did they have on everyday life? According to Puritans, what was the proper relationship between church and state?
   B. Who could vote in civil affairs, and how did widespread male political participation aid in maintaining a conformity of ideas? How were towns established in New England? How was land divided among town founders?
   C. Why was Puritanism prone to schism, and what were some of the more prominent cases of splintering?
   D. What consequences did England's Puritan Revolution have in New England? What factors contributed to a decline in religious zealousness, and how did the churches of Massachusetts deal with that decline? What was the Halfway Covenant, and how was it received? How did Puritans tolerate other dissenting religious groups such as the Quakers?

IV. How were the middle colonies founded?
   A. How was New York settled? How did the British acquire it, and why did it allow religious toleration?
   B. How were New Jersey and Pennsylvania founded? Who was William Penn, and what role did he play in the settlement of Pennsylvania? How did the Quakers differ from other dissenters in England?

C. Who immigrated to Pennsylvania? What kind of relations did the colony have with Native Americans in the seventeenth century? To what extent did Pennsylvania practice religious toleration? How did the new colony fare?

V. How did the monarchy move to consolidate its authority over the American colonies?

   A. How did the various Navigation Acts and the Staple Act regulate trade between the American colonies and England?

   B. How did the crown use King Philip's War to alter the governments of New England? How did the Glorious Revolution of 1688 affect the American colonies? Why did the colonists still value their relationship with Britain despite Britain's attempts to increase its control over them?

Teaching with The American Promise, *Second Compact Edition: Lecture Strategies*

LECTURE 1
The Religious Basis of Colonization

Begin this lecture by highlighting the theme of the textbook — "the promise of America." Ask students to consider the expectations held by the immigrants who came to New England and the middle colonies in the seventeenth century. Ask them to think about how the colonists hoped life in America would satisfy those expectations. It will become evident that students cannot understand why the colonies of Plymouth, Massachusetts Bay, or Pennsylvania were founded or how they developed without a clear understanding of the dissenting religions of seventeenth-century England. Locate the Puritan and Quaker movements socially and chronologically. Discuss the advent of the Protestant Reformation on the Continent and how Henry Tudor (Henry VIII) nationalized church institutions in England for his own political reasons. Be ready to explain why many found Henry's reforms spiritually unsatisfactory. Discuss religious toleration in England and New England. Ask your students, "What constitutes religious toleration?" and ask whether either seventeenth-century England or Massachusetts meets their definitions. Here, you might have students analyze the title page to "The World Turn'd Upside Down."

Focusing more closely on the Puritan groups who migrated to New England, explore the centrality of conversion to their religious experience. Examine the contractual nature of their "covenant" with one another and with God. Use John Winthrop's sermon (in the documents reader) to determine what was expected of Puritans in their contract with God and what were signs of their failing to live up to their contract. You might also want to bring in the *Documenting the American Promise* feature, pointing out the difficulties Puritan missionaries faced when confronting Native American populations. Also show how later generations of colonists failed to achieve the conversion experience, which prevented them from obtaining full church membership, resulting in their lack of political franchise and their inability to have their own children baptized. The Halfway Covenant, instituted a mere thirty-two years after the founding of the colony, reflected the loss of religious zeal and signaled to the community of believers that their society was in a state of decline. Ask how the people of the late seventeenth century interpreted the witch trials of the 1690s and the Indian wars of the 1670s and 1690s. Consider assigning the Bedford Series in History and Culture volume *The Sovereignty and Goodness of God*, Mary Rowlandson's captivity narrative, and ask students if these afflictions weakened the religious faith that was the root of Puritan society.

Conclude by pointing out the similarities and differences between the Quakers and Puritans. Both were seen as cults by those not a part of them. Discuss the theological differences but use extreme care at this point; you may be discussing your students' religious beliefs.

LECTURE 2
The Impact of English Politics on American Colonization

This lecture highlights the impact that politics in England had on American colonization. Suggest to students that the progress of the American colonies corresponds with the rise and fall of the Stuart dynasty. Begin with the ascension of James I to the throne and trace the succession of monarchs, pausing to cover Oliver Cromwell's brief interregnum, and ending with the ousting of James II in the Glorious Revolution. Be sure to make the connections between British politics and colonial affairs clear. Note, for example, that Charles I dissolved Parliament only one week after granting a charter to the Massachusetts Bay colony. The colony benefited greatly from the king's desire for increased power; nearly twenty thousand Puritans migrated to New England during the 1630s to escape political turbulence back home. When King Charles reconvened Parliament in 1640, Parliament declared war on the king, and the immigrants immediately stopped coming to the Massachusetts Bay colony. Instead, Puritans back in England called on those in America to come back to help fight the king. By 1647, parliamentary forces in this civil war defeated the king and executed him. The Puritans in England then established a commonwealth without a king, in which their army's general, Oliver Cromwell, acted as dictator.

Ask students what happened to the Massachusetts Bay colony's status as a "city upon a hill" once the biblical commonwealth was established in England. You might also ask students to point out the connections between the failure of Parliament's commonwealth in 1660 and the declaration of the Halfway Covenant by a synod of Massachusetts clergy in 1662. How did these events signal a decline in Puritan society? Quickly cover the Restoration and note the English conquest of New Amsterdam (renamed New York), and the founding of New Jersey and Carolina. When James II, proprietor of the New York colony, assumed the throne in the 1680s, he allowed William Penn to launch the Pennsylvania colony. Go over the king's revocation of the Massachusetts Bay charter and the formation of the Dominion of New England. Have students suggest why this move angered colonists. Ask students what effect the Glorious Revolution had on colonial affairs, paying particular attention to the rebellions in New York, Massachusetts, and Maryland. Finish with a discussion of the changes in the structure of colonial government by the 1690s.

LECTURE 3

A Social History of the Northern Colonies

Use this lecture to compare the emerging societies of the northern colonies. The Massachusetts Bay colony and its offshoots — Connecticut, Rhode Island, and New Hampshire — were densely settled territories with a largely homogeneous population. New York, New Jersey, and Pennsylvania contained more heterogeneous populations, which made their societies much different from New England's. Use Map 4.3, "American Colonies at the End of the Seventeenth Century" to demonstrate this point. Ask students to compare the manner of immigration to New England with that to the middle colonies. Who went to each, and how did they get there? Once they had arrived, how did they live?

Look at crime as a point of comparison. Use the Suffolk County court records (in the documents reader) to get students to explore what kinds of crimes were committed in the Massachusetts Bay colony, who committed them, and how the perpetrators were punished. Ask students to identify how this understanding of crime reflected a new way of life. Then ask them to consider the same crimes in the New York or Pennsylvania colonies. Would they be considered crimes, and would the punishments be the same? For the most part, the answer is yes, but distinctions can still be made. Next introduce the concept of change in societal standards and structures over time.

Change over time for these colonies can be made most clear using the New England example of witchcraft. Avoiding the religious dimensions of the witchcraft trials, ask students to identify who was most likely to be accused as a witch and who was most likely to be an accuser. Explore the social ramifications of a society that perceived itself in spiritual decline and ask students to describe the material conditions that supported that belief. Land became more scarce with a growing population; the perceived healthiness of the colony decreased as a denser population increased the chances for disease to spread; disparities in wealth became more apparent, reducing the sense of a harmonious community; and children moved from the communities in which they were raised to find land for themselves, reducing parental control and authority. Use the Bridget Bishop testimony (in the documents reader) to identify how these social problems led colonists to identify witches as scapegoats. Next ask students to consider again New York and Pennsylvania. Did they have the same problems? Why not? Show that New England was not the model that other colonies followed by demonstrating that the middle colonies, like the southern colonies, pursued a path of increasing stability while New England saw itself in decline.

Anticipating Student Reactions: Common Misconceptions and Difficult Topics

1. The Puritans and the Pilgrims Were the Same

Students frequently assume that *Pilgrim* is simply another term for *Puritan*. They get this impression from a linear reading of most texts: The Pilgrims generally drop out of the narrative of American history after surviving the first few years at Plymouth, and then the story focuses on the development of Puritan society in New England. Many students might also erroneously conclude that because both Plymouth and the Massachusetts Bay colony were established in present-day Massachusetts, the colonies were one and the same. One can correct this mistaken reading by discussing two points. First, the Puritans considered the Pilgrims minor heretics, or at least severely mistaken schismatics. The Pilgrims considered the Church of England so beyond reform that they believed the only way they could achieve salvation was to separate themselves completely from it and start anew. The Puritans, who also considered the Church of England deeply corrupt, believed such separation sought to achieve perfection on earth; and, given their Calvinist belief in the sinful nature of man, they saw such attempts as both impossible and sinfully proud. The Church of England had to be reformed, or purified, from within. Hence, the Puritans did not seek separation while they dissented from its practices.

Second, you can emphasize the differences in community organization between the colonies of Plymouth and Massachusetts Bay. Plymouth was sparsely settled with few colonists. It allowed religious toleration. Massachusetts Bay was densely settled, creating frontier communities rather than individual farmsteads in the "howling wilderness." If you assigned the History and Culture Series volume on Mary Rowlandson's captivity narrative, get students to consider Mary Rowlandson's farm during the Indian attack. Her farm included thirty-seven people in an extended family, and she literally could see her neighbors dying before her own farm was attacked. She lived in a community, which was the Puritan mode of development in Massachusetts. The Plymouth colony was much more individualistic and thus allowed more toleration of differences.

2. The Puritans Came to America to Pursue Religious Freedom

Students generally understand that the Puritans came to America to practice their religious beliefs unrestrained by a government that disagreed with them over those beliefs. Although this is generally a true statement, students make it false by assuming that seeking religious freedom for oneself logically translates into a policy of religious toleration once the formerly persecuted govern. The textbook makes clear that toleration did not necessarily follow the establishment of a Puritan government, but one cannot assume that students will overcome this misconception merely by reading part of one textbook chapter. Take them step by step, from John Winthrop's sermon on the *Arabella* (in the documents reader), in which he told the Puritans that they had to exclude others who disagreed with them to maintain their covenant with God, to the exile — forced or voluntary — of Roger Williams and Anne Hutchinson, to the persecution and execution of members of radical evangelistic sects such as the Quakers. Such practices probably do not conform to students' notions of religious freedom.

3. New England Is the Prototype of American Development

Historians have done a good job of laying this fallacy to rest, yet students continue to assume that because New England's history is so well documented, because professors and teachers emphasize its development, and because it offers an ideal of freedom and community, it must be the main source of American tradition. Ask students to compare the settlement of Massachusetts with the settlement of Virginia. Who came, and how did they get a start? Ask which pattern was replicated in the American West.

Make the point that the colonization of New England was atypical of general British colonization in North America and very different from later American settlement patterns. The Puritans did not strike out on their own to claim their lands individually. They petitioned the General Court as a group. They received their town charter, and only then were lands divided among the settlers.

Using the Bedford Series in History and Culture and the Historians at Work Series: Suggestions

When addressing the encroachment of the white Puritan New England settlements onto Native American territory, have students read Mary Rowlandson's *The Sovereignty and Goodness of God with Related Documents*, edited by Neal Salisbury. This classic captivity narrative offers a white woman's perspective on religion and Native Americans during the time of Metacomet's War (1675–1676). Also consider assigning *The Diary and Life of Samuel Sewall*, edited by Mel Yazawa, which makes available a Puritan's diary that covers five decades and documents continuity and change in Puritan thought in New England. To encourage students to compare New France and British North America, assign *The Jesuit Relations: Natives and Missionaries in Seventeenth-Century North America*, edited by Allan Greer.

Lecture Supplements and Classroom Activities

Using Multimedia Sources in the Classroom

When discussing the Salem witch trials of 1692, consider screening the docudrama *Three Sovereigns for Sarah*, distributed by PBS. The script is based on existing trial manuscripts and the writings of Sarah Cloyce, the youngest of three sisters accused of witchcraft and the only one to escape execution.

To address popular (often erroneous) conceptions about the contests between Europeans and Native Americans, consider showing the 1992 film *The Last of the Mohicans*, starring Daniel Day-Lewis. You may need to remind your students that the film represents Hollywood's interpretation of the 1839 novel by James Fenimore Cooper and is thus doubly removed from historical reality.

Historical Contingencies

Puritanism will undoubtedly be confusing to students. To have your students understand more fully the Massachusetts Bay colony's Puritanism, ask them what would have happened had the colonists there practiced religious toleration. What did the colonists fear would happen? What happened to other colonies that did practice religious toleration? (Have students consider the middle colonies, for example.) Were the Puritans able to ward off the forces of dissolution by taking such a strict stance on the issue? Why or why not?

Classroom Activities

Using *The Sovereignty and Goodness of God with Related Documents*, edited by Neal Salisbury, have students formulate a response from one of Rowlandson's captors to her narrative. Would the captor have agreed with Rowlandson's account of her captivity? Where might the two accounts diverge?

Using the Internet

The Plymouth Colony Archive Project at the University of Virginia might prove useful for your students. The site includes searchable texts including court records, colony laws, biographical profiles of selected colonists, probate inventories, wills, and maps. Direct your students to <http://etext.virginia.edu/users/deetz>.

ASSESSING RESULTS
Multiple-Choice Questions

1. The excommunication of Anne Hutchinson, detailed in Chapter 4's opening vignette, suggests that
   a. Puritanism was immune from individual interpretation of its followers.
   b. the tenet that God revealed his will exclusively through the Bible — instead of directly to a believer — was a critical feature of Puritanism.
   c. during the seventeenth century New England's Puritan zeal cooled and the goal of founding a holy New England faded.
   d. Hutchinson was inarticulate and proved to be no match for John Winthrop's brilliance, wit, and insight.

2. What did John Winthrop mean when he said that the Massachusetts Bay colony would be a "city upon a hill"?
   a. He meant that Boston should be built as a fortress against possible invasion from other European powers.
   b. He meant that all efforts should be taken to convert Indians to Christianity and to English civilization.

c. He meant that agricultural practices of the new colony should allow for small cities to develop so that nobody would need to travel far for the comforts of civilization.

d. He meant that the colony would be an example to the world of how God's plan for many could be realized on earth.

3. What was the Halfway Covenant?
   a. It allowed Pennsylvania settlers to maintain good relations with their Indian neighbors by purchasing land directly from the Indians.
   b. It allowed the grandchildren of Puritan church members to be baptized even if the children's parents were not full members.
   c. It allowed New Jersey to be divided in half between two sets of proprietors.
   d. It allowed the males of any town in Massachusetts to vote in town elections as long as they signed the town covenant.

4. Which of the following statements most accurately summarizes the position of the Massachusetts Bay colony Puritans on religious toleration?
   a. They advocated religious toleration because they had come to America to establish the principle of freedom of religious beliefs.
   b. They advocated religious toleration only for people expressing Christian beliefs.
   c. They eschewed religious toleration, believing that God had only one plan for the world and that to allow erroneous views was sinful.
   d. They did not advocate religious toleration but enforced laws requiring church attendance only on people who were community leaders.

5. How did the Glorious Revolution affect the American colonies?
   a. It caused Massachusetts Bay colony to extend its charter over all the colonies north of Maryland and renamed the new entity the Dominion of New England.
   b. It caused rebellions in Massachusetts, New York, and Maryland.
   c. It caused Bacon's Rebellion.
   d. It provided English troops to help fight the Indians in King Philip's War.

6. Why did seventeenth-century New Englanders find the testimony against accused witches so persuasive?

a. because scriptural prophecy had predicted that evil witches would one day test the Puritans' religious faith
b. because most of those accused of witchcraft were Quakers, whose beliefs were seen as heretical and of Satanic origin
c. because holding witches responsible for misfortunes and mishaps provided a convenient explanation for the disorder and instability that periodically occurred in New England communities
d. because the witches had confessed in church

7. According to Map 4.1, "New England Colonies in the Seventeenth Century," to which governing body did present-day Vermont belong?
   a. New France
   b. New Hampshire
   c. Massachusetts Bay
   d. New York

8. Excerpts from the Suffolk County Court Records, 1671–1673, reprinted in the documents reader, suggest that
   a. colonial New England courts wielded little power and were prohibited from levying fines and punishments.
   b. the courts heard only criminal cases; ecclesiastical cases were left to church tribunals.
   c. the courts shouldered part of the responsibility for maintaining piety and a godly order in colonial New England.
   d. colonial New Englanders rarely deviated from the highest aspirations of the Puritan founders.

9. John Eliot's *Indian Dialogues*
   a. was a compilation of created dialogues between converted Indians and those who resisted Christianity.
   b. rendered a faithful and exact translation of King Philip (Metacomet's) "confession of Puritan faith."
   c. documented the brutality of Wampanoags in King Philip's War against English settlers.
   d. explained the attraction Puritanism had for the majority of Native Americans living in colonial New England.

10. Identify the correct sequence of historical events and figures.
    a. Glorious Revolution, Restoration, king executed, Dominion of New England

b. New Jersey founded, Connecticut founded, New Amsterdam conquered, Rhode Island founded
c. William Penn, Anne Hutchinson, Henry VIII, John Winthrop
d. English Reformation, Pilgrims, Puritan Revolution, Halfway Covenant

PROPOSING MORE: Additional Readings

Wayne Bodle, "The 'Myth of the Middle Colonies' Reconsidered: The Process of Regionalization in Early America," *Pennsylvania Magazine of History and Biography* 113, no. 4 (1989): 527–48.

Daniel R. Coquillette, "Radical Lawmakers in Colonial Massachusetts: The 'Countenance of Authoritie' and the *Lawes and Libertyes*," *New England Quarterly* 67, no. 2 (1994): 179–211.

David Harley, "Explaining Salem: Calvinist Psychology and the Diagnosis of Possession," *American Historical Review* 101, no. 2 (1996): 307–30.

Raymond D. Irwin, "Cast Out from the 'City upon a Hill': Antinomianism Exiles in Rhode Island, 1638–1650," *Rhode Island History* 52, no. 1 (1994): 2–19.

Marilyn J. Westerkamp, "Engendering Puritan Religious Culture in Old and New England," *Pennsylvania History* 64, special issue (1997): 105–27.

Answer Key to Multiple-Choice Questions: 1-b, 2-d, 3-b, 4-c, 5-b, 6-c, 7-a, 8-c, 9-a, 10-d

COLONIAL AMERICA IN THE EIGHTEENTH CENTURY

5

1701–1770

*O*utlining Chapters: Thematic Questions

I. How were eighteenth-century colonial population growth and economic growth linked?

II. Why did New England's population lag behind that of other colonies in the eighteenth century?
 A. How did natural increase and fixed borders change traditional methods of land distribution in eighteenth-century New England?
 B. Why did a market economy develop in New England? What did farmers sell at market and what did they buy? How did fishing fit into New England's economy? How did commerce come to dominate New England's economy? What did the distribution of wealth suggest about colonial New England?

III. How did the middle colonies, particularly Pennsylvania, differ in population growth from New England and the South?
 A. Why did Germans and Scots-Irish immigrate to the middle colonies? What meaningful comparisons can be made between the two groups? Who were the redemptioners, and how did they differ from indentured servants?
 B. Why was Pennsylvania considered by some to be "the best poor [white] man's country"? Why were servants considered a bargain in Pennsylvania? Why did slavery not become an entrenched institution in the middle colonies as it did in the southern colonies? What was the middle colonies' major export? How widespread was Pennsylvania's prosperity in the 1700s? Who ranked at the top? How did religion fit into the vision of Pennsylvania society? How did the work ethic fit into that vision?

IV. What factors contributed to the tremendous population growth in the southern colonies? How did the racial transformation of the southern colonies shape the region's economy, society, and politics?
 A. How did the African slave trade affect the growth of slavery in the southern colonies? What were the two centers of southern slave culture? What was the process of enslavement? What were the conditions of the Middle Passage? How did most slaves arrive in Britain's mainland North American colonies? How did seasoning work?

B. What forms did slave resistance take? What happened at Stono, South Carolina, in 1739? How were slaves assigned work in the Chesapeake and in South Carolina? How important were family ties to slaves? In what ways did slaves attempt to retain their West African heritage?

C. How did the export of tobacco and rice (and indigo) underwrite the prosperity of the southern colonies? How did slave ownership affect distribution of wealth? What were the sources of wealth for the elite, and how did the elite maintain its grip on political offices?

V. What shared experiences served to unify the culture of the disparate colonies of British North America?

A. How did colonial consumption of British goods affect the self-image and confidence of the colonists?

B. What factors encouraged the spread of religious indifference, of deism, and of denominational rivalry in the colonies? How did the Great Awakening change the nature of American religiosity? How did this new religiosity reinforce the self-image changes caused by consumerism?

C. How did the policies of the British Empire provide a common framework of political expectations and experiences for American colonists? What relationship did colonists have with their Native American neighbors? How powerful was a colonial governor?

Teaching with The American Promise, *Second Compact Edition: Lecture Strategies*

LECTURE 1
Ethnic and Religious Heterogeneity in Colonial America

Colonial America demonstrated remarkable diversity in the eighteenth century. Consider focusing on ethnicity and religion to prove this point, going from region to region. New England was the most homogeneous, with a predominance of English descendants who practiced a mainly Puritan-derived religion. Even in New England, however, diversity was present. Have students read "Confessions of a Thief and Rapist" (in the documents reader) and ask them

to list the types of people encountered. Indians and blacks abounded among the many white inhabitants of New England. Take a moment to get students to consider the reduced religiosity in New England based on this document. Explain the Great Awakening in New England and then ask how Arthur, the confessed criminal, and others who did not commit crimes fit into this new religiosity. How widespread was deep religious devotion at the time? (Be sure to cover the "threats" that the Enlightenment, denominational rivalry, and "backsliding" posed to religiosity in New England.) Next move on to the middle colonies and explain the coming of the Germans and the Scots-Irish. With them came more diverse religions, such as the Lutheran and Presbyterian denominations. Identify the urban nature of George Whitefield's visits to America and ask how religion was transmitted to the frontier. Bring the Great Awakening to the South with the missions in Georgia and the influx of Scots-Irish down the Shenandoah Valley. Finally, discuss the ethnicity of immigrants to the South. Leave most of the discussion on slavery for the next class, but point out that southerners differentiated between ethnicities among slaves. Using the discussion of ethnicity as a starting point, begin exploring the construction of the concept of race.

LECTURE 2
Solidly Establishing Slavery

In this lecture you can introduce students to the institution of slavery. Direct students' attention to Map 5.3, "The Atlantic Slave Trade," and to Table 5.1, "Slave Imports, 1451–1870," to emphasize the solidification of the institution in the Western Hemisphere. Using the textbook and advertisements for runaway slaves (in the documents reader), reconstruct the violence that permeated slavery. Africans were kidnapped, abused, and sold to slave traders. The Middle Passage killed at least 15 to 20 percent of all Africans transported to the Americas. Here you can refer students to the account of Olaudah Equiano's capture and his experience of the Middle Passage. Slavery in the Sugar Islands met with sure death, and even coming to mainland America did not drastically improve a slave's chances for survival. Ten to 15 percent died in their first year as slaves in America, while they were "seasoned." They could not communicate with the master, who often considered them little more than livestock. Other slaves helped them make the transition from free persons embedded in systems of social relations to slaves who had no legal rights at all. At the bottom of this institution was brutal compulsion. Slaves might have been able to negotiate and resist the will of the master to a certain degree (describe such instances if possible), but ultimately the master prevailed through sheer brutality and a legal system that legitimized all that he chose to do. Ask students to consider the textbook's account of the Stono Rebellion and its consequences as a means of understanding how slavery permeated society. Finally, reintroduce your discussion of race and extend it to define the word racism. Students may need an explanation that racism means more than mere prejudice. Help students understand that racism stems from the belief in the biological inferiority of other races — in this case, nonwhites. They also need to understand that eighteenth-century racism entailed action and that it was goal-oriented: Racism amounted to the systematic oppression of a racial minority designed to maximize exploitation of that minority. There will be a lot to talk about.

LECTURE 3
The Colonial Economy in the Eighteenth Century

The British colonies in America were embedded in a system of economic relations that benefited crown and colony alike. Draw students' attention to Map 5.2, "Atlantic Trade in the Eighteenth Century," and to Figure 5.1, "Colonial Exports, 1768–1772." Ask students to consider the questions posed by Map 5.2, focusing on the ways in which trade policies influenced both Britain and the colonies. Reintroduce the original Navigation Acts of the 1650s and 1660s as they related to the American colonies. Explore the impact of the Board of Trade on American commerce (it was minimal, with the exception of the reexporting of tobacco). Show the agricultural basis of colonial prosperity (and how it rested on slave labor) and how that prosperity translated into increasing consumerism. Explore the extent of that prosperity by discussing the distribution of wealth in America compared with that of England. Who got rich in America? Did one's region make a difference in one's options? How important were merchants? Were farmers absolutely independent of the market? Use the Benjamin Franklin vignette at the start of the chapter and the *Poor Richard's Almanack* excerpt (in the documents reader) to discuss how widespread prosperity and consumerism encouraged people to think of themselves as individuals capable of making their own choices for good or evil. Finally, discuss the perks of the empire that made this prosperity possible. The crown regulated trade and collected some taxes in the process, but the colonists benefited from being included in the empire's commerce on the same basis as did citizens of England. The American colonists could trade with other British colonies and enjoyed the protection of the British navy. These advantages could not have been provided by the colonies themselves.

Anticipating Student Reactions: Common Misconceptions and Difficult Topics

1. Slavery Was a Monolithic Institution

Many students consider slavery a monolithic institution and are unable or unwilling to see the differences in ancient, medieval, African, and New World slavery. You should quickly clear up this misconception. If you assign the full text of *The Interesting Narrative of the Life of Olaudah Equiano*, edited by Robert J. Allison (in Bedford's Series in History and Culture), spend time covering the differences between African and New World slavery. This text demonstrates that the British colonists did not devise the institution of slavery — it had a long history — and that there were fundamental differences that made southern slavery the "peculiar institution": race, natural increase, and a resident planter class, among others. Be sure to illustrate the role that race played in African slavery in the New World. You will also want to cover the role of natural increase and a resident master-class in the American South. To explore the variances in the institution of slavery, point students to the differences outlined in the textbook in the tobacco and rice cultures in the American South. You may have a student who asks which system was better. Resist value judgments and stress *difference* instead. The brutality of the system should be self-evident in both cultures.

2. Colonists Were Self-Reliant Frontiersmen

Students frequently misunderstand the social and economic order of colonial America in the eighteenth century. They believe that a general self-sufficiency translates into absolute self-reliance. They fail to understand that, whether colonists were located in coastal cities or on the frontier, they continued to be embedded in a network of relations: political, economic, social, and familial. As the text makes clear, the colonists did engage in market activities, in pursuit of consumption of manufactured goods. But even when colonists failed to participate in market economic relations, there was still an exchange of goods taking place. Consumption did not necessarily mean that a cash transaction took place. One might exchange one's own labor or the loan of livestock for a manufactured good. The non-market local exchange of goods, even on the frontier, rested on the ability of merchants to obtain goods, and sometimes credit, from Britain and Europe. Use the *Poor Richard's Almanack* text (in the documents reader) to discuss how people perceived themselves as interdependent within the colonial economy. The "Confessions of a Thief and Rapist" (in the documents reader) also contains plenty of evidence of consumption and the economic interdependence of the colonies.

3. American Colonists Did Not Profit from Their Participation in the British Empire

Because the colonies ultimately rebelled against the British Empire, some students will assume that the Americans never benefited from being a part of the empire. Make the point that the American colonies' prosperity, as evidenced by the increasing consumption described in this chapter, was a direct result of their participation in the British Empire. In many ways, the colonists got the best of all worlds. The British navy protected them and their ships of commerce, while the American merchants did their best to avoid taxation whenever possible. The colonists benefited from a stable governmental system in which they (at least the elites) helped make the rules. And they benefited from governmental policies that promoted immigration. Very little was asked in return at this time. The crown profited from its American colonies, but the colonies profited as well.

Using the Bedford Series in History and Culture and the Historians at Work Series: Suggestions

There are two good autobiographies to assign in conjunction with this chapter: *The Interesting Narrative of the Life of Olaudah Equiano*, edited by Robert J. Allison, and *The Autobiography of Benjamin Franklin*, Second Edition, edited by Louis P.

Masur. Equiano's *Narrative* offers a moving first-hand account of the slave trade and the Middle Passage, and both Equiano's story and Franklin's *Autobiography* provide fascinating views of social, economic, and religious life in the eighteenth century. You may also want to consider assigning *The Commerce of Everyday Life: Selections from The Tatler and The Spectator*, by Joseph Addison and Richard Steele, edited by Eric Mackie, from Bedford's literature list.

Lecture Supplements and Classroom Activities

Using Multimedia Sources in the Classroom

When discussing the Great Awakening, you may want to consider showing your class the segment from Episode 2, "Revolution," of the PBS series *Africans in America* that covers the revival's impact on the institution of slavery.

Historical Contingencies

Have your students consider the possible course of colonial development had New England and the middle colonies adopted cash-crop agriculture. How would the patterns of settlement have been different? Would plantations have been possible in northern colonies, considering the climate? Would slavery have become more entrenched in the North if a plantation-based economy had prevailed? If your students respond yes, ask them to consider whether slavery was merely an economic institution. In other words, have students consider whether slavery reflected ideological differences between northern and southern whites or whether it was merely a response to economic needs.

Classroom Activities

Have your students debate the degree to which colonists considered themselves British (or French, Dutch, German, and so on) and the degree to which they considered themselves Americans. You might wish to have students review the conclusion of the chapter, "The Dual Identity of British North American Colonists." At this point you could bring in the *Promise of Technology* feature on the printing press to discuss the growth of public opinion and its influence on the creation of an American culture. When can (or should) historians reasonably begin to speak of something as identifiable as "American culture"? Did it exist by 1760? Why or why not?

Using the Internet

When discussing the international slave trade, direct your students to the Middle Passages Inc. site at <http://www.middlepassages.com>, which provides a slave-ship database.

The Alfa-Informatica Project at <http://odur .let.rug.nl/alfa> makes available online a number of primary documents relating to the southern colonies in the eighteenth century. From the home page, click on "Projects," then click on "The American Revolution HTML-project," then "Documents," then "1726–1750." Students will find here various documents, including essays by Benjamin Franklin and excerpts from his autobiography as well as various acts of colonial legislatures.

ASSESSING RESULTS
Multiple-Choice Questions

1. The vignette on Benjamin Franklin's adulthood, which opens chapter 5, reveals all of the following everyday experiences in eighteenth-century life, except
   a. long hours of labor subject to the authority of a parent, relative, or employer.
   b. the loneliness and privations of only children.
   c. the restless quest for escape from the ties that bound.
   d. a slackening in religious fervor.

2. New England's population
   a. decreased because of a high mortality rate and people migrating west and south in search of more arable land (that is, land fit for growing crops).
   b. grew at a faster rate than that of other colonies because of its encouragement of immigration and because of a high fertility rate.
   c. grew at the same rate as other colonies because some factors encouraged growth while others discouraged it.
   d. grew at a slower rate than did the other colonies because its Puritan orthodoxy and its limited available land discouraged new immigration.

3. Redemptioners were
   a. women convicted of crimes in England who were transported to America in hopes of being "redeemed" through hard work.
   b. free people of color who had earned their freedom by embracing Christianity.
   c. indentured servants who had the ability to negotiate the terms of their servitude with

their prospective masters after arriving in the colonies.
   d. none of the above.

4. Increased consumption in the British colonies
   a. encouraged people to think of themselves as individuals capable of making decisions that influenced the quality of their lives.
   b. discouraged savings, which was ultimately bad for the economy but stimulated American manufacturers in the short run.
   c. reduced the social distinctions resulting from disparities in the distribution of wealth because all participated in a "democracy of goods."
   d. increased the patronage power of the royal governors since the colonies needed more tax collectors to service the increased importation of goods.

5. The Great Awakening
   a. created rebellions in the colonies of Massachusetts, Maryland, and New York in opposition to Catholic tendencies of the monarchy.
   b. limited the importance of religion in people's lives, as Christians of all denominations responded to George Whitefield's call to live more secular lives.
   c. sought to convert the unchurched and revive the piety of the faithful with a new style of preaching that appealed more to the heart than to the head.
   d. reduced the religiosity of the American colonists as Anglicans, Baptists, Congregationalists, and Presbyterians interfered with one another's church services while competing for churchgoers.

6. Enlightenment thinkers
   a. tended to agree that science and reason could disclose God's laws in the natural order.
   b. argued that God's plan could be found only in the Bible.
   c. held no sway in the British colonies of North America.
   d. were influential only in the most urban areas of the northeast and therefore caused no great concern among the clergy of the established religions.

7. The function of the "dummy board" of the mulatto woman Phyllis
   a. was to mark the grave of this woman, who, as a slave, could not afford a marble tombstone.

b. was to sit in front of a window in a house to scare off potential robbers while the owners were away.
c. was purely decorative and illustrates the fine woodworking skills of the Yamasee Indians.
d. is not known.

8. According to Map 5.3, "The Atlantic Slave Trade," which region of the Americas received fewer slaves from Africa than British North America?
a. Mexico and Central America
b. West Indies
c. Brazil
d. Guiana

9. In a Boston broadside of 1768 that told of the crimes of Arthur, a thief and a rapist, Arthur
a. blamed his downfall on his desertion of his masters, his drunkenness, and his lewd behavior.
b. blamed his downfall on the excessively cruel treatment he received from his masters.
c. refused to repent for his crimes against society.
d. was forced into a life of crime by a band of ruffians that had induced him to run away from his master.

10. Identify the correct sequence of historical events and figures.
a. French and Indian War, Jonathan Edwards, *Poor Richard's Almanack*, Stono Rebellion

b. French and Indian War, Stono Rebellion, Navigation Acts, Scots-Irish immigration begins
c. Great Awakening, Scots-Irish immigration begins, Georgia founded, redemptioners
d. German immigration begins, Scots-Irish immigration begins, Stono Rebellion, French and Indian War

Proposing More: Additional Readings

A. Owen Aldridge, "Natural Religion and Deism in America before Ethan Allen and Thomas Paine," *William and Mary Quarterly* 54, no. 4 (1997): 835–38.

Michael A. Gomez, "Muslims in Early America," *Journal of Southern History* 60, no. 4 (November 1994): 671–710.

Kenneth P. Minkema, "Jonathan Edwards on Slavery and the Slave Trade," *William and Mary Quarterly* 54, no. 4 (1997): 823–34.

Allison G. Olson, "Eighteenth-Century Colonial Legislature and Their Constituents," *Journal of American History* 79, no. 2 (1992): 543–67.

Mart A. Stewart, "'Policies of Nature and Vegetables': Hugh Anderson, the Georgia Experiment, and the Political Use of Natural Philosophy," *Georgia Historical Quarterly* 77, no. 3 (1993): 473–96.

John K. Thornton, "African Dimensions of the Stono Rebellion," *American Historical Review* 96, no. 4 (1991): 1101–13.

Answer Key to Multiple-Choice Questions: 1-b, 2-d, 3-c, 4-a, 5-c, 6-a, 7-b, 8-a, 9-a, 10-d

Essay Questions, Chapters 1–5

1. The authors of the textbook note that the first Americans did not leave written accounts of their experiences in the Western Hemisphere. Scholars therefore have had to rely on artifacts and material culture to reconstruct the histories of these people. Even when scholars have access to written accounts, such as those that document European exploration and colonization of the Western Hemisphere, they often still utilize material culture to help them make sense of the past. In what ways have historians and other scholars used artifacts and material culture to explain ancient America, the Age of Exploration, and early colonization efforts? What can these artifacts tell us that written documents cannot? What are the drawbacks of these types of evidence? Be sure to refer to specific examples from the text.

2. Scholars used to refer to the period between 1492 and 1600 as the "Age of Discovery." Within the last generation or so, the term "Age of Exploration" has come into fashion. The authors of the textbook, however, have chosen "Europeans and the New World" to describe the same time period. What are the implications of each term? What factors might

have engendered the change? Why might the rubric "Europeans and the New World" encourage a more comprehensive study of the era?

3. Compare the motivations for exploration of the Spanish to those of the British. How did these motivations influence settlement patterns and the maturation of colonial societies in North, Central, and South America?

4. Historians traditionally have looked to colonial New England to explain all of colonial North America. How might the story of the colonial Chesapeake, lower South, and middle colonies challenge this assumption of the typicality of the New England experience?

5. Looking at the period from 1607 to 1760, to what extent was American history driven forward by the needs and traditions of the Old World versus the realities and possibilities of the New World?

6

THE BRITISH EMPIRE AND THE COLONIAL CRISIS

1754–1775

Outlining Chapters: Thematic Questions

I. How did the American colonies fit into the British Empire's campaigns against other European powers? How did the French and Indian War lay the groundwork for the imperial crisis of the 1760s between British leaders and American colonists?

   A. How and why did the French and English compete for control over the Ohio valley?

   B. How successful was the 1754 Albany Congress for intercolonial defense?

   C. How did William Pitt decisively change the course of the French and Indian War in Britain's favor? What were the consequences of British victory? Why have many considered the terms of the Treaty of Paris unfavorable to the British? What perceptions of each other's actions did American colonists and the British hold immediately following the war?

II. What policies did British ministers, under a new king, formulate for the American colonies as a consequence of the French and Indian War?

   A. What was Pontiac's uprising? What British policies resulted from the uprising?

   B. How did Grenville's ministry hope that the Sugar Act would improve the administration of the colonies and finance payment of the war debt?

III. What was the Stamp Act, why was it imposed, and how did Americans react to it?

   A. Why did American colonists reject both the new direct tax and the concept of virtual representation?

   B. What were the Virginia Resolves, and how did they suggest the limits of parliamentary authority over the colonies? Who were the Sons of Liberty? How did the Stamp Act encourage nonelite participation in politics in Massachusetts, and how successful were the actions of the nonelite? What lessons were to be learned from the Stamp Act crisis?

   C. What was the Stamp Act Congress, and how did it signal the possibility of intercolonial political action? How did white Americans understand their rights of liberty and property? How did black slaves react to white America's assertions of liberty? How successful was the Declaratory Act in resolving the Stamp Act crisis?

IV. Why were the Townshend duties a tactical blunder?

   A. What were the Townshend duties? What provisions were most ardently opposed? How did the Massachusetts Assembly take the lead in protesting the duties?

   B. What did the colonists hope to achieve through the resistance tactics of nonconsumption and nonimportation, and how did these tactics differ from each other? Why were both tactics difficult to enforce? What were their immediate consequences for women?

   C. What was the Boston Massacre, and whom did the courts find responsible for it? Why did John Adams and Josiah Quincy defend the British soldiers?

V. Why were all the Townshend duties, except the tax on tea, repealed?

   A. What three incidents between 1770 and 1773, during a general lull in animosities between Britain and the colonies, set the stage for increased intercolonial opposition to Britain?

   B. How did Boston differ from other colonial ports in its resistance to the Tea Act of 1773?

   C. What were the details of the five acts that the American colonists called the Intolerable Acts, and how did the colonists react to them?

   D. Why did the First Continental Congress meet? Who were its delegates, what did it propose, and how would it enforce its measures?

VI. How did authorities in the northern and southern colonies differ in dealing with the menace of domestic insurrection?

   A. Who won the battles of Lexington and Concord?

   B. How did slaves in the American colonies react to news of the open warfare between the colonists and Britain?

Teaching with The American Promise, *Second Compact Edition: Lecture Strategies*

LECTURE 1

Political and Social Determinants of Propensity for Radical Action

This lecture compares the social and political arrangements of the American colonies with those of England in the years leading up to the Revolution and suggests ways to understand how people chose sides in the conflict. The American colonies were more egalitarian than Britain but were still very unlike modern American society. While Americans had an increasing sense of

social hierarchy in which its members knew their place, their society was much more fluid than British society. But American politics remained the province of the elite. In discussing politics, show how the elite mobilized the nonelite — the lesser farmers, mechanics, and artisans — to support them in their campaigns against one another. Explain how colonial politics differed from that of England. Using the specific example of Thomas Hutchinson in the opening vignette, show how a royal governor's power was limited by his distance from the source of his power (the king) and his proximity to his adversaries (the colonial elite).

Explore the structure of colonial society. How stratified was it? What were one's chances for advancement? Have your students read the accounts of George Robert Twelves Hewes and Peter Oliver (both in the documents reader). Oliver's Tories were predominantly well-to-do and believed they should get special treatment, while in the Hewes document the working class shows a clear resentment of social distinctions. Use these accounts of the Stamp Act riots to show how notions of hierarchy were breaking down in the colonies. To discuss these class differences, try to get students to define the term *class*. They will inevitably start their definition with gradations of wealth, but if you point out that many tradespeople (for example, plumbers) can become wealthy today, students will soon see how amorphous the term can really be. Using a broad definition of class that includes gradations of wealth, occupation, education, family connections, and so forth can be helpful in arguing that more classes existed during the eighteenth century than we usually acknowledge today. Next examine how class differences help us to understand who supported the Revolution and why.

Look closely at Boston society and describe how social changes may have led to a propensity for radical action there. Wealth was not necessarily the primary indicator of whether one might support the Revolution, although it played a role. Again, it may be useful to juxtapose the excerpts from the documents reader by George Hewes and Peter Oliver. Explore why many of the political elite remained loyal, while many wealthy merchants supported the patriots. How did a group such as the Sons of Liberty fit into the social context of these times? Compare the divergence of class interests in Massachusetts with elite support for the revolutionary movement in Virginia, particularly following Lord Dunmore's proclamation in April 1775.

LECTURE 2
The Ideology of the American Revolution

This lecture should explain the intellectual environment that promoted the misunderstandings between American patriots and the British. Those patriots who came to resent the policies of George Grenville subscribed to the political theories of the English Country Party, while most Englishmen held those theories in low esteem. The Country Party held that liberty and power were constantly at war. Unpack the definitions of these terms and help students to understand that an ideology filters new information and validates it by comparing the new information to knowledge and beliefs already known to be true. The theories led Americans to expect conspiracies of power subduing liberty. Show how the British reinforced preexisting American fears of a standing army, of the ministry's ability to corrupt the political system by offering patronage positions, and of the reintroduction of Catholicism. Note that many Americans feared:

1. That a standing army could only be used to subdue a free people when there was no outside threat to the peace, particularly when the crown stationed the army away from the frontiers where they would have logically been used to put down Indian insurrections.

2. A "conspiracy of the placemen." Colonists used the term *placemen* to describe members of Parliament (MPs) who were "placed" in Parliament by the crown in its efforts to regain control of the mechanisms of British government. Because the crown could not constitutionally gain control of Parliament, it tried to do so by manipulating elections in certain districts to ensure that the royal candidate was elected. The crown could then appoint these placemen to certain bureaucratic positions, which would earn them an additional salary. In addition to believing the new tax-collecting effort of the crown encroached on the right of a society to tax itself, colonists feared that the newly created patronage position of tax collector would be offered to MPs who would then be beholden to the crown and thus be willing to restrict the colonies' efforts at self-government.

3. That an ecclesiastical conspiracy was being forced on America with the threat of an American bishop with all the trappings of

Rome. The Congregational Church in New England would therefore suffer disestablishment, and the buildings would be assumed by the Anglican Church. Additionally, the Quebec Act of 1774 officially recognized the Catholic Church, giving further proof to the patriots of the crown's tyrannical schemes for the colonies.

Use a short discussion of the readings to demonstrate the fears in the words of the people themselves. Joseph Warren (in the documents reader) referred to the Country Party ideology when he discussed being a captive to another person's caprice as the natural consequence of a standing army. Note that George Washington (in the documents reader) feared that a "fixed and uniform plan to tax" would be put into place by the ministry. Each primary document makes the ideology more sensible to the student.

LECTURE 3
An Overview of the Events Leading toward Revolution, 1754–1775

Use this lecture to introduce to students the events from 1754 to 1775 that led toward revolution, and show the evolution of the patriot movement from opposition to taxation to rebellion against the king and Parliament. You may want to have students make a time line to list the major events, and then distill the essentials of each with special notice of how ideology or class interests affected their outcomes. Start with the French and Indian War, showing that Americans assumed that the English did not appreciate their efforts, while the English believed that Americans failed to contribute their fair share toward winning the war. With increased Indian hostilities, and a barely subdued French population in Canada, Parliament stationed an army to defend the colonies from Indian attack and limited the westward encroachment on Indian territory. Examine the Proclamation of 1763 and the stationing of troops. Note that Parliament wanted the colonies to pay for their own defense, which the British thought was eminently reasonable. Thus, Parliament passed the Revenue (Sugar) Act, which actually lowered taxes but added swift punishment for criminal evasion of the law. It provoked protest in the colonies about common-law rights of taxation and trial by one's peers, and the relationship of the colonies to Parliament. Explore the question of whether the British ministry dealt with Americans in bad faith or whether Americans simply evaded their responsibilities. Define *virtual representation,* and then explain why the British suggested it and the political basis on which the Americans rejected it. Explore how Americans forced the repeal of the Stamp Act and how the Declaratory Act saved face for Parliament by reaffirming Parliament's ability to tax the colonies. When Parliament reintroduced taxes in the colonies, the Townshend duties were considered external rather than internal taxes; describe the difference and why the crown thought external taxes would be acceptable to Americans. Explain how the use of these revenue-enhancing taxes to subsidize the salaries of governors and judges threatened to corrupt the entire colonial political system.

Explain nonimportation, and show class and regional differences in implementing it. Next, outline the Boston Massacre and explain how Boston's upper and middle classes successfully defended the British soldiers accused of murder, and how the massacre reinforced notions that a standing army was a menace to the citizenry. Here, you might refer students to Paul Revere's engraving of the Boston Massacre in the text and ask them to compare Revere's strongly patriotic version with the account in the textbook. Quickly explain the significance of the *Gaspée* affair and how it led to the establishment of committees of correspondence, which became informal political institutions that existed outside the legal political system. Finally, describe the Tea Act, the Boston Tea Party, and the Intolerable (Coercive) Acts as the beginning of the final descent into open rebellion by a radicalized colonial population who thought Parliament was attempting to reduce its basic political rights. Direct students' attention to the *Documenting the American Promise* feature, "The Destruction of the Tea," when discussing the Boston Tea Party. Describe the Coercive Acts and their impact on American political ideology. The battles of Lexington and Concord forced all Americans to consider which side they should support and loosened the ties to the empire nearly completely. Explain that philosophical, social, and institutional differences between the British and the Americans made constitutional questions difficult but not impossible to resolve. Had either side been able to see the other's point of view, the crisis of the 1760s and 1770s might have been averted, and American history perhaps radically altered. You have a lot to cover here — you will need to make choices. But students will find a quick overview helpful as they try to make sense of the road to revolution.

Anticipating Student Reactions: Common Misconceptions and Difficult Topics

1. Colonists Naturally Supported the Revolution

Students come out of high school with a very Whiggish view of the American Revolution. They frequently believe that everyone in the American colonies naturally wanted independence from England, and they believe that everyone knew that the colonists would ultimately win. Because students know the outcome of the Revolution, they unconsciously assume that historical actors clearly understood what the outcome of their actions would be. To correct this error, ask them how many colonies the British had in North America during the American Revolution. Many will answer "thirteen"; others may remember Canada. Few will know about Nova Scotia or the Floridas. And practically none will even consider the dozen or so island colonies. Why then, you should ask, did none of these other colonies seek independence? Quickly discuss each of the nonrebellious regions: Canada was a recently conquered French province without traditions of self-government. Nova Scotia was the site of the main artillery base for British North America, and most of its inhabitants owed their living to supplying the military with goods. The Floridas had just been acquired from Spain in 1763, and few British subjects resided there. The island colonies were slave societies controlled by elites residing in England. Most of their ambitious citizens aspired to go to England, and the rest were so oppressed that politics of self-government had no meaning for them. Only in the well-established British colonies on the North American mainland was the question important. And even there, well-meaning and intelligent people disagreed.

2. The British Ministry Dealt with Americans in Bad Faith

Students frequently assume that because Americans believed they were getting a bad deal, the British ministry actually did deal with the Americans unfairly. It is important to have students see the whole movement toward revolution from the British perspective. The British sent troops to America during the French and Indian War to protect the colonists from the French and from the Indian allies of the French. The war was extremely costly, and the British thought it very reasonable to get the Americans to help pay for a war that greatly benefited them. So the British imposed taxes that had already been imposed on the population of Great Britain, some for over a century. At each step along the way to revolution, the ministry tried a means to gain some revenue, and then backed away when confronted with the great animosity shown by the Americans. The British saw Americans as ungrateful and cheap: They wanted to enjoy the fruits of British government without sharing the responsibility of paying for it.

3. The Revolutionary Spirit Was a "Revolution from Above"

Because history is frequently presented to students as a top-down phenomenon, students rarely consider the lower classes as having a leading role in any event in American history. Having read about the merchants and planters who "led" the revolution, students naturally think that everyone else in society just fell in line with their "betters." In the American Revolution, however, common folk frequently played the role of radical vanguard. John Adams and other wealthy patriots were infuriated when the common people took to the streets and destroyed Peter Oliver's home. They were not so much concerned about destruction of property as they were that "the mob" did not need its upper-class leaders. Sailors in Boston and artisans in Philadelphia held views about the Revolution's direction that were measurably more radical than those of their wealthier "leaders." Again, have your students read George Hewes's account of the Boston Tea Party (in the documents reader) to reinforce this point.

Using the Bedford Series in History and Culture and the Historians at Work Series: Suggestions

To have students explore more fully the issues that divided patriots and loyalists in the period leading up to and during the American Revolution, consider assigning *Benjamin and William Franklin: Father and Son, Patriot and Loyalist*, by

Sheila Skemp. This brief biography looks at the personal background and political experiences of Benjamin Franklin, ardent patriot, and his son William, the last royal governor of New Jersey, who remained loyal to the British crown. Thomas Paine's *Common Sense and Related Writings*, edited by Thomas P. Slaughter, also works well in the classroom.

Lecture Supplements and Classroom Activities

Using Multimedia Sources in the Classroom

Consider screening Episode 1, "The Reluctant Revolutionaries," of the PBS series *Liberty!*, which chronicles the road to revolution beginning with the end of the French and Indian War. You might also want to show Episode 2 of the same series, "Blows Must Decide," which picks up the story in the fall of 1774 with British troops occupying Boston and moves through the signing of the Declaration of Independence.

Historical Contingencies

Ask your students whether the American Revolution was inevitable. Had the British put down the colonists more forcefully, for example, would the revolutionary impulse have been extinguished? Had the British responded more favorably to colonists' demands in the 1760s and early 1770s, would the colonial relationship have continued past 1776? Impress on your students that the road to revolution could have veered off in many different directions.

Classroom Activities

After the first two lectures, have your class debate the nature of the Revolution. Was it an ideological revolution, led by the philosophers and rhetoricians, or a social revolution, led by the masses? Most historians reject such simplification, but students will benefit from the exercise, learning to hone their skills in historical argumentation. You may have them consider the outcome, which should be familiar in its basic form. Did the Revolution precipitate social change (did it free the slaves, did it change the status of women, and so on), or did it engender a new way of viewing politics?

Using the Internet

The University of Oklahoma's College of Law has placed on the Web a site called A Chronology of

US Historical Documents. Here, students can find the 1754 Albany Plan and the Resolutions of the Stamp Act. Direct students to <http://www.law.ou.edu/hist>.

Students may also be interested in the document titled "Anonymous Account of the Boston Massacre," made available at <http://www.ukans.edu/carrie/docs/texts/bostanon.html>.

ASSESSING RESULTS
Multiple-Choice Questions

1. The French and Indian War involved fighting
   a. in North America, the Caribbean, Europe, and India.
   b. in North America, Europe, Australia, and China.
   c. only in India and Europe.
   d. only in North America.

2. Virtual representation was based on the premise that
   a. colonial interests were represented in Parliament by virtue of the laws submitted by colonial legislative assemblies.
   b. all Englishmen, regardless of their physical ability to vote, were represented by Parliament.
   c. the colonies were opposed to internal taxation but not to external taxation.
   d. the colonies were opposed to external taxation but not to internal taxation.

3. One significant result of resistance to the Stamp Act, symbolized in Boston by the assault on Thomas Hutchinson's house and repeated throughout the colonies, was the
   a. call for separation of church and state.
   b. renunciation of legal protections of the institution of private property.
   c. call for immediate emancipation of slaves north of the Mason-Dixon line.
   d. politicization of classes previously excluded from formal political participation.

4. The British cartoon "Edenton Tea Ladies" suggested that
   a. women cared less for politics than they did for afternoon tea.
   b. patriotic American men had much to admire in their female counterparts.
   c. the British respected patriotic women who took a stand on the important issues of the day.
   d. women who meddled in politics undermined their femininity.

5. In passing the Declaratory Act, Parliament
   a. overstepped its authority by repealing the Massachusetts charter and declaring martial law in Boston.
   b. repealed the Townshend duties but declared that tea was a luxury that could withstand greater taxation.
   c. repealed the Stamp Act but declared its ability to legislate all matters concerning the American colonies.
   d. acknowledged the historic relationship between the Catholic Church and the people of Quebec when it declared that Ohio would belong to Quebec.

6. Slaves
   a. flocked to fight for the Revolution under the banner of liberty, equality, and brotherhood.
   b. took an active role in the nonconsumption/nonimportation movement by boycotting British goods following the imposition of the Townshend duties.
   c. waited to see which side would win before deciding with whom they would ally themselves.
   d. were actively recruited by the British by Lord Dunmore's proclamation.

7. Women
   a. flocked to fight for the Revolution under the banner of liberty, equality, and brotherhood.
   b. played virtually no role in the years leading up to the Revolution.
   c. took an active role in the nonconsumption/nonimportation movement by boycotting British goods following the imposition of the Townshend duties.
   d. closed the port of Boston by throwing British tea into the harbor.

8. According to Map 6.2, "North America after the French and Indian War," how much land did Britain have access to?
   a. not much more than they had before the war
   b. less then they had before the war
   c. a great deal of land, primarily land that used to be Spain's
   d. a great deal of land, primarily west and north of the Proclamation Line

9. Was Paul Revere's engraving of the Boston Massacre accurate?
   a. No, Revere depicted an organized group of soldiers purposely firing into a crowd of peaceful citizens, while this was not what

happened.

b. No, Revere depicted British soldiers cowering in fear before a rioting crowd, while the opposite was true.

c. No, but only because Revere had imperfect knowledge of how the event happened.

d. Yes, Revere's depiction and all other accounts agree.

10. Identify the correct sequence of historical events and figures.

a. French and Indian War, Albany Congress, Battle of Lexington, *Gaspée* affair

b. French and Indian War, Sugar Act, Townshend duties, Quebec Act

c. Committees of Inspection, Lord Dunmore's Proclamation, Declaratory Act

d. Stamp Act Congress, Albany Congress, First Continental Congress

PROPOSING MORE: Additional Readings

Robert A. Becker, "Politics or Principle: The Townshend Duties Crisis and the Coming of Independence," *Reviews in American History* 16, no. 3 (1988): 362–67.

John L. Bullion, "British Ministers and American Resistance to the Stamp Act, October–December 1765," *William and Mary Quarterly* 49, no. 1 (1992): 89–107.

Gregory E. David, "Thinking and Believing: Nativism and Unity in the Ages of Pontiac and Tecumseh," *American Indian Quarterly* 6, no. 3 (1992): 309–35.

Cathy Matson and Peter Onuf, "Toward a Republican Empire: Interest and Ideology in Revolutionary America," *American Quarterly* 37, no. 4 (1985): 496–531.

Answer Key to Multiple-Choice Questions: 1-a, 2-b, 3-d, 4-d, 5-c, 6-d, 7-c, 8-d, 9-a, 10-b

THE WAR FOR AMERICA

1775–1783

7

Outlining Chapters: Thematic Questions

I. What were the objectives of the Second Continental Congress?

    A. How did the Second Continental Congress assume both political and military power during 1775? Who were its delegates, and why did they refrain from declaring their immediate independence from Britain? What steps did the Second Continental Congress take to prepare for war?

    B. How did the Second Continental Congress pursue the aims of both winning the war and seeking reconciliation with Britain in 1775 and early 1776?

    C. Who was Thomas Paine, and how did his pamphlet *Common Sense* influence the cause of American independence? How did the Continental Congress come to declare independence, and why did it blame the king for all the problems between the colonies and England? What issues proved to be most contentious during the debates surrounding the drafting of the Declaration of Independence?

II. Why did both England and the American colonies assume that military victory would be tough to secure?

    A. How did the Continental Congress raise an army? How did military service become a badge of one's political allegiance, and who served in the Continental army?

    B. What was the British army's overall strategy? What political objectives restrained that strategy, and what basic assumption undergirded it?

    C. How successful were the Continental army's offense against Canada and defense of New York?

III. How did local supporters of both sides secure the political allegiance of the uncommitted?

    A. In patriot communities, what served as local government? How did women's actions change when their husbands were away in military or political service to the new country?

    B. Why did some colonists remain loyal to the British? How did the British secure the loyalty of slaves, Native Americans, and other groups dispossessed by the patriots?

C. What deeds did revolutionaries consider traitorous? How did revolutionaries punish traitors, and why did loyalists regard the label *traitor* with contempt and suspicion?

D. How was the Revolution financed, and what effect did the war have on the economy?

IV. Why was 1777 pivotal to the American Revolution?

A. How successful was Burgoyne's army in conquering upstate New York? How did the Americans win at Saratoga? Why did Americans consider this battle critical? Did British occupation of Philadelphia counterbalance American victory at Saratoga? How did war profiteering affect the American cause?

B. Why did Americans engage in "anti-Indian campaigns," and what effect did they have on the American war effort?

C. How and why did France support the Americans?

V. What was George III's new strategy for victory, 1778 to 1781? What went wrong for the British?

A. How successful was British strategy in Georgia and South Carolina from 1780 to 1781?

B. What was Benedict Arnold's treachery, and how did its discovery help the American cause?

C. Why did the British assumption that loyalists could maintain territory captured by the army in Georgia and the Carolinas prove unfounded?

D. How was General Cornwallis defeated at Yorktown?

E. Why did peace come so slowly after the final military engagement at Yorktown? What were the terms of the agreement?

Teaching with **The American Promise,** *Second Compact Edition: Lecture Strategies*

LECTURE 1
Indecision in the Early War

Although an intellectual revolution in colonial attitudes toward Great Britain had been taking place since the 1760s, many Americans were uncertain about declaring absolute independence from England in the earliest part of the war. In this lecture, explain that the fighting began and a military commander was appointed before independence was actually declared. Such actions in 1775 did not convince the king that the Continental Congress's peace overtures were sincere.

The most momentous force for intellectual revolution came from publication of the pamphlet *Common Sense.* Discuss how this pamphlet (excerpted in the documents reader) altered the intellectual landscape by changing the focal point of anger from the king's ministers to the king himself. Ask students to describe Thomas Paine's motives for publishing the pamphlet. You will also want to explore how colonists received *Common Sense.* Here you might also have students look at John and Abigail Adams's criticisms (in the documents reader). Put an end to the misconception that the patriot movement was united for independence from the start; but make clear that once independence was declared, everyone understood the significance of what the patriots had done. (Point out the John Adams letter to Abigail Adams, in the documents reader, about making July 2 a holiday of great importance. Also note the print titled "Declaration of Independence Read to a Crowd.") At this point you might direct students in a discussion of the "promise" of American independence. Ask students what independence meant to the patriots. What did they hope to gain?

LECTURE 2
The Home Front

This lecture should have two themes: (1) the American Revolution was a social as well as a political revolution, and (2) the war imposed real hardships on people for their political beliefs.

To drive home the first theme, describe the world of the American Revolution as one in which the old social hierarchies came under attack. In the midst of this civil war, Americans redefined their society. Sometimes members of the traditional elite continued as the social and political leaders, and other times new men, without established social standing, were elected to lead their communities. Use the letters of John and Abigail Adams (in the documents reader) to explore the reasons for the social restructuring taking place. Without a king at the top of a social hierarchy, the whole social order was called into question. Who would rule, and by what justification? Some knew that mere wealth would not be sufficient to allow the elite to maintain traditional deference from their social inferiors. Society had to become more egalitarian for free white males. But it did not necessarily follow that this new leveling applied to women, blacks, or Native Americans. Ask your students to consider how society remained unaltered for these socially dependent groups.

The second theme depicts a society changed as a result of the process of waging war. Committees ran local government without any higher justification for their own existence. One's local opponents could be arrested, imprisoned, exiled, or executed. Neighbors fought neighbors and confiscated their property. Men had to examine the legal status of women to determine how to deal with the wives and daughters of their opponents. The uncommitted and the pacifists were suspected as enemies and profiteers because they did not actively support the cause. Real profiteering took place with "gouging" prices, hyperinflation from unsupported Continental currency, and a swollen black market. Patriot Americans came to doubt the virtue of the people engaged in the war effort on their own side. Explore the treatment of Continental soldiers through the soldier's memoir (in the documents reader). Ask why the soldier joined the fight and how he was rewarded.

Finally, get students to consider the loyalist perspective on the war and how loyalists were abused both by the patriots and the British army. You may want to ask your students how many Americans opposed the Revolution and remained loyal to the crown. Explain that at least ninety thousand people chose to emigrate following the war and that many more probably wanted to leave but were unable to do so. Also, ask why people chose to remain loyalists during the war. The textbook and the documents reader indicate that a desire for social stability was one of the primary motivating factors and that many loyalists believed that local government was full of petty tyrants who had a more direct impact on their lives than the so-called tyranny of a distant king. (Direct your students to the statement in the textbook by Boston loyalist Mather Byles to emphasize your point.) To show students where the main strongholds of loyalist support were, refer them to Map 7.2, "Loyalist Strength and Rebel Support."

LECTURE 3
The Military Campaigns

Use this lecture to help students make sense of the military strategies of the American Revolution. Take the students from Bunker Hill to Yorktown and focus on the essentials rather than on the details of the many campaigns. Map 7.1, "The War in the North, 1775–1778," and Map 7.3, "The War in the South, 1780–1781," are particularly helpful in demonstrating military campaigns. Show that the war was long and difficult for the American revolutionaries as they fought against the world's best-equipped army. George Washington was appointed commander for political reasons rather than for his military abilities, and he rushed to Massachusetts to direct and train the militias that surrounded Boston in the aftermath of the Battle of Bunker Hill. The Continental army forced the British to evacuate Boston but then lost its offensive into Canada and its defense of New York and retreated to Philadelphia at the end of 1776. From there, discuss the general British strategy of isolating New England, the radical hotbed of the Revolution, from the rest of the colonies. Make a special note of the importance of Saratoga in formally bringing the French into the war. Discuss the British military strategy and then show the shift to a southern strategy that ultimately failed because the real battles were won in the backcountry by partisan guerrilla fighters rather than in traditional battles fought by the armies. Make the point that although the British occupied every major city in the colonies, their occupation had little real effect.

After Yorktown, the military battles ended in North America as France continued to fight Britain on other fronts. After two years of diplomatic maneuvering, the British finally offered the Americans all they wanted and more, which convinced them to sign a separate treaty without waiting for the French to make peace. In the end, the Americans did not really "win" the war so much as the British failed to pursue it with a winning strategy. Consider ending this lecture with a discussion of gun ownership in the colonies (see the *Promise of Technology* feature). Ask students to consider the logistical problems faced by colonists who needed to gear up for the revolution. What were the implications of an unarmed nation at war?

Anticipating Student Reactions: Common Misconceptions and Difficult Topics

1. The Patriots Were a United Group Determined to Achieve Independence

The revolutionaries were a mixed group with many agendas at the beginning. Many wanted a reconciliation with England that would create an autonomous position for the colonies within the empire, much like the commonwealth countries of today. Even when they agreed on the need for independence, patriots disagreed on the reasons for independence. New England wanted independence because of its extended confrontation with England and the imposition of the Coercive Acts. Virginia promoted independence to gain freedom from debts owed to British merchants. Finally, make the point that although all agreed on the need for military buildup, few outside New England would commit to an offensive posture until they were forced to by the British.

2. The Loyalists Were Self-Serving and Shortsighted

Students rarely consider the loyalists. The Revolutionary War, to most, was fought by the British army (and mercenaries) and the Continental army of the United States. If they think about loyalists at all, they think of them as the few government employees in America — the tax collectors, customs agents, royal governors, and so forth. To counter such beliefs, it is important to make the loyalists real to students. Discuss why common people were loyalists. Ask students how many people chose to leave the independent colonies rather than live without a king. The loyalists obviously did not know the revolutionaries would win, and they suffered great hardships at the hands of their patriot neighbors just as patriots suffered at the hands of their loyalist neighbors.

3. The American Revolution Was Short, Painless, and Won by American Fortitude

Lasting from 1775 to 1783, the American war for independence was lengthy by the standards of its day and in relation to all other wars fought by the United States. Only the Vietnam War was longer for Americans. And the American Revolution caused as much, if not more, disorder in America as did the U.S. Civil War. Neighbors killed one another and confiscated or destroyed property. Some merchants profited at the distress of the public by gouging prices.

By 1783 the British public was clearly unhappy with the war, and Parliament voted to bring the conflict to a speedy conclusion. Britain failed to prosecute the war because it sought not just to conquer the colonies but also to reintegrate them into the empire. Hence, political objectives limited military tactics, while incompetence weakened the military's ability to carry forward a winning strategy.

Finally, make sure students understand the crucial role France played in the war by supplying soldiers, equipment, training, and an effective and coordinated land-sea strategy that dealt the British a fatal blow at Yorktown. Americans made revolution without first consulting the French, but the outcome might have been different without France's official and clandestine support.

Using the Bedford Series in History and Culture and the Historians at Work Series: Suggestions

Thomas Paine's *Common Sense and Related Writings,* edited by Thomas P. Slaughter, is of course appropriate for this chapter. To give students a nuanced picture of the loyalist position during the American Revolution, again you might consider assigning *Benjamin and William Franklin: Father and Son, Patriot and Loyalist,* by Sheila Skemp. Students will find William Franklin's loyalist position fascinating in light of his father's famous stance for liberty. *What Did the Declaration Declare?,* edited by Joseph J. Ellis, offers students the chance to explore leading historians' interpretations of the meaning of the Declaration.

Lecture Supplements and Classroom Activities

Using Multimedia Sources in the Classroom

The remaining videos from PBS's *Liberty!* series work well with this chapter. Episode 3, "The Times That Try Men's Souls," picks up the story the day after the signing of the Declaration of Independence and covers the war through the end of 1776. Episode 4, "Oh Fatal Ambition!," touches on America's efforts to enlist the aid of the French and details Burgoyne's defeat at Saratoga, providing the evidence of American ability that France needed before committing to the patriots' cause. Episode 5, "The World Turned Upside Down," considers British efforts to exploit the contradiction inherent in America's efforts to fight a war in the name of liberty while also justifying slavery. The episode also covers Britain's southern policy, its defeat at Yorktown, and the signing of the Paris Peace Treaty. You may also want to consider showing the rest of Episode 2, "Revolution, 1750–1805," from the PBS series *Africans in America,* which examines the influence of revolutionary ideology on American slaveholding and the ways in which slaves used that ideology to their advantage.

Historical Contingencies

Have students consider the prospects for American victory had the French not intervened. Be sure to explain that foreign recognition and aid, critical in any war, is of paramount concern during a civil war. Ask students what France brought to the struggling colonies, and have them consider seriously what the course of events may have looked like had France remained unresponsive to the calls of the patriots. You might also have them consider how history would have been different if the colonies had lost. How might the colonies have been reintegrated into the British Empire? Whose history would we be studying in this survey course?

Classroom Activities

You may want to have students debate whether the war for American independence was a radical or conservative revolution. Consider assigning *What Did the Declaration Declare?*, edited by Joseph J. Ellis, to help them understand the historical trends and influences that shaped the drafting of that document.

Using the Internet

The University of Oklahoma's College of Law has made available online a number of documents relevant to the revolutionary era. Direct students to <http://www.law.ou.edu/hist>.

ASSESSING RESULTS
Multiple-Choice Questions

1. What did Abigail Adams mean when she told her husband John to "Remember the Ladies"?
   a. Abigail was telling John that he should remember to send his family (which was entirely female) enough money to support themselves while he was away.
   b. Abigail was reminding John that the women who served in the Continental army as cooks, laundresses, and nurses should receive the same bonuses as did the men in their enlistment.
   c. Abigail was explaining that the upheavals of society during the war would require the special efforts of Congress to help support the soldiers' wives and widows.
   d. Abigail was suggesting that the goal of independence from a tyrannical king raised a parallel goal — the end of tyranny of husbands over their wives.

2. What were the original objectives of the Second Continental Congress?
   a. to attack Spanish America to create a new bond between the northern and southern colonies
   b. to declare independence from England and to ally the colonies with France
   c. to free all the slaves north of the Mason-Dixon line by offering freedom in return for service in the army
   d. to prepare for war while pursuing reconciliation with England

3. Why were loyalists more vocal about their beliefs during the period 1774–1776 than they were later?
   a. After 1776, the loyalists concentrated on quietly seeking out traitors to the patriots' cause to undercut their support and defeat them from within.
   b. After 1776, all the loyalists left America.
   c. With the British army on their side after 1776, loyalists felt no need to argue, only to fight.
   d. Until late in 1776, the possibility of full-scale rebellion was still uncertain, which meant that vocalizing beliefs might make a difference.

4. At what battle did America's victory bring France into the war?
   a. Bunker Hill
   b. Kings Mountain
   c. Saratoga
   d. Yorktown

5. How did Benedict Arnold's treason aid the war effort?
   a. It allowed Americans to differentiate between their own supporters, who sometimes seemed to lack virtue, and the truly greedy people, like Arnold, who supported the British.

b. It encouraged loyalists to relax their defenses in the belief that more patriots would soon sell out their cause as had Arnold, which ultimately led to numerous patriot victories.

c. It revealed English plans that might not have come to light had he not been captured after his meeting with Arnold.

d. George Washington passed along ingenious disinformation through Arnold, which derailed British efforts that might have succeeded in destroying the independence movement.

6. Why was the image "Death of Jane McCrea" an important propaganda tool?

a. The patriots used the story to show how the British army abandoned the loyalists.

b. The American army used the story to stir up outrage against the British for allying themselves with Native Americans.

c. The Continental Congress kept its internal opposition in check with this and similar ideas of how defectors from the patriot cause were treated by the British.

d. The British used the sentiment to justify continuing the war by claiming that the American revolutionaries were just a bunch of murderous criminals.

7. According to Joseph Plumb Martin's account in the documents reader, did he and other volunteers benefit from their service in the Continental army?

a. Yes. Had Martin and others not volunteered, they would have been ineligible to obtain government jobs after the war ended.

b. Not directly, although Martin's service to his country did help him to find a good republican wife.

c. No. Congress failed to deliver on promises of adequate food, clothing, cash, and land bounties.

d. Yes. Had Martin and others not volunteered, they would have been drafted, losing any chance for the land and cash benefits they later received.

8. According to Map 7.3, "The War in the South, 1780–1781," from which state did General Cornwallis proceed immediately prior to the battle of Yorktown?

a. North Carolina
b. Georgia
c. Massachusetts
d. Nova Scotia

9. The *Promise of Technology* feature on muskets and rifles suggests that

a. extensive gun ownership in America in the second half of the eighteenth century guaranteed that the colonists were well prepared to do battle with the British.

b. gun ownership in America in the second half of the eighteenth century was surprisingly limited, posing real logistical problems for the colonists who needed to gear up for the Revolution.

c. annual muster days staged in towns throughout the colonies guaranteed that militia men were well trained and ready to do battle with the British.

d. muskets proved to be an effective weapon in battle.

10. Identify the correct sequence of historical events and figures.

a. Saratoga, Ticonderoga, Yorktown, Valley Forge

b. King George's southern strategy, New England campaign, Ben Franklin sent to Paris, Treaty of Paris

c. Battle of Bunker Hill, Olive Branch Petition, *Common Sense*, Declaration of Independence

d. *Common Sense*, Battle of Bunker Hill, Declaration of Independence, Ticonderoga

PROPOSING MORE: Additional Readings

Marilyn S. Blackwell, "The Republican Vision of Mary Palmer Tyler," *Journal of the Early Republic* 12, no. 1 (1992): 11–35.

Mark A. Clodfelter, "Between Virtue and Necessity: Nathaniel Greene and the Conduct of Civil Military Relations in the South, 1780–1782," *Military Affairs* 52, no. 4 (1988): 169–75.

Don N. Hagist, "The Women of the British Army during the American Revolution," *Minerva: Quarterly Report on Women in the Military* 13, no. 2 (1995): 29–85.

Keith Mason, "Localism, Evangelicalism, and Loyalism: The Sources of Discontent in the Revolutionary Chesapeake," *Journal of Southern History* 56, no. 1 (1990): 23–54.

Alan Taylor, "From Fathers to Friend of the People: Political Personas in the Early Republic," *Journal of the Early Republic* 11, no. 4 (1991): 465–91.

Answer Key to Multiple-Choice Questions: 1-d, 2-d, 3-d, 4-c, 5-a, 6-b, 7-c, 8-a, 9-b, 10-c

BUILDING A REPUBLIC

1775–1789

8

*O*utlining Chapters: Thematic Questions

I. With what questions did the framers and ratifiers of the Articles of Confederation grapple?
   A. How were the Articles of Confederation written, and how did they come to embody a decentralized government? What problems did this decentralized government pose?
   B. Why did Maryland, Delaware, New Jersey, Rhode Island, and Pennsylvania wish to give the Congress administrative control of the western lands up to the Mississippi River?
   C. What factors contributed to the inefficacy of the Congress under the Articles of Confederation? Why did a modest executive branch emerge, despite the Articles' silence on that issue?

II. Why were state governments at the center of each citizen's political identity in the first decade of independence?
   A. Why did states draw up constitutions, and how did those constitutions generally structure the state governments? How did the state constitutions differ from colonial political traditions? Why did states choose to limit the authority of governors and upper houses of state legislatures? Why did some states add bills of rights?
   B. Why did the state constitutions require people to own property to qualify to vote and hold office? What was the effect of such property qualifications?
   C. How did some framers propose to alter the republican language of equality to accord with the presence of slavery in the new country? How did slaves, freedmen, and women each interpret the language of republican equality? How did the republican language of equality in the state constitutions and in the Declaration of Independence affect the institution of slavery in the new country?

III. Why are the years 1781–1788 often referred to as the "critical period"?
   A. What factors contributed to the economic depression of the 1780s? What solutions did Robert Morris propose, and what opposition did those solutions face?

B. How did national land policy evolve in the 1780s? What debates surrounded that policy? How did the policy encourage deep sectional differences?

C. Why did old revolutionaries oppose Shays's Rebellion? In what way did the protesting farmers pose a threat to men like John Adams and James Bowdoin?

IV. How did the U.S. Constitution come into existence?

A. Why was the Philadelphia convention proposed? What was its agenda, and who served as its delegates?

B. What were the Pennsylvania and New Jersey Plans, and how did the Philadelphia convention reconcile them? How did the proposed constitution deal with slavery?

C. How and why did the proposed constitution place limits on direct democracy?

V. By what process was the U.S. Constitution ratified?

A. Who were the proponents of the U.S. Constitution, and what was their strategy to win ratification?

B. Who opposed the Constitution, and why did they fear it?

C. What carried ratification in the large hold-out states of Virginia and New York?

Teaching with The American Promise, *Second Compact Edition: Lecture Strategies*

LECTURE 1

The Problems of Creating a Framework of Government

This lecture should suggest that government is always a series of experiments. Political institutions require constant tinkering, and concepts adopted at one point may be abandoned at another. This lecture asks, "Why are constitutions written? How should the institutions of government be organized?" Take the students step by step through the process of creating a government where no constitution officially exists. Compare efforts of the various states in their constitution-writing process, and then compare the states to the national government. (Here, you might want to draw your students' attention to

Map 8.1, "Cession of Western Lands, 1782–1802," to emphasize the debates that surrounded the drafting of the Articles.) Discuss what the proper role of the government should be. Explore the assumptions behind decisions regarding how power is allotted to the various institutions of government. When discussing the preservation of liberty as a function of government, ask students to consider the issue of religious freedom covered in the *Historical Question* feature. How was the separation of church and state interpreted at the different levels of government?

LECTURE 2

Strengths and Weaknesses of the Articles of Confederation

This lecture explores the life of the Articles of Confederation, the United States' first constitution. Make it clear that the Articles were written as a wartime document to aid a league of states in fighting a common foe. Despite its weaknesses, which you should catalog for your students, Americans liked the Articles of Confederation because they had relatively little effect on their lives while still establishing an important level of government. Explain the details of how government under the Articles was organized **and how it operated**. Note that it was ineffective **because** it was limited by design. There were, **however**, significant decisions made during the mere eight years of the Articles' operation. America formulated a national land policy and a plan for creating new states that would eventually join the Union. Point out that all the states north of Maryland either outlawed slavery or provided for the eventual emancipation of the slaves within their borders. (Draw your students' attention to the spot map that shows the legal changes to slavery, 1777–1804.) Discuss the issue of slavery in the territories.

Nevertheless, it was the weaknesses of the Articles that those involved with national government noticed most. Mention the economic upheaval of the 1780s that resulted in Shays's Rebellion. Stress that Congress was weak and ineffective but that, as noted earlier, many preferred it that way. Make the point that the citizens of the states wanted governmental sovereignty to reside in the state governments (refer to the previous lecture). They wanted to ensure that government could not deprive them of their liberties. Throughout this lecture, have students consider the ways in which the architects of the Articles of Confederation understood the "promise" of the new country.

LECTURE 3

The Constitution as a Mechanism for Distributing Power

This lecture discusses the historical redistribution of power envisioned by the writers of the Constitution. The constitution written at the Philadelphia convention was touted as a better framework for national government, but better for whom? Clearly women, blacks, and poor white males did not expect the new Constitution to alter their lives radically for the better. Discuss the misconceptions about equality of opportunity for the "dependent populations." The Constitution ignored women, enshrined slavery, and left decisions regarding qualifications for voting and officeholding to state governments, which were run by wealthy elites. Here, have students discuss Mercy Otis Warren's observations of the Constitution (in the documents reader). The western areas of most states, which had less political power than the longer established eastern portions, generally opposed ratification. Those few who actually exercised power understood how the Constitution could redistribute political power within the new country, hence the long debate over the Virginia and New Jersey Plans at the Philadelphia Convention and the battle over ratification. Briefly explore the details of the Virginia and New Jersey Plans and how they were reconciled. Ask how small and large states hoped to gain or hoped to minimize their loss of political power with the Constitution. How did it compare with power arrangements under the Articles of Confederation? Then consider the process of ratification. (Be sure to have students discuss essay number 10 of James Madison's *Federalist*, in the documents reader.) While ratification was not a certainty, some states ratified immediately. Why? Other states showed great internal division because certain groups recognized that they stood to lose while their opponents would gain political power. Why were they so concerned about the redistribution of power? What were its possible effects? Focus on these questions when introducing the Antifederalists. Explain that they were not men of small vision but rather men fearful of what the redistribution of power by the Constitution would do to them. Their legacy is

the Bill of Rights. Finally, ask students if they think the Constitution has been used to redistribute power at any other times in American history. You might have them consider, for example, the ways in which the success of the New Jersey Plan ensured George W. Bush's election in 2000.

Anticipating Student Reactions: Common Misconceptions and Difficult Topics

1. *The Definition of Equality Is Static and Fixed*

Students frequently assume that early Americans did not believe in equality of opportunity because they did not practice equality according to today's definitions. Explain to students that the concept of equality has always been an important part of the American rhetoric, but that the definition of equality has evolved continuously over the course of American history. This chapter allows the instructor to explore the ways in which notions of social hierarchy, especially during the framing of the Constitution, limited notions of equality. Most eighteenth-century political leaders considered women, blacks, and the lower classes "dependent" populations because they owed their livelihood to someone else — a husband, a master, or a client/patron. As dependents, they were not expected to participate in political or social decisions because they lacked the "independence" to form their own conclusions. Have students use documents (in the documents reader) covering Mercy Otis Warren as a case study. Why should a brilliant woman hide her intelligence? What opportunities did women have in the early republic? Did those opportunities change with class or racial differences? Blacks similarly were considered dependent even though some states formally renounced slavery. Have your students compare the sections in the textbook that discuss emancipation in the northern states with the selection from Thomas Jefferson's *Notes on the State of Virginia* (in the documents reader), in which Jefferson stereotyped blacks and suggested that emancipation was a dead letter in the South. (Also available is the Series in History and Culture volume, Thomas Jefferson's *Notes on the State of Virginia with Related Documents,* by David Waldstreicher.) Why did the North reject slavery at this particular time, and why did the South remain wedded to the institution? How did racism contribute to emancipation? Did emancipation mean that blacks experienced social and political equality? And, finally, when discussing free white males, make clear that property qualifications excluded from one-quarter to one-half of all white males from the franchise. The playing field was level only for those allowed to play: The dependent groups were allowed only as spectators.

2. Ratification of the Constitution Was Certain

Students frequently believe that the Constitution was a done deal. Most assume that because the Articles of Confederation so obviously needed repair, they couldn't possibly rival the Constitution. To avoid this teleological construction and to reintroduce the idea that history is always contingent, point out that the Articles actually reflected the ideals of limited central power. They delegated minimal authority to a distant national government. Americans fought the Revolution for local autonomy, and even if the Articles were not perfect, local government still provided most governmental needs of the citizenry. Emphasize that all segments of American society were reluctant to endorse a new, more powerful yet untried framework for government, particularly one that flew in the face of accepted political theory. Even after the Constitution took effect following ratification by the first nine states, either Virginia or New York could have derailed it by refusing to join the Union under its provisions. Either state was self-sufficient enough to become an independent country and could have easily destroyed the United States simply by refusing to join and thus physically dividing the nation. Ask your students to consider what actions any of the ratifying assemblies should have taken if unconvinced by essay number 10 of James Madison's *Federalist* (in the documents reader) and what effect those actions would have had on the union.

3. The Antifederalists Were Men of Small Vision

If students are at all familiar with the Antifederalists, they probably think that (1) they were backward-looking reactionaries who opposed modernity and (2) not only were they incapable of imagining the greatness that awaited the United States under the Constitution, but they probably came from the poorer and less educated ranks of American citizens as well, and hence their vision was limited to their immediate local needs. This interpretation, of course, ignores the southern planters who supported Antifederalist causes. It

also ignores the many well-known heroes of the American Revolution who opposed the Constitution — Patrick Henry, Samuel Adams, George Mason, and (anonymously) Mercy Otis Warren. These well-meaning, civic-minded, and intelligent opponents of the Constitution saw that document as a return to many of the same sorts of institutions that they had opposed in the Revolution. What they wanted most was a pledge that the national government would never violate their "inalienable" rights, and thus they called for a national bill of rights. Point out that the Constitution's Bill of Rights is the Antifederalist legacy to the present, and ask how many would have been convinced by the Federalists that such a document was unnecessary. Use the discussion of the separation of church and state in the *Historical Question* feature to show students how issues resolved themselves differently at the state and national levels.

Using the Bedford Series in History and Culture and the Historians at Work Series: Suggestions

Thomas Jefferson's *Notes on the State of Virginia with Related Documents*, by David Waldstreicher, works well in the classroom. A useful book that deals with some of the issues and confrontations over the Constitution is *Declaring Rights: A Brief Documentary History*, edited by Jack N. Rakove. Another worthwhile assignment is *The Federalist*, also edited by Jack N. Rakove. Eve Kornfeld's *Creating American Culture, 1775–1800: A Brief History with Documents* examines the ways in which America's leading intellectuals sought to invent a story of nationhood during the Revolutionary era. Edward Countryman's *What Did the Constitution Mean to Early Americans?* offers students the chance to explore the far-reaching implications of the Constitution.

Lecture Supplements and Classroom Activities

Using Multimedia Sources in the Classroom

Consider showing the final episode of the PBS series *Liberty!*, "Are We to Be a Nation?," which details the economic crisis of the 1780s, the squabbling between the states, the Philadelphia convention, and the ratification process.

Historical Contingencies

Have your students consider the question "What if the Antifederalists had prevailed?" Such a discussion may allow students to delve more deeply into the Antifederalist position and force them to take it seriously. Consider assigning *Declaring Rights* (see previous section) to facilitate discussion.

Classroom Activities

Have your students debate the meaning of the Constitution to the various groups of early Americans. Your students may find Edward Countryman's *What Did the Constitution Mean to Early Americans?* helpful on this score.

Using the Internet

The University of Oklahoma Law Center has placed the text of the Articles of Confederation online. Direct students to <http://www.law.ou.edu/hist/artconf.html>. Students may find it useful to compare the Articles with the text of the Constitution, found in Appendix I of *The American Promise*.

The Library of Congress has made available the Federalist Papers. Direct students to <http://lcweb2.loc.gov/const/fed/fedpapers.html>. You may want to have them compare these writings with the Anti-Federalist Papers, found at <http://www.constitution.org/afp.htm>.

ASSESSING RESULTS
Multiple-Choice Questions

1. James Madison's passion for political philosophy
    a. made him "too intellectual" for his fellow revolutionaries, and thus he was barred from "practical activities," such as hammering out a new federal constitution.
    b. made him sickly and enervated and therefore ill suited for the rigorous debates that surrounded the drafting of the Constitution.
    c. led him to oppose the ratification of the Constitution on ideological grounds.
    d. served him well in his roles as one of the main architects of the U.S. Constitution and one of its staunchest defenders.

2. Why did Maryland delay ratification of the Articles of Confederation?
    a. It wanted a national policy for the gradual emancipation of all slaves north of the Mason-Dixon line.
    b. It wanted aid in putting down a rebellion of indebted farmers who refused to pay state taxes.

c. It wanted the states with unsettled western land claims to donate their claims to the national government.
    d. It wanted the inclusion of a bill of rights to guarantee the citizens personal liberties against a distant government.

3. Why did most states require a certain level of property ownership to qualify for voting or holding political office?
    a. It was believed that concentrating political power in the hands of the wealthy would encourage economic development.
    b. It was believed that such qualifications would encourage the poorer classes to work hard and save money.
    c. It was believed that keeping a single list of property owners to regulate the collection of taxes and to keep track of voters was more efficient than maintaining separate lists for each.
    d. It was believed that only property owners possessed the necessary independence to make wise political decisions.

4. What was the difference between the paper money printed by the states and the banknotes issued by the Bank of North America during the critical period?
    a. State money constantly depreciated because the states printed money as they needed it; banknotes could be redeemed with hard money kept in the bank's vault.
    b. The bank printed money as needed to regulate the economy; the state currencies were backed by taxes stored in each state treasury.
    c. The state currencies were legal tender; banknotes were only promissory notes issued in the name of the bank's president, Robert Morris.
    d. There was no difference whatsoever; they were all convertible to gold or silver on demand.

5. How was sectionalism created during the critical period?
    a. The eastern states imposed high taxes to retire their war debts; the western states, without war debts, sold their public-domain lands to generate operating capital.
    b. The northern states tied themselves to trade with England; the southern states traded with the Caribbean.
    c. The northern states all provided for the eventual emancipation of slaves within their borders; southern states did not.

d. The eastern states consciously built large cities; the western states sought to maintain their rural nature.

6. What made Antifederalists oppose the Constitution most strongly?
   a. fear that the document would cause class warfare because the Federalists were all wealthy
   b. fear that the Constitution would prove weak and ineffective since the president could veto legislation if he disagreed with Congress
   c. fear that sectional loyalties would eventually cause a civil war in such a large republic
   d. fear that a distant government would infringe on people's liberty

7. How did the federal guarantee of religious liberty differ from religious freedoms granted by the individual states?
   a. State government guarantees of religious toleration applied only to Christian denominations.
   b. The federal guarantee went beyond toleration of religion and made an individual's civil status independent of his or her religious beliefs.
   c. State government guarantees of religious liberty were based on a positive guarantee of political participation for all, despite religious differences; the federal government's sense of toleration was a negative guarantee, prohibiting Congress from interfering with the individual's right to pray.
   d. All state governments prohibited Catholics or non-Christians from voting or holding office.

8. According to Map 8.1, "Cession of Western Lands, 1782–1802," which of the following states had a disputed land claim with Britain?
   a. Pennsylvania
   b. Georgia
   c. Virginia
   d. Maine (Massachusetts)

9. Which of the following statements, excerpted from his *Notes on the State of Virginia* in the documents reader, best represents Thomas Jefferson's views on emancipation?
   a. He favored emancipation but did not believe it was possible.
   b. He favored emancipation and supported the bill for immediately freeing all the slaves of Virginia.
   c. His racism prevented him from seeing the injustice of slavery.
   d. His paternalism made him believe that slavery benefited both master and slave alike.

10. Identify the correct sequence of events.
    a. Virginia Bill of Rights, Articles of Confederation ratified, Shays's Rebellion, Philadelphia convention
    b. Treaty of Paris, Virginia Bill of Rights, Constitution ratified, Northwest Ordinance
    c. Articles of Confederation ratified, state constitutions written, *The Federalist*, Annapolis convention
    d. Shays's Rebellion, Treaty of Paris, Bank of North America chartered, state constitutions chartered

PROPOSING MORE: Additional Readings

John H. Aldrich and Ruth W. Grant, "The Antifederalists, the First Congress, and the First Parties," *Journal of Politics* 55, no. 2 (1993): 295–326.

Joan R. Gundersen, "Independence, Citizenship, and the American Revolution," *Signs* 13 (1987): 59–77.

Larry M. Lane and Judith J. Lane, "The Columbian Patriot: Mercy Otis Warren and the Constitution," *Women and Politics* 10, no. 2 (1990): 17–32.

Richard P. McCormick, "The 'Ordinance' of 1784," *William and Mary Quarterly* 50, no. 1 (1993): 112–22.

Jack N. Rakove, "Smoking Pistols and the Origins of the Constitution," *Reviews in American History* 22, no. 1 (1994): 39–44.

Rosemarie Zagarri, "The Revolution against the Revolution," *Reviews in American History* 22, no. 1 (1994): 45–50.

Answer Key to Multiple-Choice Questions: 1-d, 2-c, 3-d, 4-a, 5-c, 6-d, 7-b, 8-a, 9-a, 10-a

THE NEW NATION TAKES FORM

9

1789–1800

Outlining Chapters: Thematic Questions

I. What were sources of stability and change in the 1790s?
   A. Whom did George Washington appoint to his first cabinet, and on what basis did he choose them?
   B. How were the ten constitutional amendments, known as the Bill of Rights, proposed and ratified? What purpose did the Bill of Rights serve? Why was the right to vote, later viewed by most as a fundamental liberty, conspicuously absent from the Bill of Rights? What qualifications did most states impose in terms of voting? How did New Jersey deviate from the pattern?
   C. How were courtship, marriage, and motherhood reevaluated in light of republican ideals? How were gender roles altered by this reevaluation?

II. What economic changes affected America in the 1790s?
   A. Why, and how, did Americans in both northern and southern states engage in commercial agriculture?
   B. What sorts of transportation improvements were made beginning in the 1790s, and how did they differ from east to west and north to south?
   C. How did commercial banking arise, and how did banks operate?

III. What was Alexander Hamilton's three-part economic program, and why did it engender controversy?
   A. What was Hamilton's plan for funding the public debt, and why did he include assuming state debts as well? How did Hamilton propose that the federal government raise the money necessary to meet the interest payments on the national debt? Why did James Madison and Thomas Jefferson oppose Hamilton's plan?
   B. Why did Hamilton believe a national bank necessary? How was it to be organized, and who would control it? Who opposed the plan, and why? How did Hamilton propose to encourage American manufacturing?
   C. What philosophical differences about government were exposed by the actions of the farmers of Pennsylvania and the actions of the federal government during the Whiskey Rebellion?

IV. How did domestic and international armed conflicts affect American life during Washington's second administration?
   A. How did American policy toward the Indians foster tension in the Ohio valley in the 1790s? How did American population growth and

settlement affect Indian relations? How can the fighting between American settlers and Native Americans be characterized? What effect did the Treaty of Greenville have on the Native Americans?

B. What impact did the French Revolution, the Reign of Terror, and the state of war between France and England have on American politics? What was Washington's response to the war, and how successful was it?

C. What were the terms of John Jay's treaty with the British? How was it received in the United States? How were votes in Congress reflective of other philosophical splits in the House and Senate?

D. What precipitated the Haitian Revolution? Why did it strike fear in the hearts of many white Americans? What influence did it have in slave communities in the United States?

V. Who were the Federalists and the Republicans?

A. How were John Adams, a Federalist, and Thomas Jefferson, a Republican, elected president and vice president in 1796? Why did Adams retain Washington's cabinet, and how did that decision give Alexander Hamilton undue influence?

B. What was the XYZ affair, and how did it lead to the Quasi War with France in 1798?

C. How did the Alien and Sedition Acts operate, and who were their intended victims? How did opposition to the Alien and Sedition Acts create the idea of nullification? How did President Adams ultimately deal with the French, and how did his handling affect his bid for reelection?

Teaching with The American Promise, *Second Compact Edition: Lecture Strategies*

LECTURE 1

The Tension between Competing Values in the 1790s

This lecture demonstrates how the early 1790s were marked by the radical ideas emanating from the American Revolution as opposed to the traditional notions of hierarchy. Start with the debate that surrounded the proper form of address for the new American president. The vignette at the beginning of the chapter discusses the disdain

most Americans had for the granting of titles. Congress considered many exalted titles, which seem silly to us today, before it settled on the more egalitarian address of "Mr. President." Yet even Washington originally endorsed some of the proposed titles. Other indicators of the tension between radical egalitarianism and traditional hierarchy appeared in child-rearing and educational policies. Use the documents reader to explore changes in both of these areas. Have your students discuss the ideas of William Manning (in the documents reader). Next introduce the idea of "republican motherhood" and discuss the education of women through the valedictory addresses of Molly Wallace and Priscilla Mason (in the documents reader). Finally, discuss the changes in the electorate. Why were women and free blacks allowed to vote in New Jersey for thirty years? Use this discussion to demonstrate that republican motherhood, although creating the possibility for future change, acted in unison with traditional values based on hierarchy and patriarchy.

LECTURE 2

Politics and Economic Change at the End of the Eighteenth Century

Use this lecture to demonstrate that Alexander Hamilton established a forward-looking economic political agenda in the last decade of the eighteenth century. His preference for appropriate deference to the elite according to the traditional notions of hierarchy, however, caused him to be suspected of aristocratic pretensions and of seeking to establish, if not an American aristocracy, then at least an oligarchic political elite. Thus, his agenda immediately sparked suspicions not only among his enemies, the former Antifederalists, but also among his former allies who had supported ratification of the Constitution. Explore Hamilton's wide-ranging economic program: (1) the funding of the national debt with assumption of outstanding state debts, (2) chartering a central bank (the Bank of the United States), and (3) encouraging American industrial independence. At this point, be sure to discuss Hamilton's *Report on the Subject of Manufactures* (in the documents reader). Use this lecture to address the myth that politics and economics operate in separate realms and the myth that a continually expanding industrial base is desirable. Discuss the details of Hamilton's economic plans. Conclude with discussions of the opposition to Hamilton's seemingly modern economic agenda. Pay particular attention to the argument about the unconstitutionality of the Bank of the United States. The Constitution was less than five years old at a point when Hamilton claimed nearly unlimited expansionary powers under the "necessary and proper clause." Certainly it sparked controversy then, and it will elicit a response from your students today.

LECTURE 3
European Conflict and the Coalescing of American Political Parties

This lecture ties together international and domestic politics to show the creation of the two-party system in the United States. Pay particular attention to the American and British reactions to the French Revolution. First, discuss the misconception that the "founding fathers" built the two-party system into American politics from the beginning and that it has always been seen as a positive form of institutionalized conflict. Direct your students' attention to Washington's farewell address (excerpted as in the documents reader) to highlight his philosophical opposition to political parties. Then show how the French Revolution divided American opinion and how the war between France and England created a diplomatic crisis for the United States that eventually led to the Quasi War with France. Be sure to tie in the Jay Treaty and the XYZ affair. With war fever rampant, the Federalist-controlled Congress passed the Alien and Sedition Acts, which were aimed at the domestic enemies of the Adams administration rather than at the country's foreign adversary. Explain the details of these acts and whom they affected. Discuss the questions posed at the end of the *Documenting the American Promise* feature, "The Crisis of 1798: Sedition." Finally, conclude with Jefferson's and Madison's introduction of the concept of nullification in the Kentucky and Virginia Resolutions. Not only had external affairs divided Americans into separate camps, but one camp now planned to ignore the First Amendment rights of its opponents, and the other looked for remedies for their oppression outside the Constitution. Use the development of responses to constitutional issues to frame the rest of the political discussions leading up to the Civil War. The Virginia and Kentucky Resolutions were only the first salvo in the war over how to resolve problems for which the Constitution provides no framework.

Anticipating Student Reactions: Common Misconceptions and Difficult Topics

1. Americans Have Always Believed in a Two-Party System
Americans of the 1790s believed that factions (parties) were a sign of disease in the body politic. Only one group — a group imbued with public virtue — could make laws for the country, laws that would promote the harmony of interests of all segments of society. They did not imagine that institutionalized conflict, such as that of the United States with its two-party system, would result in good government. They could only see it resulting in civil war, as one group sought to benefit itself at the expense of another. The development of the Federalist and the Democratic-Republican parties toward the end of the eighteenth century seemed to validate this belief as the Federalists created the Alien and Sedition Acts — laws we would clearly define as both partisan and unconstitutional — to reduce the power of their opponents. The Democratic-Republicans responded with the Virginia and Kentucky Resolutions, which put forth the position that the states could nullify an unconstitutional law passed by Congress. Certainly, nobody foresaw this turn of events during the ratification of the Constitution. Such measures by each side represented a view of the other party as evil, corrosive, and self-serving. Ask your students to discuss what today's hard-core partisans think of their opponents. People today continue to debate the merits of a two-party system. Some now think institutionalized conflict is the same as institutionalized "gridlock." (Here, you might want to discuss the election of 2000, in which American voters seemed unable to choose between Democratic Party candidate Albert Gore and Republican Party candidate George W. Bush.) Explain that the two-party system is "good" for the country as long as it works, but that it has no constitutional or philosophical reason for continuation. You might end by comparing America's modern two-party system with other nations' multiparty systems, identifying strengths and weaknesses of each.

2. Americans Have Always Viewed Increasing Industry Positively
Many students might not understand that in the 1790s Americans were quite ambivalent about in-

dustrialization. The experience of England seemed to show that industrialization increased misery and poverty or at least centralized these conditions, as people were forced off their ancestral lands and, with no other place to go, entered factories. Thomas Jefferson called for America to remain an agricultural land and to resist encroaching industry. With agriculture came land-ownership, which gave citizens the necessary independence from outside influence to allow them to make the best political decisions for the country. But Alexander Hamilton had a competing vision of independence — one of national economic independence rather than personal economic independence. Only the legislative agenda of industrializers such as Hamilton and the social forces that kept people from achieving personal independence resulted in America's achievement of a manufacturing economy. Ask your students which they would have preferred to be in the last decade of the eighteenth century — farmers or factory workers. Most will answer farmers, since farming was the best means of personal independence. Then ask which occupation was best for the country. Point out that the answer manufacturing makes sense only in the context of later developments. Nobody knew what the future would hold.

3. Politics Has Little or No Effect on the Economy

Students are imbued with present-day cynicism about the ability of government to make any real changes in their lives. They don't realize that much of the world around them works the way it does because legislation shapes the way institutions work. Clearly the 1790s demonstrate that governmental action is a tangible force for economic change. Hamilton proposed three economic programs that altered both the political landscape and the economic order of the new country. Although only two of his programs (funding of the national debt and chartering a central bank) received congressional approval at the time, the third (tariff protection of American industries) would eventually be adopted as well and cause just as much controversy. By creating these institutions, the Congress of the 1790s affected the economy of both the nineteenth and twentieth centuries. Americans today still care about these three issues, and decisions about them have just as much impact as they did in the 1790s. To drive home this point, ask your students to comment on how the United States is changing into a postindustrial society. Are the causes of change strictly economic? Are the economic sources influenced by legislation? What are the options? Tie this discussion back to the 1790s and show how great economic transitions require a great deal of legal restructuring of economic institutions.

Using the Bedford Series in History and Culture and the Historians at Work Series: Suggestions

When discussing constitutional issues during this period, you might assign *Declaring Rights: A Brief Documentary History,* edited by Jack N. Rakove. *Judith Sargent Murray: A Brief Biography with Documents,* by Sheila Skemp, offers a good introduction to women's roles during this period, especially the issue of republican motherhood.

Lecture Supplements and Classroom Activities

Using Multimedia Sources in the Classroom

When discussing gender roles during the early national period, consider screening the PBS documentary *A Midwife's Tale,* which is based on Laurel Thatcher Ulrich's Pulitzer Prize–winning account of Martha Ballard, a midwife in Maine during the decades following the American Revolution. In addition to chronicling Ballard's life as a midwife and her struggles against poverty, disease, and domestic abuse, the documentary interweaves footage of historian Ulrich piecing together the fragmentary evidence of Ballard's world.

When discussing the Haitian Revolution, consider showing part three of the PBS series *Africans in America,* "Brotherly Love," which documents the event's influence in the United States.

Historical Contingencies

Ask your students to consider the trajectory of American development had Hamilton's economic program been rejected. What if Americans had held to Jefferson's ideal of the virtuous, independent yeoman farmer? What problems could the country have avoided? What problems would it have likely encountered? Again, remind students that the fact that Americans followed Hamilton's vision does not suggest that Americans had no choice in the matter. Their course was not predetermined.

Classroom Activities

Have your students debate the relative merits and drawbacks of the Federalist-sponsored Alien and Sedition Acts. Your students should grasp immediately that the Sedition Act infringes on the constitutionally guaranteed liberties of free speech and the Alien Act oversteps the powers of Congress enumerated in the Constitution. Ask your students, however, if Congress has the "right" to subvert the Constitution during times of crisis. Students may find Adams's strategy to quash his political opposition a bit too blatant to endorse the two acts. Remind students of their original position when discussing Lincoln's suspension of habeas corpus during the Civil War, the passage of the Sedition Act in World War I, and the internment of Japanese Americans during World War II. How far, according to your students, can the federal government "bend" the Constitution to "protect" the republican form of government?

Using the Internet

Direct your students' attention to sites relevant to the Alien and Sedition Acts. The Avalon Project: Documents in Law, History, and Diplomacy at Yale University offers texts of the acts as well as texts of the Virginia and Kentucky Resolutions. Go to <http://www.yale.edu/lawweb/avalon/avalon.htm> and click on "18th Century Documents." You can also send students to <http://www.constitution.org/rf/vr_02.htm>, which is the page of the Constitution Society's Web site that includes the debates surrounding the drafting of the Virginia Resolutions.

ASSESSING RESULTS
Multiple-Choice Questions

1. How did the political role of women change during the early republic?
   a. Women, as well as property-owning blacks, were given the right to vote, starting in small states such as New Jersey, to broaden and more fully democratize the electorate.
   b. Women were to serve as the conscience of an increasingly market-oriented United States, chastising shopkeepers and merchants who gouged the public with high prices.
   c. Women were to exercise their private virtue in raising their sons and to inculcate in them the public virtue necessary for good government.
   d. Women continued to have no political role in America.

2. Who opposed Alexander Hamilton's Bank of the United States, and why?
   a. John Adams opposed it because he thought it gave Hamilton undue influence over his cabinet.
   b. Jefferson and Madison opposed it because they believed it unconstitutional.
   c. Eastern merchants opposed it because they feared it would drain all the currency from the seaports and deposit it on the frontier.
   d. New Englanders opposed it because they thought their distance from the Philadelphia-based institution would increase the cost of doing business.

3. How did American agriculture change in the 1790s?
   a. American agricultural production remained largely unchanged from previous years.
   b. An extended drought, together with unwise tillage practices, caused massive destruction of topsoil, and created the nation's first "dust bowl."
   c. Americans grew more grains related to alcohol production, in order to make a profit, despite the new federal excise tax.
   d. Americans began the large-scale cultivation of wheat and cotton for sale on the international market.

4. John Jay's treaty with
   a. the Indians at Greenville, Ohio, forced the Indians to relinquish most of the Ohio valley but guaranteed that their remaining lands would be safe from further encroachment from settlers.
   b. France required the payment of bribes to three French officials and the unsecured loan of $12 million to France.
   c. England failed to negotiate the immediate compensation for seizure of American ships.
   d. the Spanish promised to keep the Mississippi River open to all traffic and proclaimed an alliance in the European wars.

5. The Alien and Sedition Acts
   a. were used by the Republican Party of Thomas Jefferson to limit the voting power of immigrants, because they usually voted Federalist.
   b. were carefully written to preserve order during times of impending war, but also

preserved the First Amendment rights of freedom of speech and freedom of the press.

c. compelled Jefferson and Madison to write the Virginia and Kentucky resolves, which first proposed the theory of nullification.

d. compelled Alexander Hamilton to oppose secretly the election of John Adams by the electoral college, which resulted in Thomas Jefferson's election as vice president.

6. What is evident from the textbook's cartoon of the Matthew Lyon fight in Congress?
   a. Although tempers frequently flared and there was much heated rhetoric in Congress, members never lost their dignity by resorting to physical violence.
   b. Formal duels between political opponents were occasionally staged on the floor of Congress.
   c. Federalists and Republicans, despite their differences, observed a strict code of honor when Congress was in session.
   d. Occasionally political conflict erupted into physical brawling in Congress.

7. In what future state were the Battle of Fallen Timbers, St. Clair's Defeat, and Fort Greenville located?
   a. Ohio
   b. Indiana
   c. Illinois
   d. Michigan

8. Washington's farewell address
   a. sought to establish principles of national behavior that were based on unity rather than party factionalism.
   b. urged the incoming administration to enter into a permanent alliance with England.
   c. urged the incoming administration to enter into a permanent alliance with France.
   d. underscored the importance of national parties to manage political conflict.

9. The Whiskey Rebellion demonstrated that
   a. cash-short farmers deeply resented the high taxes levied on wheat and rye.
   b. merchants deeply resented paying high prices for alcohol.
   c. the government was willing to change its policy in the face of popular opposition to an act passed by Congress.

d. the tension between minority rights and majority rule had ceased to be palpable by the 1790s.

10. The Haitian Revolution
    a. failed to inspire American slaves in their quest for freedom and liberty.
    b. led to the first and only independent black state to arise out of a successful revolution by slaves.
    c. was so far removed from Americans' consciousnesses that it provoked no reaction from American slaveholders.
    d. sparked several large-scale slave rebellions across the United States.

11. Identify the correct sequence of historical events and figures.
    a. Hamilton's Funding and Assumption Plan approved, Virginia and Kentucky Resolutions, Bank of the United States chartered
    b. Bill of Rights ratified, George Washington inaugurated, Alien and Sedition Acts passed, Jefferson becomes vice president
    c. St. Clair's Defeat, Battle of Fallen Timbers, Whiskey Rebellion, Quasi War
    d. XYZ affair, Jay Treaty, Neutrality Proclamation, Treaty of Greenville

PROPOSING MORE: Additional Readings

John H. Aldrich and Ruth W. Grant, "The Antifederalists, the First Congress, and the First Parties," *Journal of Politics* 52, no. 2 (1993): 295–326.

Benjamin B. Klubes, "The First Federal Congress and the First National Bank: A Case Study in Constitutional Interpretation," *Journal of the Early Republic* 10, no. 1 (1990): 19–41.

Jan Lewis, "The Republican Wife: Virtue and Seduction in the Early Republic," *William and Mary Quarterly* 44, no. 4 (1987): 689–721.

Philippa Strum, "On Theorizing about Rights," *Reviews in American History* 21, no. 1 (1993): 151–55.

Ray Thomas, "'Not One Cent for Tribute': The Public Addresses and American Popular Reaction to the XYZ Affair," *Journal of the Early American Republic* 34, no. 3 (1983): 389–412.

Answer Key to Multiple-Choice Questions: 1-c, 2-b, 3-d, 4-c, 5-c, 6-d, 7-a, 8-a, 9-a, 10-b, 11-c

REPUBLICAN ASCENDANCY 10

1800–1824

*O*utlining Chapters: Thematic Questions

I. In what ways can Thomas Jefferson's presidency be considered a revolution?

    A. Why was the election of 1800 considered a surprise? Why was the election thrown into the House for a final decision?

    B. What inspired Gabriel, a Virginia slave, to plan a rebellion? What was the legacy of his ill-fated revolt?

    C. What was Jefferson's vision of the Republican simplicity? How did widespread landownership guarantee liberty, according to Jefferson? How did Jefferson implement his vision of limited government?

    D. Who were the "midnight judges," and what precedent was set by the Supreme Court, in the case *Marbury v. Madison,* regarding them? How did John Marshall change the way the Supreme Court operated?

    E. How did the United States purchase the Louisiana Territory from France? Why did Jefferson commission Lewis and Clark to explore the trans-Mississippi West? What were the results of this mission?

II. How did European and Indian wars intrude on American life in the first decade of the nineteenth century?

    A. What effect did renewed fighting between England and France have on American commerce with those countries? What was the *Chesapeake* incident, and how did the United States respond to it? What was the Embargo Act? How successful was it, and what effect did it have on the U.S. economy?

    B. How did James Madison attempt to stop European interference with American neutrality? How successful were his attempts during his first two years in office?

    C. Why did Madison fear that war with England would embroil the American western frontier? Who were Tecumseh and the Prophet, and how did they unify the Indians of the Ohio valley? How did William Henry Harrison deal with them?

III. Why did the United States declare war on Great Britain in 1812? How did the war proceed?

    A. Why, and by what process, did the United States declare war on England? Who were the War Hawks, and what was their agenda? Why were American attempts to capture Canada largely unsuccessful? Why were the New England states disloyal during the war? How did Americans turn the tide of the war? How did Andrew Jackson first gain national notoriety?

B. What were the British offensives of 1814? Why was the Battle of New Orleans significant?

C. Why was the Federalist Party discredited because of the war? What was the Hartford Convention, and what did it advocate? Who won the war? What group benefited the most from the war? What group lost the most?

IV. How did the status of white women change in the early republic?

A. What underlying assumption about the proper relations between men and women came from British common law? How did divorce laws change? How did these laws and ideas affect slave women?

B. How did gender relations change within Protestant denominations? How did these relations differ between mainstream and fringe Protestant groups? What were the short-term and long-term implications of these changes?

V. What was the "Era of Good Feelings"?

A. What was unusual about Missouri when it requested admission as a state in 1819? What was the Tallmadge Amendment, and what were the terms of the Missouri Compromise of 1820?

B. What was the Monroe Doctrine, and why did President Monroe issue it?

C. How was the election of 1824 different from almost every other American presidential election, and what was the "corrupt bargain"?

D. How successful was John Quincy Adams as president?

Teaching with The American Promise, *Second Compact Edition: Lecture Strategies*

LECTURE 1
The Revolution of 1800

Even prior to Thomas Jefferson's election in 1800, many viewed his anticipated victory as a revolution. Political rhetoric became so heated that

slaves in Virginia thought the time was ripe for a slave uprising. Discuss Gabriel's rebellion and the rhetoric that inspired it. Use "A Jeffersonian Sailmaker's Fourth of July Address" (in the documents reader) to explore whether the language of equality was meant to apply to anyone other than white males. Does the account of Gabriel's rebellion suggest that slaves accepted the assumption that the language of liberty and equality applied only to white males? Next, discuss in detail how Jefferson actually won the election. Then address both Jefferson's style of presidency and his vision of the ideal American society. Use the photo of Jefferson's clothing to discuss the simplicity of his vision. Move from style to substance and ask how the Indians fit into Jefferson's vision. Use "President Jefferson's Private and Public Indian Policy" (in the documents reader) to discuss what plan Jefferson had for Indian lands. Ask what Tecumseh and the Prophet could have expected from the federal government if they had not fought to organize the various tribes against American encroachment. Finally, return to politics and the ongoing convergence of politics and institution-building by discussing the "midnight judges" and how the Supreme Court justice John Marshall established the precedent of judicial review. Make a point of listing the various methods of dealing with questions regarding the Constitution. Thus far, politicians and intellectuals had proposed only two options: nullification and judicial review. This discussion will prepare students for the next lecture, when you introduce the third option: secession.

LECTURE 2
Another Era of War

Begin your lecture on the War of 1812 by discussing how European wars led to different definitions of neutrality under which the United States sought to trade profitably with all the belligerents. Both Britain and France, however, sought ways to limit American trade with its primary adversary. Confiscation and impressment were two of the means both belligerents used to influence American policy. The United States was unable to mount an effective counterstrategy. Discuss the embargo of 1807–1809 and how it affected the popularity of Jefferson. Why did he institute it, and what did he hope to achieve? Point out how the embargo destroyed part of the U.S. economy without generating the desired effects. Ask students, "How did Madison reintroduce a limited embargo, and how was he duped?" Introduce the War Hawks and their agenda. Next show that their plan, coupled with concerns about British encroachment in the West, greatly undermined the myth of impressment as the determinative cause of the War of 1812. Discuss how the country was unprepared for the war and unrealistically expected to "liberate" Canada from British protection. Ask why the British burned Washington (because an American force had burned Toronto). Show how the war divided the country; explain that Federalist New England opposed the war and was openly courted by the British in hopes of removing war from the country. Follow this discontent to the Hartford Convention, and discuss the two important effects of that meeting: (1) secession of one section of the country from the rest was openly discussed for the first time; (2) the Federalist Party was destroyed by its seemingly treasonous behavior at the convention. Emphasize the origins of secession and add this option to the list of means of dealing with constitutional questions. Point out that the Constitution was less than thirty years old, yet all the ideas about dealing with constitutional issues that led to the Civil War were already in place. Also show that although the Federalists ran in New England elections into the 1820s, the Hartford Convention effectively put an end to their party. Finally, emphasize that the United States did not really win anything in its second war with Great Britain. England's policies toward neutrals did not change, and the United States won no territory as a result of the war. Only the Battle of New Orleans, which took place after the Treaty of Ghent was signed, convinced the British to honor its provisions. That battle also had longer-term impacts by introducing a western military leader to the American public.

LECTURE 3
The Era of Good Feelings

The phrase "Era of Good Feelings" is the historian's shorthand for the time when the United States operated as a one-party state, with the Democratic-Republican Party as the country's only national party. Several important events took place during the Era of Good Feelings, among them the Missouri Compromise, the Monroe Doctrine, and the "corrupt bargain." Contemporaries viewed the first and the third as significant at the time, and historians regard the first and the second as important in the long run. Despite

the so-called good feelings, serious divisions within the country developed on the issue of the extension of slavery, starting with the admission of Missouri to statehood. (Here you can refer to Map 10.2, "The Missouri Compromise, 1820.") Of course, the issue never would have arisen had the country not expanded with the Louisiana Purchase, so you should quickly review that topic. Next, point out the length of time it took before Missouri was allowed to join the Union even though it had met all the existing criteria for admission. Ask students to consider what distinguished Missouri from other territories. Why did slavery suddenly start to bother people of the North? Clearly there was a moral dimension to their opposition, but other aspects existed as well. Leave an opportunity to return to this discussion in future lectures. Emphasize the formula for settling all future discussions of the issue: (1) maintain a balance in the Senate between slaveholding and nonslaveholding states; (2) limit all future expansion of slavery to territory south of Missouri's southern border (36° 30′). Discuss how America's leaders thought about the entire issue. Next, quickly introduce the Monroe Doctrine, showing that it meant very little at the time. (Ask students to explain the doctrine and give an example of its use. Ask them to criticize it from the viewpoint of one of the United States' Latin American neighbors.) Finally, cover the "corrupt bargain." Describe how John Quincy Adams won the presidency through the House of Representatives over the more popular Andrew Jackson. (Here you can use Map 10.3, "The Election of 1824.") Explain why the appointment of Henry Clay as Secretary of State could be viewed both as unethical and as dangerous to the future of the country.

Discuss some of the social developments that were under way during the first thirty years of the nineteenth century. Have students consider women's legal status in the early republic, comparing the lack of power here to the different kinds of roles women began to play in the religious sphere. Use the account on pages 226–27 of the textbook to explore the beginnings of the Second Great Awakening and women's roles in it. (Note that the main coverage of the Second Great Awakening occurs in Chapter 11.) Ask students why women were merely "exhorters" rather than actual preachers. Refer them to the anecdote and image of Jemima Wilkinson. Ask them why she styled herself as a person without sex or gender.

Finally, explore the question of race in an age of increasingly democratic participation. Ask students to consider Gabriel's rebellion, what rhetoric might have inspired it, and whether Gabriel and his followers were doomed from the start.

Anticipating Student Reactions: Common Misconceptions and Difficult Topics

1. Impressment of Sailors Was the Sole Cause of the War of 1812

Most students believe that American outrage over impressment was the only cause that prompted the United States to fight the British. The textbook clearly illustrates that other issues guided U.S. policy. To demonstrate that concerns about the western frontier played a larger role than impressment, ask students from which part of the country most of the sailors originated. When they identify New England, ask if New England supported the war. Then explore the reasons why the westerners and southerners supported the war and examine the agenda of the War Hawks. Why were they especially concerned about the British in North America?

2. The United States Won the War of 1812

As in the American Revolution, the British decided that pursuing a victory in the War of 1812 was too difficult. American victories (or British failures) caused Great Britain concern. With the exception of the Battle of New Orleans, most of the U.S. army engagements were fiascoes. The U.S. navy, on the other hand, outmaneuvered the British on the Great Lakes and threatened to cut off communications with the western portions of British North America. With the threat to the West and the stalemate on the coast, the British negotiated and signed the Treaty of Ghent, which did not settle any of the pretensions for which America had gone to war. Because the Battle of New Orleans resulted in the defeat of a major British land expedition, however, the British honored the treaty by withdrawing their forces, unlike their actions at the end of the American Revolution. Thus, the Americans fought a stalemate war, in which they gained very little other than a greater sense of self-importance.

3. The Missouri Compromise Line Stretched All the Way to the Pacific

Many students erroneously assume that the 36° 30′ line extended all the way to the Pacific coast. Debates over the extension of slavery into territories

won from Mexico, the Compromise of 1850, and much of the sectional rancor of the 1850s in general therefore make little sense to these students. To them, the Missouri Compromise solved all tricky constitutional questions on the extension of slavery into the territories. Take the opportunity to demonstrate to students that the 36° 30′ line bisected territory secured from the Louisiana Purchase only. (Have students refer to Map 10.2, "The Missouri Compromise, 1820," to illustrate your point.) Have students debate the virtues and limitations of the compromise. Ask them to predict the success of the compromise to quell debate about the extension of slavery into the territories.

Using the Bedford Series in History and Culture and the Historians at Work Series: Suggestions

This chapter introduces students to Lewis and Clark and their journey across the continent. You might consider assigning portions of the fascinating journals the men kept along the way, excerpted in *The Lewis and Clark Expedition: Selections from the Journals*, edited by Gunther Barth.

Lecture Supplements and Classroom Activities

Using Multimedia Sources in the Classroom

Ken Burns's documentary *Thomas Jefferson* works well in the classroom and complements the textbook's discussion of his presidency. You might also consider showing segments from *Lewis and Clark: The Journey of the Corps of Discovery*, which uses the famed explorers' journals and stories from Native American oral tradition to recreate their expedition.

Historical Contingencies

Have students consider the possible course of American history had opponents blocked the acquisition of the Louisiana Purchase. Would slavery have become a divisive issue? Remind students that much of the sectional rancor over slavery stemmed from opposition to the extension of slavery into the territories. Would the failure of the United States to secure the Louisiana Purchase have set a precedent for future attempts to acquire land? Could the boundaries of 1787 "contain" the issue (and institution) of slavery?

Classroom Activities

Most students do not consider the Louisiana Purchase controversial. Remind them that the decision, however, generated heated discussion at its implementation. Have the class debate the constitutionality of the acquisition. Be sure to remind students that Jefferson opposed many of Hamilton's policies on constitutional grounds, arguing that the Constitution made no mention of a national bank and so on. Ask students to find the section in the Constitution that provides for the acquisition of new territory not already claimed by the United States. (See the Constitution of the United States in the appendices.) When they fail, ask them on what grounds Jefferson and his supporters could (and did) justify their decision. Did Jefferson exceed his authority? Under what circumstances should the federal government exceed its constitutional authority?

Using the Internet

Excerpts of the Lewis and Clark journals can be found online at the site called American Studies @The University of Virginia. Direct your students to <http://xroads.virginia.edu>, tell them to click on "Hypertexts," and then "Lewis & Clark Journals."

The citation and full text of *Marbury v. Madison* can be found at Historic Supreme Court Decisions — by Party Name. Direct your students to <http://supct.law.cornell.edu/supct/index.html> and tell them to search for *Marbury v. Madison*.

ASSESSING RESULTS
Multiple-Choice Questions

1. Meriwether Lewis came to appreciate bringing the Indian wife and infant son of a French Canadian trapper along on his expedition to explore the Louisiana Purchase because
    a. Sacajawea, who knew the languages of the tribes all the way to Oregon, served as the interpreter for the expedition.
    b. Sacajawea was the only one to keep a written journal of their travels and therefore provided a day-to-day source of information for the formal report made to the Congress at the end of the expedition.
    c. the Native Americans they met along the way knew that war parties did not bring women and infant children, and thus the expedition was considered peaceful.
    d. Sacajawea prevented their capture by Mexican authorities by interceding on the expedition's behalf when they accidentally crossed into Mexican-claimed territory, near present-day Denver.

2. Why did Thomas Jefferson advocate widespread landownership?
    a. He wanted to limit the power of the wealthy, and widespread landownership would diminish the amount of property amassed by the elites.
    b. He believed that landownership would tie down a migrant population and produce greater national wealth.
    c. He believed in property qualifications for voting; and, to make the electorate more democratic, he advocated making landownership easier.
    d. He believed land, particularly agricultural land, conveyed the personal independence necessary for citizens to make political decisions without being influenced by employers or patrons.

3. *Marbury v. Madison*
    a. required that the United States trade only with the first country (England or France) that agreed to stop seizing American ships, and also required an embargo of all trade with the other.
    b. established the precedent of electing both the president and the vice president on a single ticket.
    c. required the election of 1800 to be decided by Congress because both Aaron Burr and Thomas Jefferson received the same number of electoral votes.
    d. established the precedent of judicial review of the constitutionality of actions of the president and Congress.

4. How did William Henry Harrison discredit the Prophet?
    a. He killed the Prophet's brother, Tecumseh.
    b. He called upon Tenskwatawa to perform some miracle.
    c. He demonstrated that the Shawnee were in league with the British.
    d. He destroyed Prophetstown.

5. Why did the United States become a one-party system following the War of 1812?
    a. James Madison arrested the leaders of the opposition party and banned them from further elections.
    b. The Federalists merged with the War Hawks and took control of the Republican Party.

c. John Quincy Adams's popularity drained the Republican Party of its members.

d. The Hartford Convention discredited the Federalist Party as disloyal and treasonous.

6. The Missouri Compromise
   a. required Missouri to outlaw the importation of new slaves.
   b. banned slavery in all territories west of Missouri.
   c. required Missouri to free all slaves born after a certain date, upon their twenty-fifth birthday.
   d. maintained a balance in Congress between the slave and the free states.

7. The lady's fan decorated with Jefferson's image that opens the chapter
   a. was used by Jefferson's wife, Martha, at the inaugural ball honoring her husband.
   b. was an accessory that allowed a woman to make a political statement.
   c. was commissioned by Jefferson's political opponents to humiliate him by connecting his image with a fancy feminine accessory.
   d. was given to Sacajawea by the explorers Lewis and Clark.

8. Aaron Burr, the vice president of the United States, killed Alexander Hamilton in a duel
   a. because Hamilton publicly questioned Burr's integrity, which cost Burr election as governor of New York.
   b. because Hamilton killed Burr's nineteen-year-old son in a duel three years earlier.
   c. because Hamilton attempted to form a separate country in the southwestern part of the United States.
   d. because Hamilton backed Jefferson for president, costing Burr the election.

9. Tecumseh responded to the eroding of his people's land by unfavorable treaties with the United States by
   a. allying himself with the United States against the British, hoping that the United States would repay his loyalty with the return of his people's ancestral lands.
   b. embarking on a campaign to return his people to their ancient ways.
   c. accommodating new realities and advocating farming, trading, and intermarriage with the Americans.
   d. appeasing his anger with large quantities of alcohol.

10. Identify the correct sequence of historical events and figures.
    a. Monroe Doctrine, "corrupt bargain," Treaty of Ghent
    b. Battle of Tippecanoe, Gabriel's rebellion, Battle of New Orleans
    c. Revolution of 1800, *Marbury v. Madison*, Hartford Convention, Missouri Compromise
    d. President Thomas Jefferson, President James Monroe, President John Quincy Adams, President James Madison

PROPOSING MORE: Additional Readings

Barry Balieck, "When the Ends Justify the Means: Thomas Jefferson and the Louisiana Purchase," *Presidential Studies Quarterly* 22, no. 4 (1992): 679–96.

Louis Billington, "Female Laborers in the Church: Women Preachers in the Northeastern United States, 1790–1840," *Journal of American Studies* 19 (1985): 369–94.

Roger H. Brown, "Who Bungled the War of 1812?," *Reviews in American History* 19, no. 2 (1991): 183–87.

Donald R. Hickey, "New England's Defense Problem and the Genesis of the Hartford Convention," *New England Quarterly* 50, no. 4 (1977): 587–604.

Graham Russell Hodges, "Gabriel's Republican Rebellion," *Reviews in American History* 22, no. 3 (1994): 128–32.

Stuart Leibiger, "Thomas Jefferson and the Missouri Compromise: An Alternative Interpretation," *Journal of the Early Republic* 17, no. 1 (1997): 121–30.

Answer Key to Multiple-Choice Questions: 1-c, 2-d, 3-d, 4-d, 5-d, 6-d, 7-b, 8-a, 9-b, 10-c

Essay Questions, Chapters 6–10

1. Drawing on your knowledge of colonial and post-Revolution America, discuss the degree to which the War for Independence was a social revolution. In other words, in what ways did the status of Americans change once the colonies became liberated from Britain? Did independence mean something other (or more) than the end of British colonial rule?

2. At what point did a distinctly American culture, as opposed to a British colonial culture, develop?

3. Did the development of American society, 1789–1824, fulfill the "promises" of the American Revolution?

4. How many "revolutions" occurred in America between 1776 and 1824?

11 THE EXPANDING REPUBLIC

1815–1840

*O*utlining Chapters: Thematic Questions

I. What were the major aspects of the "market revolution"?
  A. How did improved transportation change America? Why was the federal government reluctant to become involved in funding internal improvements? How important were new technologies to the "transportation revolution," and how safe were they? How did railroads begin to give canals competition?
  B. Why did American textile factories target young women as employees, and how important were women to the development of industry in the 1820s and 1830s? What attraction did factory work hold for women? How successful were women in organizing labor unions, and how successful were unions in raising their wages? How did the organization of labor in the shoemaking industry differ from that of the making of cloth and yarn?
  C. How did banks affect the Jacksonian economy? How did they operate? How did laws for creating corporations change the way America did business? How did an explosion in the number of American lawyers aid the development of an economy that emphasized entrepreneurship?
  D. What caused the economic depression in 1819? How severe was the economic contraction? What role were banks thought to have played in it?

II. What changes in American politics led to the creation of the second American party system?
  A. Why was voter turnout so high in the 1830s? By 1828, how did candidates organize their campaigns differently from previous campaigns? What new role did the press play in political campaigns? How did the Democratic and Whig Parties come into existence?
  B. What scandals and questions of character influenced the election of 1828, and how did the character issues help to define the emerging national parties?
  C. How did Jackson reinforce his image of representing the common man? What was Jackson's approach to the government?

III. How did American culture change during the Jacksonian era?
  A. What was the new theory regarding gender roles in America? What was the driving force in creating divisions between masculine and feminine roles? How was housework rendered invisible? Why was the doctrine of separate spheres acceptable, even when it was disregarded in many ways?
  B. What necessitated increased literacy in the first third of the nineteenth century? What institutions arose to meet that need, and how were they funded and operated? How equal was the education of the sexes? What two paths did young men take after common school? What new anxieties arose about the morals of youths, and why?
  C. Why was there an explosion of newspapers in the 1830s? What popular amusements were widely available to Americans beginning in the 1830s? How did the American theater demonstrate the fluidity of popular culture? How was oratory affected by the new public amusements?

IV. What was the central tenet of the Second Great Awakening, and how did it shape American religion?
  A. How did the Second Great Awakening start, and what was its main means of promotion? How did ministers elicit conversion? How did church membership change because of the Second Great Awakening, and which churches benefited most? Who were the primary targets of recruitment? How did Charles Grandison Finney promote this religious awakening? How did this movement promote social reforms?
  B. How did the temperance movement evolve, and how did it move from mere moral suasion to a political agenda? What was the "moral reform" movement? What role did women play in the moral reform movement?
  C. How did the abolitionist movement evolve, and how did it differ from earlier antislavery campaigns? What were the goals of the new movement, and who joined it? What opposition did the abolitionist movement face, and why? What role did women play in the abolitionist movement?

V. How did Jackson's administration define the Democratic Party?
  A. What was Jackson's Indian policy, and how did it differ from the policies of previous administrations? By what means did the various cultures oppose it? Why are the Cherokee of special interest, and how successful were they in opposing Jackson? What precedent did *Worcester v. Georgia* establish, and how did Jackson defy it?
  B. What was the "Tariff of Abominations"? Why did South Carolina advocate its nullification? How did South Carolina start a constitutional crisis, and how were its immediate concerns resolved? What were the theoretical issues of the crisis, and were they solved at that time?
  C. How did Jackson dismantle the Bank of the United States? What were the causes of the long depression known as the Panic of 1837?
  D. Why did Martin Van Buren serve only one term as president?

Teaching with The American Promise, *Second Compact Edition: Lecture Strategies*

LECTURE 1
Jacksonian Economic Improvements

This lecture focuses on the social aspects of the economic changes of Jacksonian America. First discuss the evolution of the concept of the market from a place where goods were exchanged to an arena for commodity exchange. Explain that as the market drew in more Americans, basic institutions underwent fundamental change on several fronts. The economy quickened through a revolution in transportation infrastructure. Before the transportation revolution, market exchanges took place primarily on a local level because transportation was either excessively expensive or physically impossible. Outline how turnpikes operated and how they represented an improvement over common roads. Show how the building of the Erie Canal by the state of New York set off an explosion of similar canal-building experiments and how railroads began to compete with canals as transportation projects. Have students look at Map 11.1, "Routes of Transportation in 1840," to demonstrate the vying modes of transportation.

Next, introduce the idea of industrialization. Dispel the belief that early industrialization is best represented by large factories. Preface your remarks by noting that the heart of increased and inexpensive industrial production in the early nineteenth century hinged on reducing production of an item into small, manageable tasks done by semiskilled women or children. Draw your students' attention to the 1850 daguerreotype of a woman at the loom. Discuss Slater's Mill and the Lowell system of factories as important cultural components of American industrialization, but not as its essence. Preview your discussion of the "doctrine of separate spheres" when you discuss why women provided cheap labor and why they were unable to obtain greater wage gains through strikes. Also describe the increasing desire for a "protective" tariff by northern manufacturers and their representatives in Congress.

Next, explore how banking operated, giving special notice to the process of exchanging a bank's notes at a distant location. Explain how banks proliferated as a means to "grow" the economy prior to dismemberment of the Second Bank of the United States, and how they grew explosively once that one remaining brake on the economy was removed.

Finally, confront the myth that the twentieth century's Great Depression had no precedent. Explain the business cycle and its low point. Discuss the cause, depth, and length of each of the depressions, giving special notice to the Panic of 1837. If this lecture seems too large to fit your schedule, you may wish to limit it to a detailed discussion of one of the major economic changes: transportation, industrialization, or finance.

LECTURE 2
The Culture of Jacksonian America

This lecture should focus on how a belief in the ability to shape one's own identity and future created a conscious desire to shape society as well. First, show how the economy intruded on perceptions of gender roles — explain that work was redefined as labor for wages, a concept that obscured the importance of work done by women at home. Explain why home was redefined as a refuge from the world and how the middle-class woman's role was to preserve that refuge.

Next, describe the Second Great Awakening and the means used by ministers to promote sal-

vation. Explore camp meetings, the use of emotion to elicit conversion, and the role of women in religious affairs. Direct students to the picture of Charles G. Finney's Broadway Tabernacle and ask them what aspects of that setting worshipers might have found inviting. Move on to make the point that evangelical Protestantism, along with the causes of education, temperance, and moral reform, were frequently promoted by the striving mercantile classes, whose ideology of self-sufficiency and self-discipline meshed well with these movements for spiritual and social reform. Explain each of these movements and include a discussion of abolitionism as well. Take special care to demonstrate why some perceived abolitionism as an extremist movement, and explain how both the South and the North reacted to it. Dispel the myth that all northerners were inherent abolitionists. Demonstrate the volatile nature of this movement by having students read Elijah Lovejoy's letter about his confrontation with an antiabolitionist mob (in the documents reader).

Finally, use Sarah Grimké's "Letters on the Equality of the Sexes" (in the documents reader) to explore how the movement for women's rights evolved out of participation in the abolitionist movement, and make the point that some perceived the idea of women's rights as even more radical than abolitionism.

LECTURE 3
Sectional Crisis and the Revolution in Partisan Politics

There were four major political developments during the Jackson administration, any one of which could constitute a full lecture. They include (1) increased political participation, (2) protective tariffs and the nullification crisis, (3) the politics of dealing with Native Americans (particularly the Cherokee removal), and (4) the "monster" bank. You can use the following lecture strategy, which presents these developments all at once to provide an overview, or you might narrow the focus of your lecture to one or two of these topics and add more detail.

To demonstrate the evolution of political parties and the ongoing sectional split, you should first explain the increase in political participation. Show how the politics of the Jacksonian era were in many ways a natural outgrowth of the ideals of Jefferson's Republican Party, which sought universal white male suffrage. Next explore how transportation improvements, coupled with the demands from commercial enterprises for increased literacy, created a communications revolution that brought political messages to the common man. Politicians then organized networks of politically like-minded newspapers and tied them to their parties for patronage. Local organizations used rallies and other means derived from popular culture to lure potential voters to their cause.

Once you establish the means of participation, introduce specific political issues. Start with the issue of the protective tariff of 1828, and show how manufacturers desired a tariff barrier to eliminate foreign competition for the American market. Explain that southerners, in particular, found themselves oppressed by the proposed tariff because it would raise the cost of goods to them without any immediate benefit. But also show that many argued that the Constitution only allowed tariffs that raised revenue to run the government: anything above that or for any other purpose was unnecessary and unconstitutional. This issue ultimately led to the nullification crisis, in which South Carolina rescinded the protective tariff within its borders. In a showdown, the Jackson administration offered both carrot and stick, reducing the tariff to manageable levels but threatening military invasion if South Carolina did not back down. The crisis served notice that the Union was extremely fragile and was becoming more so with ongoing sectional antagonisms, particularly exacerbated by the abolitionist movement.

Jackson also pursued other issues such as the removal of all Indians east of the Mississippi River. Use "Cherokees Debate Removal" (in the documents reader) to explore the means of carrying out the removal and to discuss specifically the Trail of Tears. Be sure to direct students to Map 11.3, "Indian Removal and the Trail of Tears." Also look at Jackson's war with the Second Bank of the United States and show how it contributed to the further development of separate national parties. Use "President Jackson's Farewell Address" (in the documents reader) to explain why Jackson saw the bank and other corporations as "monsters." Finally, take a few minutes to dispel any misconceptions that today's Republican Party traces its roots back to Thomas Jefferson's Republican Party. You might consider drawing a time line to help students focus on the development of the different party systems in the United States.

Anticipating Student Reactions: Common Misconceptions and Difficult Topics

1. Most, If Not All, Northerners Supported Abolitionism

Although students usually understand that southern-bred abolitionists, like the Grimké sisters, were a rarity, they believe that most, if not all, northerners supported the abolition movement. Although many northerners opposed slavery, most did not favor abolitionism because it seemed too radical. Southerners sought to keep the abolitionists' insurrectionary pamphlets out of the mail for fear of such literature falling into the hands of slaves, who might think that the northern public would support another Gabriel's rebellion. Explain to your students that northern whites, on the other hand, generally opposed both slavery and emancipation. Slavery brought Africans to the United States; emancipation would allow their descendants to wander at their own will. Northerners and southerners shared a deep-seated feeling of white superiority, and most sought ways to ensure that blacks occupied a powerless position in society.

2. Today's Republican Party Originated with the Republican Party of Thomas Jefferson

Some of your students will believe that today's Republican Party is the same as Thomas Jefferson's party. Although you will need to jump forward and back chronologically, devote part of a class to creating a time line (as suggested for Lecture 3) to delineate the periods of the first and second American party systems. Show the decline of the Federalists as a national party following the Hartford Convention, and then show the rise of the Whigs and Democrats out of Jefferson's Republican Party. Jump ahead and briefly show when the Whig Party declined and today's GOP was organized. One pedagogical tool (although not entirely accurate) is to talk about parties organized around principles of economic development (the parties of business — the Federalist, Whig, and modern Republican Parties) as opposed to parties organized around maximizing personal liberty (the parties of the people — Jefferson's Republican, Jackson's Democratic-Republican, and modern Democratic Parties).

3. The Great Depression of the 1930s Was a Solitary Event without Precedent

Many students fail to appreciate the repetition of the business cycle that marks the economy's journey through boom and bust throughout the 120 years before the twentieth century's most famous panic. (Economists invented the term *depression* in the early 1930s because it did not sound as dire as *panic*. Your students may be familiar with the modern term: *correction*.) You might consider drawing a time line for your class to show the major economic low points: 1819, 1837, 1857, 1873, 1893, and so on up to 1929. Take a few moments to explain the contributing factors, the length, and the depth of each of the depressions. A useful pedagogic device is to show the correlation in the antebellum period between economic downturns and both destabilizing banking practices and fluctuating agricultural commodity prices.

Using the Bedford Series in History and Culture and the Historians at Work Series: Suggestions

If you want to provide more background on political conflicts in Jacksonian America, consider assigning *Andrew Jackson v. Henry Clay: Democracy and Development in Antebellum America,* by Harry L. Watson. To explore the complex issues of Indian removal, have students read Theda Perdue and Michael D. Green's study, *The Cherokee Removal: A Brief History with Documents.* To supplement your discussion of reform movements, consider assigning *William Lloyd Garrison and the Fight against Slavery: Selections from* The Liberator, edited by William E. Cain. You may also want to have students read *Welfare Reform in the Early Republic,* edited by Seth Rockman.

Lecture Supplements and Classroom Activities

Using Multimedia Sources in the Classroom

When discussing Jacksonian Indian policy, consider showing segments from the second episode of the PBS documentary *The West,* "Empire upon the Trails," which covers the Indian removal and the Trail of Tears.

Historical Contingencies

To encourage students to question the significance of the nullification crisis, ask them, "What if South Carolina had seceded because of the nation's tariff policies?" Would other southern states have followed South Carolina's lead? Would the Civil War have been fought earlier? Would the nation have been willing to risk a civil war over the tariff issue? Ask students to identify other national policies with which southern ideologues disagreed. Could the debates over internal improvements or the national bank have been enough to spark the Civil War? Or would only the crisis over the extension of slavery into the territories be serious enough to precipitate disunion? This exercise should encourage students to think seriously about the role of slavery in eventual secession and the course of the Civil War.

Classroom Activities

Consider having students debate the legality of South Carolina's position on nullification. Were protective tariffs unconstitutional, as Calhoun and others argued? Did states have the authority to judge the constitutionality of acts of Congress? Is nullification constitutional? Is secession constitutional? This exercise should prepare students for future discussions on secession, the coming of the Civil War, and the ultimate fate of Reconstruction.

Using the Internet

Citations and full texts of *Worcester v. Georgia* can be found at Historic Supreme Court Decisions—by Party Name. Direct students to <http://supct.law.cornell.edu/supct/index.html> and tell them to search for *Worcester v. Georgia.*

Students can learn much about the abolitionist movement from the Library of Congress's Web site. The American Memory site at <http://memory.loc.gov> makes available African American pamphlets on slavery and freedom. Tell students to click on "History" under "Collection Finder" and then click on "African American Pamphlets, 1824–1909." "The African American Mosaic" makes available online images from that exhibit, including reproductions of *The Liberator* as well as other abolitionist items. Direct students to <http://www.loc.gov/exhibits/african/intro.html>.

ASSESSING RESULTS
Multiple-Choice Questions

1. What did Americans see in the life and character of Andrew Jackson that reflected the mood of the country?
   a. the desire to create a permanent underclass of blacks, Indians, and women
   b. the fear of the social manifestations of the market revolution
   c. the ability of people or countries to shape their own destiny
   d. the necessity of maintaining one's honor, even if dueling were required

2. The key element in the mill factory system was
   a. the rapid mechanization of industrial processes based on developments in scientific knowledge.
   b. the proliferation of outwork conducted in the home.
   c. the development of steel.
   d. that women would work for low wages.

3. The national political parties of the second American party system were
   a. the Republican Party and the Democratic Party.
   b. the Democratic Party and the Whig Party.
   c. the Federalist Party and the Republican Party.
   d. the Democratic Party and the Populist Party.

4. What was the "doctrine of separate spheres"?
   a. Congress's ability to legislate economic issues should be limited to banking and finance, which are a form of interstate commerce.
   b. Slavery should not be allowed to extend into territories in which the lands are best suited for small farms that could be reserved for working-class whites.
   c. Women should maintain the home as a moral refuge from a corrupt world while men should take jobs for wages outside the home.
   d. The eastern Indian cultures must be "removed" to the unorganized territory west of the Mississippi River to help them maintain their traditional culture.

5. The Second Great Awakening mainly benefited which denominations?

   a. Episcopalians, Congregationalists, and Unitarians
   b. Methodists, Baptists, Presbyterians, and other evangelical groups
   c. Dutch Reformed, Lutherans, and Catholics
   d. Jews, Muslims, and other non-Christians

6. What was the underlying threat of South Carolina's opposition to tariff reform in the late 1820s and early 1830s?
   a. By advocating the ability of a state to rescind federal law, South Carolina ultimately threatened to dissolve the union of the states.
   b. By advocating the ability of a state to rescind the federal tariff, South Carolina threatened the income of the federal government and would have required a reduction in its services.
   c. By advocating the ability of a state to pass legislation affecting national transportation improvements, South Carolina threatened to undermine the ability of the Supreme Court to rule on the constitutionality of state and federal laws.
   d. By advocating the ability of a state to pass legislation affecting a national institution, such as the Bank of the United States, South Carolina threatened to dissolve the national economy and implement a separate state currency.

7. How did Finney's Broadway Tabernacle reflect popular amusement in America's cities?
   a. Its plain architecture, hard seats, and lack of decoration emphasized the importance of humility and a simple lifestyle.
   b. Its curtains concealed Finney's guest speakers until he summoned them, which confounded the congregation and added to the emotional effect of the sermons.
   c. Its theatrical layout made all members of the congregation approximately equal in their distance from the speaker and thus "democratized" the tabernacle.
   d. Its triangular shape allowed segregation of the church by class, so that the rich need not be seated with the middle class, nor the middle class with the poor.

8. From which part of the country were most of the Indians "removed" in the 1830s?
   a. the upper South: mainly Tennessee, Kentucky, and the southern tips of Indiana and Illinois

b. the old Northwest: mainly Illinois, Wisconsin, Michigan Territory, and the unorganized territory west of Illinois

c. the lower South: mainly Georgia, Alabama, Mississippi, and Florida

d. the West: mainly Louisiana, Arkansas Territory, and Missouri

9. Early steamboats

a. proved one of the safest modes of transportation, causing fewer than two dozen major accidents between 1811 and 1851.

b. were often floating palaces, providing swank accommodations to ladies and gentlemen who paid first-class fares.

c. were sluggish and inefficient, and therefore did not influence transportation until the 1850s, when entrepreneurs began to improve their design.

d. offered speed but not luxury, thereby limiting their usefulness for commercial ventures.

10. Identify the correct sequence of historical events.

a. Garrison's *Liberator* started, American Colonization Society formed, Trail of Tears, David Walker's *Appeal*

b. Trail of Tears, *Worcester v. Georgia*, Indian Removal Act

c. Panic of 1819, Second Bank of the United States chartered, Tariff of Abominations, Panic of 1837

d. Erie Canal completed, Tariff of Abominations, nullification crisis, specie circular

Proposing More: Additional Readings

Daniel Feller, "Politics and Society: Toward a Jacksonian Synthesis," *Journal of the Early Republic* 10, no. 2 (1990): 135–61.

Michael V. Namorato, "New Insights on Old Issues," *Reviews in American History* 23, no. 1 (1995): 51–57.

Mary P. Ryan, "The Empire of the Mother: American Writing about Domesticity, 1830–1860," *Women and History* 2–3 (1982): 1–170.

Carroll Smith-Rosenberg, "Beauty, the Beast, and the Militant Woman," *American Quarterly* 23 (1971): 562–84.

David O. Whitten, "The Depression of 1837: Incorporating New Ideas into Economic History Instruction: A Survey," *Essays in Business and Economic History* 13 (1995): 27–40.

Answer Key to Multiple-Choice Questions: 1-c, 2-d, 3-b, 4-c, 5-b, 6-a, 7-c, 8-c, 9-b, 10-d

THE FREE NORTH AND WEST

12

1840–1860

Outlining Chapters: Thematic Questions

   I. What fundamental changes transformed the American economy, 1840 to 1860? Why might this transformation be termed an *industrial evolution*?

     A. What had limited agricultural production in the United States and what technological improvements increased production? What other factors increased farmers' yield? How did the federal government promote increased agricultural production?

     B. What economic factors made mechanization desirable in the United States, and what was distinctive about the "American system"? How did manufacturing and agriculture mesh to form a national economy?

     C. How did railroads develop in antebellum America? How did they stimulate growth in other industries? How did private investment and federal aid combine to spur growth in the railroad industry?

  II. What were the promises and realities of free labor?

     A. What was the ideal of free labor? What did antebellum Americans regard as the virtues of the free-labor system? What were the system's limitations?

     B. How equal was the distribution of wealth in antebellum America, and how likely was successful upward economic mobility? To what did antebellum Americans attribute economic inequalities?

     C. How extensive was immigration between 1840 and 1860? What groups immigrated to America at that time? How did they differ from one another, and how did they fit into the American vision of free labor?

 III. What was the "evangelical temperament," and what sorts of reforms did evangelical Protestants propose? What reformers questioned the limitations of evangelical reform, and what alternatives did they propose?

     A. What was transcendentalism, and how did it ultimately reflect American individualism? What sort of utopian reform movements evolved in the nineteenth century, and how did they operate?

     B. How did the women's rights movement evolve from other reform movements? How did women's rights activists challenge social norms of male domination? What did women's rights activists propose at the Seneca Falls meeting, and what opposition did they face, 1848–1860?

C. How did abolitionist thought develop in the 1840s and 1850s? How did northern free blacks participate in abolitionism?

IV. How did the American nation expand its boundaries?

A. What was "manifest destiny," and how did it justify American westward expansion?

B. With what country did the United States share "joint occupation" of Oregon? What propelled migration to Oregon beginning in the 1830s? How did Plains Indians differ from Eastern Woodland Indians, and how did white settlers affect them? How did the policy of placing Indians on reservations begin? What hardships did settlers have to endure in migrating to Oregon, and what did they find when they got there? How did men and women experience the move to Oregon differently?

C. Who were the Mormons? What did they believe? Why did they move to Utah, and how did they survive in the desert?

D. How did Americans become interested in the Mexican territories of New Mexico, Texas, and California? How did Texas and California break away from Mexico, and why did they succeed?

V. By what process did the United States annex its western territories in the 1840s?

A. How did John Tyler become president, and how did he betray the Whig Party's agenda?

B. What issues surrounded the debate on the annexation of Texas and Oregon? What roles did annexation play in the presidential election of 1844, and how were the territories finally annexed?

VI. What attitudes of the United States made war with Mexico likely?

A. How did the Polk administration originally plan to obtain Mexico's northern provinces? How did the United States provoke a war with Mexico? How did the opposition party view the war? How well did the Mexicans fight back?

B. How was victory finally secured in Mexico, and what were the terms of American victory? What were the consequences of the Mexican-American War?

Teaching with The American Promise, *Second Compact Edition: Lecture Strategies*

LECTURE 1
How Did America Become So Productive?

Begin this lecture by looking at demographic changes in America, and ask students why America attracted immigrants. When someone inevitably answers that it attracted people seeking freedom, ask why these immigrants didn't go elsewhere, such as Argentina or Canada (both of which attracted many immigrants). America's appeal extended beyond freedom. Suggest to students that the extreme shortage of labor in ratio to its increasing productive capacity made America seem attractive to immigrants. Wages were high, and opportunities to purchase land were readily available. Concentrate on land purchase, and ask how the federal government encouraged such purchases. Explain that federal subsidies of land sales engendered greater agricultural output by putting more land under tillage, which in turn allowed for the growth of large cities.

Ask whether immigration, urbanization, and increased tillage alone account for America's pattern of productivity. What about technological improvements? Without getting bogged down in minutiae, describe the advances in technology aimed at improving agriculture. Next, explore the ways in which railroads improved the movement of goods, people, and information. Using Map 12.1, "Railroads in 1860," show how railroads altered the sense of distance between locations. Ask students about changes in industry and direct them to consider the "American system" of manufacturing. Was it about interchangeable parts? Ask whether any student has heard that Eli Whitney invented interchangeability of precision parts of complex machines. Using the details from the "Anticipating Student Reactions" section about interchangeability, clear their misconceptions and discuss how tariff barriers aided industrialization more than the slow adoption of technology in the first half of the nineteenth century.

Finally, introduce free-labor ideology and suggest how that concept contributed to American productivity more than any other single event, idea, or change. Once you have described what its proponents saw as the main benefits of the free-labor system, make it clear that this system, while it drove the economy, also left many behind. Discuss how immigrants, Native Americans, African Americans, and white women fared under the free-labor system. Use the chapter's opening vignette about Lincoln's father to show how the system separated families. Finally, use "The Anxiety of Gain" and "A Farmer's View of His Wife" (both in the documents reader) to explore the negative aspects of free-labor ideology.

LECTURE 2
Antebellum Reform Movements

This lecture demonstrates the unforeseen consequences of society's adoption of free-will theology and free-labor ideology, both of which affirm that the individual can shape his or her own destiny. Begin by suggesting to students these unintended consequences compelled many reformers to action, hoping to ensure the promise of America. Refer your students to "The Anxiety of Gain" document discussed in the previous lecture. "Rugged individualism" failed many Americans, leaving them poor despite their hard work. They worried that the cyclic nature of the economy could set them back. Thus, if individual effort failed to create success, society must be changed to facilitate rewarding such efforts. As a result of these concerns, a number of utopian communities came into existence to attempt different ways of rendering society. Explain to students the variety of communal living experiments from the 1830s to the 1870s. (You might want to draw their attention to the painting of Mary Cragin, a member of the Oneida community.) Ask them to consider how these communities were viewed by their neighbors, and then describe the long trek of the Mormons to Utah to escape persecution, using Map 12.2, "Trails to the West."

Next, explain the reform movements of the nineteenth century by demonstrating that the ideology of individualism encouraged political movements. You might begin this section of your lecture by asking students to think about the ways in which these reformers understood the promise of America and how they acted on that understanding. Describe how women came to the fore in a number of reform movements, particularly abolitionism, and learned how to organize themselves. (Use the photograph of the outdoor antislavery meeting in 1850 to show how men and women, blacks and whites, worked together in the abolitionist cause — albeit not on equal terms.) Then refer to the "Farmer's

View of His Wife" document mentioned in the previous lecture to discuss what attitudes were acceptable about the place of women in the mid-nineteenth century. The farmer was unacceptably out of step with society, but society did not give women a much higher place than it did the farmer. Finally, move to the Seneca Falls Declaration (in the documents reader) and describe and discuss the extent, means, and success of the early feminist movement.

LECTURE 3
Manifest Destiny and Territorial Expansion

This lecture shows the expansionist nature of the United States and how it acquired and consolidated territory to become a transcontinental nation. Begin by referring students to Map 12.5, "Territorial Expansion by 1860." Ask if the United States was preordained to become a transcontinental nation, and discuss the contingent nature of history. Ask students what parts belonged to the United States at the beginning of the 1840s and what parts of present-day America were owned by another country or were in dispute. Then, referring to Map 12.2, "Trails to the West," which shows the westward trails, explain how one might get to western parts of North America from the United States and what sorts of economic ties were developed in the early nineteenth century. Mention that the United States' claims to Oregon dated back to its exploration by Lewis and Clark and that British claims dated back even earlier, to exploration by Sir Francis Drake. Spain had explored and settled portions of the American Southwest and settled on a common border with Oregon by treaty with the United States in 1819. None of these claims took into account the indigenous peoples who controlled most of the territory. By the 1840s, Americans believed that God had ordained them to be prosperous and to control the American continent.

Make clear that Mexico, which inherited the Southwest when it gained independence from Spain, was seen as an impediment to American expansion. Most Americans saw Mexico as a weak nation constantly wracked by civil war in its futile attempts to build a sovereign country and populated by an inferior people of mixed-race origins. Explain the original welcome extended by Mexico in the 1820s, in hopes of peopling its sparsely settled northern provinces.

Next, explain the ways in which America secured control of the province in 1836. Use Map 12.3, "Texas and Mexico in the 1830s," to demonstrate that although Texas had bordered the next Mexican province at the Nueces River, the Republic of Texas claimed, but did not occupy, all lands east and north of the Rio Grande up to its source in present-day Colorado (including Santa Fe, the capital of another Mexican province). Next, explore why the United States did not immediately annex Texas and mention that, almost simultaneously, the United States attempted to purchase Alta California from Mexico. By 1844, annexation of Oregon and Mexico became the central issue of the presidential campaign. Using the map of the trails (Map 12.2), explain the situation in Oregon and how it was quietly resolved in 1846. At this point, you might want to have students discuss the term *manifest destiny*, which so accurately expressed Americans' conviction that God had ordained that the United States would occupy the entire continent, peopling the land with a "superior" race of Anglo-Americans.

Explain why the United States went to war with Mexico. First, describe the nature of John Tyler's presidency and why he created the issue of annexation. Once elected in 1844, James Polk provoked the Mexican government into attacking American troops sent into the disputed area claimed by Texas but occupied by Mexico, and then asked for a declaration of war. Many northerners opposed the war, in part because they feared it would extend slavery; but the war was generally popular, especially in the South and the West. The Mexicans fought harder than expected of an "inferior" race of people, and the war dragged on. Using Map 12.4, "The Mexican War, 1846–1848," describe the strategies Polk designed to force Mexico to relinquish its northern provinces, particularly how he grabbed the provinces of New Mexico and Alta California.

Then show the effects of expansion and how it changed the demographic composition of the newly won western territories. Next, introduce the discovery of gold with the *Historical Question* feature and the "Gold Fever" document (in the documents reader). Ask your students to consider what happened to Americans' fascination with free-labor ideology, which exalted the daily duty of work, in the abundance of wealth generated by the gold rush. Did Americans allocate mining rights fairly to all newcomers? And finally, use the photograph of the Chinese gold miner to discuss demographic heterogeneity resulting from the gold rush.

Anticipating Student Reactions: Common Misconceptions and Difficult Topics

1. Eli Whitney Created Interchangeable Parts That Proved the Basis of American Industrial Superiority

Students sometimes erroneously learn in grade school that Eli Whitney perfected a system of interchangeable parts for the manufacture of a weapon on a federal contract, which quickly led to the superiority of American manufacturers and boosted American economic clout. Whitney did sign a contract to manufacture interchangeable parts, but he failed to deliver the goods on time and defrauded the government with samples so finely handcrafted that they appeared interchangeable. His fraud, however, did initiate a system, known as the "American system," of crafting precision equipment, machines, and tools to approximate interchangeability. Thus, different workers could be assigned to manufacture only certain parts of a machine using jigs and patterns, and then these parts were filed down to make them fit as they were assembled. One could not take a piece off one machine and add it to another, but each piece did come out of the same manufacturing process, which was much different from the previous handcraft industry, wherein the craftsman manufactured all parts of the end product from start to finish. Only by the 1860s did any real returns come from continued federal investment in interchangeability, and the technology did not lead to real gains in productivity until late in the nineteenth century, when industrialists pursued mass-production processes. Although the American system of manufacturing had a certain simple elegance that was otherwise absent from preindustrial manufacturing, it failed to influence the American economy until well after the Civil War.

2. Communes and Protest Movements Happened Only in the 1960s

Communal living thrived well before the Age of Aquarius. Before hippies proposed alternate modes of structuring society in the 1960s and before civil rights, antiwar, and women's rights activists learned to protest in the television age, America had a well-established pattern of protest and a thirst for improving society. By the 1840s, as the textbook points out, Americans took the ideas that undergirded free-will salvation and free-will labor ideology and applied them to "improve" on their society. Communal living arrangements were used for a variety of religious, reform, and intellectual experiments, ranging from the Shakers (who practiced celibacy), the Mormons (who practiced polygamy), and the Oneida Perfectionists (who practiced complex marriage), to Robert Dale Owen's experiment in communal ownership of the means of production. Mention also the various Fourierist communities that experimented with the organization of "meaningful" labor, the intellectual commune at Brook Farm outside Boston, and the anti-slavery experiment at Neshoba outside Memphis. Americans worried about their society and sought new ways to organize it to lessen that anxiety. They also had specific protest projects for which they labored. They took to heart the zeal for self-improvement made manifest by free-will theology and desired to improve life on earth as well as their own moral character. They outlawed alcohol and sought to reduce intemperance. They improved public education, introduced prisons, and reformed hospitals and asylums. They protested slavery, women's codified subordination, and "Mr. Polk's War" as well. In short, theirs was a society attempting to define itself as it went through radical economic and demographic changes.

3. A Continental United States, Ranging from the Atlantic to the Pacific, Was Inevitable

Because current boundaries of the United States reach from the Atlantic to the Pacific, students tend to believe that America was destined to be a continental nation. As demonstrated in earlier chapters, however, America feared that the regional differences in a large nation would inevitably lead to centrifugal forces that would rip it apart. And clearly those fears were fulfilled by the Civil War. But the idea of inevitability is the most dangerous idea to students of history. It assumes that some sort of fate, or divine mandate, guided human affairs rather than acknowledging that humankind makes history through the actions, ideas, and decisions of individuals. Help your students to appreciate that history is contingent on those actions and decisions.

Using the Bedford Series in History and Culture and the Historians at Work Series: Suggestions

There are a number of books in the Bedford Series in History and Culture that work well with this chapter. When discussing transcendentalism, consider assigning *Margaret Fuller: A Brief Biography with Documents*, edited by Eve Kornfeld. Students, who may be familiar with Fuller's more famous counterparts — Ralph Waldo Emerson and Henry David Thoreau — should find Fuller's philosophy fascinating. You may want to have students read Herman Melville's *Benito Cereno*, edited by Jay Fleigelman, or Nathaniel Hawthorne's *The Blithedale Romance*, edited by William E. Cain, titles in Bedford's Cultural Editions series from Bedford's literature list. Frederick Douglass's *Narrative of the Life of Frederick Douglass, An American Slave, Written by Himself*, edited by David W. Blight, and *William Lloyd Garrison and the Fight against Slavery: Selections from* The Liberator, edited by William E. Cain, complement the textbook's discussion of abolitionism. William Wells Brown's *Clotel*, edited for Bedford's Cultural Editions series by Robert Levine, will evoke questions and comments from students. *The Japanese Discovery of America: A Brief History with Documents*, edited by Peter Duus, supplements the textbook's account of manifest destiny and allows students to gain an appreciation for another nation's view of antebellum America.

Lecture Supplements and Classroom Activities

Using Multimedia Sources in the Classroom

Two episodes of the PBS video series *The West* work particularly well in conjunction with this chapter. When discussing the influence of the manifest destiny ideology, consider showing Episode 2, "Empire upon the Trails, 1806–1848," which covers the movement west and the debate over the annexation of Texas. When discussing the *Historical Question* feature, "Who Rushed for California Gold?," and related documents, consider showing Episode 3, "The Speck of the Future, 1848–1856," which covers the discovery of gold in California and tells the story of over fifty thousand fortune hunters who moved west, scrambling for riches and forever altering the landscape.

Historical Contingencies

Have students consider the possible course of American history had Polk not purposely provoked a war with Mexico. Take advantage of any discussion of this issue to ask for counterhistorical scenarios that might have altered the shape of the United States. For instance, Britain could have gone to war with the United States over Oregon, which would have created a two-front war. An understaffed U.S. army then would have had to fight a powerful empire on land and sea, while simultaneously attempting to take Mexico's northern provinces. And as the next chapters will demonstrate, had the United States not acquired its western territory, those centrifugal forces might not have been sufficient to drive the country apart in a war between the states.

Classroom Activities

Have students debate the viability of free-labor ideology in a society that was becoming increasingly industrialized. Free-labor ideology means that laborers own their means of production and sell the fruits of their labor for a just price. That laborer is thus independent (or free) from the dictates of a "master" or a boss. Factories, however, require capital to purchase the means of production (machines), which are housed under one roof. Very few laborers could hope to raise that kind of capital in antebellum America. Workers, therefore, no longer sold the fruits of their labor but rather sold their labor itself for a wage determined by an increasingly distant market. Workers were no longer independent (or free) but dependent on wages. Ask students to consider, then, whether Lincoln's words on the virtues of free labor were tenable in an increasingly industrialized and mechanized America.

Using the Internet

The Huntington Library makes available images and texts from its Votes for Women exhibit. Here, students can find the "Declaration of Sentiments," issued at the 1848 Seneca Falls Convention; articles from *The Lily*, an antebellum feminist newspaper that advocated woman's suffrage; and other material pertinent to the women's rights movement. Direct students to <http://www.huntington.org/vfw/main2.html>.

Columbia University's Bartleby project puts online great books of western civilization. Here, students can find essays by Ralph Waldo Emerson, Henry David Thoreau, and other transcendentalists. Direct students to <http://bartleby.com>.

ASSESSING RESULTS
Multiple-Choice Questions

1. What was the basis for the transformation in the American economy?
   a. Increased agricultural production transformed the economy.
   b. Decreasing job opportunities in the countryside drove workers into factories in the cities.
   c. Increased immigration of the Irish provided the skilled labor, previously deficient in America, needed to fill all the jobs in America's expanding industry.
   d. An influx of European money expanded the American economy.

2. The term "free labor"
   a. meant that workers were not compelled to work but chose to do so freely, unlike slaves and apprentices, and it celebrated hard work, self-reliance, and independence.
   b. meant that female laborers could be paid less than male laborers because it was commonly believed that a woman already had a man supporting her.
   c. was an expression of protest, complaining of the low standard of living imposed on workmen by the "lords of the looms," the capitalists who controlled the industrial development of the country.
   d. was an expression that meant to eliminate whites' competition with blacks for jobs and argued that blacks were only competent as slaves.

3. The Seneca Falls Convention
   a. assembled the tribes of the Great Plains and instituted the policy of putting Indians on reservations.
   b. first assembled the leaders of the women's rights movement and issued a declaration that women should receive political and civil equality.
   c. was convened by the Mormons immediately following the death of Joseph Smith, and delegates voted to move to Utah to escape the violent persecution by their fellow Americans.
   d. called for a new society based on complex marriage in which every man in a community would be married to every woman in that community.

4. The war between Mexico and the United States began because
   a. President Polk sent troops into territory claimed by Mexico to provoke the Mexican army into attacking so he could claim that Mexico started the war.
   b. of the senseless massacres of Texans at the Alamo and at Goliad, which brought the Americans into Texas's war for independence.

   c. President Tyler annexed the gold-rich California, which incited Mexico to declare war on the United States.

   d. the Mexican dictator Santa Anna, sensing that a revolution would soon overthrow him if he did not quickly find a way to redirect Mexican anger from the corruption of his regime, invented a pretext for declaring war on the United States.

5. The daguerreotype of an outdoor antislavery meeting around 1850 shows
   a. that women were segregated into a special area of the meeting so they would not be corrupted by male political activity.
   b. that blacks were excluded from the ranks of abolitionists altogether.
   c. that blacks and white women worked together with white male abolitionists.
   d. that Chinese and Indians were included in the abolitionist cause to pursue more perfect equality for all.

6. What effect did the discovery of gold in California have on the ethnic diversity of the western United States?
   a. a major effect of forcing the incorporation of Oregon Territory into the United States, introducing large populations of Russians, Eskimos, Indians, and British
   b. no effect whatsoever; Americans found the gold and exploited it for Americans
   c. a minimal effect of uplifting the downtrodden Hispanics of California who had just lost all their property as an immediate consequence of the Treaty of Guadalupe Hidalgo
   d. a dramatic effect of increased ethnic diversity combined with increased discrimination and even wholesale murder of ethnic minorities

7. According to the excerpt from Walter Colton's California diary (in the documents reader), what effect did "gold fever" have on the people of Monterey, California?
   a. The Americans in Monterey immediately clamored for protection by the U.S. government and asked for annexation.
   b. The men left for the mines, but the women remained behind to maintain their places of business.
   c. Only the ethnic minorities — the Chinese, blacks, and Hispanics of Monterey — left for the gold fields; the whites continued to work at their jobs, ignoring the lure of

quick riches and claiming that well-done work was a virtue in itself.
   d. Almost the entire population of the town abandoned their chosen work, be it farming, blacksmithing, or keeping a boarding house, and lit out for the gold fields.

8. According to Figure 12.1, "Antebellum Immigration, 1820–1860,"
   a. immigration continually waxed and waned, showing no discernible pattern in the antebellum period.
   b. the peak of German immigration came in the 1830s.
   c. total immigration peaked between 1848 and 1860.
   d. total immigration peaked between 1820 and 1830, when the United States was still a relatively young country and opportunity for newcomers seemed unlimited.

9. Utopian reformers
   a. rejected the popular evangelical Protestant belief that insufficient self-control caused the most important social problems of the era.
   b. believed that perfection could be attained only by embracing fully the competitive values of the larger society.
   c. attracted over 250,000 followers by the eve of the Civil War.
   d. denounced the notion of communalism, a popular European utopian concept, as a radical idea, antithetical to American values.

10. John Tyler,
   a. elected in a landslide, had a public mandate for his policies.
   b. seeking the Democratic Party's nomination in 1844, championed the annexation of Texas to curry favor with party leaders and voters.
   c. seeking the Whig Party's nomination in 1844, championed the American system to curry favor with party leaders and voters.
   d. eager to shore up Whig Party support, signed Henry Clay's bill for a new national bank.

11. Identify the correct sequence of historical events and figures.
   a. B&O Railroad started, John Deere patented the steel plow, telegraph invented, gold discovered in California

b. Maine prohibition law passed, Seneca Falls Declaration written, Massachusetts integrates public schools, Mormons settled in Utah

c. "manifest destiny" coined, Bear Flag Revolt, Texas declares independence from Mexico, Treaty of Guadalupe Hidalgo

d. James K. Polk elected U.S. president, Bear Flag Revolt, William Henry Harrison elected U.S. president, John Tyler becomes president

PROPOSING MORE: Additional Readings

Peter Karsten, "Labor's Sorrow? Workers, Bosses, and the Courts in Antebellum America," *Reviews in American History* 21, no. 2 (1993): 447–53.

Jean Matthews, "Race, Sex, and the Dimensions of Liberty in Antebellum America," *Journal of the Early Republic* 6, no. 3 (1986): 275–91.

Michael A. Morrison, "Martin Van Buren, the Democracy, and the Partisan Politics of Texas Annexation," *Journal of Southern History* 61, no. 4 (1995): 695–724.

Elizabeth Varon, "Tippecanoe and the Ladies, Too: White Women and Party Politics in Antebellum Virginia," *Journal of American History* 82, no. 2 (1995): 494–521.

Judith Wellman, "The Seneca Falls Women's Rights Convention: A Study of Social Networks," *Journal of Women's History* 3, no. 1 (1991): 9–37.

Answer Key to Multiple-Choice Questions: 1-a, 2-a, 3-b, 4-a, 5-c, 6-d, 7-d, 8-c, 9-a, 10-b, 11-a

THE SLAVE SOUTH 13
1820–1860

O*utlining Chapters: Thematic Questions*

I. What was the essential difference between the North and the South in the antebellum period?
   A. What was the relationship between the spread of cotton production and the spread of slavery? What accounted for the tremendous growth in the slave population?
   B. How did the relative numbers of blacks and whites vary in northern and southern states, and what effect did that difference have on their societies? How did southern society alter its defense of slavery after 1820, and why? On what pillars of support did proslavery ideologues rest their defense? How did white supremacy unite white southern society?
   C. What elements characterized the southern economy? What were the major cash crops grown, and what were the differences in geography and capitalization needed to start a plantation in any of these crops? How did the plantation economy aid the development of the northern economy, and why did the two diverge? How did industrialization, urbanization, and immigration influence the Old South? Why did some southern reformers criticize the South's reliance on a plantation economy, and what opposition did they face?

II. How was a plantation physically organized, and what were the roles of the plantation master and mistress?
   A. How did the master manage his plantation? What was "paternalism," and how did it affect the southern institution of slavery? What characterized the southern sense of honor? Why were planters expected to follow the tenets of patriarchy?
   B. What virtues were southern ladies expected to possess, and how did southern chivalry force women into a subordinate role? What duties did the plantation mistress perform, and who answered to her? In what ways did gender ideals and reality clash in the Old South? What lay at the heart of plantation mistresses' critique of miscegenation?

III. What sort of life did slaves lead, and in what sort of occupations were they employed?
   A. How hard were slaves worked? At what age did they begin working, and when were they retired? How did a slave's sex affect work assignments? What percentage of slaves were field hands, house servants, skilled

artisans, drivers? What was work like in each of these occupations?

B. How did family life and religion contribute to an autonomous slave culture? How did slave families organize themselves, and how long did such unions last? Why did many African Americans embrace Christianity, and which of its features did they emphasize? In what ways did traditional African beliefs continue to influence the lives of slaves in the Old South?

C. What were the various ways in which slaves could resist the will of their masters, and what were the limits to such resistance? Why were there relatively few slave rebellions in the Old South? How did slave resistance challenge the planters' notion of paternalism?

IV. Why did free blacks in the South pose an ideological dilemma for white Southerners?

A. What accounted for the presence of free blacks in the Old South? How did state legislatures move to curtail their liberty? How much freedom did free blacks enjoy?

B. What sorts of achievements did urban, skilled free blacks make? How did such achievements compare with those of rural blacks? What differences were there between light-skinned and dark-skinned free blacks? How did free blacks respond to the institution of slavery?

V. Who were the "plain folk" of the Old South?

A. What factors characterized the plantation belt yeomen, and how were they involved in the plantation economy?

B. How did upcountry yeomen differ from their counterparts in the plantation belt? What was the yeoman's relation to the plantation economy? How did formal education and evangelical Christianity influence yeoman society?

C. Who were the poor whites, and what were their ambitions? How were their ambitions curtailed by the prosperity of the cotton economy? What was the difference between "poor whites" and yeomen?

VI. What was the balance of political power between slaveholding and nonslaveholding whites in the South? How did planter-class hegemony ensure the loyalty of nonslaveholders to the slaveholding regime?

A. How did increased democratization of the electoral process in the South affect voter turnout and partisanship? How did southern Whigs differ from southern Democrats?

B. How and why did planters continue to dominate southern politics despite the increasing democratic reforms? How did planters win elections among a nonslaveholding majority? What advantages did they gain by controlling legislatures? How did slaveholders answer southern critics of slavery?

VII. In what respects was the South considered a fundamentally unique region by 1860?

Teaching with The American Promise, Second Compact Edition: Lecture Strategies

LECTURE 1
The Political Economy of the Old South

This lecture should explain the intersection of politics and economics in the slave South. First, confront the anticipated misconception that the Old South lasted for an extended period of time. The Old South began in the 1790s (and some historians even push the date forward to 1820) with the invention of the first effective cotton gin, which created the means for southern agriculture to supply northern and European manufacturers with the cotton needed to spur the industrial revolution in those societies. You might want to draw students' attention to the photo of a cotton gin. Make clear that without an extended and extensive demand for cotton, the Old South would never have existed. Use Map 13.2, "The Agricultural Economy of the South, 1860," to show the areas of slave-based agriculture in the South and to discuss how the type of work done by slaves in each of those production systems compared with others. Then use Map 13.1, "Cotton Kingdom, Slave Empire: 1820 and 1860," depicting the expansion of cotton production and the expansion of slavery, to show how they meshed. Next discuss the southern economy and explain that although nascent industrialization and urbanization occurred in the South, the plantation economy fueled the South's growth.

Now shift gears to introduce politics as an arm of economic development. Because the planter elite dominated southern politics, the laws enacted protected the economic interests of the planter class. Describe and explain the disproportionate power of the planter class. Show how the interests of these groups permeated society and how the planters aggressively counterattacked the intrusion of free-labor ideas. Use the James Henry Hammond piece (in the documents reader) to introduce the proslavery argument that slavery represented a "positive good." Prepare your students for the next lecture by asking them to consider how slavery limited and directed the lives of southern whites.

LECTURE 2
Whites in the Old South

This lecture should illustrate how slavery affected all white Southerners. First, describe the different classes of white Southerners and give some notion of their respective percentages of the white population and their geographic concentrations. Be sure to distinguish plantation belt and upcountry yeomen, and note their differing relations to the plantation economy. Use the Frederick Law Olmsted piece (in the documents reader) to discuss the lifestyles of poor whites. After covering notions of class differences, introduce gender roles and expectations in the Old South, and explain how patriarchy and chivalry set southern women up for domination by white men. Next, tackle the perception that slavery affected only the slaves. To reinforce the idea that Southerners feared slaves, recount the vignette of Nat Turner found at the beginning of the chapter, and refer again to the Olmsted extract to show how nonslaveholding whites feared slaves. You might also want to discuss Nat Turner's confessions (in the documents reader) and ask students why Turner's account may have elicited fear in the hearts of white Southerners. Refer to William Lloyd Garrison's *The Liberator* and to David Walker's *Appeal*, both mentioned in the chapter's opening vignette, to suggest that southern whites increasingly feared the "outside agitator," who, according to white Southerners, provoked "content" slaves to rebel with their seditious propaganda. Finally, show how southern society evolved into an almost martial society to police itself against disobedient or disruptive slaves, by looking at the plantation rules of Bennet Barrow (in the documents reader). Ask students to comment on how the constant need to punish slaves might have affected those inflicting the pain. Finally, discuss how the South silenced white dissent about slavery.

LECTURE 3
African Americans in the Old South

The third lecture discusses the African Americans in slavery. Begin by explaining paternalism. Ask students if the slaveholders practiced true

reciprocity in dealing with their slaves, or if paternalism was a convenient fiction for continued slaveholding. Direct students to Bennet Barrow's plantation rules again and ask if they seem reasonable in their context. Then ask students to comment on the effectiveness of the rules, compared to the punishments Barrow gave his slaves as examined in the *Historical Question* feature. Would James Henry Hammond have condemned Barrow's rules in his proslavery piece? Explain that although white society may have claimed that overly cruel masters were considered pariahs, it failed to institute any legal defense of slaves against such abuse. Use the photograph of Gordon in the *Historical Question* feature to reinforce this idea. After showing the systematic violence used to coerce African Americans to work, address the myth that slaves were utterly dominated by their masters. Describe the various methods of resistance and the means for expanding slave autonomy. But also point out that resistance and autonomy had limits, with dire consequences if a slave pushed beyond them.

Dedicate at least half of your lecture to describing a slave's life. Be sure to cover the introduction of Christianity and its metamorphosis in the hands of the slave community. Explore family life outside the view of the big house. Cover the ways in which the master's power to sell his slaves affected the dynamics of family life for slaves.

Finally, discuss the dilemma of free blacks. They existed as thorns in the side of a society in which whites believed that all blacks should be slaves. Discuss the middle ground of black freedom in the South and the continued limits imposed on free blacks by whites. Also describe the social difference between light- and dark-skinned free blacks. Explore the advantages light-skinned free blacks may have obtained from their white relatives.

Anticipating Student Reactions: Common Misconceptions and Difficult Topics

1. The Old South Lasted a Long Time
Students frequently think that the Old South lasted a very long time, in part because of its name, but also because of the somewhat static descriptions of its society by historians. What we know as the Old South really started taking shape in the 1790s and ended in 1865, so at the most it lasted seventy years, or about three gen-

erations. Slavery predated the Old South, but both institutions died together because slavery was at the heart of southern society. Descriptions of that society frequently depict it at its height, in the 1850s, and as such fail to show many of the changes that took place to make it a viable system. Explain that the duration of the Old South was tied to the expansion of the cotton culture, beginning with the creation of the first workable cotton gin in 1793. Explain the growth of the slave system of the Old South as a process of frontier expansion, with a generation of settlers followed by generations of increasingly sophisticated social systems developed to maintain the slave regime.

2. The Institution of Slavery Affected Only the Lives of Slaves

Students rarely think about the impact that maintaining slaves had on the masters or on nonslaveholding whites in the slave society of the Old South. Yet slavery affected almost every aspect of southern life, from its ideology and intellectual life to its social and political structures based on white supremacy. The South developed forms of institutionalized violence to regulate the use of slaves. White society created slave patrols, composed of roving gangs from the lower classes of white society, to monitor the mobility of both free blacks and slaves. White families feared that slaves would murder them by poisoning their food, by burning their houses while they slept, or by starting general rebellions, such as Nat Turner's. Society was on special alert for a particular type of criminal called a slave stealer, who lured slaves away from home and then spirited them to other states to sell them. White Southerners devised laws to punish slaves differently from whites for similar crimes, in part to instill fear and obedience in slaves and in part to protect the human property of the master from destruction by the state. Manual labor was frequently defined as slave labor, and thus poor whites were cut off from economic advancement for fear of lowering themselves to the status of slaves. The progeny of female slaves raped by their masters was evident to all, and although such acts of rape were generally condemned by society, mixed-race slaves on nearly every plantation pointed to the ability of the institution of slavery to cripple white morality. In short, slavery affected every aspect of life for white and black Southerners alike.

3. African American Slaves Were Utterly Dominated by Their White Masters and Overseers

Students rarely consider resistance in any other terms than outright rebellion. Thus, they frequently infer that slaves obeyed their masters and passively waited for someone else to save them from their fate. To counter such misperceptions, direct the students to questions of resistance and autonomy. How did slaves resist the will of their masters on a day-to-day basis? Masters deluded themselves into believing that these forms of resistance were really racially inherent character flaws, that blacks were inferior people who would always lie, cheat, steal, argue, feign illness, run away, and so on. Furthermore, masters admitted privately that they could not limit the day-to-day autonomy of slaves outside their work life. Slaves worked with what they had and made the best of a bad situation. When slaveholders offered a few days off to slaves during the Christmas season (when little work in the fields could be done anyway), slaves took it as their right in succeeding years. Once a privilege was granted, it could not easily be taken away without fomenting discontent that resulted in greater sabotage and work stoppages. Such workplace resistance and desires for autonomy take place in all societies, but slave resistance and autonomy had specific limits as well, for if the slaves were caught, the masters meted out harsh punishments. Execution was used only in the most extreme cases; usually masters simply whipped troublemakers or sold them, passing on the problem to someone else. Slaves faced limits as to the extent of their resistance and search for autonomy.

Using the Bedford Series in History and Culture and the Historians at Work Series: Suggestions

If possible, allow time for a vital supplementary reading for this chapter and assign the *Narrative of the Life of Frederick Douglass*, Second Edition, edited by David W. Blight. One of the most famous slave narratives, the *Narrative* effectively conveys the brutality of slaves' experiences and their yearning and struggles for freedom. To go into greater depth about issues of slavery and resistance in the antebellum South, consider also assigning *The Confessions of Nat Turner and Related Documents,* edited by Kenneth S. Greenberg. This volume reprints the complete text of the *Confessions* plus additional documents such as newspaper accounts of the incident. Greenberg's introduction provides a historical context for Turner's Rebellion and a discussion of the debates over slavery that the rebellion engendered. Yet other interesting supplements are *The Slave Conspiracy Trials of 1741,* by Serena Zabin, and *Defending Slavery,* by Paul Finkelman.

Lecture Supplements and Classroom Activities

Using Multimedia in the Classroom

When discussing slave resistance, you may want to show Episode 3, "Brotherly Love, 1790–1831," of the PBS series *Africans in America,* which compellingly details, among other topics, the Denmark Vesey and the Nat Turner rebellions. You may also want to show a biographical documentary on Frederick Douglass, *Frederick Douglass: When the Lion Wrote History,* also distributed by PBS. To give a general overview of the westward expansion of slavery, the entrenchment of pro-slavery ideologues, and the eventual demise of slave-based plantation economy in the Old South, consider screening Episode 4, "Judgment Day, 1831–1865," of the PBS series *Africans in America.*

Historical Contingencies

Ask your students to consider the possible course of American history if the master-class elite in the South had not been able to exert hegemonic influence over lower-class whites. Would yeomen and poor whites have united with slaves along class lines to overthrow planter-class domination? Or would race have continued to divide the two groups in the Old South? Ask students to consider whether racism would have triumphed over class interests.

Classroom Activities

Have students debate the political implications of the arguments surrounding the degree to which slaves developed an autonomous culture. Those who argue for complete slave autonomy in the slave quarters, for example, run the risk of minimizing the devastating effects of institutionalized slavery on a race of people. Students who are comforted by the notion that slaves were able to lead meaningful lives outside the direct control of their masters may find the minimalization of the horrors of the institution of slavery unattractive. Those who argue that masters controlled all aspects of slave culture, even in the quarters, run the risk of suggesting freed slaves and their descendants had very little on which to build their lives outside the institution of slavery. Students who stress the brutality of slavery may find the "impoverished legacy" untenable. Few historians put the matter so starkly, but do convey to your students that historians disagree widely in their interpretations of the relative autonomy of slave culture.

Using the Internet

The University of North Carolina at Chapel Hill has made available online hundreds of texts and manuscripts on the American South. Students will find a wealth of information on the Old South at this site, which includes slave narratives, works of fiction, personal papers, and defenses of the slaveholding regime. Tell students to go to the home page for Documenting the American South at <http://docsouth.unc.edu>. Students may also find the thousands of Works Progress Administration (WPA) slave narratives useful, which the Library of Congress has made available online. Tell your students to exercise caution, however. WPA workers conducted these interviews in the 1930s, decades after the fall of slavery. Moreover, most of the interviewers were white Southerners (except those from Fisk University) who were not necessarily immune from the racism of their time and place. Former slaves may not have been willing to be especially forthcoming to white interviewers. Nonetheless, these interviews, if read carefully, contain a wealth of information on the institution of slavery.

ASSESSING RESULTS
Multiple-Choice Questions

1. Which statement best describes Nat Turner's slave rebellion?
   a. Dozens of whites were killed by slaves following a man who claimed to be a prophet.
   b. Abolitionists led a raid on a federal arsenal at Harpers Ferry, Virginia, and expected a general slave uprising to follow.
   c. Thousands of blacks massacred the white population in the French colony of San Domingue in the Caribbean following the French Revolution.

d. A free black in Charleston organized members of his church to burn Charleston following the Missouri Compromise.

2. Which statement best characterized the South's plantation economy?
   a. Southern tobacco production stifled all other forms of economic and agricultural diversification.
   b. With the South's capital tied up in slaves, Southerners did not develop any transportation facilities, financial institutions, or factories.
   c. The South's economy failed to diversify as much as the North's, but profits in southern agriculture were generally comparable to northern profits.
   d. The annual profits for southern investments in slaves far exceeded the returns on anything in which Northerners could have invested.

3. Which statement best describes paternalism in the Old South?
   a. It defined slavery as a set of reciprocal obligations between masters and slaves, in which the master provided slaves with basic care and guidance in exchange for the slave's labor and obedience.
   b. It defined a person's social standing, chances for political advancement, and self-esteem, and it sometimes required dueling as a defense against slander or assault.
   c. It gave the female head of household complete domination over the extended family of the plantation, both white and black.
   d. It assumed that women were weak and put them under the protection of their fathers.

4. Slaves resisted their masters
   a. almost never, because they accepted the paternalist bargain in which they promised obedience.
   b. only in extreme cases of cruelty and then by fomenting large-scale rebellion.
   c. only in the states bordering free territory, and then by escaping to Canada.
   d. often, by lying, stealing, pretending to be stupid, feigning illness, breaking tools, and running away.

5. Which of the following is true about the "plain folk" of the Old South?
   a. Upcountry yeomen largely rejected the ideals of the plantation economy and sought to maintain their own self-sufficiency as a vision of individual independence.
   b. Plantation-belt yeomen largely rejected the ideals of the plantation economy and sought to maintain their own self-sufficiency as a vision of individual independence.
   c. Poor whites differed from southern yeomen in that yeomen were landless and without any opportunity for economic advancement.
   d. Urban artisans and workers made up the largest group — the plain folk.

6. Why did planters continue to dominate southern politics despite universal white male suffrage throughout the South?
   a. Cynicism about the ability of politics to solve the important problems affecting nonelite lives led to low voter turnout, which allowed elites to vote themselves into office.
   b. Planters threatened yeomen and poor whites with economic retaliation if they failed to support the elite.
   c. Continued planter domination resulted from the persistence of notions of hierarchy and of the habits of deference as well as seeing planters as examples of successful upward mobility, which many of the nonelite hoped to emulate.
   d. The nonelite believed that they were unfit to serve in public office.

7. Map 13.1, "Cotton Kingdom, Slave Empire: 1820 and 1860," demonstrates that
   a. in 1820 the majority of slaves lived in cotton producing areas of Alabama, Mississippi, and Louisiana.
   b. by 1860 few slaves lived along the Atlantic seaboard; they had all been drawn inward to work on cotton plantations.
   c. there is no positive correlation between the location of cotton plantations and the spread of the slave population.
   d. as the production of cotton soared, the slave population increased dramatically.

8. How effective were the punishments meted out by Bennet H. Barrow, the master of the Highland Plantation, as discussed in the *Historical Question* feature?
   a. Somewhat effective: Barrow stated that he found the more brutal punishments to

have better results, particularly with children and pregnant women.

b. Their efficacy is not entirely known: His overseer performed most of the punishments outside Barrow's knowledge and so failed to record their causes.

c. Extremely effective: After castrating three of his slaves, Barrow later bragged of having gained perfect dominion over his slaves.

d. Not effective: After 160 whippings of Barrow's 129 slaves over a 23-month period, the behaviors drawing such punishments continued unabated.

9. Figure 13.1, "Black and White Population in the South, 1860," demonstrates that
   a. no state had a slave majority.
   b. several southern states had slave majorities.
   c. more slaves lived in the Lower South than in the Upper South.
   d. both Delaware and Maryland had free black populations that exceeded 30 percent.

10. What did the poor white farmer in Mississippi whom Frederick Law Olmsted described in *The Cotton Kingdom* think of the lives of slaves on the neighboring plantations?
   a. He thought they were well treated, given plenty of food, and educated to their capacity.
   b. He thought they would attack all the whites in the neighborhood if not properly watched over.
   c. He thought they had a hard life, full of work and devoid of leisure.
   d. He thought they should be freed and sent north to give more employment opportunity to southern whites.

11. Identify the correct sequence of historical figures and events.
   a. decreased ability of landless southern whites to purchase land, democratization of southern politics, creation of relatively large free black sector of southern population
   b. cotton gin invented, cotton production begins, sugar production begins, tobacco production begins
   c. paternalism embraced to justify slavery, dueling adopted as a form of defending one's honor, patriarchy adopted to order one's household, Christianity became a large factor in the lives of slaves
   d. cotton gin invented, Denmark Vesey's execution, Nat Turner's revolt, Frederick Law Olmsted tours the South

Proposing More: Additional Readings

Joyce E. Chaplin, "Creating a Cotton South in Georgia and South Carolina, 1760–1815," *Journal of Southern History* 57, no. 2 (1991): 171–200.

J. William Harris, "The Organization of Work on a Yeoman Slaveholder's Farm," *Agricultural History* 64, no. 1 (1990): 39–52.

Alex Lichtenstein, "Coercion Had Its Limits," *Reviews in American History* 23, no. 1 (1995): 20–25.

Stephanie McCurry, "The Two Faces of Republicanism: Gender and Proslavery Politics in Antebellum South Carolina," *Journal of American History* 78, no. 4 (1992): 1245–64.

Jeffrey R. Young, "Ideology and Death on a Savannah River Rice Plantation, 1833–1867: Paternalism Amidst 'A Good Supply of Disease and Pain,'" *Journal of Southern History* 59, no. 4 (1993): 673–706.

Answer Key to Multiple-Choice Questions: 1-a, 2-c, 3-a, 4-d, 5-a, 6-c, 7-d, 8-d, 9-c, 10-c, 11-d

14 THE HOUSE DIVIDED

1846–1861

Outlining Chapters: Thematic Questions

I. What were the political legacies of America's victory in its war with Mexico?
   A. Why was the question of extending slavery to federal territories the focus of constitutional debate from 1846 to 1860? What was the Wilmot Proviso? Why did Northerners, regardless of party affiliation, generally support it? Why did Southerners oppose it so vehemently? What was the fate of the Wilmot Proviso? What was the doctrine of "popular sovereignty," and why did its proponents consider it an acceptable solution?
   B. Why did the issue of expansion of slavery into the territories cause disaffected Whigs and Democrats to bolt from their respective parties? How successful was the new Free-Soil Party in the election of 1848?
   C. What precipitated a congressional crisis in 1850? What were the terms of Henry Clay's proposed compromise, and how did the North and the South receive them? What was William H. Seward's "higher law" theory? Why did a Senate committee combine Clay's compromises into the Omnibus Bill, and why did Clay believe Congress would pass it? Why did the Senate committee's strategy backfire? How did Stephen Douglas save the Compromise of 1850?

II. Why did the Compromise of 1850 ultimately fail?
   A. Why was the Fugitive Slave Act the most explosive of the Compromise measures?
   B. How did Harriet Beecher Stowe's novel *Uncle Tom's Cabin* galvanize northern opposition to the "peculiar institution" and invite wrath from southern slaveholders?
   C. Why did Franklin Pierce win the election of 1852? Why did Pierce focus on overseas expansion, and why did the United States purchase 30,000 square miles of Mexico in 1853?
   D. Why did Stephen Douglas desire a transcontinental railroad, and how did his desire lead to the Kansas-Nebraska Act? Why did it specifically repeal the Missouri Compromise?

III. What destroyed the second American party system in the 1850s, and how was the electorate realigned?
   A. What caused the death of the Whig Party by the mid-1850s? Why did the power of the Democratic Party decline as well?

B. How did nativism and the demands for free soil/free labor spawn the birth of two new political parties? How successful were the Know-Nothing and the Republican Parties in attracting disaffected Whigs and Democrats to their folds?

C. Why did the election of 1856 signal the rise of the Republican Party and the demise of the Know-Nothing Party?

IV. How was the Republican Party able to capitalize on its northern base, and what events convinced Northerners that the South could not be trusted?

A. How was Kansas settled and organized? Why did guerrilla warfare break out in Kansas between proslavery and antislavery factions? Why did Preston Brooks cane Charles Sumner on the Senate floor? How did the Republican Party capitalize on "Bleeding Kansas" and "Bleeding Sumner"?

B. What were the terms of the Supreme Court's majority decision in the *Dred Scott* case? On what grounds did the minority dissent? What effect did the decision have on the doctrine of popular sovereignty? Why did the decision strengthen the Republican Party?

C. Why did Abraham Lincoln find his political home in the Republican Party? What were his views about slavery and about African Americans? On what grounds did he appeal to northern voters?

D. How did the panic of 1857 and the Lecompton constitution influence the 1858 Illinois Senate race between Stephen Douglas and Abraham Lincoln? Where did the two candidates stand on popular sovereignty and racial equality? What was the "Freeport Doctrine," and why did Southerners repudiate it? Why did Lincoln lose the election?

V. How did the events of the late 1850s lead to the collapse of the Union in 1861?

A. Why did John Brown attack the federal arsenal in Harpers Ferry, Virginia? How did his execution turn him into a martyr in the eyes of many Northerners? What did Southerners think of his exploits?

B. Why was the Democratic Party unable to select one candidate or adopt one platform in the election of 1860? How did the Republican Party broaden its appeal? Why did it choose Lincoln as its candidate? How did the four major candidates divide the electorate?

C. How did secessionists interpret the election of 1860? Why were Southerners divided on the issue of secession? How quickly after Lincoln's election was the Confederate States of America established? What concessions was Lincoln willing to make to appease the South?

Teaching with The American Promise, *Second Compact Edition: Lecture Strategies*

LECTURE 1
The Failure of Compromise

This lecture introduces students to the problems and assumptions underlying the extension of slavery into the territories and explores the effects of the solutions to this issue on previous compromises between North and South. The U.S. victory in the Mexican War left a number of questions on the issue of slavery unresolved. Both the North and the South wanted the conquered territory for their own economic advantage. Emphasize that the debate surrounding slavery in the 1840s largely centered on political and economic gain, and not on the morality of the institution, as many students might expect. Explain that Pennsylvania Democrat David Wilmot proposed his Proviso to reduce northern alienation from the Democratic Party for failing to pursue the Oregon question as vigorously as the Polk administration had pursued expansion at Mexico's expense.

Explain that sectional politics had not yet destroyed the power of the national political parties; both the Democrats and the Whigs received electoral votes from all sections of the country. Explain the terms of Henry Clay's Omnibus Bill and why it did not pass until Stephen Douglas broke it into separate bills. Cover Lewis Cass's doctrine of "popular sovereignty," and use Map 14.2, "The Compromise of 1850," to show which areas were subject to that idea and which ones still adhered to the Missouri Compromise. Ask students what part of the Missouri Compromise was completely repealed by the Compromise of 1850, and why the South should have feared the repeal.

Next, explore the prickly issue of the Fugitive Slave Act and how its enforcement alienated Northerners and its lack of enforcement disgusted Southerners. Introduce the railroad agitation of the 1850s, and explore why Stephen Douglas reopened the issue of the extension of slavery into the territories. Use Map 14.3, "The Kansas-Nebraska Act, 1854," to show where slavery could possibly be extended and the areas generally expected to be contested. Direct students to Lincoln's statement (in the documents reader) regarding popular sovereignty in Kansas, and ask what he expected to be its outcome. Finally, explain why the Kansas-Nebraska Act explicitly repealed the remaining operative clauses of the Missouri Compromise.

LECTURE 2
Political Realignment

This lecture examines the demise of the second American party system and the birth of the present party system. Discuss how the failure of the two Whig presidencies to produce results of the Whig agenda contributed to the decline of the Whig Party. Explore how the growing sectional conflict weakened the Democrats and killed the Whig Party. Use Map 14.4, "Political Realignment, 1848–1860," to demonstrate the trend from nationally based parties to regionally based parties. Explore the program of the American Party and the original single issue of the Republican Party. Refer your students to the discussion under the heading "The Old Parties: Whigs and Democrats" and then encourage them to explain why Whigs and northern Democrats migrated to the Republican Party. You may have to prod them by asking them to use Lincoln as a model.

Next, use the *Uncle Tom's Cabin* poster to discuss how Northerners imagined that slavery operated; then show how the South responded. Use this discussion to explore the myth that the coming of the Civil War was entirely the South's fault. Show how failure to compromise because of fundamental differences led to increasing division within the political structure so that, by 1860, secession actually seemed a reasonable course to many Southerners and that some Northerners, though only a few, actually applauded the departure of the "slavocracy." Finish by reviewing the ways in which the Republican Party broadened its appeal in the 1860 election.

LECTURE 3
Victims of Violent Conspiracy

This lecture shows the depth of animosity and distrust engendered by the failures to compromise in the 1850s. Open by asking your students to consider whether the Civil War was inherently

inevitable, but then tell them to hold their answers until the end of class. Show how both the North and the South came to believe they were victims of a conspiracy by the other section. Southerners cried that they had been swindled into giving up parity in the Senate in exchange for a worthless fugitive slave law. Northerners felt victimized as well, as the southern-dominated Supreme Court ruled that Congress never had constitutional authority to restrict slavery, that blacks were not citizens, and that the laws protecting the safety of free blacks in the North from the hands of southern slave catchers were illegal.

Demonstrate the slippery slope from the passage of the Kansas-Nebraska Act to the election of Lincoln by showing how openly violent national politics had become. New England ran guns along with its immigrants to Kansas in an effort to make the territory a free state. Missouri slaveholders flocked to Kansas to vote in the territorial elections and intimidate the antislavery majority that had settled there. Use the chapter's opening vignette and the John Brown piece (in the documents reader) to discuss the Sack of Lawrence and the acts of John Brown. Cover the ways in which the proslavery party stole the elections in Kansas and framed a proslavery state constitution that the Buchanan administration proposed accepting. Two other events stand out as milestones of distrust. The caning of Charles Sumner convinced Northerners that southern society was violently barbaric. John Brown's raid at Harpers Ferry suggested to Southerners that all Northerners were abolitionists who would provoke slave rebellions that would kill all white Southerners. Note that the panic of 1857 convinced Southerners that their economic system was superior to that of the North, since the panic had little effect on the South and Northerners believed Southerners had conspired with Europeans to damage the northern economy. Republicans fiercely denounced the power of the "slavocracy" to control the country.

Next, explain the splintering of the Democratic Party in the election of 1860 and how Lincoln won the election even though he failed to carry a single southern state. Use the Charleston *Mercury* headline to start discussing how Southerners went about seceding from the Union; be sure to point out that not all Southerners supported secession. Now return to the question of the inevitability of the Civil War, and suggest how the course of history might have developed differently. At Lincoln's inauguration in March 1861, few were convinced that war would come.

Anticipating Student Reactions: Common Misconceptions and Difficult Topics

1. Morality, and Not Economics, Governed the Debates about Slavery

Although the issue of the morality of slavery grew to be an increasingly divisive one, the real issue underlying sectional hostilities was the extension of slavery into the territories. Southerners believed that slavery could not continue to thrive as an economic system if they were denied the opportunity to put more acreage under tillage. Because the staple agriculture of the South exhausted the soil of its nutrients, planters had to move westward in search of fertile soil. Preventing planters from carrying their slaves into the western territories would effectively destroy the institution of slavery in the United States. Southerners believed that limiting slavery to where it already existed would exhaust the soil and force them to abandon staple crop agriculture and to emancipate the now unnecessary slave labor force. So, from the southern point of view, continued geographic expansion of slave territory was essential to the survival of slavery, and Northerners agreed.

Northerners adhering to a free-labor, free-soil ideology believed that western lands should be reserved for creating small farms for hardworking white people. Northerners also practiced soil-exhausting agriculture and thus needed new land on which to expand agricultural production and maintain their ambitions for an improved standard of living. Thus, they saw themselves as competing with Southerners for limited lands for future agricultural production. Competition with slave labor would mean that the land-use patterns of the West would come to resemble those of the plantation belt rather than those of the Midwest. Northerners would lose not only the economic future for their children but also the culture in which their children were raised, since as smallholders in a plantation they would resemble southern yeomen.

If the conquest of Mexico led to the expansion of slavery, then hardworking white families of the North would have to work shoulder to shoulder with blacks, whom they considered an inferior race. The West, they believed, was taken from Mexicans and Indians (other people they believed to be racially inferior to themselves) for the explicit benefit of the "superior" white race. Thus, the fight over extension of slavery into the western territories was not just a smoke screen for the debate on the morality of slavery, but contained economic, cultural, and ideological dimensions as well.

2. The South Was Solely Responsible for the Coming of the Civil War

Regardless of geographical origins, many students may believe that because the South maintained the immoral institution of slavery and seceded from the Union, it must have caused the Civil War. Now is your opportunity to show students that history rarely demonstrates that any one side of a conflict or event has a monopoly on truth and justice. Both the North and the South caused the Civil War by misinterpreting each other's motives and failing to seek real reconciliation to settle grievances fairly. Following the introduction of the Wilmot Proviso, the country increasingly divided along sectional lines, which destroyed the ability of the national parties to find workable compromises. The political settlements of the 1850s lacked success because both sides failed to make them work.

The Compromise of 1850 exemplifies such failure. It passed not because it was worked out in the real spirit of compromise, but because of the parliamentary skills of Stephen Douglas, who divided the bill into separate pieces and aligned sufficient votes to get each piece passed. When the voting was completed, however, an overwhelming majority of both houses of Congress had voted against some portion of the compromise package. The nature of this failure to compromise rested on fundamental disagreement over the issue, and you can explore how fundamental disagreements endanger the country with a look at modern issues, such as abortion. Be careful not to get entangled in the arguments themselves. A quick overview of the topic will suffice to demonstrate the potential for violent division of the electorate — a division that moderates on both sides would abhor. Quickly move back to the issues of the 1850s and explore with your class the myriad of ways in which both sections slid toward secession.

3. Lincoln Was a Radical Abolitionist

Perhaps because Lincoln bears the nickname "the Great Emancipator" many students equate his 1850s position on slavery with that of the radical abolitionists. Remind students that Lincoln opposed the extension of slavery into the territories, but, as the textbook points out, he believed that the Constitution sanctioned slavery in those states where it already existed. Unlike William

Lloyd Garrison, he did not condemn the Constitution as a "pact with the devil" or a "document dripping with blood." And unlike David Walker and John Brown, Lincoln did not advocate "violence, bloodshed, and treason" to bring about the demise of the institution. Make clear to your students that Lincoln, on the eve of the Civil War, held moderate antislavery views.

Using the Bedford Series in History and Culture and the Historians at Work Series: Suggestions

To explore further the debates over slavery and the western territories in antebellum America, consider assigning *Dred Scott v. Sandford: A Brief History with Documents*, edited by Paul Finkelman. *Abraham Lincoln, Slavery, and the Civil War*, edited by Michael P. Johnson, offers students a thorough review of Lincoln's views on slavery and the coming of the Civil War.

Lecture Supplements and Classroom Activities

Using Multimedia Sources in the Classroom

Episode 4 of the PBS series *Africans in America*, "Judgment Day: 1831–1861," chronicles the growing strength of the abolitionist movement during the mid-nineteenth century and the widening divide between North and South on the issue of slavery. "Roots of Resistance: A Story of the Underground Railroad," part of the PBS *American Experience* series, highlights the significance of the passages that led black men and women to freedom during the mid-nineteenth century.

Historical Contingencies

In hindsight, major events such as the Civil War often seem inevitable. Ask students to consider some counterfactual events that could have conceivably altered history. What if southern "filibusterers" had captured Cuba in the 1850s? Would the acquisition of Cuba have satisfied those who wished to extend the territorial boundaries of slavery? What if the conditions in Europe had lessened the impact of the panic of 1857 on the North? Would this have reduced Southerners' smugness about the superiority of their economy? Would New England have seceded from the Union, as William Lloyd Garrison had proposed? What if one or more of the states of the Lower South had failed to secede from the Union? Would the Confederacy have come into existence, or would the federal government have had the opportunity to deal with each state individually?

Classroom Activities

To examine the fundamental differences of opinion in the 1850s on the legality of slavery, direct your students to the question of whether the Constitution protected slavery, as interpreted by Frederick Douglass and Jefferson Davis (both in the documents reader). Then have students debate whether the Constitution is a "proslavery" document.

Using the Internet

The University of Missouri at St. Louis's site Virtual St. Louis provides a wealth of information pertaining to this chapter. Direct students to <http://www.umsl.edu/~virtualstl/default.htm>. From there, tell students to click on "Dred Scott." Here, students can find a host of documents and images relating to *Dred Scott v. Sandford*, including speeches by Abraham Lincoln, census data, the Fugitive Slave Act of 1850, the Kansas-Nebraska Act, the seven Lincoln-Douglas debates, majority and minority opinions in the *Dred Scott* case, maps, and playbills.

ASSESSING RESULTS
Multiple-Choice Questions

1. On what grounds did Dred Scott sue for his freedom?
   a. He had won his freedom by serving in the Mexican War in his master's place.
   b. He had been born free and was stolen off the streets by slave catchers who sold him into slavery.
   c. He was born in a state that abolished slavery by freeing all slaves born after a certain date when they reached the age of thirty-five, but he was sold south when he was a teenager.
   d. He had lived as a slave in a state and a territory in which slavery was prohibited.

2. What was the effect of the Wilmot Proviso?
   a. It allowed territorial legislatures to determine if slavery would be allowed in the territory.
   b. It prevented the United States from annexing all of Mexico.

c. It realigned the American electorate from along party lines to along sectional lines.

d. It refused to admit Kansas into the Union as a slave state.

3. What attracted voters to the Know-Nothing Party?
   a. its condemnation of immigrants and Roman Catholics
   b. its insistence on repealing the Missouri Compromise
   c. its desire to push for the immediate emancipation of slaves throughout the country
   d. its expansionist plans for conquering Cuba

4. What legislation led to the "Sack of Lawrence"?
   a. the Wilmot Proviso
   b. the Kansas-Nebraska Act
   c. the Lecompton constitution
   d. the Omnibus Bill

5. What was the cumulative effect of the events of the 1850s?
   a. The violence of action and of rhetoric drove the electorate to support extremist positions in support of their own section against the other section.
   b. Fear of ongoing violence destroyed the economy and led to the panic of 1857.
   c. The "slavocracy" gained conclusive political ascendancy by gaining control of the Senate.
   d. The Republican Party repudiated free-labor ideas to broaden its appeal to a national coalition of voters.

6. The spot map, "Secession of the Lower South, Dec. 1860–Feb. 1861," demonstrates that after Lincoln's election
   a. seven slave states seceded from the Union before the fall of Fort Sumter.
   b. only South Carolina and Mississippi seceded before the fall of Fort Sumter.
   c. all fifteen slave states had seceded before the fall of Fort Sumter.
   d. seven slaves states remained loyal to the Union, even after the firing on Fort Sumter.

7. On what grounds did Dr. Harriet K. Hunt, in the *Documenting the American Promise* feature, protest the payment of her city taxes?
   a. The payment of taxes without representation always leads to tyranny, and thus the state would tyrannize her in the same way that men held dominance over women and kept them as property.

b. Her inability to vote while being forced to pay taxes gave her the same status as a free black or an Indian, a scandalous affront.

c. Her inability to vote while being forced to pay taxes put her in the same position as minors or aliens, except they had the means to gain the franchise while she did not.

d. All of the above.

8. What is readily apparent from Map 14.5, which shows the electoral vote of the 1860 presidential race?
   a. Bell's Constitutional Union Party led in the lower South.
   b. Stephen Douglas would have won the election if he had won his home state.
   c. Because the election was so close, it hinged on the vote of the western states of California and Oregon.
   d. Lincoln was strictly a regional, rather than a national, candidate.

9. On what basis did Jefferson Davis, in the documents reader, insist that the Constitution protected slavery in all territories?
   a. Slavery was a form of property, and all forms of property were protected by the Constitution.
   b. The Three-fifths Compromise recognized slaves in apportionment of representation.
   c. The Constitution specifically allowed eliminating the slave trade but did not specifically establish a framework for eliminating slavery.
   d. The Preamble to the Constitution asserted positive rights of the federal government but did not mention negative actions it could assert in dealing with preexisting institutions such as slavery.

10. According to the chapter's opening vignette, John Brown's raid on the arsenal at Harpers Ferry
    a. proved such a debacle that white Southerners discounted the entire affair.
    b. was well calculated and, although ultimately unsuccessful, initiated the largest slave insurrection in Virginia's history.
    c. renewed the sectional tension that had lain dormant throughout the 1850s.
    d. provided white Southerners with proof of their growing suspicion that Northerners actively sought to incite slaves in bloody rebellion.

11. Identify the correct sequence of historical events and figures.
   a. Wilmot Proviso, Kansas-Nebraska Act, *Dred Scott*, Harpers Ferry
   b. Lecompton Constitution, Gadsden Purchase, Omnibus Bill, Lincoln-Douglas debates
   c. "Bleeding Kansas," *Uncle Tom's Cabin*, popular sovereignty introduced, the caning of Sumner
   d. presidencies of James Buchanan, Millard Fillmore, Zachary Taylor, Franklin Pierce

Proposing More: Additional Readings

Gary Collison, "'This Flagitious Offense': Daniel Webster and the Shadrach Rescue Cases, 1851–1852," *New England Quarterly* 68, no. 4 (1995): 609–25.

William E. Gienapp, "Nativism and the Creating of a Republican Majority in the North before the Civil War," *Journal of American History* 72, no. 3 (1985): 529–59.

Robert E. McGlore, "Forgotten Surrender: John Brown's Raid and the Cult of Martial Virtues," *Civil War History* 40, no. 3 (1994): 185–201.

Sarah Robbins, "Gendering the History of the Anti-slavery Narrative: Juxtaposing *Uncle Tom's Cabin* and *Benito Cereno, Beloved* and *Middle Passage*," *American Quarterly* 49, no. 3 (1997): 531–73.

John S. Vishneski III, "What the Court Decided in *Dred Scott v. Sandford*," *American Journal of Legal History* 32, no. 4 (1988): 373–90.

Answer Key to Multiple-Choice Questions: 1-d, 2-c, 3-a, 4-b, 5-a, 6-a, 7-c, 8-d, 9-a, 10-d, 11-a

THE CRUCIBLE OF WAR 15

1861–1865

Outlining Chapters: Thematic Questions

I. What issues faced Abraham Lincoln and Jefferson Davis as they began their terms as presidents of their respective nations?

   A. What did Fort Sumter symbolize to Northerners and Southerners? Why were the first shots of the Civil War fired by Southerners in Charleston, South Carolina?

   B. What effect did the fall of Fort Sumter have on the secession debates in the Upper South? Why did Maryland, Delaware, Missouri, and Kentucky stay in the Union? Why did West Virginia come into existence?

II. What did combatants on each side believe they were fighting for, and why did they each believe their cause would prevail?

   A. Why did all classes of white Southerners fight for the Confederacy, and why did they avoid naming slavery as the cause of their fight? Why did Northerners fight?

   B. Why did the Confederacy believe it would win the war, despite overwhelming evidence that suggested a different outcome? How did King Cotton bolster the South's confidence in its ability to win the war? What was the South's war strategy? What was the North's? Why did both sides miscalculate?

   C. What leadership skills did Lincoln and Davis provide for their respective nations? What sorts of tasks did the leaders confront in organizing for war? How did the Union and Confederacy finance the war?

III. Where were the major military campaigns during the first year and a half of the Civil War, and which proved most decisive?

   A. What significance did the Battle of Manassas hold for Federals and Confederates? How decisive were the battles of the eastern theater under Lincoln's generals McClellan, Pope, and Burnside? How did Lee become commander of the Confederate forces? How did Lee's fighting style differ from that of the Union generals?

   B. Why was the control of the western theater critical for both sides? What strengths did Ulysses S. Grant bring to his command, and what strategy did he craft for the Union? How did the war stand at the end of 1862?

C. How effective was the Union naval blockade of the South? Why was King Cotton diplomacy a failure for the South?

IV. How was the Civil War transformed from a war to preserve the Union to a war to end slavery?

   A. Why did Lincoln originally assume a conservative position on emancipation? How did abolitionists regard Lincoln's position? How did Congress engage the issue? How did slaves force emancipation onto the political agenda, despite Lincoln's reluctance to address it?

   B. Why did Lincoln finally issue the Emancipation Proclamation, and what did it actually do? How did the North react to the proclamation?

   C. What roles did African Americans play in the Union military effort, and why? What effect did military participation have on African Americans?

V. How did the exigencies of the Civil War quell the white South's expectations for an independent Confederacy?

   A. What drastic actions did the Confederate government take to prepare for war, and were they enough? Why have the Confederacy's war efforts been termed a "revolution from above"?

   B. How widely and how equally were wartime deprivations felt in the South, and what effect did they have on southern unity?

   C. How did the war affect the power relations of masters and slaves who were far from the war's front lines? How did slaves act during the war? How did southern women contribute to the war effort?

VI. How did "total war" affect the North's culture and economy?

   A. Why did Congress finally pass a package of government programs for enhancing the economy after it had opposed similar measures for almost seventy years? How did these government programs affect industrial, agricultural, educational, and financial institutions?

   B. In what ways did northern women of all classes and geographic areas contribute to the Union war effort?

   C. How did the politics of the two-party system strengthen the ability of the North to wage war? What sort of dissent did Lincoln actively silence, and what effect did his efforts have on free speech gener-

ally? Was northern conscription fair and equitable? How did black efforts at gaining legal equality fare in the North?

VII. What strategy did Grant prescribe for northern victory?

   A. What happened at the Battles of Vicksburg and Gettysburg, and what effect did the two events have?

   B. Why was Grant named commander of all northern armies, and what tactic did he and his subordinates William T. Sherman and Philip H. Sheridan use to break the will of the southern people?

   C. What was the significance of the 1864 election? What obstacles did the Republican Party face? What changes did the Republican Party make to broaden its appeal?

   D. How did the Confederacy collapse in the late winter and early spring of 1865?

Teaching with **The American Promise,** *Second Compact Edition: Lecture Strategies*

LECTURE 1

Chronology and Strategy

This lecture introduces students to the Civil War, emphasizing its chronology and the strategies pursued by both sides. Start with the process of secession; refer back to Chapter 14 and recount the factionalization of the Democratic Party and Lincoln's success in winning the 1860 presidential election. Using Map 15.1, "Secession, 1860–1861," explain why the first seven southern states seceded and what steps President Buchanan and President-elect Lincoln took to stop the nation from rupturing. Next, describe the significance of the federal base in Charleston harbor and what effect the fight over it had on the southern states. Discuss why four border slave states did not secede. Address the anticipated misconception that the South was a united front throughout the war by discussing disagreements over secession, disgust with conscription, and rejection of disunion by many geographic subsections of the South. Bring the North into the picture by reemphasizing how Lincoln kept the loyal slave states from seceding by avoiding any talk about emancipation and by suppressing civil liberties when he thought he could get away with it. Next, quickly discuss the campaigns of 1861–1862, using Map 15.2, "The Civil War, 1861–1862," to show why action in the western theater proved decisive. Be certain to mention Vicksburg and Gettysburg together as the turning point in the war, referring to the spot maps of the battles. Then, using Map 15.3, "The Civil War, 1863–1865," explain how Grant, with Sherman and Sheridan, perfected a "scorched-earth" policy to convince a defiant South that it was truly defeated. Discuss William T. Sherman's explanation of "the Hard Hand of War" (in the documents reader) to emphasize the psychological nature of northern strategy.

Be sure to point out that northern and southern strategy differed in many ways. Both sides thought they would win the war quickly, but the devastation of the earliest battles convinced leaders that the war could be won only after a long campaign. The South thought it could outwait the North and force it to accept the South's departure from the Union as northern resolve wavered. This war of attrition, southern leaders thought, would bring in European allies for the South and would dishearten the North with its many divided loyalties. Discuss the failure of King Cotton diplomacy, and ask whether the South accurately assessed the mood of the North. Also appraise the degree to which the Union's blockade of the South hampered its war effort. The North, on the other hand, chose to expand its army and increase the production of war materiel as necessary to obtain its objective. By 1863, the North accepted Grant's strategy of destroying as much of the South as possible to destroy the South's ability and desire to wage war. Use the *Historical Question* feature, "Why Did So Many Soldiers Die?," to convey to students that the carnage of the Civil War was much higher than that of previous wars as a result of battles fought with outdated tactics and modern guns.

LECTURE 2
Total War

This lecture explores the newness of modern warfare and shows how the Civil War was the first "total war." Begin by drawing on the section "'And the War Came'" to describe how Abraham Lincoln and Jefferson Davis each had to organize and gear his country for war. Explore how the productive means of each section became critical to the war effort and why the North had a clear advantage in both materiel and personnel. Suggest to students that, beginning with the Civil War, war involved entire societies, not just armies in the field. Show how, when southern

Democrats abandoned the Congress, the Republican agenda centralized much of the economic decision-making process in the United States and, accordingly, increased the power of the national government. List and explain the features of that agenda and conclude with the financial instruments created by Congress at that time. Address the anticipated misconception regarding the recent development of deficit spending at this point, and show how it made maximum northern mobilization possible.

Next, discuss the human side of the war. How did those on the home front and those on the front line negotiate conflicting forces? Return to the *Historical Question* feature, and explain how technological advances in armaments and reliance on outdated military tactics produced significantly larger numbers of casualties in the Civil War than in any other war in American history. Discuss why the wounded died so frequently, focusing primarily on the lack of medical knowledge. Conclude the discussion of casualties by discussing the Walt Whitman piece on wounds (in the documents reader).

Because of the loss of men, both sides instituted the draft for the first time in American history. Explain how the conscription laws worked and how they divided both northern and southern societies along class lines. Then move to the question of gender; ask about the role of women in the war: How did life change for those serving as nurses and those working at home while the men were away? You might ask students to consider what the war "promised" women on the home front. What expectations did they have? End the lecture with an explanation of why Lincoln refused to let the war interfere with the country's electoral process and how the election of 1864 turned out.

LECTURE 3
The Crucible of Race

This lecture covers the evolution of northern policy regarding African Americans. Open this lecture with a discussion of the documents regarding war aims (in the documents reader). Be prepared to deal with students who maintain that slavery was not the central issue that caused the war. Look back to the chapter's opening vignette about Frederick Douglass to see how African Americans realized from the start that the war would affect slavery. Ask students to think about the ways in which African Americans interpreted the war as the means by which the Union could fulfill the "promise" of America. Show how and why Lincoln's policy toward emancipation changed. Explain how events taking place outside the control of the federal government necessitated the reevaluation of what to do about slavery. Thousands of slaves freed themselves and flocked to the Union cause. Use the photograph of the contrabands crossing the Rappahannock River to convince students that slaves had both the means and the desire to affect their own destiny. Explore the writings of a slave in Union-occupied New Orleans (in the documents reader) to see what at least one newly freed slave thought of his former masters and of his cautious liberators. Discuss the actions Congress took to liberate the slaves legally, despite Lincoln's reticence. Be sure to cover whom each of the acts and proclamations actually freed.

Ask students how both sides used African Americans in the early stages of the war. Note that the Confederate military could not have fielded the army the way it did without using slaves for menial work, thereby freeing up white men for fighting. The North originally began using free black volunteers the same way, but African Americans wanted to prove their worthiness for freedom on the battlefield and pushed to be allowed to fight. Here, you may want to refer students to the photograph of the 107th U.S. Colored Infantry. Segregated units arose in the Union army, with black soldiers and white officers — all thrown into some of the fiercest battles of the war. Discuss how racial prejudice affected the outcomes and punishments meted out by court martial for black soldiers. How did immigrants react to conscription to fight to free the slaves? Discuss how African American valor in service to the country affected the way in which white Americans viewed blacks at the end of the war.

Anticipating Student Reactions: Common Misconceptions and Difficult Topics

1. Slavery Was Not the Central Issue That Caused the Civil War

One of the most common misconceptions brought into the first half of the American history survey is that the Civil War was about economics, philosophical differences, or political culture — anything but slavery. But when pushed to explain the differences between the North and

South, students should eventually see that slavery was at the root of every major difference they may propose. Point out that the economic differences stemmed from the North's increasing efforts to diversify the economy based on free labor, while the South's staple-crop agriculture remained based on slave labor. Southerners championed states' rights (largely a "lost cause" explanation not used in the immediate prewar environment) because it protected slavery. Cultural differences can be traced to the existence or absence of slavery in the two sections. Southern wariness of an active federal government that "interfered" in local politics stemmed from the concern that it would dismantle slavery. Southerners similarly worried about a loosely interpreted Constitution; although Southerners maintained that the Constitution protected slavery, they feared that Northerners had a corrupt understanding of the document. Many students learned history based on an interpretation that took Southerners' words at face value: Their avoidance of mentioning slavery meant that it was not a cause. Correct this interpretation by directing students back to slavery.

2. Each Section Was Completely United in Its Defiance of the Other's Actions

Each section was divided over the issues of secession and war. In the North, Lincoln suppressed the legal government of Maryland because it would have prompted secession. He also suppressed free speech and jailed antiwar agitators, whom he and his party called "Copperheads," to bolster the war effort. Most of the suppressions took place in border states — states with close ties to the South. In the South, Unionists opposed the war and aided the federal army whenever possible. Large portions of the Appalachian upcountry, primarily in western North Carolina and eastern Tennessee, experienced real civil war as neighbor killed neighbor over a difference of loyalties, with the Unionists finally winning the upper hand. At least one county in northern Alabama seceded from the state to protest Alabama's secession from the Union. Texas executed more than one hundred Unionists in Galveston after a hasty trial, while Missouri, Arkansas, Alabama, and the Carolinas continued a legacy of extralegal executions through bushwhacking opponents. Class divided both North and South as well, as the conscription laws operated to give the wealthy a legal means of dodging the draft. In the North, one needed to pay only $300 to avoid the draft. A Southerner could opt out by proving that he oversaw twenty or more slaves or worked in an industry essential to the war effort. In both sections, wealth or skill was one's ticket out of the deadly fray. And thus the war came to be called "a rich man's war and a poor man's fight," as it was perceived that the rich would benefit from government investments in war production but the wealthy would take very little part in actual battle.

3. The Federal Government Did Not Begin Deficit Spending until FDR and the Great Depression

Students are frequently "presentist." They believe that government spending, being a perennial argument in the politics of their own lives, could not have historical roots. Yet one need only look at the financing of every war the United States has fought to see that government rarely has the money available to finance a war effort. During the Revolutionary War, the states that provided funds to the Continental army borrowed the money or printed "fiat" money, both of which caused high rates of inflation. The War of 1812 caught the U.S. government without proper financial instruments for borrowing and transporting the large sums needed to field large armies. Thus, after the war, those responsible for its management spearheaded a campaign to create those instruments: They created the Bank of the United States and funded internal improvements. The war with Mexico also required the United States to borrow from its own citizens, with a promise to pay them back. The Civil War, however, institutionalized that process, as it required a much higher order of spending to achieve its ends. Modern warfare is expensive and requires more money in a short period of time than can be garnered through normal taxation. Both the U.S. and the Confederate governments sold bonds, raised taxes, and issued soft money for which they had no specie backing. Deficit spending — meaning spending more than the government takes in — is not a recent phenomenon in American history.

Using the Bedford Series in History and Culture and the Historians at Work Series: Suggestions

Michael P. Johnson's *Abraham Lincoln, Slavery, and the Civil War* makes available to students essential documents on secession, war strategy, political campaigns, and freedom from Lincoln's archives.

Lecture Supplements and Classroom Activities

Using Multimedia Sources in the Classroom

Ken Burns's acclaimed series *The Civil War* works well in the classroom. Consider showing Episode 5, "The Universe of Battle — 1863," which covers the transformative role that the Battles of Gettysburg and Vicksburg had on the outcome of the war, as well as African Americans' and women's wartime participation. You might also want to show a segment from the biographical documentary *Frederick Douglass: When the Lion Wrote History*, distributed by PBS Video, which covers the influential leader's wartime activities. The 1989 Hollywood film *Glory*, which tells the story of the famed Massachusetts 54th Regiment, also works well in the classroom.

Historical Contingencies

To underscore the central importance of slavery to the Civil War, ask students if they think the Union would have won had Lincoln not issued the Emancipation Proclamation. What if the North maintained throughout the entire course of the war that it was fighting to preserve the Union, rather than to free the slaves? Even if the Union had won without this pivotal transformation, what would the "reconstructed" Union have looked like had slavery persisted?

Classroom Activities

Have students debate whether a democratic government has the right to suspend civil liberties during national emergencies. Remind students of the positions they took when discussing the Alien and Sedition Acts of the Adams administration. What are the differences between peacetime and wartime society? Do the exigencies of war absolve the government for its actions? What threats, legitimate or perceived, did Clement Vallandigham pose to the Union war effort? Did the suspension of *habeas corpus* aid the Union war effort? In what ways did the stifling of free speech in the Confederacy affect its war efforts?

Using the Internet

The Library of Congress's American Memory Project may prove especially useful to students wishing to research the Civil War online. The Library has made available, for example, 1,118 photographs of the war, most taken under the supervision of Mathew Brady. Direct your students to <http://memory.loc.gov/ammem/cwphtml/cwphome.html>. Students might also find the African American Pamphlet collection informative. Direct students to <http://memory.loc.gov/ammem/aap> and tell them to search the term "Civil War." The University of North Carolina's Documenting the American South project should be equally valuable to students. Direct them to <http://docsouth.unc.edu> and tell them to click on "The Southern Homefront, 1861–1865" for relevant material.

ASSESSING RESULTS
Multiple-Choice Questions

1. When Frederick Douglass heard news from Charleston in April 1861 that Southerners had fired on the American flag, he
   a. sank into a deep depression because he was a pacifist and abhorred bloodshed.
   b. marched over to the nearest recruitment office and enlisted as a private in the federal army.
   c. celebrated the outbreak of fighting because he understood that a war to save the Union would undoubtedly affect slavery.
   d. urged President Lincoln to pursue a cautious course because he hoped the conflict could be resolved without bloodshed.

2. What single issue was the ultimate cause of the American Civil War?
   a. slavery
   b. the nature of the Union
   c. economic competition between the sections
   d. differences in cultural sensibilities

3. Why did King Cotton diplomacy fail?
   a. The Union blockade kept all southern ships in port and thus prevented them from transporting cotton.
   b. In 1860, there was a bumper crop of cotton, and Egypt and India began supplying the needs of the market.
   c. Southern factories used every bit of the cotton the South produced to make uniforms and other items needed for maintaining an army in the field.
   d. The cotton plantations, particularly the larger ones, were not as productive during the war, as all the white men had joined the Confederate army.

4. Why did Congress pass a package of programs to enhance the Union economy during the Civil War?

   a. With so many men heading west to avoid the draft, Congress felt it needed to give them a reason to stay and fight.
   b. Because southern Democrats left Congress when their states seceded, northern Republicans were finally able to enact their economic agenda.
   c. Congress sought to offset the economic distress felt by so many smaller businessmen as the war effort drained the economy of investment capital.
   d. Because the Confederate Congress already enacted a similar package that served to centralize power in the national government, the U.S. Congress felt it had no choice but to do likewise.

5. Why did many consider the Civil War "a rich man's war and a poor man's fight"?
   a. Class distinctions largely disappeared as rich and poor fought as comrades in arms, on both sides.
   b. Conscription and other hardships fell unequally on rich and poor.
   c. At the beginning of the war, the wealthy proposed that they pay a sharply graduated income tax to help pay for the war, as they numerically were incapable of providing as many men as were the other classes.
   d. The rich bought bonds as well as fought in the armies of both sides and, therefore, waged a "total war," while the poor could only fight.

6. What role did African Americans play in the Union military effort?
   a. The North limited black participation in the military to nonfighting roles of keeping camp, cooking, and so forth.
   b. Ultimately, the North provided for black enlistment in fighting units.
   c. The North allowed African Americans to join military units but limited participation to the navy.
   d. The North prohibited black participation in the military.

7. The Emancipation Proclamation liberated slaves
   a. in Confederate and Union states.
   b. only in loyal slaveholding border states.
   c. in loyal slaveholding border states and in federally occupied states of the Confederacy.
   d. in Confederate states still in rebellion on the effective date of the order.

8. According to the *Historical Question* feature, why was there such a high fatality rate among wounded soldiers?
   a. Doctors had a reputation for alcoholism and simply botched many operations.
   b. Most soldiers came from lower-class origins and thus were more likely to die from wounds because they were not in the best health before being wounded.
   c. Both the North and the South felt that trying to save wounded soldiers was a waste of resources.
   d. Doctors lacked basic knowledge of germ theory, and many routinely infected their patients through their ignorance.

9. According to Map 15.1, "Secession, 1860–1861," what were the last four states to secede from the Union?
   a. North Carolina, Florida, Texas, and Tennessee
   b. Texas, Virginia, Kentucky, and Missouri
   c. Virginia, Arkansas, Tennessee, and North Carolina
   d. Virginia, Kentucky, Missouri, and Arkansas

10. Why did President Lincoln issue the Emancipation Proclamation?
   a. Because the high number of casualties in the war demanded it; freeing slaves would weaken the South's force and help the North win more quickly.
   b. Lincoln believed the Declaration of Independence insisted that all men were created equal, so slaves should be free.
   c. Lincoln claimed that in issuing the proclamation he was answering to a "higher authority" than mere laws.
   d. The *Dred Scott* decision required freedom for all slaves taken to free states, and Lincoln claimed that all states that seceded immediately became free states when they passed their ordinances of secession.

11. Identify the correct sequence of historical events.
   a. Lee appointed commander of Army of Northern Virginia, Dorothea Dix named superintendent of female nurses for the North, Andrew Johnson becomes vice president, Grant becomes commander of all Union armies
   b. National banking system created, upper South secedes, slaves of rebel masters declared free by the Union, Homestead Act
   c. Greenbacks introduced, Confederate draft initiated, Emancipation Proclamation, New York draft riots
   d. Battle of Vicksburg, Emancipation Proclamation, Lee surrenders, Lincoln is reelected

PROPOSING MORE: Additional Readings

Anne J. Bailey, "A Texas Cavalry Raid: Reaction to Black Soldiers and Contrabands," *Civil War History* 35, no. 2 (1989): 138–52.
Peter S. Carmichael, "'Oh, for the Presence and Inspiration of Old Jack': A Lost Cause Plea for Stonewall Jackson at Gettysburg," *Civil War History* 41, no. 2 (1995): 161–67.
Drew Gilpin Faust, "Altars of Sacrifice: Confederate Women and the Narratives of War," *Journal of American History* 76, no. 4 (1990): 1200–28.
William C. Harris, "Conservative Unionists and the Presidential Election of 1864," *Civil War History* 38, no. 2 (1992): 298–318.
James L. Huston, "A Political Response to Industrialism: The Republican Embrace of Protectionist Labor Doctrine," *Journal of American History* 70, no. 1 (1983): 35–57.
Gary Scharnhorst, "From Soldier to Saint: Robert Gould Shaw and the Rhetoric of Racial Justice," *Civil War History* 34, no. 4 (1988): 308–22.

Answer Key to Multiple-Choice Questions: 1-c, 2-a, 3-b, 4-b, 5-b, 6-b, 7-d, 8-d, 9-c, 10-a, 11-c

16 RECONSTRUCTION

1863–1877

Outlining Chapters: Thematic Questions

I. What were the challenges and controversies facing efforts at reconstruction even before the end of the war?

   A. What was Lincoln's reconstruction plan under the terms of his Proclamation of Amnesty, and why did congressional radicals oppose it? What did Congress propose as an alternate to Lincoln's plan?

   B. What kind of labor systems evolved in the Union-occupied areas of the South during the war? On what grounds did white Southerners predict the failure of the new labor plan? On what grounds did African Americans criticize the new system? Why did blacks think the federal government would distribute land to freedmen?

   C. What did freedom mean to the ex-slaves in terms of mobility, work hours, education, family security, and religious independence?

II. What course did presidential reconstruction take under Andrew Johnson?

   A. What was the course of Andrew Johnson's rise to political power, and why was he Lincoln's vice president? How did he alter Lincoln's reconstruction plan?

   B. In what ways did southern state delegations defy the mild terms of presidential reconstruction? What were the black codes, and why did southern legislatures create them? How did Andrew Johnson's administration respond to them? Whom did the newly reconstructed southern state governments elect to federal offices?

   C. How did conservative white southern Mississippians miscalculate the ease with which the South would be admitted back into the Union? How did Johnson's opposition to the Freedmen's Bureau Act and the Civil Rights Act galvanize the Republican Party?

III. How did Congress take the lead in reconstruction, and how did blacks and white women respond?

   A. What was the centerpiece of the Fourteenth Amendment, and how did it alter voting rights? What were the political consequences of altered voting rights? How successful was Johnson in his attempt to circumvent radical Republican efforts at reconstruction?

B. What did the Military Reconstruction Act do to the ten unreconstructed southern states? What made congressional reconstruction "radical"? Why did some radical Republicans believe congressional reconstruction did not go far enough?

C. For what political reasons was Andrew Johnson impeached, and what were the legal justifications of the case? Why did the Senate fail to convict him?

D. How did the Fifteenth Amendment complete the agenda of congressional reconstruction? Who felt betrayed by the wording of the Fourteenth and Fifteenth Amendments, and why?

IV. How did congressional reconstruction alter political and everyday life in the South?

A. What three groups composed the majority of the southern Republican Party, and what did each group seek out of this coalition? What threatened the Republican Party in the South? Who protected it in the South, and how effective was that protection?

B. How well did the ethnicity of Republican officeholders reflect the ethnicity of those who elected them? What changes did the new southern state constitutions introduce to southern society? What was the agenda of the Republican Party of the southern states, and how effective were the programs to implement that agenda?

C. How did sharecropping become the primary means of organizing southern agriculture, and why? In what ways did the system introduce changes to southern agriculture, and in what ways did it perpetuate old patterns?

V. Why did northern Republicans abandon southern republicanism?

A. What was the nature of politics during the Grant administration? What splinter group proposed civil service reform and southern "home rule"? What accomplishments did his administration achieve, and what failures did it suffer? What happened to the U.S. economy during Grant's administration?

B. When did the North gradually start to abandon reconstruction? What part did racism play? What role did the Supreme Court play in undermining reconstruction?

C. How did southern "redeemers" characterize southern Republican government?

What were the Democrats' best tools for driving whites from the Republican Party and for eliminating black voting power?

D. What was so peculiar about the election of 1876, and how did it end reconstruction once and for all?

Teaching with The American Promise, *Second Compact Edition: Lecture Strategies*

LECTURE 1

Presidential versus Congressional Reconstruction

This lecture explains the origins of reconstruction, from its presidential phase, through its moderate congressional phase, to its radical competition. Referring to the first anticipated misconception of this chapter, ask your students when reconstruction began, and why. Ask them to consider the Union army field commanders who had to make decisions about runaway slaves (known as "contraband"). When did reconstruction begin for them, and how did they impose it in the areas they controlled? Next, students must consider the various plans political leaders devised to reincorporate the "rebellious" section of the country back into the framework of the nation. Ask your students what sort of terms they would have imposed and how their plans would have differed from those actually used. Use this opportunity to list the terms of Lincoln's Proclamation of Amnesty and Reconstruction. Then compare his plan with the additional requirements under Johnson's plan.

To render the evolution of congressional reconstruction understandable, shift gears from straight politics to political economy. Direct your students to the question of rehabilitating the southern economy. How was agricultural labor to be organized? Show how this question led to unanticipated developments: (1) the long-term development of sharecropping and (2) the establishment of the black codes. Use a discussion of the Mississippi Black Code (in the documents reader) to emphasize that southern whites were not ready to grant any sort of real freedom to blacks. This virtual reenslavement of the freedmen by the enactment of the black codes enraged both radicals and moderates in the North. They believed they had won the war, and they did not intend to lose the peace. Show how Andrew Johnson's intransigence led Congress to take more radical action and ultimately led to his impeachment. Finally, list the terms of the radical plan of congressional reconstruction — here, refer students to the spot map of the Reconstruction Act of 1867 — and describe the purpose of the Freedmen's Bureau, the Civil Rights Act, and the Fourteenth Amendment.

LECTURE 2
The Meanings of Freedom

This lecture demonstrates how newly emancipated slaves experimented with the various meanings of freedom and how freedom has both a social and a political context. Begin by referring your students to the *Documenting the American Promise* feature, "The Meaning of Freedom." What are the different types of freedom referred to in the first two documents? The first was the freedom to find one's family and to protect it against abuse, and the second was to define the family in such a way that no exterior forces could deny its existence. Use the chapter-opening photo of the freedmen's school primer to reinforce the general types of freedom. What does this image say about African Americans who had only tasted freedom for a little while? Explain that African Americans separated themselves from the white-dominated churches to gain freedom from oversight into the most personal aspects of their lives. Refer back to Lecture 1 and show how sharecropping promised the same sort of freedom by allowing the cropper to determine if his wife and children would work alongside him in the fields and what hours would be spent at labor. Use Map 16.1 to show how the freedmen moved their residences to gain privacy, both from the landlord and from their neighbors.

To consider aspects of freedom, begin with the Alabama Black Convention transcript (in the documents reader) and the Tennessee Freedmen Convention petition in the *Documenting the American Promise* feature to examine what party black people considered the party of freedom and why they thought that way. Explore the right to assemble. Show how southern whites feared this right in much the same way they feared slave rebellions. Explain that it was white prejudice and hatred that forestalled successful biracial political society during reconstruction, and address the misconception that reconstruction governments were uniquely corrupt. Talk about the Gilded Age corruption in the North, and direct students to think about the political cartoon in the text showing President Grant falling into a barrel of scandals held together by various corrupt political "rings." Explain that examining someone's competence in governing is a subjective question. Were the reconstruction governments corrupt? The answer is abundantly yes. But compare the corruption of these governments with the corruption of white-controlled governments in the North at the same time or with white-controlled governments in the South following reconstruction. The level of corruption is indistinguishable. During reconstruction, however, competence to govern was judged by one's race.

LECTURE 3
Redemption

This lecture shows how southern whites overthrew reconstruction and why northern whites abandoned it. First discuss the ongoing campaign of violence waged by white Southerners against black and white Republicans. Explore the various means of intimidation that were used to silence Republicans. The reign of terror included economic coercion, assault, and murder. A black could be threatened with expulsion from the farm where he worked for attending a rally or voting Republican in an election. The army could not deal with the violence because it was too small to be effective, and local law enforcement remained in the hands of those who either perpetrated the crimes or at least sympathized with them. Use Elias Hill's testimony before the Ku Klux Klan Committee (in the documents reader) to give students a firsthand account of the typical sort of violence. Ask about the legacy of this sort of paramilitary terrorism. Were KKK members really only trying to defend themselves, or were they attempting to subjugate blacks through intimidation and murder?

Show how northern weariness, political opportunism, and racism contributed to the overthrow of reconstruction. Discuss the northern Republican's report on reconstruction (in the documents reader). Explain that most moderates felt that once blacks were given the basic political tools of the right to vote, they should find their own way in the world. No large-scale confiscations had taken place as a result of the war.

Ask whether confiscations could have redistributed southern property to the freedmen as payment for their enslavement. Northerners did not anticipate the ferocity with which white Southerners would wage their campaign of violence against black Southerners. Increasingly, "home rule" for the South, which meant withdrawing what Union troops remained, sounded like a reasonable request. Discuss the mythology of the "Lost Cause" (refer students to the photo of the quilt adorned with Lee's image), and explain how white southern justifications for the extreme violence of "reclaiming" government were self-serving. Explain the election of 1876 and the Compromise of 1877 to your students. Explain that both sides cheated in the election: the Democrats stole the election through the campaign of violence waged against Republican Southerners, and the Republicans stole it back by stuffing ballot boxes in the three southern states they still controlled. Next, show how extraconstitutional means were used to resolve the crisis. Then ask why a backroom deal removed federal troops from the South and why southern Republicans were abandoned by the national party. Introduce the last of the anticipated misconceptions at this point. Ask your students whether there were any long-term consequences to the way reconstruction was handled.

Anticipating Student Reactions: Common Misconceptions and Difficult Topics

1. Reconstruction Began after the Civil War Ended

Lincoln officially began reconstruction in 1863 with his Proclamation of Amnesty and Reconstruction, but it really began as soon as the Union army occupied any of the slaveholding states that were in rebellion. With the army near at hand, the slaves took advantage of the change in power to free themselves or at least to renegotiate the terms of their enslavement. With wartime occupation of large parts of the South, the Union army had to come to terms with the problem of restructuring the southern labor system. In the Sea Islands of Georgia and South Carolina, the army experimented with turning over plantations abandoned by their masters to the slaves who occupied them. In the Mississippi valley,

however, the army developed a system of "compulsory free labor" that foreshadowed much of the treatment blacks would experience after the war ended. With emancipation, the freedmen suddenly stopped playing the role of servile creatures, a role forced on them to survive while living under the lash. The outward change in attitude surprised the former masters, who refused to believe that they had been cleverly duped by their slaves and, therefore, believed that blacks were fickle and "ungrateful" for all the masters had done for them. Ask students to consider the implications of pushing back the date of reconstruction to late 1861. How does the account of reconstruction change?

2. Reconstruction Governments in the South Were Uniquely Corrupt

The idea that southern Republican governments during reconstruction were somehow more consistently corrupt than governments in any previous period in American history comes from Redeemer propaganda against those governments. That propaganda reflected the racism and class sentiment of its originators. The white elites who had previously held power in the southern states chafed at being excluded from power, and they assumed that Republican-controlled legislatures filled with blacks and nonelites could not intelligently govern. Thus, any mistake or misstep was immediately used to demonstrate the inherent incompetence of those groups in power. By the end of the nineteenth century, the myth of black incompetence and carpetbagger corruption achieved the status of fact in the South, and this "fact" was then communicated to the rest of the country through histories of the era written by white Southerners. This myth ignores both the facts of reconstruction and the context of late-nineteenth-century political culture.

3. Reconstruction Had No Long-Term Impact and Is Irrelevant Today

Reconstruction still influences the nation and will continue to do so for the foreseeable future. By understanding the violence with which the South opposed the political, social, and legal consequences of emancipation, students can make sense of the ongoing racial problems of the twentieth century. It is also important to show the origins of overwhelming black poverty in reconstruction. When explaining that ex-slaves got "nothing but freedom" when they were set free — no land or monetary compensation, no reward for two hundred years of slave labor in developing the nation's economy — ask your students how the government in the nineteenth century helped other groups through federal legislation, pointing to homestead legislation, tariffs, and internal improvements. Few Americans have started with literally "nothing but freedom."

Using the Bedford Series in History and Culture and the Historians at Work Series: Suggestions

Consider assigning John David Smith's *When Did Segregation Begin?* to have students explore the origins of the Jim Crow South.

Lecture Supplements and Classroom Activities

Using Multimedia Sources in the Classroom

Consider showing the last episode of Ken Burns's acclaimed *Civil War* series, "The Better Angels of Our Nature." Ask students if they agree with Burns's "romance of the reunion" interpretation of the war's aftermath.

Historical Contingencies

Remind students that Lincoln's reconstruction plan was a wartime measure designed to bring back waffling Confederate states to the Union. There is no evidence to suggest that Lincoln intended to stick with his 10 percent plan at the end of the war. Ask students to consider the possible direction of reconstruction had Lincoln not been assassinated. Would Lincoln have adopted a harsher, more radical course? Would he have been able to steer his way clear through Congress, or would he have faced problems similar to those Johnson faced? Had Lincoln lived, would the freed men and women have received something more than "nothing but freedom"?

Classroom Activities

Have students debate whether "forty acres and a mule" would have solved many of the problems faced by the freed men and women during reconstruction. Remind students that successful farming depends, in part, on access to cash, credit, and the market. Would land alone have addressed these issues? Remind them, too, that

redistributing land to blacks would have done much to destroy the power base of the Old South.

Using the Internet

The University of Maryland's Freedmen and Southern Society Project makes available online selections from the projected nine-volume series *Freedom: A Documentary History of Emancipation, 1861–1867.* Direct your students to <http://www .inform.umd.edu/EdRes/Colleges/ARHU/ Depts/History/Freedman/home.html>. Cornell's Supreme Court Collection makes available the full text of major Supreme Court cases. Direct students interested in the Court's role in reconstruction to <http://supct.law.cornell.edu:8080/ supct>. Tell students to search the site by case name.

ASSESSING RESULTS
Multiple-Choice Questions

1. In 1865, General Carl Schurz proclaimed the Civil War a "revolution half accomplished" because
   a. it failed to secure anything meaningful for the freed slaves.
   b. he predicted that emancipation would signal economic collapse and social anarchy in the South.
   c. although it signaled the defeat of the Confederacy it would not end white racism or black subservience in the South.
   d. reconstruction provided an economic underpinning to freedom but failed to provide political change.

2. Rumors that the federal government would distribute forty acres and a mule to every freedman originated
   a. in the wording of the Fourteenth Amendment, which denied amnesty to a large class of former Confederate officials.
   b. in Sherman's land and labor experiment and the enacting legislation of the Freedmen's Bureau.
   c. in reports that English expansion of cotton production in Egypt and India had grown so much during the American Civil War that cotton planting would never again be profitable in the United States.
   d. with southern Democrats who hoped to separate the newly enfranchised freedmen from the Republican Party by raising freedmen's expectations of land distribution.

3. What was the basis of Lincoln's presidential reconstruction?
   a. Lincoln proposed the confiscation of all property of everyone who had served the Confederacy in any way, as well as the execution of major Confederate political and military officials.
   b. Lincoln proposed dividing the southern states into five military districts and required states to ratify the Thirteenth Amendment and renounce the Confederate war debt in exchange for readmission.
   c. Lincoln proposed readmitting southern states once 10 percent of the 1860 electorate of a state took an oath pledging future loyalty to the Union.
   d. Lincoln proposed granting amnesty only to former Confederates who owned more than $20,000 in property at the end of the war.

4. The Fourteenth Amendment
   a. declared the pardons granted by Johnson to former Confederates null and void, thereby barring secessionists from formally participating in federal, state, and local elections for the rest of their lives.
   b. abolished slavery.
   c. overturned the *Dred Scott* decision by declaring "anyone born or naturalized in the United States" to be a citizen.
   d. gave African American men the right to vote.

5. What was the most effective strategy used by Democratic "Redeemers" in overturning Republican dominance in the South?
   a. regaining the right to vote for the disfranchised former Confederates
   b. intimidating and murdering their opponents
   c. promoting economic advancement in a diversified economy
   d. stuffing the ballot box in presidential elections in South Carolina, Florida, and Louisiana

6. In the *Documenting the American Promise* feature, Reverend A. B. Randall reported from Arkansas that
   a. African Americans saw emancipation as only the first step toward freedom, which they equated with responsibility, competency, and good citizenship.
   b. the freedmen refused to allow their marriages to be recorded because of their multiple "marriages" during slavery, when

they were sold from one plantation to another.
   c. black soldiers should quickly marry their sweethearts, for if they died in battle their wives would be eligible for federal benefits.
   d. most former slaves who requested his services to marry them were usually younger and without any families to stop them from quick and thoughtless wartime marriages.

7. The purpose of the 1867 Tenure of Office Act was to
   a. strengthen the Senate's role in the selection of the cabinet.
   b. limit the president to two terms in office.
   c. prevent the president from replacing cabinet members who opposed his views on reconstruction.
   d. purge Johnson's cabinet of those who opposed Congress's plans for reconstruction.

8. Map 16.2, "The Reconstruction of the South,"
   a. corrects the myth that reconstruction lasted a long time by demonstrating that conservative southern whites "redeemed" their states in only a matter of months or a very few years.
   b. shows that by the election of 1876, Republican governments could be found in six of the eleven former Confederate states.
   c. demonstrates that Mississippi was the first state to be readmitted to the Union.
   d. proves that reconstruction lasted a long time by demonstrating that Union troops were stationed in all eleven states of the former Confederacy until 1877.

9. The "black codes" of Mississippi
   a. stipulated that freedmen, free Negroes, and mulattos could testify in court against one another but not against white men.
   b. declared that any black person without employment would be considered a vagrant whose labor could be sold at auction to pay the resulting fines or who could be sentenced to involuntary labor.
   c. required the children of slave parents to petition the courts to have their parents' marriage made legal so that they could inherit from their parents.
   d. required the black population of the state to own land to qualify for voting privileges.

10. Identify the correct sequence of historical events.
    a. Military Reconstruction Act, Sherman grants South Carolina coast land to black

refugees, Johnson impeached, Proclamation of Amnesty and Reconstruction

b. Equal Rights Association founded, Lincoln assassinated, Freedmen's Bureau established, panic of 1873

c. presidential reconstruction, black codes, Fifteenth Amendment, election of Hayes as president

d. all persons born in United States made citizens, slavery outlawed throughout the United States, Congress makes racial discrimination illegal, discrimination of voting rights on the basis of race is outlawed throughout the United States

Proposing More: Additional Readings

Ira Berlin, Steven F. Miller, and Leslie Rowland, "Afro-American Families in the Transition from Slavery to Freedom," *Radical History Review* 42 (1988): 89–121.

Elsa Barkley Brown, "Negotiating and Transforming the Public Sphere: African American Political Life in the Transition from Slavery to Freedom," *Public Culture* 7 (1994): 107–46.

Michael Fitzgerald, "Radical Republicanism and the White Yeomanry during Alabama Reconstruction, 1865–1868," *Journal of Southern History* 54, no. 4 (1988): 565–96.

Eric Foner, "The Meaning of Freedom in the Age of Emancipation," *Journal of American History* 81, no. 2 (1994): 434–60.

Jay R. Mandle, "Continuity and Change: The Use of Black Labor after the Civil War," *Journal of Black Studies* 21, no. 3 (1991): 414–27.

Answer Key to Multiple-Choice Questions: 1-c, 2-b, 3-c, 4-c, 5-b, 6-a, 7-c, 8-a, 9-b, 10-c

Essay Questions, Chapters 11–16

1. Compare Andrew Jackson's America to that of Abraham Lincoln. What types of shifts occurred in American society, culture, and politics? How fundamental were those shifts?

2. Historians of the American South have wrangled over the degree to which the Old South deviated from the larger trends in American antebellum society. How distinct from the North was the Old South on the eve of the Civil War? Was the Civil War fought between two separate nations in name only, or had the South developed a fundamentally different society? Be sure to address politics and culture as well as economics.

3. Interpretations of the Civil War's origins have generally fallen into two categories. The first interpretation, the "irrepressible conflict" school, argues, in part, that the war was the inevitable outcome of the struggle between two fundamentally opposing views on the extension of slavery into the territories. The second interpretation, or the revisionist "blundering generation" school, argues instead "that only the inability of political leaders to cope with essentially compromisable problems, and the sectional passions inflamed by irresponsible agitators on both sides, led to a needless war." Drawing on your knowledge of events from 1846 to 1861, do you believe that the Civil War was inevitable?

4. Your textbook notes that the Civil War was a total war. What did it mean to the Union and the Confederacy to be involved in a total war? How did it affect the warring nations' strategies and the ultimate outcome of the war?

5. Historians have debated the nature of reconstruction. Some have suggested that reconstruction was a time of profound social and political change. Others, however, have questioned whether anything of enduring importance occurred at all. Based on your knowledge of antebellum and reconstruction-era America, do you believe that reconstruction fundamentally altered America? Or was it, in the words of one historian, "essentially nonrevolutionary and conservative"?

THE WEST AND THE CITY: AMERICANS ON THE MOVE

17

1870–1900

*O*utlining Chapters: Thematic Questions

I. What factors contributed to the "land fever" for the western territories?
   A. Who moved west, what were their motivations, and what distinguished the different groups vying for western land? What hardships did these migrants face? What opportunities did they encounter?
   B. Why was the American dream of landownership denied to some segments of the population? Who were the dispossessed?

II. How did the face of rural America change over the second half of the nineteenth century?
   A. How did the economy of the New South resemble that of a colony dependent on its mother country? What solutions did New South boosters propose to remedy the situation? How successful were the solutions?
   B. What factors contributed to an agricultural revolution that transformed American farming? What did this revolution signal to the traditional American family farm?
   C. In what ways did farmers become increasingly drawn into a world market?

III. Why has the American West been depicted as the site of a clash of cultures?
   A. Who populated the Great Plains and the Far West?
   B. What precipitated the final removal of American Indians from their ancestral lands? How did removal affect traditional Indian cultures?
   C. How did Native Americans resist white encroachment on their ancestral lands? How successful were these efforts?
   D. What was the "west of the imagination"? Who created it? Who believed in it?

IV. What factors engendered the rise of the city in the late nineteenth century?
   A. What demographic patterns and technological innovations account for the "urban explosion"? What attractions and incentives did the city offer to migrants?
   B. Who were the new immigrants? How did they differ from the old immigrants? How did the new immigrants change the landscape of the American city? Who called for immigration restrictions, and why?

C. What factors shaped the social geography of the city? How did the city become the home to both the nation's poor and its millionaires?

V. What were the competing images and realities of city life in late-nineteenth-century America?

   A. How did big-city government operate? What were political machines? Who were the political bosses, and how did they differ from reform politicians?

   B. How did the physical landscape of American cities change in the late nineteenth century? What technological advances allowed for these changes?

Teaching with The American Promise, *Second Compact Edition:* Lecture Strategies

LECTURE 1

Homesteaders and Farmers in Rural America

This first lecture highlights three main themes of westward migration. Start by conveying the sheer expansiveness of the land settled and the vast number of people who migrated west. Encouraged by the Homestead Act of 1862 and aided by the new railroads, Americans settled more territory in the last three decades of the century than they had in the previous history of the country.

Second, you will want to describe the patterns of daily life of the settlers. Once west of the Mississippi River, many settlers faced a life of hardship, deprivation, and loneliness. The letters of the Swedish woman who settled in Kansas (in the documents reader) evocatively portray the hard life many farmers experienced on the prairie. Beset by violent acts of nature, surrounded by an unforgiving landscape, confronted with unfriendly national economic policies, chronically in debt, and culturally isolated, farmers rarely found "God's country," which they so actively sought. Draw your students' attention to the words from the popular ballad that captured the bitter resignation of migrants too poor to leave. Suggest that those who did not own land and had no hope of landownership — tenants, sharecroppers, and migrants — were at a greater disadvantage than other settlers. Be sure to explain the crop lien system, a vicious circle in which many poor farmers were trapped. The dispos-

sessed, mired in a system of debt, dependency, and exploitation, nevertheless became a growing part of the American workforce by the century's end.

Third, you can end the lecture by describing how farm life changed rapidly in the last decades of the century. Farmers increasingly adopted new technologies, transforming farming from a way of life into a business venture. Agricultural specialization, ties to world markets, and mechanization allowed American farmers to increase their output greatly. Still, even as farm production soared, industrial output outstripped it, compelling many farmers to leave the fields and head to the factories.

LECTURE 2

The West

In this lecture, you can dispel common myths about the American West. Contrary to popular legend, the American West was home to more than just heroic cowboys and savage (but noble) Indians. Indeed, the West experienced an influx of immigrants, as did the rest of the nation, in the late nineteenth century. This lecture should first suggest the variety of ethnic groups that settled the West. Europeans, Asians, Canadians, Latin Americans, and African Americans all helped to populate the land from the Mississippi to the Pacific Ocean. Here you can impress on your students that these newly arrived inhabitants of the West were no more immune to the resentment and hostility of native-born Americans than were the immigrants who poured into American cities. Have students discuss "Observations of Chinese Immigrants" (in the documents reader) at this juncture. Violence often erupted between groups competing for land and resources, but the most deadly clashes occurred between whites and Native Americans who had been living on the land since before the "age of discovery." You can point out that, although the U.S. government had guaranteed the protection of Indians who had inhabited the western territories, the California gold rush, land fever, and border wars severely tested the government's willingness to protect Native Americans. Settlers continually encroached on these sacred ancestral grounds and Indians resisted, touching off a series of wars on the plains that lasted from 1861 until 1890. Here you might direct students to Map 17.2, "The Loss of Indian Lands, 1850–1890," and to In-mut-too-yah-lat-lat's vivid explanation of the reasons for Native American resistance (in the documents reader).

Finally, explain to students that the U.S. government simultaneously engaged in wars with Indians and began a process of Americanizing them, destroying Indian culture in the process. The 1887 Dawes Act, for example, broke up reservations and gave each Indian an allotment of land, thereby introducing the foreign concept of individual landownership while having the added benefit (for the United States) of reducing Indian lands from 138 million acres to 48 million acres. With the defeat of the Sioux in 1890 at Wounded Knee, many cultures received a crushing blow.

LECTURE 3
The Rise of the City

Although much of the nation remained heavily rural in the last decades of the nineteenth century, American cities nonetheless experienced tremendous growth. Urban population tripled in the last three decades of the century, from 10 million in 1870 to 30 million in 1900. First, you can cover the groups that populated the new American cities. Immigrants (primarily from southern and eastern Europe) and migrants from America's rural areas accounted for this population explosion. Here you may wish to bring up Michael Gold's account of his father's move from Romania to New York City (in the documents reader), which aptly describes the experience shared by many immigrants. Native-born Americans often resented the influx of new arrivals, segregating them in urban ghettos to an unprecedented degree. You can suggest to your students that more than the social geography of the city changed. Immigration and industrialization altered the physical geography as well, with skyscrapers, streetcars, public libraries, suspension bridges, and city parks dotting the new urban landscape. The streetcar allowed the urban middle class, which once lived in close proximity to the working masses, to escape the immigrant poor by relocating to the newly developing suburbs. To emphasize the change in social geography, draw students' attention to the photo of the Brooklyn Bridge.

You will also need to discuss the exigencies of urbanization. The new cities required new services — public sanitation, public utilities, electric street lights — and overseeing many of these new services was a new breed of politician, the city boss. Although usually minor elected officials, city bosses often wielded more power than mayors and other high-ranking politicians. Through bribery and graft, city bosses rewarded their supporters with favors such as jobs on the city payroll and lucrative franchises for subways and streetcars. George Washington Plunkitt's explanation of city politics and the uses of "honest graft" (in the documents reader) will provide students with a colorful firsthand account of the machinations of a city boss. Counter the image of the all-powerful city boss, however, with the other players on the political field. Negotiating with the bosses were the reform politicians, who though less flamboyant than their more famous counterparts nonetheless played an important function in the political life of the American city. The burgeoning city thus accommodated many voices, from the immigrant to the native, from the wealthy to the indigent, from the corrupt to the well-intentioned. End your lecture on the complexities and varied experiences of urban life in the late nineteenth century with a discussion of the 1893 Columbian Exposition and America's divided mind about the city.

Anticipating Student Reactions: Common Misconceptions and Difficult Topics

1. *Migration during the Late Nineteenth Century Consisted Primarily of Europeans Crossing to the Northeastern Shores of the United States*

The image of immigration many students hold is the popular one of central or southeastern Europeans traveling in steerage with their meager belongings, passing through Ellis Island and settling on the Lower East Side of New York City, or perhaps then emigrating to the Wild West. While this represents one common pattern, it is important to convey the varied character of the mass movement of populations that took place during the mid- to late nineteenth century. Make the point that those "on the move" were Native Americans, Asians, and Hispanic peoples, as well as Europeans, who were journeying both to and within America, and in all different directions, from the country to the city, from Latin America to El Norte, from Canada to New England, from China to California, and so on. To reinforce this point, you might refer students to the opening vignette's description of a homesteader moving west, a country boy leaving for the city, a young girl leaving Russia for America. Map 17.3, "The Impact of Immigration to 1910," is also useful for conveying that, by 1910, the immigrant population was spread across the country (with the exception of the South), not just concentrated in the Northeast.

2. The "Melting Pot" of America Has Always Welcomed New Arrivals

Students may be surprised to discover the levels of prejudice and hostility that native-born Americans (wary of religious and cultural differences) exhibited toward the new immigrants who arrived in the United States at the turn of the century. One of the most successful nativist groups, the American Protective Association, advocated the restriction of immigration, stringent naturalization requirements, barriers to the employment of aliens or Catholics, and the teaching of the "American" language in public schools. You can make the point that not only did such paranoid fringe groups as the APA promote restrictive policies but also many of America's leading citizens were in the vanguard of those urging limits on immigration. In 1891, for example, Massachusetts senator Henry Cabot Lodge proposed that illiterates be barred from immigrating to the United States. Although Presidents Cleveland, Taft, and Wilson vetoed bills with this particular restriction, Congress overrode Wilson's last veto in 1917. Congress handed nativists other victories, usually without contest. In 1882, Congress responded to strong anti-Chinese sentiment by closing off the United States to Chinese laborers for ten years. In that same year, Congress prohibited the immigration of people with criminal records or signs of mental instability. Responding to the demands of organized labor, Congress barred contract workers in 1885. People with communicable diseases and polygamists were barred in 1891; in 1903, Congress excluded prostitutes, anarchists, and epileptics; and in 1907, the mentally retarded were prohibited from immigrating to the United States.

3. The Civil War and Reconstruction Put an End to Oppression of and Discrimination against Blacks

Students don't always grasp that although American slavery ended with the Civil War, blacks continued to suffer from oppression and discrimination, especially in the South. You can make them aware of the extent to which South-

ern Democrats, backed by the U.S. Supreme Court, ensured legal and extralegal discrimination against African Americans in the South after Reconstruction. Even before the Supreme Court handed down its landmark decision in *Plessy v. Ferguson* in 1896, it had ruled to uphold segregation. In the civil rights cases of 1883, the Court invalidated the 1875 Civil Rights Act of Congress, which had guaranteed all persons, regardless of race, the right to use public facilities. When a number of African Americans charged that they were being denied these rights, the Court narrowly interpreted the law, declaring that such places as hotels, railroads, and theaters were not "public" institutions because they were owned by individuals. In other words, according to the Court, the Fourteenth Amendment protected citizens from violations of their civil rights by states only; it did not protect them from violations by private individuals. *Plessy v. Ferguson* revalidated legal segregation by instituting the "separate but equal" clause.

In 1898, the Supreme Court affirmed disfranchising devices, such as poll taxes and literacy tests, used in southern states against African Americans. *Mississippi v. Williams* states that as long as race was not a specified criterion for disfranchisement, the Fifteenth Amendment was not violated. Extralegal methods of discrimination included violence more often than not. Between 1889 and 1909, over seventeen hundred African Americans were lynched by angry whites. Sexual explanations often masked economic motives. Between 1880 and 1889, for example, over 60 percent of those lynched in the state of Georgia were accused of committing sexual offenses against white women. Finally, to return to the chapter's main theme, make the point that blacks seeking to escape the South and hopeful of finding new opportunities in northern cities were yet another component of the great mid- to late-nineteenth-century movement of peoples.

Using the Bedford Series in History and Culture and the Historians at Work Series: Suggestions

When discussing the Indian wars of the late nineteenth century, you may find it useful to have your students read *Our Hearts Fell to the Ground: Plains Indian Views of How the West Was Lost*, edited by Colin Calloway. Another way to approach the West is by reading Bill Brown's *Reading the West: An Anthology of Dime Westerns,* a title in the Cultural Editions series from Bedford's literature list. Jacob Riis's *How the Other Half Lives,* edited by David Leviatin, offers students an account of immigration into America's cities and will prove useful when discussing racial, ethnic, and religious stereotypes. Titles from Bedford's Cultural Editions series well worth assigning are Rebecca Harding Davis's *Life in the Iron Mills,* edited by Cecelia Tichi, and Stephen Crane's *Maggie,* edited by Kevin J. Hayes. *Plunkitt of Tammany Hall,* by William L. Riordon, edited by Terrence J. McDonald, gives a lively account of one of the most infamous political bosses and should spark interesting class discussion. You might also use *Plessy v. Ferguson: A Brief History with Documents,* edited by Brook Thomas, to discuss Jim Crow "justice," as mentioned under Classroom Activities. Readings from *Does the Frontier Experience Make America Exceptional?,* the Historians at Work volume edited by Richard W. Etulain, will surely get students thinking more about Frederick Jackson Turner's thesis.

Lecture Supplements and Classroom Activities

Using Multimedia Sources in the Classroom

PBS Video offers a number of good documentaries on the American West. "Ghost Dance," from the series *The West,* depicts the Oklahoma land rush, the influx of immigrants into western mining communities, and Native American resistance to white encroachment on tribal land. Two other episodes from that series also work well in the classroom: "Fight No More Forever," which details the lives of those who stood in the way of America's westward expansion (Sitting Bull of the Lakota, Chief Joseph of the Nez Perce, and Brigham Young of the Mormons) and "Geography of Hope," which covers the efforts of Congress and the reformers to "Americanize" Indians. *Geronimo and the Apache Resistance* and *Last Stand at Little Big Horn* offer more detailed discussions of Native American resistance. When discussing the section of the text entitled "The West of the Imagination," consider showing "Wilderness and the West," part of PBS's *American Vision* series. *Journey to America,* also distributed by PBS, gives a good overview of the "new immigrants" who came to the United States during the late nineteenth and early twentieth centuries. For a more detailed discussion of immigration and urbanization, consider showing *The Forward: From Immigrants to Americans,* distributed by Direct Cinema Limited; this film documents one of the most influential and successful Yiddish-language daily newspapers in the United States, the *Forward.* When discussing the changes to the urban landscape during the late nineteenth century, consider showing *Brooklyn Bridge,* distributed by Direct Cinema Limited; this documentary chronicles the struggles to build the bridge and its transformation into a symbol of American strength and ingenuity.

Historical Contingencies

Have your students consider possible courses for the American West had the South won the Civil War. Would the North have had the resources to station troops in the American West? Would the North have pursued its expansionist policies in the trans-Mississippi West? What would the implications of Confederate victory have been for the Southwest?

Classroom Activities

Using *Plessy v. Ferguson: A Brief History with Documents,* edited by Brook Thomas, from the Bedford Series in History and Culture, have students debate the validity of Homer Plessy's contention that legislation can be an effective tool to combat racial prejudice. Do your students agree? Or do they side with Justice Henry Billings Brown, who argued that social equality cannot be mandated but rather must be based on "natural affinities"?

Using the Internet

The University of California, Riverside, has made available online a photographic collection of Ellis Island, 1900–1920. Direct students to <http://cmp1.ucr.edu/exhibitions/immigration_id.html>.

ASSESSING RESULTS
Multiple-Choice Questions

1. Which of the following groups competing for western land in the mid- to late nineteenth century gobbled up the most territory?
   a. speculators
   b. homesteaders
   c. railroad entrepreneurs
   d. sharecroppers

2. What industry did the New South dominate?
   a. iron
   b. tobacco
   c. cotton
   d. mining and lumber

3. Which of the following best characterizes American farming in the second half of the nineteenth century?
   a. decreased profits
   b. a turn toward agribusiness
   c. increased dependency on self-sufficiency
   d. increased stature and prominence in American popular culture

4. Which of the following statements best characterizes the American West during the second half of the nineteenth century?
   a. The West remained unaffected by the ethnic and religious tensions that plagued the East.
   b. The West was linked inextricably to the urban East by capital investment and by iron rails that carried western goods to world markets.
   c. Western industries, such as cattle and ranching, remained free from the corporatization process that came to dominate farming in the East.
   d. The American West was a remarkably peaceful place in which violent episodes between competing factions rarely erupted.

5. Adherents to the Ghost Dance religion
   a. shunned all elements of Christianity.
   b. preached unification and assimilation with the whites.
   c. looked forward to a return of Indian ways and the defeat of the white man's ways.
   d. aroused sympathy from agents of the Bureau of Indian Affairs.

6. The death knell for Indian resistance to white encroachment on government-protected hunting and burial grounds sounded at
   a. Wounded Knee.
   b. Sand Creek.
   c. Custer's Last Stand.
   d. the Bozeman Trail.

7. Which of the following are factors in the new wave of immigration into American cities at the turn of the twentieth century?
   a. deteriorating economic and political conditions in Western Europe and religious persecution

   b. religious persecution of Catholics and cheap land in America
   c. the need for labor in the South and cheap land in the South
   d. the need of American industries for cheap, unskilled labor and the pursuit of religious freedom

8. The rise of the big city in the late nineteenth century engendered which of the following?
   a. social, racial, and ethnic segregation
   b. social, racial, and ethnic integration
   c. high voter turnout
   d. the demise of central business districts

9. Jacob Riis's 1890 *How the Other Half Lives*
   a. sympathetically portrayed the conditions of African Americans under Jim Crow.
   b. exposed the lavish lifestyles of New York's richest families.
   c. gave an account of the lives of New York's working class.
   d. alerted the American public to the atrocities committed against Native Americans in the West by the federal government.

10. In the documents reader, Michael Gold's father
   a. immigrates to America to escape having to serve in the Russian army.
   b. comes to New York City and after many trials makes a fortune in the corset business.
   c. realizes after a month in the United States that the American dream was a big lie and returns to Romania.
   d. comes to the United States, experiences some advances and setbacks, and ultimately becomes a house painter.

11. Identify the correct sequence of historical figures and events.
   a. Turner's frontier thesis, massacre at Wounded Knee, Brooklyn Bridge, Dawes Act
   b. Custer's Last Stand, Homestead Act, *How the Other Half Lives*, Chicago fire
   c. Custer's Last Stand, Chinese Exclusion Act, massacre at Wounded Knee, Turner's frontier thesis
   d. Oklahoma land rush, Homestead Act, Brooklyn Bridge, Chicago fire

Proposing More: Additional Readings

James R. Barrett, "Americanization from the Bottom Up: Immigration and the Remaking of the Working Class in the United States, 1880–1930," *Journal of American History* 79, no. 3 (1992): 996–1020.

Daniel Czitrom, "Underworlds and Underdogs: Big Tim Sullivan and Metropolitan Politics in New York, 1889–1913," *Journal of American History* 78, no. 2 (1991): 536–58.

Glenda Riley, "Women on the Great Plains: Recent Developments in Research," *Great Plains Quarterly* 5, no. 2 (1985): 81–92.

Charles R. Wilson, "Racial Reservations: Indians and Blacks in American Magazines, 1865–1900," *Journal of Popular Culture* (1976): 70–80.

Gavin Wright, "The Strange Career of the New Southern Economic History," *Reviews in American History* 10 (1982): 164–80.

Answer Key to Multiple-Choice Questions: 1-c, 2-b, 3-b, 4-b, 5-c, 6-a, 7-a, 8-a, 9-c, 10-d, 11-c

18 BUSINESS AND POLITICS IN THE GILDED AGE

1870–1895

Outlining Chapters: Thematic Questions

I. In what ways were old industries transformed in the late nineteenth century, and what new industries were born?
   A. Why are the railroads considered America's first big business? What factors contributed to the growth of the railroad industry?
   B. How did the growth of the railroad industry contribute to the growth of the steel industry? How did Andrew Carnegie capitalize on the steel manufacturing process? What is vertical integration?
   C. How did John D. Rockefeller come to dominate the oil-refining industry, and in what ways did he move to consolidate his enterprises? What are trusts? How do holding companies differ from trusts?
   D. In what ways did electricity and the telephone transform American industry?

II. What factors engendered the move from competition among American businesses to consolidation?
   A. Who was J. P. Morgan, and what is finance capitalism? How did Morgan move into the steel industry? What is an oligopoly?
   B. Who advocated social Darwinism in the United States, and how did the philosophy differ from Andrew Carnegie's "Gospel of Wealth"? How did social Darwinism provide a rationale for corporate consolidation, the growing disparity between rich and poor, and Jim Crow segregation?
   C. In what ways did the Supreme Court uphold laissez-faire economics?

III. What role did party politics play at the national level?
   A. In the late nineteenth century, what role did party politics play in American culture? In what ways did party politics reflect sectional, religious, and ethnic divisions in the United States?
   B. Why were the parties tainted by allegations of corruption? Who were the Stalwarts, Half-Breeds, and Mugwumps, and what role did they play in party politics?
   C. How did the assassination of President James A. Garfield in 1881 prompt national civil service reform?

D. What issues shaped the presidential election of 1884? Why have some historians referred to the election as a "political circus"?

IV. What economic issues defined the Gilded Age, and how did those issues lead to a party realignment in the 1890s?

    A. What controversies surrounded the tariff in the late nineteenth century? What groups favored the tariff? What groups opposed it? How did the tariff influence party politics?

    B. What role did the federal government play in the protection and limitation of trusts? What industries were most affected by the government's action? What role did the Supreme Court play in regard to trusts?

    C. What was the fight for free silver?

Teaching with The American Promise, *Second Compact Edition: Lecture Strategies*

LECTURE 1
New Industries, New Management

This lecture discusses how American industry expanded at a phenomenal rate in the decades following the Civil War. First, start by suggesting to students that a number of factors — among them abundant sources of raw materials and energy, a seemingly endless supply of cheap labor, Americans' ingenuity, and the growth of the railroad — contributed to this expansion. Second, point out that new industries — steel, oil refining, electric power, and the telephone and telegraph — required new forms of management and organization. Here you will want to mention that entrepreneurs such as Jay Gould, Andrew Carnegie, and John D. Rockefeller sought security for their newly formed corporations. No longer satisfied with the traditional guarantees afforded to corporations, these men devised new methods of organization to shore up their power and dominance in their respective industries. Both informal agreements such as pools and the more formal arrangements of trusts and holding companies allowed them to gobble up their competition and institute instead certain forms of central control.

Be sure to explain that these tycoons received support from J. P. Morgan, a leading financier of the late nineteenth century, and from the **Supreme** Court, which in a series of cases strengthened the movement toward corporate consolidation by striking down any federal or state regulation of industry. Introduce students to a popular view of business tycoons by showing them the cartoon of Jay Gould as a pirate and the *Puck* political cartoon depicting Jay Gould and others. Also have them discuss the attacks levied against Standard Oil by Henry Demarest Lloyd and Ida M. Tarbell, excerpted in the *Documenting the American Promise* feature. Finally, you will want to mention that both social Darwinism, promoted by Yale professor William Graham Sumner, and Andrew Carnegie's "Gospel of Wealth" served to bolster corporate consolidation, prevent regulation, and justify the concentration of wealth in the hands of America's elite. To demonstrate your point, direct students' attention to Figure 18.2, "Merger Mania, 1895–1905." You may wish to close with a discussion of Carnegie's "Gospel of Wealth" and Sumner's *What Social Classes Owe to Each Other* (both in the documents reader).

LECTURE 2
Party Politics in the Late Nineteenth Century

In this lecture, convey to students that party politics held a fascination for most Americans in the decades following the Civil War. Remind your students that if the presidents themselves seemed dull, the hoopla that surrounded their elections to the White House captivated the electorate. Allegations of scandal and corruption pervaded politics, but voter participation during this period was at an all-time high. Students should understand that most Americans had grown resigned to the degree to which their politicians were involved in scandal and graft, and certainly the corruption and party factionalism that characterized the Grant administration continued in the following decades. Discuss the allegations of scandal that tainted the presidential administrations of the late nineteenth century. Suggest that although President Rutherford B. Hayes continued to use the spoils system in handing out government posts, rewarding members of the Republican Party, the party bosses were never satisfied with Hayes's dispensation of federal perks and made it impossible for Hayes to seek reelection in 1880.

Note that the assassination of President James A. Garfield in 1881 by a deranged man claiming affiliation with a rival Republican faction dramatically demonstrated the need for an overhaul of the civil service system. The Pendleton Act, signed into law by President Chester A. Arthur in 1883, provided such a reform. Remind students that the Democrats were no more immune from the taint of scandal than their rivals were. Highlight the election of 1884, during which the Democratic presidential candidate Grover Cleveland had to own up to the fact that he had sired an illegitimate child, although, as the textbook notes, the paternity of the child was never proved. Cleveland's opponent, James G. Blaine, had been associated with shady bond dealings, however. In the end, Blaine's association with a mud-slinging preacher who linked the Democratic Party to alcoholism, the Pope, and secession irreparably damaged his bid for the presidency.

LECTURE 3

Free Silver versus the Gold Bugs

Start this lecture by pointing out that, at first, the debate centered on paper currency. Remind students that to fund the Civil War, the federal government had printed greenbacks, which were not backed by hard money (gold and silver) and therefore contributed to inflation. Here you will need to explain the rationale of both those who supported and those who opposed the expansion of the money supply. Supporters of cheap money (debtors from the West and the South) formed the Greenback Labor Party in the 1870s, arguing that the nation needed an expanding monetary system to keep pace with the nation's growing population and commercial expansion. Creditors, mostly from the Northeast, opposed an expanding monetary system because it allowed debtors to pay back their loans with devalued currency. In 1879, the federal government supported the creditors by tying the nation's currency to the gold reserves, which made money tighter. Although the Greenback Labor Party's coalition fell apart after the election of 1880, the issue of currency reform remained on the forefront of national politics.

At this point, underscore that free silver, and not greenbacks, became the rallying cry of those who advocated an expanding monetary system. Remind your students that the silver bonanza in western mines in the 1860s and 1870s led to a flood of silver on the market, which drove down the price of silver relative to gold. Debtors (and those in the mining industry) thus saw silver as the answer to a tightening money supply. In 1873, however, a lame-duck Republican Congress struck a blow to silver advocates by demonetizing the metal, thereby limiting even further the money in circulation. A Democratic Congress sought to appease silver advocates by passing the Bland-Allison Act in 1878, which required the government to buy silver and issue silver certificates, and the Sherman Silver Purchase Act in 1890, which increased the amount of silver the government must buy. Neither of these two acts eased the economic plight of debtors, who soon demanded the "free and unlimited coinage of silver." President Grover Cleveland, a gold-bug Democrat who solidly backed the gold standard, refused to yield on the issue and, even more egregious to some, forced the Congress to repeal the Sherman Silver Purchase Act in 1893. Preview Chapter 20 by ending your lecture with the suggestion that the currency debate would assume even greater volatility in the 1890s as agrarian discontent, labor unrest, and unemployment all increased dramatically.

Anticipating Student Reactions: Common Misconceptions and Difficult Topics

1. Agrarian Discontent

Many students have a tough time understanding the rise in agrarian discontent during the late nineteenth century that gave rise to the Grange movement and culminated in the People's Party. Because of overproduction, the growth of new farms under cultivation, and increasing competition from the world market, American farmers had been suffering from a decline in commodity prices since the end of the Civil War. Moreover, railroads and middlemen who handled produce often cheated farmers by charging high transportation and storage rates while offering rebates to high-volume industrial traffickers like John D. Rockefeller. High tariff rates also placed the American farmer at a disadvantage because they protected manufactured goods (pricing them out of reach for the average farmer) but failed to protect agricultural products. Finally, farmers were chronically in debt either because of high mortgages or the crop lien system, and their debt increased with falling commodity prices. Frustrated with Congress, which refused to listen to their demands on currency reform, farmers began organizing, recognizing that only demonstrations of power and solidarity would bring about social and economic change.

2. The Gilded Age Presidents Were All Party Tools Who Didn't Think or Act Independently

Many students may be familiar with the factionalism and corruption that characterized politics in the late nineteenth century. They may therefore fail to appreciate the efforts made by some politicians to act independently. The assassination of James A. Garfield catapulted Chester A. Arthur, an entrenched member of the Stalwart faction, to the presidency. Almost immediately, however, he distanced himself from Roscoe Conkling's gang by prosecuting his old cronies for receiving kickbacks on contracts for postal routes. He later vetoed a pork-barrel measure that surely would have benefited many Republicans in Congress. He also vetoed the Chinese Exclusion Act (see Chapter 17) because he believed it violated the Burlingame Treaty of 1868. Finally, Arthur aligned himself with the reform minority by signing the Pendleton Civil Service Reform Act in an effort to end cronyism in national politics and by appointing a commission to study tariff rates. His actions as president so angered leaders of the Republican Party that they refused to nominate him in the 1884 election, choosing instead the more predictable, and entrenched, James G. Blaine of Maine.

Using the Bedford Series in History and Culture and the Historians at Work Series: Suggestions

When discussing J. D. Rockefeller and the rise of Standard Oil, consider assigning *Muckraking: Three Landmark Articles,* edited by Ellen F. Fitzpatrick. This book includes journalist Ida M. Tarbell's critical attack on Standard Oil, "The Oil War of 1872," which appeared in *McClure's Magazine* in January 1903. *Thomas Edison and Modern America,* edited by Theresa M. Collins and Lisa Gitelman, is a superb volume with which to present the Gilded Age to students.

Lecture Supplements and Classroom Activities

Using Multimedia Sources in the Classroom

The rise of Andrew Carnegie and the development of the modern steel industry are detailed in the PBS documentary *The Richest Man in the World:*

Andrew Carnegie. Segments from *The Telephone, Edison's Miracle of Light,* and *The Iron Road,* all by PBS, are also useful in the classroom. To supplement the material in the text, consider showing *Mr. Sears' Catalogue,* which details the growth of the mail-order business in late-nineteenth-century America, and "The Gilded Age," part of the *American Vision* series, which looks at artistic movements in Gilded Age America.

Historical Contingencies

Have your class consider the possible course of American development had the railroads not been invented. Although the question is a bit hackneyed, it should get students thinking about the importance of the railroad to the modern American infrastructure. Could industry have developed the way it did without railroads to move people, goods, and information quickly, cheaply (at least for the leading industrialists), and efficiently? What other industries grew alongside the railroad industry?

Classroom Activities

You might end your lecture on nineteenth-century politics by asking students to compare the late-nineteenth-century political scene with that of today. Why was voter turnout so much higher then, and why is our electorate seemingly so much more apathetic today? How do the scandals of the late nineteenth century compare with those of the late twentieth century? What role did "private morality," then and today, play in electoral politics? What role should it play? Ask students what has changed and what has remained the same.

Using the Internet

The University of Virginia's Crossroads Project makes available online a series of Gilded Age political cartoons. Direct your students to the "Mugwumps and the Masses: Political Cartoons of the Gilded Age Politics" home page at <http://xroads.virginia.edu/~MA96/PUCK/shome.html>.

Students can chart the growth of the railroad industry by viewing a series of railroad maps made available online by the Library of Congress's American Memory project. Direct students to <http://memory.loc.gov/ammem/gmdhtml/rrhtml/rrhome.html>.

ASSESSING RESULTS
Multiple-Choice Questions

1. Contemporary critics lambasted President Grover Cleveland's action to save the nation's gold reserves in 1895 because it

a. unduly taxed the working class.
b. allegedly allowed J. P. Morgan to reap an enormous profit and gave him unprecedented power.
c. took the nation off the gold standard.
d. favored debtors over creditors.

2. America's first "big business" was the
a. railroad industry.
b. steel industry.
c. oil refining industry.
d. meatpacking industry.

3. In the "Gospel of Wealth," Andrew Carnegie
a. argued that the Bible provided justification for the country's wealth being held by a few.
b. argued the merits of welfare capitalism.
c. offered a strong critique of laissez-faire economics.
d. defended the concentration of wealth in the hands of America's leading industrialists, declaring that the wealthy knew how to use their riches for the public good.

4. In a series of cases that affected American corporations during the 1880s and 1890s, the Supreme Court moved to
a. uphold antitrust legislation.
b. strengthen railroad regulation.
c. champion labor unions.
d. extend the protections guaranteed under the Fourteenth Amendment to corporations.

5. The *Puck* cartoon of railroad tycoons illustrates
a. the fear and respect with which much of the country viewed the powerful railroad barons.
b. concern about the power these men wielded and how their activities might affect the country.
c. that the political cartoonists in the Gilded Age took care to be both subtle and tactful when caricaturing powerful men.
d. that those who built the railroads worked together effectively to ensure that the lines meshed well and that the whole system ran on time.

6. The Republican Party seized on the tariff issue in the 1880s, seeking to unite all of the following constituencies except
a. industrialists.
b. labor.
c. western producers of raw materials.
d. southern farmers.

7. The Supreme Court case that severely hampered the 1890 Sherman Antitrust Act's ability to "bust trusts" by distinguishing manufacturing from trade was
a. *Munn v. Illinois.*
b. *Wabash, St. Louis, and Pacific Railroad v. Illinois.*
c. *E. C. Knight v. American Sugar Refining Company.*
d. *Muller v. Oregon.*

8. The Crime of 1873 refers to
a. the demonetization of silver.
b. the free and unlimited coinage of silver.
c. the demonetization of gold.
d. the return to a bimetallic system.

9. Mark Twain and Charles Dudley Warner coined what phrase to describe late-nineteenth-century America?
a. The Age of Welfare Capitalism
b. The Era of Good Feelings
c. The Age of Discontent
d. The Gilded Age

10. Identify the correct sequence of historical events and figures.
a. President Garfield assassinated, first transcontinental railroad, Carnegie's "Gospel of Wealth," Sherman Antitrust Act
b. first transcontinental railroad, President Garfield assassinated, Pendleton Act, Carnegie's "Gospel of Wealth"
c. Standard Oil invents the trust, Edison invents the lightbulb, *Munn v. Illinois,* McKinley Tariff passed
d. *Munn v. Illinois,* Pendleton Act, Sherman Antitrust Act, first transcontinental railroad

PROPOSING MORE: Additional Readings

G. Blodgett, "The Political Leadership of Grover Cleveland," *South Atlantic Quarterly* 82, no. 3 (1983): 288–99.

R. Garson, "Social Darwinism and the Liberal Tradition: The Case of William Graham Sumner," *South Atlantic Quarterly* 80, no. 1 (1981): 61–76.

A. Munslow, "Andrew Carnegie and the Discourse of Cultural Hegemony," *Journal of American Studies* 22, no. 2 (1988): 213–24.

Michael O'Malley, "Specie and Species: Race and the Money Question in Nineteenth-Century America," *American Historical Review* 99, no. 2 (1994): 369–95.

Answer Key to Multiple-Choice Questions: 1-b, 2-a, 3-d, 4-d, 5-b, 6-d, 7-c, 8-a, 9-d, 10-b

AMERICA'S WORKERS: LIFE AND LABOR

19

1870–1890

Outlining Chapters: Thematic Questions

I. Who were America's new industrial workers?
  A. What was the rural periphery, and what factors encouraged workers to leave it in favor of the industrialized core?
  B. How did ethnic rivalry and racism serve to divide skilled from unskilled workers and thus discriminate against "nonwhite" workers?
  C. What were the similarities and differences in the lives and working conditions of different groups of American workers?
  D. What was the family economy, and how did women and children contribute to it? How did race and ethnicity influence the types of work performed by women and children?

II. Who were the new managers and white-collar workers?
  A. What was the new managerial class, and what conditions accounted for its emergence?
  B. How did women's opportunities for employment expand in the 1880s?
  C. In what ways does the department store afford a good setting in which to examine the working life of the new white-collar class?

III. How did the growth of industrial capitalism transform home and family life during the late nineteenth century? What factors characterized the home lives and leisure activities of American workers?
  A. What was the "cult of domesticity," and how did it affect household organization? This cult purveyed a certain image of womanhood — to whom did this image apply? To whom did it not apply? How did the cult of domesticity engender changes in hiring patterns of household help? Under what conditions did domestic servants labor?
  B. What were mill towns and company towns, and in what ways do they demonstrate the effect of industrial capitalism on traditional patterns of work and home life?
  C. In what leisure activities did the working class participate? What were the "cheap amusements" that attracted working-class patrons?

IV. What factors contributed to the rise of the labor movement in late-nineteenth-century America?
  A. What was the significance of the Great Railroad Strike of 1877? What lessons did workers learn from the strike?

B. What were the Knights of Labor and the American Federation of Labor? How were their visions of American labor similar, and how were they different? How did their goals for the labor movement differ?

C. What was the Haymarket affair, and what role did radicalism play in the outcome? What was the significance of the riot?

V. What role did utopian visions for a better life play in American culture?

A. Who was Henry George, and what was the single tax?

B. Who was Edward Bellamy, and how influential was his work *Looking Backward*?

Teaching with The American Promise, *Second Compact Edition: Lecture Strategies*

LECTURE 1
Lives of the Workers

This lecture introduces students to the lives of the working class in the late nineteenth century. According to Chapter 17, new patterns of immigration profoundly affected the workplace. Ethnic diversity and racial prejudice often pitted skilled workers (who often came from northern Europe) against the unskilled (many from southern and eastern Europe). The increased mechanization of the workplace served to displace skilled workers in favor of lower-paid, unskilled workers, exacerbating tensions. Here, refer students to "Labor Contractors and Italian Immigrants" (in the documents reader). Racial prejudice, which took its most blatant form in the treatment of African Americans and Asians, also fostered a social construction of "whiteness," which allowed northern Europeans to view eastern and southern Europeans as racially inferior. Poverty, however, was a common denominator for many working-class families, regardless of national origin.

At this point, you may wish to discuss the testimony of the textile worker before the U.S. Senate Committee on Relations between Capital and Labor (in the documents reader). Ask students to speculate on what options were available to this man. What kind of future could he and his family look forward to? Then make the general point that the inability of the male wage-earner to support his family led women and children to take low-paying and sometimes hazardous jobs to contribute to the family wage. Next, explain that although many workers shared the experience of poverty, working conditions varied considerably. Draw students' attention to the photos of the Chinese railroad workers and the "breaker boys." Have them read the domestic servants' descriptions of their experiences (in the documents reader). These images and documents — along with the chapter's vignettes on the lives of the common laborer, the skilled worker, the factory operative, the sweatshop garment worker, and the miner — speak to the diversity of workers and workplaces.

LECTURE 2
The New Managerial Class

This lecture demonstrates how rapid industrialization and corporate consolidation promoted the growth of a new managerial class — a cadre of workers who stood between the owners of a corporation and its workers on the shop floor. This new class was often engaged in sales, clerical, or service-related work and bespoke a transition from manufacturing to service industries. The new managerial class drew its ranks primarily from the white middle class. It was possible for a skilled worker to rise to the position of technical executive in the age before professional engineering and business schools trained such workers. As businesses became larger, the greater volume of correspondence and the need for more elaborate and exact records led to the hiring of more office workers. To demonstrate your point, have students look at the photograph of clerical workers. You should mention that office management frequently turned to women to fill clerical positions not only because women generally worked for lower wages than men did but also because they tended to be better educated than the males available to fill these positions. Women also found white-collar employment in department stores, the new consumer palaces designed to lend magic and glamour to everyday items. Although women who worked in department stores often considered themselves superior to women who worked in factories, their working conditions and paychecks often did not warrant such feelings. They were subjected to gender segregation, low wages, and arbitrary discipline from the floorwalkers.

LECTURE 3
The Labor Movement

This lecture focuses on how workers sought, by collective action, to counteract their loss of control in the workplace and the growing anonymity of corporate capitalism. Begin by mentioning that although workers had organized in craft unions for decades, the labor movement of the late nineteenth century had a different tenor as workers acted to better their conditions through politics and reform movements and increasingly through labor unions. (To convey something of labor's growing self-awareness and sense of empowerment, you might have students read the document in the documents reader in which workers satirize their bosses.) Next, move on to the Great Railroad Strike of 1877, when workers on the Baltimore and Ohio Railroad walked off their jobs to protest a cut in wages that occurred simultaneously with an increase in dividends paid to shareholders. Using Map 19.1, "The Great Railroad Strike of 1877," you can show how the strike spread across the country and explain that it affected numerous industries. The unorganized and spontaneous strike suffered from a lack of leadership and was eventually put down by the federal government, but it served as a stimulus to labor organizing.

Turn your attention to the Knights of Labor, which soon became the dominant voice of labor during the 1880s. The Knights, under the leadership of Terence V. Powderly, advocated a "universal brotherhood" of all laborers — from the master craftsman to the unskilled worker. The Knights also promoted other large-scale reform measures such as public ownership of the railroads and the income tax. Discuss one of the Knights' chief rivals, the American Federation of Labor, founded by Samuel Gompers. Unlike the Knights, the AFL was an organization of skilled craft unions. Gompers scoffed at the broad reform goals of the Knights of Labor and promoted instead short-term, concrete economic goals.

Discuss next the setback labor unionism faced in the wake of the Haymarket affair. After a bomb was thrown into the ranks of police who had come to Chicago's Haymarket Square to disperse the remnants of a peaceful band of anarchists, public opinion came to associate unionism with radicalism. Here, you might direct students' attention to the image of the pamphlet *The Chicago Riot*, which offered a decidedly one-sided account of the Haymarket affair. In response, Gompers refocused the labor movement, using strikes and boycotts judiciously so as not to alienate popular support. You might want to end this lecture by discussing the ways in which American workers sought to act on their vision of the promise of America. Ask students to consider what workers believed capital, management, and the government owed to them. Be sure to draw students' attention to the anthem of the "eight-hour movement."

Anticipating Student Reactions: Common Misconceptions and Difficult Topics

1. Radicalism and American Workers

In light of the Haymarket affair, students may wonder to what degree American workers, especially those involved in unions, were influenced by radical philosophies. In the United States, as in Britain and continental Europe, a number of social critics focused on the nature of work in modern society. Whatever differences may have separated these thinkers (and there were many), the critics did agree that capitalism debased work by depriving the working class of control over the means of production and by reducing economic activities to their commercial value. To rid society of what they considered the ills of capitalism, radicals advocated giving workers ownership of the means of production — tools, factories, mines, machines. Radicals did differ on how the capitalist system should be abolished. Some socialists optimistically believed that a socialist party in a democracy could win a majority and legislate capitalism out of existence. Others, such as the Industrial Workers of the World (IWW), were not quite so sanguine. These radicals argued that only violence could abolish capitalism. Eugene V. Debs, leader of the American Railway Union, helped organize the Socialist Party of America, which had a modicum of success in the early twentieth century. Socialists, however, were constantly under attack from conservatives, who were quick to associate all reformers with pernicious revolutionaries and anarchists, thus discrediting the movement. And because the ownership of private property was a cherished part of the American dream and a carefully guarded principle of American jurisprudence, socialists would make little headway in America, even among the workers.

2. "Eight Hours for What We Will"

While students usually know that workers fought for improved working conditions and better pay, they are sometimes unaware that one of the major goals of the labor movement in the late nineteenth century was the eight-hour workday. One of the main reasons workers agitated for a shorter workday was that they desired more time to pursue leisure activities. Because free time is something most of us in the early twenty-first century take for granted, students may be surprised to learn that workers in the late nineteenth century had to fight for this right. The anthem reprinted in the textbook captures the spirit of the eight-hour movement: "Eight hours for work, eight hours for rest, eight hours for what we will!" Ironically, some students may be familiar with our current society's glorification of working long hours, as celebrated in corporate culture or in popular television dramas that revolve around the workplace. Students may not realize that their notion of "long hours" is based on the assumption that eight hours is the length of a normal working day.

Introduce cultural history by discussing what working people did with their time off. Great pleasure palaces, such as Coney Island, Euclid Beach, Paragon Park, and Ponce de León Park, as well as dance halls and baseball fields, dotted the American urban landscape, all designed to offer the American worker respite from the drudgery of the workplace. Refer your students to the photograph of Coney Island's official guidebook to give them a sense for what kinds of entertainment were available. American entrepreneurs had commodified leisure activities, capturing the desires of their willing, paying customers.

Using the Bedford Series in History and Culture and the Historians at Work Series: Suggestions

Edward Bellamy's *Looking Backward: 2000–1887,* edited by Daniel H. Borus, and William Dean Howells's *A Traveler from Altruria,* edited by David W. Levy, both provide excellent examples of late-nineteenth-century utopian literature in its historical context. Both offer an entertaining look at utopian visions of the future.

Lecture Supplements and Classroom Activities

Using Multimedia Sources in the Classroom

To convey the conditions under which railroad workers labored, consider showing *The Iron Road,* produced and distributed by PBS Video. The first episode of Ken Burns's series *Baseball* chronicles the rise of the sport in concomitance to the rise of the city. The PBS video *Coney Island* offers students a look at cheap amusements and the commodification of entertainment in the late nineteenth century. You might also consider showing *Journey to America,* also distributed by PBS Video, which documents the wave of "new immigrants" who came to America during the late nineteenth century.

Historical Contingencies

Have students consider what America would look like had the Knights of Labor, workers, business, and government quickly and peacefully settled grievances in Chicago. Why did each vision of workers' rights seem practical or impractical? Have them consider the factors that gave rise to the Haymarket Riot — the conditions needing to be addressed and the solutions they proposed. Ask them if America's capitalist economy could have developed along more democratic lines than it has if labor issues had been handled different in the last decades of the nineteenth century. Is the capitalist system predicated on the existence of a few tycoons and masses of workers?

Classroom Activities

Set up a mock negotiation session between owners, managers, and union workers. Have workers demand an eight-hour workday, higher wages, or improved working conditions. Provide managers and owners with details on their own profits and the costs of implementing the workers' demands. At what point do the negotiations break down?

Using the Internet

The Chicago Historical Society and Northwestern University have made available an electronic archive of materials from the CHS's extensive Haymarket holdings. Tell students to go to <http://www.chicagohistory.org/hadc/intro.html>.

Assessing Results
Multiple-Choice Questions

1. The Great Railroad Strike of 1877
   a. was led by socialist Eugene V. Debs.
   b. was put down instantaneously by federal troops, who killed hundreds of workers in confrontations across the country.
   c. proved the downfall of President Rutherford B. Hayes, whose inability to handle the crisis lost him the Republican nomination in 1880.
   d. underscored the problems caused by rapid industrialization and highlighted labor's many legitimate grievances.

2. Which of the following statements best characterizes the new industrial workforce of the late nineteenth century?
   a. Industrialists increasingly depended on laborers from both the American and the global agricultural periphery.
   b. Skilled and unskilled workers joined unions to represent their shared concerns.
   c. Child labor decreased in response to stiff federal and state regulations.
   d. Women left the workforce in greater numbers than they had in previous decades.

3. The corporate consolidation movement of the late nineteenth century
   a. spurred the growth of a new rank of middle managers, who stood between the executives of a company and its workers.
   b. decreased the number of workers in the office.
   c. hampered the opportunity for women to enter white-collar jobs.
   d. prohibited the advancement of skilled craftsmen to executive positions.

4. Which of the following statements best describes the "cult of domesticity"?
   a. Its ideology dictated that a woman's place was in church.
   b. Its image of womanhood was appropriate for women of the middle and upper classes as well as their working-class counterparts.
   c. Ironically, it created opportunities for certain women to pursue club work, reform, and woman suffrage, thereby expanding women's horizons outside of the home.
   d. It led to a dramatic change in patterns of women's rights.

5. Which of the following factors did not motivate George M. Pullman to construct a company town for his workers?
   a. He was a reformer.
   b. He wished to curb labor unrest and prevent unionization.
   c. He was part of the Chicago school of architecture, and he envisioned a working class town as his next big project.
   d. He wished to provide his workers with the opportunity to become homeowners.

6. Industrialization and urbanization dramatically altered American workers' free time by
   a. giving rise to the commercialization of entertainment.
   b. reinforcing traditional notions and rituals of courtship.
   c. ending the gender segregation in leisure activities during the period after courtship and marriage.
   d. obliterating the importance of religious, familial, and cultural rituals for newly arrived immigrants.

7. The Noble and Holy Order of the Knights of Labor under the direction of Terence Powderly
   a. excluded master craftsmen from its ranks.
   b. focused exclusively on short-term, concrete goals such as the eight-hour day, higher wages, the right to collective bargaining, and the outlaw of yellow-dog contracts.
   c. was a major participant in the Great Railroad Strike of 1877.
   d. embraced a wide spectrum of reforms, including free land, income tax, public ownership of railroads, equal pay for equal work performed by women, and the abolition of child labor.

8. As a result of the Haymarket bombing
   a. membership in the Knights of Labor skyrocketed.
   b. many people associated labor unions with radicalism.
   c. the Illinois state legislature banned labor unions.
   d. many major corporations caved in to workers' demands for an eight-hour day.

9. According to the *Historical Question* feature, in attempting to measure "success" in late-nineteenth-century America, historians have come to realize that

a. each immigrant group had its own unique definition of success.

b. the rich stayed rich, and the poor remained poor to middling.

c. Jews in New York City fared much better than Italians.

d. Horatio Alger's formulaic novels of "rags to riches" rang true for most immigrants.

10. The consensus among the domestic servants that journalist Helen Campbell interviewed (in the documents reader) was that

a. domestic work was preferable to work in a factory or mill, being both safer and more relaxing.

b. the mistresses of the household where they were employed tended to treat them like members of the family, but unwanted advances from males in the family were all too familiar occurrences.

c. working in someone else's home full time meant that they were almost always on call and had very little personal liberty.

d. they disliked working as maids but lacked the skills or the inclination to try working at other jobs.

11. Identify the correct sequence of historical events and figures.

a. Great Railroad Strike, American Federation of Labor founded, Haymarket bombing, Knights of Labor founded

b. Gompers founds Organized Trades and Labor Unions, Great Railroad Strike, Haymarket bombing, Knights of Labor founded

c. Great Railroad Strike, Pullman builds model town, Haymarket bombing, Knights of Labor's influence declines

d. Pullman builds model town, first professional baseball team, Steeplechase amusement park opens on Coney Island, Knights of Labor founded

PROPOSING MORE: Additional Readings

Leon Fink, "The New Labor History and the Powers of Historical Pessimism: Consensus, Hegemony, and the Case of the Knights of Labor," *Journal of American History* 74, no. 1 (1988): 115–36.

Michael Kazin and Steven J. Ross, "America's Labor Day: The Dilemma of a Workers' Celebration," *Journal of American History* 78, no. 4 (1992): 1294–323.

J. Laslett, "Haymarket, Henry George, and the Labor Upsurge in Britain and America during the Late 1880s," *International Labor and Working-Class History* 29 (1986): 68–82.

Kathy Peiss, "'Charity Girls' and City Pleasure: Historical Notes on Working-Class Sexuality, 1880–1920," in *Powers of Desire: The Politics of Sexuality,* ed. Ann Snitow, Christine Stansell, and Sharon Thompson (New York: Monthly Review Press, 1983).

Robert Weir, "Powderly and the Home Club: The Knights of Labor Joust among Themselves," *Labor History* 34, no. 1 (1993): 84–113.

R. Jackson Wilson, "Experience and Utopia: The Making of Edward Bellamy's *Looking Backward,*" *Journal of American Studies* 11, vol. 1 (1977): 45–60.

Answer Key to Multiple-Choice Questions: 1-d, 2-a, 3-a, 4-c, 5-b, 6-a, 7-d, 8-b, 9-a, 10-c, 11-c

FIGHTING FOR JUSTICE AND EMPIRE 20

1890–1900

O*utlining Chapters: Thematic Questions*

I. What types of reform did American women engage in during the last decade of the nineteenth century?
  A. Who was Frances Willard, and what was the Woman's Christian Temperance Union? How did this organization differ from earlier organizations devoted to securing temperance? In what ways did the WCTU move beyond its original scope to include a variety of reform issues in its agenda?
  B. Who were the leaders of the woman suffrage movement at the close of the century, and what were their strategies?
  C. Who was Ida B. Wells, and why did she begin an antilynching campaign? What were her tactics and how successful were her efforts?
II. What economic and social ills plagued American farmers and laborers at the turn of the century?
  A. What were the Farmers Alliances, and what were their goals? What rested at the core of the alliances' economic program? How successful were the alliances? What was the Populist movement? Who were its leaders? What were their specific calls to action?
  B. What caused workers at Andrew Carnegie's Homestead, Pennsylvania, steel plant to go on strike? What were their demands? What was the result of the strike?
  C. Who was Eugene V. Debs? What role did he play in the Pullman strike of 1894? What was the result of the strike?
III. What was the political climate of the depression of 1893?
  A. Who was Jacob Coxey, and what was Coxey's "army"? What plans did Coxey propose to alleviate the suffering of the poor and unemployed? How did the nation respond to Coxey's army?
  B. What was the People's Party? What was its platform? What successes did it enjoy in securing its agenda?
  C. What were the defining issues of the election of 1896? What was the atmosphere surrounding the election? What did the election results portend for the future of American politics?

IV. What motivated American expansionism in the late nineteenth century?
   A. What were the twin pillars of American foreign policy in the late nineteenth century? How did these pillars advance American economic interests overseas?
   B. How did American concerns for both financial gain and religious conversion influence American foreign affairs at the turn of the century?
V. What factors contributed to the emergence of the United States as a world power?
   A. What were the causes of the Spanish-American War, and why was it dubbed a "splendid little war"?
   B. What issues surrounded the debate over American imperialism?

Teaching with The American Promise, *Second Compact Edition: Lecture Strategies*

LECTURE 1
Women and Reform

Women participated in reform movements in the late nineteenth century in unprecedented numbers. Although barred from the franchise in most states, American women nevertheless sought to create new political alliances and effect change through new reform organizations. Your lecture should cover three main reform movements in which women participated: temperance, suffrage, and antilynching.

Begin with one of the most successful of the women reformers, Frances Willard. In 1881, she became president of the Woman's Christian Temperance Union (WCTU), a grassroots organization formed in 1874, and dramatically altered the course of the temperance movement in the United States. She urged WCTU members to agitate for social action, rather than relying on prayer, to eliminate drunkenness. (Here you might want to refer students to the WCTU flyer promoting temperance.) Willard greatly expanded the activities of the WCTU, involving her organization in non-temperance issues such as woman suffrage and improving work conditions.

Woman suffrage was a major reform issue at this time, although not as prominent as temperance. (Be sure to bring Frances Willard's demand for the "home protection ballot" into your discussion of the suffrage movement.) In 1890, the two separate suffrage organizations, the National Woman Suffrage Association and the American Woman Suffrage Association, merged to form the National American Woman Suffrage Association (NAWSA), which launched campaigns at the state level to gain the vote for women.

Finally, close your lecture with a discussion of Ida B. Wells, an African American who represents another type of woman reformer. After hearing of the lynching of one of her friends in 1892, Wells began a vigorous antilynching campaign. Wells's investigations into lynchings uncovered the degree to which economic conditions and shifting social structures, compounded by white southerners' desire to maintain supremacy, contributed to the unprecedented frequency of lynchings. She also debunked the myth that lynchings protected white womanhood. Although anachronistic, Billie Holiday's recording of "Strange Fruit" powerfully captures the horrors of lynching, and you might consider playing it for your class. Note that although Congress did not meet Wells's demands for federal antilynching legislation, her activities succeeded in bringing the issue to the nation's attention. Be sure to point out to your students the image of Wells's 1892 pamphlet "Southern Horrors."

You may wish to end class by having students discuss the ways in which these women reformers called on America to live up to its promises. Have students review the last sentence of the Reconstruction Amendments, for example, and ask them how those who demanded woman suffrage and antilynching legislation sought to force Congress to fulfill its obligations.

LECTURE 2
Agrarian and Working-Class Discontent

This lecture conveys the degree to which Americans flocked to organizations to create new political alliances to work for change. You will first want to discuss the American farmers who were agitating for reform in the 1880s and 1890s. Beset by a variety of economic woes, farmers organized in Farmers Alliances throughout the South and the Midwest. Cover the issues that galvanized the Farmers Alliance, such as credit merchants, railroads, trusts, and the money power. Also point out that the alliance considered farmers members of the working class and that, to broaden its base and capture the support of the American labor movement, the Southern Farmers Alliance supported the Knights of Labor, calling on its members to boycott Jay Gould's railroad. By the late 1880s, the Farmers Alliances had become increasingly politicized. Farmers tried to establish a series of farmers' cooperatives to enhance their buying and selling power, but after meeting with stiff opposition from bankers and merchants they soon foundered. Note, however, that the farmers gained experience in political agitation and subsequently drafted a platform of demands that included railroad regulation, currency reform, and laws against land speculation. Discuss the ways in which the alliance movement gave rise to the Populist movement and the People's Party. Call attention to the Populists' demands, outlined in the Omaha Platform of 1892 (in the documents reader), and the photograph of the People's Party Convention delegate's badge.

Moving on, cover the ways in which American workers continued to agitate for better working conditions, better pay, and shorter workdays. Two of the most violent disputes between labor and capitalists — the Homestead lockout and strike of 1892 and the Pullman strike of 1894 — raised fundamental questions about the rights of workers and the sanctity of private property. Here you might have students read the debate between Samuel Gompers and N. F. Thompson on labor unions (in the documents reader). Be sure to draw your students' attention to the illustration of the attack of the Homestead strikers on the Pinkerton men.

End your lecture with a discussion of depression-era politics. Use the story of Coxey's army to suggest the level of desperation felt by the nation's poor and unemployed. Cover the election of 1896, the divisive issue of free silver, the debate over fusion, and the demise of the Populist movement. To have students appreciate the legacies of the Populists' downfall, have them read the account of the Wilmington race riot of 1898 (in the documents reader). You may wish to end your lecture by having students reflect on the ways in which both farmers and labor leaders demanded that America live up to its promise. The Omaha Platform will be especially useful on this score.

LECTURE 3
The Quest for Empire

This lecture stresses that the nation entered the twentieth century after a war for expansion, questioning the direction in which it was headed. Although the United States had remained largely aloof from the scramble for overseas colonies in the late nineteenth century, its leaders were acutely aware of the profits to be reaped from global expansion. U.S. foreign policy rested on the twin pillars of the Monroe Doctrine, asserting the unfettered U.S. control of the Western Hemisphere, and the Open Door policy in Asia, which granted the United States access to markets in that region. (Here you might ask students to examine and analyze the "Open Door" cartoon.) The desire for new markets for U.S. products influenced U.S. policy abroad, as did missionary zeal, patriotism, and jingoism.

Next, describe to your students the events of the Spanish-American War and the rise of the United States as a world power after its defeat of Spain in the "splendid little war." (Map 20.3, "The Spanish-American War, 1898," allows you to explain the Spanish-American War in some detail.) Americans were initially outraged at the brutality with which the Spanish colonial government treated Cubans who had been fighting for their independence since 1895, and Americans' moral indignation grew as journalists sensationalized the plight of the Cuban revolutionaries. The sinking of the *Maine* off the coast of Cuba served to intensify Americans' antipathy toward the Spanish. You will want to have students discuss the *Historical Question* feature "What Sank the *Maine*?" Make it clear that financial interests also motivated the United States to enter the fray. American business had millions of dollars invested in Cuban sugar plantations. Skirmishes between the Cuban revolutionaries and the Spanish nearly halted trade, and that was bad for U.S. business.

Also note that the United States wanted easier access to Asian markets, and a defeated Spain would likely yield control of not only Puerto Rico, but also Guam and the Philippine Islands. With U.S. aid, the Cubans finally secured their independence from Spain, but the Platt Amendment to the peace treaty gave the United States the right to intervene in Cuba whenever it pleased. Thus, a war begun by the United States for humanitarian interests resulted in greater U.S. imperialism.

Be sure to make the point that not all Americans were caught up in the late-nineteenth-century lust for empire. Have students read and discuss "Mark Twain on the Blessings-of-Civilization-Trust" (in the documents reader) for alternative views on American imperialism.

Anticipating Student Reactions: Common Misconceptions and Difficult Topics

1. The Money Supply

Students frequently have a hard time understanding the motivations behind the demands for free silver in the 1890s. Remind them that the 1896 election hinged on this issue. Begin by explaining the chronic indebtedness experienced by many farmers. Note the prevalence of sharecropping and tenancy in the South and the high costs of migrating to the West. Also note the drop in farm commodity prices during the second half of the nineteenth century, and ask students to consider the effect of falling prices on farmers' ability to repay their debts. Then have them speculate as to why those in debt would favor a loose money supply (and why creditors would favor a constricted money supply). You might need to point out that a looser money supply has an inflationary effect on prices. Your students might leap to the conclusion that inflation is a telltale sign of an unhealthy economy. Remind them, however, that farmers owe a fixed amount no matter what the money is worth. Inflation signals that the money is worth less than when debtors had borrowed the money. Creditors benefit from a tight money supply because the money is worth more than when they loaned it out. If your students still seem to be struggling with this point, ask them if they took out student loans to go to college. Then ask why they might want the money they repay the creditor to be worth less than the money they borrowed. Exaggerate the case. Have them personify the crediting agency as one individual who can do whatever he or she wishes with your students' money. The students will owe the money regardless of its worth; ask them if they would rather have the creditor be able to buy a mansion with their money or a bottom-of-the-line hatchback car with no frills. Most will choose the latter.

2. Lynchings Occurred Only Infrequently and Mostly during the First Few Years Following the Civil War

If students know anything about lynching, they may assume that episodes of mob violence happened rarely and largely died out after Reconstruction. You might begin with a discussion of the crime. What distinguishes lynching from murder? Why is this distinction important? Ida B. Wells's tireless publicizing of the issue, detailed in the textbook, not only made it abundantly clear that the problem was much bigger and more widespread than people realized but also debunked the myth most commonly used to justify this horrific brand of extralegal "justice." That is, whites usually claimed that lynchings occurred in retaliation against black men who had sexually violated their women, but Wells exposed the "threadbare lie that Negro men assault white women" and showed that this excuse often masked mob violence against blacks who were doing well economically in the community or who in some other way did not conform to the standard of subservient behavior that white society expected from African Americans. In 1892, Wells reported that 241 lynchings had occurred across twenty-six states; she later continued to record and describe incidents of lynchings in a series of publications. Between 1882 and 1931, according to the National Association for the Advancement of Colored People, 3,318 black men, women, and children were lynched "at the hands of parties unknown." End by discussing why antilynching activists demanded a federal antilynching law.

3. Theodore Roosevelt and the Spanish-American War

Students may well be familiar with the popular image of Theodore Roosevelt leading his Rough Riders in a heroic charge up San Juan Hill, but they might not know that this image reflected the popular, romanticized version of the battle and bore little relation to the actual event. In that sense, the image itself can be seen as emblematic of the hypocrisy of a war that was billed as a campaign to "liberate" Cuba but was actually fought at the behest of bankers, businessmen, newspaper moguls, and other powerful U.S. interests. Have students look at the lithograph of Roosevelt and his Rough Riders.

Make the point that while the image suggests that the U.S. army was ready for action, in reality American troops were few, poorly led, and ill prepared. True, the regular standing army of about 28,000 troops was a well-disciplined and highly professional force, but more than 223,000 raw recruits had volunteered after President William McKinley asked Congress to declare war. Secretary of War Russell Alger had promised McKinley that he could get 40,000 men to Cuba within ten days after the war broke out. It took him seven weeks to get fewer than half that number of men to the island. In fact, thousands of volunteers were stranded in Tampa, Florida — without guns, uniforms, or other equipment. Many contracted diseases while eating rotten food, living in poor sanitary conditions, and waiting in the hot sun to be transported to Cuba. Remind students that the U.S. navy was in much better shape than the army — despite our romantic image of Roosevelt on San Juan Hill, the navy proved the real key to the outcome of the war.

Using the Bedford Series in History and Culture and the Historians at Work Series: Suggestions

Consider assigning *Southern Horrors and Other Writings: The Anti-Lynching Campaign of Ida B. Wells, 1892–1900*, edited by Jacqueline Jones Royster, when covering women reformers of the 1890s. *Southern Horrors* collects three of Wells's powerful antilynching pamphlets and gives students the opportunity to explore popular racial and sexual conventions of the late nineteenth century. Charlotte Perkins Gilman's *The Yellow Wallpaper*, edited by Dale M. Bauer, in the Cultural Editions series from Bedford's literature list is another popular and well-received supplement covering women.

Lecture Supplements and Classroom Activities

Using Multimedia Sources in the Classroom

Ida B. Wells: A Passion for Justice chronicles the life of the antilynching crusader and works well in a discussion of militant women of the 1890s. *One Woman, One Vote* covers the seventy-year struggle for woman suffrage — from Seneca Falls in 1848 to the passage of the Nineteenth Amendment in 1920. The segments on the formation of NAWSA also work well in a class devoted to women reformers. When discussing U.S. involvement in overseas expansion, consider using *Hawaii's Last Queen*, which details Liliuokalani's efforts to protect the sovereignty of her island in the face of opposition from wealthy plantation owners and the U.S. government. Segments from *TR: The Story of Theodore Roosevelt* on the Spanish-American War also work well in a discussion of U.S. imperialism. All of these documentaries are distributed by PBS Video.

Historical Contingencies

Ask students to speculate on the possible course of American history had William Jennings Bryan won the election of 1896. Would victory have ensured that Populism would have remained a powerful reform impulse? What would have been the implications of a strengthened labor movement and weakened business interests? Would Jim Crow "justice" have continued in the South, or would Bryan's victory have ushered in a movement toward African American equality?

Classroom Activities

Have students debate the merits and drawbacks of U.S. imperialism. Students can represent business leaders, missionaries, humanitarian workers, jingoistic politicians, and so on. Should the United States have been involved in overseas expansion? What are other ways the United States could have been involved?

Using the Internet

Students interested in learning more about the Spanish-American War can visit "The World of 1898" Web site, offered by the Library of Congress. Tell students to go to <http://www.loc.gov/rr/hispanic/1898>. The site makes available online resources and documents about the war and also provides links to other relevant Library of Congress Web sites, such as the American Memory project.

ASSESSING RESULTS
Multiple-Choice Questions

1. The groups that converged on St. Louis in February of 1892
   a. were united in their desire to build a new political party that would better represent the needs of the people than either the Democratic or Republican Parties.
   b. included representatives from the Knights of Labor, the Woman's Christian Temperance Union, the American Communist Party, and the Farmers Alliance.
   c. nominated former General James B. Weaver of Iowa as the Populist candidate for president.
   d. nominated William Jennings Bryan as the Populist candidate for president.

2. The Woman's Christian Temperance Union, under the direction of Frances Willard,

differed radically from earlier temperance efforts in that it
a. concerned itself solely with the consumption of alcohol in private homes.
b. was active only in the largest urban areas.
c. concerned itself with nontemperance issues, such as woman suffrage, along with advocating total abstinence from alcohol.
d. viewed the consumption of alcohol as a sin.

3. Which of the following statements best characterizes lynching in the late nineteenth century?
a. Most African American victims were lynched in states outside the former Confederacy.
b. The number of lynchings steadily declined throughout the late nineteenth century, suggesting the immediate success of the antilynching activities of Ida. B. Wells.
c. Congress passed significant antilynching legislation in the 1890s.
d. Lynchings had more to do with economics and the shifting social structure in the South than with any real or alleged offenses committed by the victims.

4. Farmers in the 1880s and 1890s complained bitterly about all of the following except
a. an expanding money supply.
b. a constricted money supply.
c. exorbitant railroad and warehouse rates.
d. land speculators.

5. The 1892 Homestead lockout and strike and the 1894 Pullman strike
a. won public sympathy to the cause of labor.
b. raised fundamental questions about the rights of laborers and the sanctity of private property.
c. testified to the growing strength of labor unions in the last two decades of the nineteenth century.
d. ultimately crushed the empires of two of the nation's largest corporate capitalists.

6. Coxey's army, which marched from Ohio to Washington, D.C., in the summer of 1894,
a. convinced Congress to pass major relief legislation for dispossessed Americans.
b. forced Congress to repeal vagrancy laws.
c. engendered a groundswell of public sympathy for the plight of the poor and unemployed.
d. dramatized the plight of the poor and unemployed.

7. The 1896 presidential election
a. saw the lowest voter turnout in a presidential election in the nineteenth century.

b. garnered the largest victory for the Populists to date.
c. saw urban labor rally behind William Jennings Bryan and the Democratic ticket.
d. centered on the free silver versus gold standard debate.

8. When historians speak of the twin pillars of American foreign policy in the late nineteenth century, they refer to the U.S. government's insistence on
a. American control of the Western Hemisphere, as outlined in the Monroe Doctrine, and an Open Door policy in Asia.
b. an Open Door policy in the Western Hemisphere and American control of Asia, as outlined in the Monroe Doctrine.
c. absolute freedom of the seas and open covenants agreed on openly.
d. protective tariffs and absolute freedom of the seas.

9. Which of the following factors motivated the United States to fight in the 1898 Spanish-American War?
a. The American public's lingering distrust of Spain.
b. Americans' fear of the radicalism of the Cuban revolutionaries.
c. American's desire for greater and easier access to Europe by securing former Spanish colonies that blocked U.S. entry to Europe.
d. Americans' desire to protect U.S. business interests and investments.

10. According to Map 20.3, "The Spanish-American War, 1898," which of the following places in the Philippine and Cuban arenas saw major action during the Spanish-American War?
a. Mindanao and Jamaica
b. Luzon and Havana
c. Manila and San Juan Hill
d. Hainan and Tampa

11. Identify the correct sequence of historical events and figures.
a. Farmers Alliance organized, People's Party founded, Spanish-American War begins, Coxey's army marches
b. Boxer Rebellion, Open Door policy, Homestead lockout, Cross of Gold speech
c. Farmers Alliance organized, Homestead lockout, Pullman strike, Spanish-American War begins
d. Pullman strike, Homestead lockout, Spanish-American War begins, Boxer Rebellion

PROPOSING MORE: Additional Readings

M. Barkun, "Coxey's Army as a Millennial Movement," *Religion* 18, no. 4 (1988): 363–89.

G. Bederman, "'Civilization,' the Decline of Middle-Class Manliness, and Ida B. Wells's Antilynching Campaign, 1892–1894,"*Radical History Review* 52 (1992): 5–30.

W. F. Holmes, "The Southern Farmers' Alliance and the Jute Cartel," *Journal of Southern History* 60, no. 1 (1994): 59–80.

C. D. Laurie, "Extinguishing Frontier Brushfires: The U.S. Army's Role in Quelling the Pullman Strike in the West, 1894," *The Journal of the American West* 32, no. 2 (1993): 54–63.

L. Schneider, "The Citizen Strikers: Workers, Ideology in the Homestead Strike of 1892," *Labor History* 23, no. 1 (1982).

J. Turner, "Understanding the Populists," *Journal of American History* 67, no. 2 (1980): 354–73.

Answer Key to Multiple-Choice Questions: 1-a, 2-c, 3-d, 4-a, 5-b, 6-d, 7-d, 8-a, 9-d, 10-c, 11-c

Essay Questions, Chapters 16–20

1. Historians have debated the nature of Reconstruction. Some have suggested that Reconstruction was a time of profound social and political change. Others, however, have questioned whether "anything of enduring importance occurred at all." Based on your knowledge of Reconstruction and the Gilded Age, do you believe that Reconstruction fundamentally altered America? Or was Reconstruction, in the words of one historian, "essentially nonrevolutionary and conservative"?

2. Throughout the second half of the nineteenth century, representatives from the South and the West maintained that their regions were held hostage to the East. They charged that northern and eastern industrialists treated the South and the West as if they were colonial outposts, subject to the exploitation of the urban and industrial centers. To what degree did these regional representatives accurately diagnose the situation? Did the South and West experience similar processes of industrialization and urbanization as the North and East, or did they remain isolated from these larger trends?

3. What were the competing conceptions of justice, freedom, and equality circulating during the second half of the nineteenth century? On what basis did various groups justify these conceptions? Ultimately, which of these conceptions most accurately reflect(s) "the promise of America"?

4. In 1873, Mark Twain and Charles Dudley Warner published their novel *The Gilded Age*, which satirized America as a land of money-grubbers and speculators. The novel resonated with late-nineteenth-century readers and continues to do so with historians. In fact, historians have appropriated its title to characterize the late nineteenth century — America's Gilded Age — as an age of materialism and cultural shallowness. Citing specific historical examples, discuss the appropriateness of this title for America in the late nineteenth century.

5. During the late nineteenth and early twentieth centuries, numerous reform and radical movements emerged in America. Some of these movements sought to reinforce traditional American values and institutions, while others threatened to abolish them completely. Compare any three of these movements — labor reform, socialism, Populism, woman suffrage, immigration reform, political reform — and discuss the ways in which they sought to affect American society. Be sure to consider the goals, constituencies, successes, and failures of each movement you discuss. Ultimately, what movement(s) posed the greatest threat to "traditional" American values and institutions? What movement(s) achieved the greatest and most far-reaching success?

6. Did the Populist movement represent a culmination of late-nineteenth-century reform movements, or did it represent a radical departure from those traditional efforts to

improve American society? Defend your response.

7. Choose any three of the following trends or phenomena of late-nineteenth-century American life: immigration restriction, Jim Crow segregation and disfranchisement, the destruction of Native American cultures in the American West, business consolidation, the growing disparity between rich and poor, and U.S. overseas expansion. In what ways could the proponents of social Darwinism explain these trends or events? What holes, if any, do you see in their arguments? Ultimately, is social Darwinism a satisfactory analytical tool for understanding America in the late nineteenth century?

PROGRESSIVE REFORM FROM THE GRASS ROOTS TO THE WHITE HOUSE

21

1890–1916

*O*utlining Chapters: Thematic Questions

I. Who were the progressive reformers? What factors united them, and what issues divided them? What motivated progressive reformers at the grass-roots level?

A. How did progressives set out to "civilize" the city? How did the settlement house, social gospel, and social purity movements fit into this agenda?

B. What attitudes did progressives hold toward the working class? How did progressives attempt to reform the lives of the urban poor? What factors limited the success of cross-class alliances?

II. How did progressivism operate in theory and in practice?

A. How did progressives transform the theories of social Darwinism?

B. How do the political careers of Cleveland mayor Thomas Lofton Johnson, Wisconsin governor/senator Robert La Follette, and California governor Hiram Johnson epitomize progressive reform at the local and state levels?

III. In what ways did Theodore Roosevelt capture the reform spirit at the national level?

A. What was Theodore Roosevelt's Square Deal? What did he believe to be the most "vital question" facing the country at the dawn of the twentieth century?

B. What were Roosevelt's views on governmental regulation of corporations? What powers did he wish the government to possess in terms of regulation? How did Roosevelt's policies change once he was elected to a second term?

C. What policies guided Roosevelt in foreign affairs?

D. In what ways did William Howard Taft fail to continue the progressive agenda outlined by Roosevelt?

E. Why did Roosevelt choose to enter the 1912 presidential race as a third-party candidate? How successful was the Bull Moose Party?

IV. Was Woodrow Wilson a progressive president?

A. What were Wilson's views on tariff and banking reform? What specific pieces of legislation were passed on these issues during his tenure as president? What were his views on trusts? What were his views on federal regulation?

B. Why have historians dubbed Wilson "the reluctant progressive"?

V. What were the limits of progressive reform?

A. How did socialism, syndicalism, and the birth control movement represent radical alternatives to progressivism?

B. Why did some reformers see progressivism as a tool for men only?

C. In what ways did progressive activists view racism as reform?

Teaching with The American Promise, *Second Compact Edition: Lecture Strategies*

LECTURE 1

Progressive Reform at the Grassroots and State Levels

This lecture introduces students to progressive reform and demonstrates the transformation of the reform movement from grassroots to state-wide levels. Remind students that from the outset the progressives were a diverse group with a variety of motivations, interests, and goals. The social gospel of activists and theologians such as Walter Rauschenbusch motivated some reformers, while others feared that the social upheaval of the 1890s would continue unless some sort of corrective action was taken. Targets included wealthy individuals and powerful corporations, both of which reformers distrusted. Some progressives also feared the new immigrants. The reformers were united in all of the following: their belief that environment, and not heredity alone, determined human potential; their sense of optimism that conditions could be corrected without radically altering America's economy or institutions; their profound trust in experts and scientific investigations; and their willingness to take action.

After introducing the varied concerns of the progressives, turn the class's attention to the specific work undertaken by the reformers. Stress the role that women reformers, who were attracted to grassroots activism, played in the progressive movement. The vignettes on Jane Addams of Hull House and the Women's Trade Union League will provide students with an understanding of the kinds of issues that motivated reformers as well as the kinds of actions these progressives could take at the local and state levels. You might also want to refer back to Ida M. Tarbell's attack on Standard Oil, one of the landmark "muck-

raking" articles published in the Progressive Era, to discuss the far-reaching effects of women's reform. Be sure to discuss as well political reform at the local and state level. The accounts of Cleveland mayor Thomas L. Johnson, Wisconsin politician Robert La Follette, and California governor Hiram Johnson will make your point clear. You can end your lecture with a discussion of Jane Addams's "The Subjective Necessity for Social Settlements" (in the documents reader).

LECTURE 2

Progressivism in the White House: Roosevelt, Taft, and Wilson

In this lecture, turn your class's attention to how the reform movement entered national politics by tackling the social problems engendered by urban industrialism. Begin with Teddy Roosevelt's ascension to the presidency in 1901. Roosevelt had promised the American nation and, more important, Republican Party bigwigs that he would continue the policies of his predecessor. But Roosevelt was a progressive, and it did not take long for him to break away from party leadership and transform the office of the presidency into a "bully pulpit." Cover his first targets — those large corporate trusts that he believed abused their power. Remind students that Roosevelt was not antibusiness. Indeed, he recognized that consolidation was inevitable and not necessarily contrary to the public interest. Roosevelt believed that it was possible to distinguish between "good" and "bad" trusts, and that only those harmful to the public at large should be prosecuted under federal antitrust legislation. Mention that Roosevelt faced stiff opposition to his regulatory impulses from the Republican-dominated Congress during both his terms as president, but he dealt with this opposition with characteristic savvy and vigor. His handling of railroad regulation and food and drug inspection should illustrate to your students his ability to deal with Congress.

Discuss the fact that Roosevelt's handpicked successor, William Howard Taft, displayed no such flair with Congress. Moreover, he managed to alienate Roosevelt himself on the tariff issue, on conservation, and especially on the issue of trusts. By 1912, Roosevelt was so disenchanted with Taft that the former president formed a third party — the Progressive Party (nicknamed the Bull Moose Party) — and ran on its ticket. Draw students' attention to the Bull Moose poster. Roosevelt's move split the Republican Party, ensuring that Democrat Woodrow Wilson became the twenty-eighth president.

End your lecture with a discussion of Wilson's presidency. Wilson secured crucial tariff and banking reform as well as antitrust and federal trade acts. But he soon declared that progressivism had run its course. Wilson reevaluated his position after the Republicans won significant victories in the state and congressional elections of 1914. No longer professing the end of progressive reform, Wilson came to champion many of Roosevelt's causes.

LECTURE 3
The Limits of Reform

Use this third lecture to convey to students the limits of progressive reform. Never a radical movement, progressivism always had as its goal the preservation and strengthening of traditional American social, political, economic, and cultural institutions. Contemporary critics and many historians have correctly assessed the limits of progressivism, charging that it served only the needs of white men. The accounts of Socialist Party leader Eugene V. Debs, birth control advocate Margaret Sanger, woman suffrage leaders Carrie Chapman Catt and Alice Paul, and "race men" Booker T. Washington and W. E. B. Du Bois will help students to understand the limits of reform. (Draw your students' attention to documents on Washington, Du Bois, radical activist Mother Jones, and the member of the Industrial Workers of the World in the documents reader.) Students should appreciate that the limits of reform compelled these other, more radical activists to agitate for more comprehensive changes in America's social, economic, and political structures.

Anticipating Student Reactions: Common Misconceptions and Difficult Topics

1. Child Labor

One of the problems progressive reformers attempted to address that students may find particularly interesting was the issue of child labor. Students are often amazed to learn the ages at which some children were put to work, and they may find it incredible that attempts to end child labor were met with resistance from employers and even parents. You might have students discuss the chapter-opening artifact — the progressive poster attacking child labor.

2. Jim Crow, Progressivism, and the Career of W. E. B. Du Bois

Students might be surprised to learn that the conditions for blacks in America actually worsened during the Progressive Era. In fact, historians refer to this time as the nadir in American race relations. Make it clear that the period saw the systematic disfranchisement of black voters and the rise of racial segregation. Remind them that Jim Crow had the sanction of the U.S. Supreme Court; in 1896 the Court upheld the legality of segregation in *Plessy v. Ferguson*; in 1898, the Court upheld the legality of state constitutions that disfranchised voters through literacy tests (as long as race was not a stipulated criterion) in *Williams v. Mississippi*. Point out that the Roosevelt and Wilson administrations had abysmal records on civil rights.

Highlight the career of W. E. B. Du Bois, one of the most forceful and eloquent voices for African Americans since Frederick Douglass. Du Bois, born in Massachusetts, was the first black person to earn a Ph.D. from Harvard. In his most famous work, *The Souls of Black Folk* (1903), Du Bois offered a strong critique of Booker T. Washington's accommodationist policies. (See the documents reader.) Du Bois's 1905 Niagara movement, which demanded suffrage and civil rights for African Americans, provided the foundations for the establishment in 1909 of the National Association for the Advancement of Colored People (NAACP). The NAACP's interracial membership further championed the Niagara movement's radical position on matters of racial equality. Du Bois edited *The Crisis* magazine for the NAACP. He later joined the Communist Party, gave up his American citizenship, and moved to Ghana for the rest of his life.

Using the Bedford Series in History and Culture and the Historians at Work Series: Suggestions

Jacob Riis's *How the Other Half Lives*, edited by David Leviatin, provides students with a vivid, but biased, portrayal of tenement life and the living conditions of New York City's immigrant poor in the late nineteenth century. It is especially useful when discussing the racial, ethnic, and religious stereotypes perpetuated by progressive reformers. You might also want to use Jane Addams's *Twenty Years at Hull House*, edited by Victoria Bissell Brown, when covering motivations and actions of progressive reformers. Another good volume for covering politics and progressivism is *The 1912 Election and the Power of Progressivism,* edited by Brett Flehinger. You might also assign *What Was Progessivism?* by Glenda E. Gilmore, which gives students a closer look at progressive Americans who searched for solutions to the social problems caused by industrialization and urbanization. *Muckraking: Three Landmark Articles,* edited by Ellen F. Fitzpatrick, can help introduce your students more fully to the role of journalism in spurring progressive reform. *Muller v. Oregon: A Brief History with Documents,* edited by Nancy Woloch, works well when examining the intellectual roots of progressive reform and the effect of pragmatism in American jurisprudence. If you want your students to learn more of Du Bois's philosophy, consider assigning *The Souls of Black Folk,* edited by David Blight and Robert Gooding-Williams. When discussing Jim Crow segregation, assign *Plessy v. Ferguson: A Brief History with Documents,* edited by Brook Thomas. Frederick E. Hoxie's *Talking Back to Civilization: Indian Voices from the Progressive Era* is an account of Native Americans' challenges to government policies during the Progressive Era. John David Smith's *When Did Southern Segregation Begin?* and Booker T. Washington's *Up From Slavery,* edited by W. Fitzhugh Brundage, will provoke thoughtful discussion, too.

Lecture Supplements and Classroom Activities

Using Multimedia Sources in the Classroom

"America 1900," part of the PBS series *The American Experience,* and "1900: Age of Hope," part of *The People's Century,* both convey the sense of optimism with which reformers greeted the new century. To give a more in-depth look at progressivism in the White House, show *TR: The Story of Teddy Roosevelt,* also distributed by PBS Video.

To examine race relations in the Progressive Era, consider using D. W. Griffith's epic *Birth of a Nation,* a racist film that celebrates the overthrow of Reconstruction.

Historical Contingencies

Have students consider the possible course of American history had William McKinley not been assassinated. Would progressivism have found its way to the national stage? Ask students to name legislation passed under Roosevelt, Taft, and Wilson that might not have been passed under McKinley. How did that legislation affect American society? What would America have looked like had that legislation not passed?

Classroom Activities

Have students debate the merits of establishing a ten-hour workday for working women. Why did progressive reformers believe women needed such protection? How do reformers' demands for a shortened workday mesh with their demands for suffrage and equality? Why did the Supreme Court refuse to uphold a law limiting the workday for men in the case of *Lochner v. New York* (1905) but uphold a similar law for women three years later in the case of *Muller v. Oregon?* Ask your students if the court's reasoning makes sense to them.

Using the Internet

The Special Collections Division of Michigan State University has begun to scan documents from its American Radicalism Collection and post them on its Web site. Students who wish to research the Industrial Workers of the World or the birth control movement can go to <http://digital.lib.msu.edu/onlinecolls>.

There are a number of Web sites devoted to the Votes for Women project. The Library of Congress has two relevant collections available in its American Memory project. Direct students to <http://memory.loc.gov>. Using the "Collection Finder," students can locate "Women's Suffrage — Books and Pamphlets" and "Women's Suffrage — Photographs and Prints." The University of Maryland, College Park, through its Women's Studies Database, has made available a vast assortment of information on women activists. Direct students to <http://www.mith2.umd.edu/WomensStudies>.

ASSESSING RESULTS
Multiple-Choice Questions

1. Jane Addams's Hull House
   a. afforded educated women an unprecedented opportunity to become involved in urban reform.
   b. proved it was possible to deal with urban problems while remaining outside the realm of politics.
   c. barred men from participating in her settlement house programs.

d. strongly influenced Chicago's reform movement but made little impact on national efforts to reform U.S. cities and politics.

2. Which of the following statements best describes progressive reformers?
   a. They believed that heredity alone determined human potential.
   b. Despite their efforts at reform, they remained profoundly skeptical that America could be changed without radically altering its fundamental institutions.
   c. They remained highly skeptical of experts and scientific investigations.
   d. They displayed a decided willingness to take action.

3. The "uprising of twenty thousand" refers to the
   a. 1902 strike in Pennsylvania's anthracite coalfields.
   b. 1909 strike led by members of the International Ladies' Garment Workers Union.
   c. 1903 separation of the Panamanian isthmus from Colombia and the ultimate U.S. recognition for the new Panamanian government.
   d. 1913 strike in Colorado's mines led by the United Mine Workers and Mother Jones.

4. In 1900, Teddy Roosevelt believed that the most vital issue facing the nation was
   a. the debate over the government's power to control trusts.
   b. foreign policy issues.
   c. the government's ability to manage national resources.
   d. the call for direct election of senators.

5. A key component of Woodrow Wilson's 1912 New Freedom campaign platform was its demand for
   a. direct election of senators.
   b. woman suffrage.
   c. recall of judges.
   d. tougher antitrust legislation.

6. The National Woman's Party, founded by Alice Paul in 1916,
   a. advocated the state-by-state method of securing woman suffrage.
   b. advocated a federal constitutional amendment guaranteeing woman suffrage.
   c. rejected the tactics of direct action and civil disobedience in order to secure woman suffrage.
   d. worked closely with the older organization, the National American Woman Suffrage Association, to secure woman suffrage.

7. W. E. B. Du Bois, a champion of the rights of African Americans in the late nineteenth and early twentieth centuries, pushed for
   a. focusing on educating blacks in vocational skills.
   b. accommodation.
   c. repeal of all laws that enforced desegregation.
   d. moving blacks to Africa.

8. Map 21.2, "The Panama Canal, 1914," shows that the Panama Canal
   a. cut travel distance between New York and San Francisco by more than half.
   b. defined the border between modern-day Panama and Costa Rica.
   c. passed through two different Latin American countries.
   d. was approximately eighty miles in length.

9. According to the document in the documents reader, what was Mother Jones's reaction to Mrs. Palmer's plan to bring working-class people and capitalists together?
   a. She thought the interests of labor and capital were too divergent for such a meeting to accomplish anything.
   b. Although she hoped the meeting would bear positive results, she worried that disagreements between the two groups might result in violence.
   c. She thought it was a step in the right direction but chastised Mrs. Palmer for not inviting representatives from woman suffrage groups.
   d. She threatened to picket the front of Mrs. Palmer's mansion if she attempted to convene such a meeting.

10. Identify the correct sequence of historical events and figures.
    a. *Plessy v. Ferguson*, IWW founded, Jane Addams opens Hull House, Alice Paul launches National Woman's Party
    b. WTUL founded, IWW founded, Triangle Shirtwaist Company fire, Margaret Sanger opens first birth control clinic
    c. Federal Reserve Act, NAACP founded, Taft elected president, *Plessy v. Ferguson*
    d. *Muller v. Oregon*, *The Souls of Black Folk*, Socialist Party founded, IWW founded

PROPOSING MORE: Additional Readings

D. D. Bruce, "Booker T. Washington: 'The Man Farthest Down' and the Transformation of Race," *Mississippi Quarterly* 48, no. 2 (1995): 239–53.

Maureen A. Flanagan, "Gender and Urban Political Reform: The City Club and the Woman's City Club of Chicago in the Progressive Era," *American Historical Review* 95, no. 4 (1990): 1032–50.

R. W. Fox, "The Culture of Liberal Protestant Progressivism, 1875–1925," *Journal of Interdisciplinary History* 23, no. 3 (1993): 639–60.

John Hope Franklin, "The Birth of a Nation: Propaganda as History," in *Race and History: Selected Essays, 1938–1988* (Baton Rouge: Louisiana State University Press, 1989), 10–23.

August Meier and John H. Bracey, "The NAACP as a Reform Movement, 1909–1965: 'To Reach the Conscience of America,'" *Journal of Southern History* 59, no. 1 (1993): 3–30.

D. Steigerwald, "The Synthetic Politics of Woodrow Wilson," *Journal of the History of Ideas* 50, no. 3 (1989): 465–584.

A. Testi, "The Gender of Reform Politics: Theodore Roosevelt and the Culture of Masculinity," *Journal of American History* 81, no. 4 (1995): 1509–33.

Answer Key to Multiple-Choice Questions: 1-a, 2-d, 3-b, 4-a, 5-d, 6-b, 7-c, 8-a, 9-a, 10-b

WORLD WAR I: THE PROGRESSIVE CRUSADE AT HOME AND ABROAD

22

1914–1920

Outlining Chapters: Thematic Questions

I. What was Woodrow Wilson's prewar foreign policy? What principles guided this policy?
   A. What was Wilson's policy toward Latin America? In what Latin American country did Wilson face his most serious and controversial involvement?
   B. What events in Europe precipitated the onset of the "Great War"?
   C. What was the principle of neutrality? Why did Wilson adopt this policy? How did the realities of war test America's commitment to neutrality?
   D. Why did the United States enter the war?

II. In what ways was the war a "crusade for democracy"?
   A. In what ways was the U.S. army ill prepared to fight when it was called to arms in 1917? How did the troops prepare?
   B. What was the progressive stake in the war? Why did progressives support the war effort?
   C. What new opportunities did women face during the war? How did the U.S. involvement in the war advance the cause of woman suffrage?
   D. What factors contributed to the "great migration" of African Americans during the war? Where were they going? What were they leaving behind?
   E. What was the struggle over national purpose?
   F. What was the U.S. military strategy once involved in the war? What was the American way of fighting?

III. How was the peace compromised?
   A. What were Wilson's "Fourteen Points"? When did he announce them? What was their purpose?
   B. What terms were agreed on at the Paris Peace Conference?
   C. What was the domestic reaction to the Treaty of Versailles?

IV. What changes took place in the postwar U.S. economy and society?
   A. Why was there economic hardship and labor upheaval after the war? How did middle-class America respond to this unrest?
   B. What was the "Red scare"? What factors engendered it? Why did it eventually lose credibility?

Teaching with **The American Promise,** *Second Compact Edition: Lecture Strategies*

LECTURE 1

Wilson's Prewar Foreign Policy

This lecture on the roots of American involvement in World War I should cover Woodrow Wilson's prewar foreign policy. Suggest that although Wilson displayed very little interest or aptitude for foreign policy when he ran for president in 1912, he soon discovered that he could not remain aloof from the world after assuming the office. He rooted his foreign policy in his firm belief that America should provide a moral example in international affairs; he believed in the sanctity of human rights, the right of law, the right of self-determination, and free trade.

Show that Wilson found it difficult to maintain his idealistic policy in Latin America, especially in Mexico; but when war broke out in Europe, Wilson felt no compunction to intervene. Wilson immediately proclaimed U.S. neutrality, urging Americans to be neutral and impartial. Ask students to consider why Wilson chose to follow such a course. Remind them that he was not convinced that Germany was solely to blame for the hostilities; he did not believe the United States had a vital stake in the outcome of the war; he feared the reaction from America's immigrant populations; and, perhaps most important, he believed that only a neutral nation could broker a peace between the warring nations.

Neutrality proved to be a hard course to follow, however. Wilson himself was an Anglophile, as were many members of his cabinet. Wilson's firm conviction in the sanctity of absolute freedom of the seas, coupled with the German policy of unrestricted submarine warfare, made it nearly impossible for Wilson to restrain from siding with the Allies. Moreover, the U.S. need to bail out its slumping economy made trading to the belligerents an especially attractive policy. When the European economies proved too exhausted from fighting the war, the United States loaned them money to buy U.S. goods. Once again, Wilson found it difficult to remain neutral. The United States loaned Great Britain nearly ten times the amount it loaned Germany. By the time the U.S. public had learned of the Zimmermann telegram, it was ready for a new policy.

LECTURE 2

The United States and the "Great War"

The second lecture covers U.S. involvement in World War I. Remind students that Germany's continued policy of unrestricted submarine warfare finally compelled Wilson to action. Emphasize that the president declared from the outset that the U.S. goal was not to destroy Germany but rather to make the world "safe for democracy." Have the class discuss his request to Congress for a declaration of war (in the documents reader). Emphasize that despite Wilson's heady rhetoric, however, the United States was woefully unprepared. Cover the ways in which the Wilson administration geared the nation to fight the war. The government instituted loyalty programs in public schools, created a number of agencies to manage the economy, began a department on propaganda (the Committee on Public Information), and enacted a series of repressive measures to ensure the support of the American people. Eugene V. Debs's speech about capitalist warmongers (in the documents reader) provides an interesting opposing view. Have students take a look at the propaganda poster urging Americans to enlist. You might take some time to discuss the chapter-opening artifact — a 1914 magazine cover that would seem to convey rather vividly the American press's support for the U.S. entry into World War I.

Moving on, discuss how the domestic economy, increasingly fueled by African Americans' and women's labor, mobilized war industries. Wilson signed a Selective Service bill into law, which transformed the tiny volunteer army into a large and powerful fighting force, and new training camps turned raw recruits into professional soldiers. Even the "American way of war" changed, with General John J. Pershing refusing to allow his troops to fight alongside French and English troops for fear of stalemate. Instead, Pershing advocated heavy frontal pressure combined with swift surprise attacks on the enemies' flanks. The Allies proved victorious, but not without suffering heavy losses. End the class by having students consider what African Americans, women, and progressive reformers hoped that U.S. involvement in the war would do to help the country fulfill its promise. Ask students to think about how each group thought the war effort might transform American society. At this point, you may wish to have the class discuss the *Historical Question* feature "What Did the War Mean to African Americans?"

LECTURE 3
Wilson's Postwar Vision

The third lecture covers Woodrow Wilson's postwar vision. In his famous "Fourteen Points" speech to Congress, Wilson announced his plans for the postwar world even before the war had ended. Discuss how the first five of these points reaffirmed the basic liberal ideas that Wilson had championed before the war: open covenants agreed on openly, absolute freedom of the seas, free trade, reductions of arms, and the recognition of the rights of colonized peoples. The next eight points were concerned with the right to self-determination. But it was the final point, the creation of a league of nations, on which Wilson rested his hopes for securing his vision of a postwar peace. Point out to students that Wilson jeopardized his chances, however, when he refused to take any members of the Republican Party to the peace negotiations in Paris, thereby ensuring the party's opposition to the resulting treaty.

Suggest that the European allies' insistence on assigning blame for the war to Germany, their reluctance to turn their African and Asian colonies over as mandates to an international body, and Britain's resistance to absolute freedom of the seas did not make Wilson's task at the negotiating table easy. Then turn your attention to the opposition Wilson faced at home. The irreconcilables and the reservationists in the U.S. Senate, for example, refused to support a treaty that bound the United States to a league of nations. When the peace treaty reached the Senate in March 1920, it was six votes short of the two-thirds majority needed for passage. European nations organized the league in Geneva, but the United States never became a member, and Wilson died without seeing the new world order he so desired. End the lecture by having students contrast Wilson's vision with the realities of postwar America. Be sure to bring in the dubious constitutionality of the Palmer Raids (in the documents reader).

Anticipating Student Reactions: Common Misconceptions and Difficult Topics

1. Crises in the Balkans

Students may have a tough time understanding the series of crises in the Balkans in the early decades of the twentieth century that ultimately caused World War I. Before getting into the details, however, establish that World War I was about much more than the assassination of Archduke Ferdinand in Sarajevo. Emphasize that the main issue was the balance of power among the major European empires and their competition for colonies and resources on the world stage.

Having made this point, help students gain a clear view of the geography of south-central Europe. Explain that the Ottoman Empire, although in an advanced state of dissolution, maintained a band of territory from Constantinople westward to the Adriatic. To the south lay an independent Greece. To the north, on the Black Sea, lay an autonomous Bulgaria and an independent Romania. In the center and west of the peninsula lay the landlocked independent kingdom of Serbia, adjoined by Bosnia-Herzegovina, which had been administered by Austria since 1878 even though it legally belonged to Turkey. The growth of Slavic nationalism in the late nineteenth century convinced many of the subject peoples of the Austro-Hungarian Empire — including Bosnians, Croats, and Slovenes — to seek independence by joining Serbia, the center of Slavic nationalism and the site at which a new national state might be formed at the expense of the Austro-Hungarian Empire.

On June 28, 1914, in Sarajevo, a Bosnian Serb assassinated Archduke Ferdinand, heir to the throne of the Austro-Hungarian Empire, to proclaim his desire to break away from the empire. Austria-Hungary then declared war on Serbia, and the whole preexisting system of interlocking European alliances meant that the great European powers — Allied and Central — were suddenly at war with each other. In support of Austria-Hungary, Germany declared war on Russia and its ally France. Determined to support its Slavic brethren, Russia came to Serbia's aid. Great Britain declared war on Germany, and so forth. Thus the lines were drawn, and fighting began in August 1914.

You might want to note that the armistice did not end ethnic tensions in the Balkans. In 1918, the nation of Yugoslavia was created as the Kingdom of the Serbs, Croats, and Slovenes. It became a federal state with six republics in 1946 but increased demands for independence threatened Yugoslavia. The country split up in 1991 when four breakaway republics declared independence: Bosnia-Herzegovina, Croatia, Macedonia, and Slovenia. Ask students to reflect on how the ethnic tensions present at the turn of the twentieth century are manifested today.

2. Modern War

Most students have probably heard of "trench warfare" and, in fact, most will associate the term with World War I. Many will be eager to learn more about the military deadlock that at times paralyzed armies and was broken only by quick forays into "no-man's-land" and machine-gun fire. Be prepared to discuss, however briefly, the 1916 Battle on the Somme as an example of this trend in warfare. Contrast this battle, if you wish, with the "American style of war" introduced by General John J. Pershing. Also be prepared to discuss the new technological means that were used by both sides to break the military stalemate. The most successful example of technology was the German submarine, which completely flummoxed the Allied leaders as they attempted to draft policy response. You can also talk about chemical weapons (which so disgusted the international community that their use was later banned by the Geneva Convention of 1925), tanks, and airplanes. These technological advances helped transform World War I into the first modern war, fought for unlimited ends.

Using the Bedford Series in History and Culture and the Historians at Work Series: Suggestions

Consider assigning *Black Protest and the Great Migration: A Brief History with Documents*, by Eric Arnesen, when discussing the Great Migration, labor, racism, and black activism.

Lecture Supplements and Classroom Activities

Using Multimedia Sources in the Classroom

When discussing U.S. military involvement in World War I, consider showing your students the PBS documentary *The Great War: 1918*, which is particularly useful when covering how servicemen coped with the realities and horrors of modern warfare. When discussing the suffrage activists' use of Woodrow Wilson's rhetoric in World War I to secure women's right to vote, consider showing the PBS documentary *One Woman, One Vote*.

Historical Contingencies

Have your students speculate on what would have happened had William Jennings Bryan not resigned from the State Department. Remind them that his departure signaled the end of the last voice for neutrality in the Wilson administration. Would Bryan's continuation at the State Department have guaranteed a more neutral course for America? Could he have kept America out of the war? Or would his voice have been overwhelmed by pro-Allied leaders in the administration? What would have been the probable course of World War I had America stayed out of the fighting?

Classroom Activities

Consider setting up a debate on the pros and cons of the government's actions to suppress civil liberties during the Great War. Do national emergencies justify the suspension of constitutional guarantees and liberties? Must the Constitution be "bent" to be saved? You may want to circulate to your students the texts of the Espionage and Sedition Acts, found at Brigham Young University's Harold B. Lee Library Web site (<http://www.lib.byu.edu> — search the HBLL site for "Sedition Act"). Remind your students of the positions they took when discussing the Alien and "Sedition Acts" of 1798 and Lincoln's suspension of habeas corpus during the Civil War. You may want to close the debate by asking if Eugene V. Debs's speech (in the documents reader) posed a legitimate threat to the United States and its war efforts.

Using the Internet

In addition to the Web site mentioned above, you may want to direct students to "Photos of the Great War," an image archive hosted by the University of Kansas at <http://www.ukans.edu/~kansite/ww_one/photos/greatwar.htm>.

ASSESSING RESULTS
Multiple-Choice Questions

1. What three countries comprised the Triple Alliance?
   a. Great Britain, France, Russia
   b. Germany, Austria-Hungary, Italy
   c. Germany, Austria-Hungary, Russia
   d. Great Britain, France, United States

2. U.S. public support for entry into the war increased dramatically when the British leaked

secret information about a proposed alliance between Germany and Mexico in a document known as
   a. the Zimmermann telegram.
   b. the Wilhelm telegram.
   c. the white paper.
   d. the *Lusitania* file.

3. U.S. entry into the war transformed the domestic economy by
   a. opening an unprecedented number of industrial jobs to women and African Americans.
   b. allowing corporate leaders to crush the cause of labor by legally prohibiting the eight-hour day, the living wage, and the right to collective bargaining.
   c. curbing U.S. production and efficiency.
   d. instituting enormous wartime taxes that completely drained corporate profits.

4. Allied leaders opposed Wilson's Fourteen Points because the proposal jeopardized their postwar plans, which included all of the following except
   a. acquisition of enemy territory.
   b. reduction of arms.
   c. new colonial empires.
   d. war reparations.

5. At home, the Treaty of Versailles
   a. received firm support from America's German, Irish, and Italian populations, who believed that justice had finally been served.
   b. barely squeaked by the U.S. Senate in 1920.
   c. found its most vocal supporter in Senator Henry Cabot Lodge, who went on a grueling speaking tour to secure its passage.
   d. was defeated by the combined opposition of Republican irreconcilables and reservationists in the U.S. Senate.

6. Which of the following statements best characterizes the postwar United States?
   a. Prewar and wartime progressive campaigns — such as those intended to improve working conditions, public health, and educational opportunities — continued unabated.
   b. The end of war production and the flood of U.S. veterans on the labor market caused unemployment to rise sharply.
   c. Business embraced labor unions.
   d. Many people moved to the countries of their ethnic origin.

7. According to the *Historical Question* feature "What Did the War Mean to African Americans?,"
   a. black men, led by W. E. B. Du Bois, largely condemned World War I as a "white man's fight" and sought refuge as conscientious objectors in Canada.
   b. blacks achieved great advances because of the opportunities to prove their value as soldiers overseas and in the war industries at home.
   c. black soldiers experienced in military training and service the same level of discrimination that they encountered in civilian life.
   d. black soldiers unexpectedly received full recognition for their heroism on the battlefields of France.

8. According to Map 22.5, "Europe after World War I," which of the following nations was created by the Treaty of Versailles?
   a. Romania
   b. Poland
   c. Luxembourg
   d. Bulgaria

9. In a speech delivered in Canton, Ohio (in the documents reader), Eugene V. Debs blamed which of the following for U.S. entry into the war?
   a. German immigrants who served as spies for the Kaiser and fomented war fever in America
   b. German soldiers, whom Debs believed raped Belgian women as German troops moved to take over France
   c. Mexican officials who had pledged to ally their country with Axis powers in an attempt to overtake America
   d. capitalist warmongers

10. Many progressive reformers championed America's war efforts because
   a. mobilization ensured centralization of power and renewed government activism.
   b. mobilization ensured decentralization of power and a scale-down in government activism.
   c. they thought Wilson's domestic policy, New Freedom, was too bold and they recognized that Wilson would be forced to abandon it to fight the war.
   d. they wanted to remake German society in America's image.

11. Identify the correct sequence of historical events.
  a. Zimmermann telegram, armistice signed, Nineteenth Amendment ratified, prohibition begins
  b. *Lusitania* **sunk**, Zimmermann telegram, Bolshevik Revolution, Paris peace conference
  c. Nineteenth Amendment ratified, *Lusitania* sunk, Espionage Act passed, armistice signed
  d. Selective Service Act, Espionage Act, prohibition begins, Paris peace conference

PROPOSING MORE: Additional Readings

Mark Ellis, "'Closing Ranks' and 'Seeking Honors': W. E. B. Du Bois in World War I," *Journal of American History* 79, no. 1 (1992): 96–124.

Dimitri D. Lazo, "A Question of Loyalty: Robert Lansing and the Treaty of Versailles," *Diplomatic History* 9, no. 1 (1985): 35–53.

Ute Mehnert, "German Weltpolitik and the American Two-Front Dilemma: The 'Japanese Peril' in German-American Relations, 1904–1917," *Journal of American History* 82, no. 4 (1996): 1452–77.

J. Olinammentorp, "Not Precisely War Stories: Edith Wharton's Short Fiction from the Great War," *Studies in American Fiction* 23, no. 2 (1995): 153–72.

T. J. Roland, "Irish-American Catholics and the Quest for Respectability in the Coming of the Great War," *Journal of American Ethnic History* 15, no. 2 (1996): 3–31.

Answer Key to Multiple-Choice Questions: 1-b, 2-a, 3-a, 4-b, 5-d, 6-b, 7-c, 8-b, 9-d, 10-c, 11-b

FROM NEW ERA TO GREAT DEPRESSION 23

1920–1932

Outlining Chapters: Thematic Questions

I. What did Secretary of Commerce Herbert Hoover mean when he declared that America had entered a "new era"?

   A. How did the exigencies of postwar politics and the election of 1920 define the New Era? What did Warren G. Harding mean when he advocated a "return to normalcy"?

   B. How did the passage of the Eighteenth and Nineteenth Amendments reflect the nation's desire to return to normalcy?

   C. How did America's retreat from the world confirm America's commitment to normalcy? How did the Harding administration's anti-immigration policies and the trial of Nicola Sacco and Bartolomeo Vanzetti reflect antiforeign hysteria?

   D. How did the policies of the federal government during the Harding and Coolidge administrations and the rulings of the national judiciary support American business?

   E. How did Henry Ford's phenomenal success in the automotive industry confirm the nation's attitude toward business? What were the ways in which new techniques in specialization and new programs in scientific management furthered the growth of American business?

   F. How did American consumers respond to this growth?

II. What was the culture of the New Era, and what were its discontents?

   A. What were the ways in which the film industry contributed to the culture of the 1920s?

   B. Who were the great cultural icons of the age, and why was America fascinated by heroes?

   C. Why are the 1920s referred to as the Jazz Age? How did the Jazz Age influence the behavior of young women in America?

   D. Who were the "New Negroes"? In what ways did African Americans become more militant following World War I? How did they assert their militancy? Who were the writers and artists of the Harlem Renaissance, and how did they respond to the dominant culture of their era?

E. Who were the writers of the Lost Generation, and how did they respond to the dominant culture of their era?

III. How did rural America resist the encroachment of "modernity"?

 A. What factors allowed for the rebirth of the Ku Klux Klan, and how did the reorganized Klan differ from its predecessor?

 B. What were the issues surrounding the Scopes trial, and how did its outcome confirm rural America's resistance to modernism?

 C. Who was Al Smith, and how did America respond to his bid for presidency?

IV. What factors led to the Great Crash of 1929?

 A. What did Herbert Hoover believe to be the proper relationship between government and the economy? Why was the economy unstable in 1929? Why was Hoover blind to the economy's instability?

 B. Why did the stock market crash in 1929, and what were the crash's repercussions?

 C. How did Hoover respond to the crash? What were the limits of individualism in solving the crisis?

V. How did the Great Depression affect the lives of ordinary Americans?

 A. What was the human toll of the Great Depression?

 B. In what ways did wealthy Americans respond to the Great Depression? How did middle-class Americans respond?

 C. How did the American working class respond to the Great Depression?

Teaching with **The American Promise,** *Second Compact Edition: Lecture Strategies*

LECTURE 1
"Normalcy"

This lecture should convince students that many Americans in the 1920s longed for a retreat from the upheavals of the previous decade. When President Warren G. Harding promised the American people a "return to normalcy" in a 1920 campaign speech, he capitalized on the nation's weariness from a world war unprecedented in its destruction, the threats to the cherished democratic and capitalist order that socialism represented — especially in light of the 1917 Russian Revolution — and the intrusion of progressive re-

form in the workplace and the private sphere. Harding's speech carried considerable currency with much of the American public. Here you may wish to note that America's refusal to support Woodrow Wilson's coveted League of Nations confirmed that the nation had tired of worldly involvement and preferred to remain isolated from foreign affairs. Also mention that the passage of the Eighteenth and Nineteenth Amendments bolstered America's desire to return to normalcy. Have students discuss the *Historical Question* feature "Was Prohibition a Bad Idea?" to evaluate the effectiveness and the legacies of the "noble experiment." Note also that the nation's attitude had changed toward the government's involvement with American business. The Supreme Court's decisions to oppose any federal regulation regarding wages, hours, and conditions of labor suggested that the reform impulse of the earlier Progressive Era no longer lingered. Indeed, Calvin Coolidge's position on the proper relation between government and business (in the documents reader) outlines a theory held by many Americans. And for a time, America appeared to thrive under this return to normalcy.

Demonstrate that by 1922, the economy had recovered from its initial postwar slump and entered a period of vigorous growth. The phenomenal success of Henry Ford in the automotive industry suggested that the government's hands-off policy benefited American business. Moreover, the effectiveness of new techniques in specialization and scientific management, coupled with welfare capitalism, implied that American business could monitor itself without the interference of the federal government. Finally, American consumers' desire to purchase manufactured goods and partake in commercial pastimes — sports, amusement parks, movies, radio — illustrated their acceptance of this return to normalcy.

LECTURE 2
Critics of American Culture

This lecture makes clear to students that mainstream culture in the 1920s was not without its critics, and not everyone championed the return to normalcy. Start by covering the writers of the Lost Generation, such as Ernest Hemingway, who chafed at the crass commercialism of the consumer culture and spurned the conventionality and provinciality of American life, choosing instead to live in exile. You might then describe the disaffected youth of the 1920s who rejected the moral conventions of their parents, flaunting their newfound sexual freedom. The theories of Sigmund Freud became the lens through which many young people looked at the world, allowing for a frank and open appraisal of sexuality. You may then wish to cover the African American artists and writers of the Harlem Renaissance who celebrated their rich culture through poetry, art, music, theater, and dance. (Here, you can refer students to Aaron Douglas's painting *Noah's Ark*.) Ironically, many associated with the Harlem Renaissance depended on white patronage for their livelihoods. To suggest the depths to which some Americans resisted the dominant white culture, you might introduce Marcus Garvey's proclamations on the inability of that culture to embrace African Americans and his eventual call for blacks to return to Africa (in the documents reader).

Urban intellectuals were not the only ones who rejected modern American culture, however. At this point you should make it clear to students that many rural Americans also rejected the encroachment of modernity, but for different reasons. Discuss how the rebirth of the Ku Klux Klan, the Scopes trial, and the hostility leveled at presidential candidate Al Smith bespeak the degree to which some resisted the dominant culture. Be sure students read Imperial Wizard Hiram Evans's comments on the Klan's cross-regional appeal (in the documents reader).

LECTURE 3
The Causes of the Crash

Despite tremendous growth during the early 1920s, the nation's economy was fundamentally unstable. First, mention that while certain sectors of the economy grew during the decade, agriculture, the largest sector, remained weak. Farmers continued to receive low prices for their goods and suffered from chronic indebtedness. Overproduction and underconsumption, fueled by a massive imbalance of wealth, also contributed to the economy's instability. Make sure that students understand that not all Americans shared in the prosperity of the 1920s.

Next, demonstrate that an unstable international economy further contributed to the national economy's underlying weakness. European nations, unable to pay off the loans they incurred during the Great War, borrowed even more money from the United States to pay off their old loans and finance their trade. Moreover, the United States erected trade barriers, which pre-

vented foreign nations from selling their goods in the United States, which in turn hampered their ability to buy U.S. goods. Finally, make the point that the government's retreat from economic regulation also accounted for the economy's instability. Explain that an unregulated stock market allowed for buying on margin, which in turn encouraged average speculators to invest beyond their means. When nervous investors began unloading their overvalued stock, the price of stocks began to plummet. These speculators were forced to meet their margin loans, and the panic began that would result in the worst economic depression in American history. President Herbert Hoover's commitment to private philanthropy rather than governmental involvement did not spur the growth of the economy or restore Americans' confidence in it. The nation was ready for a different solution.

Anticipating Student Reactions: Common Misconceptions and Difficult Topics

1. *The United States Was Completely Isolationist in the 1920s*

Students may assume that America's disillusionment with Woodrow Wilson's idealistic rhetoric and its distrust of the League of Nations caused the United States to retreat from foreign affairs altogether during the 1920s. But although the isolationist mood swept across the nation in the years following World War I, the United States could hardly sever its ties with the rest of the world completely. It might be worth pointing out that American business leaders held foreign investments, the U.S. government earnestly endeavored to collect on war debts, and the nation maintained overseas possessions, especially in the Pacific. In addition, the United States signed a number of treaties in the 1920s. The Washington Disarmament Conference met in 1921; and delegates from the United States, Britain, Japan, France, and Italy signed the Five-Power Naval Treaty, which limited tonnage and construction of capital ships. The United States also signed the Four-Power Treaty (along with Britain, Japan, and France, agreeing to respect other nations' possessions in the Pacific and to refer disputes to an outside arbitration) and the Nine-Power Treaty (which formally pledged all signatories to support the Open Door principle first articulated at the turn of the century). In 1928, the United

States signed the Kellogg-Briand Pact, along with sixty-one other nations, which demanded all who signed to "condemn recourse to war . . . and renounce it as an instrument of national policy." Finally, the United States continued its tortured relations with Nicaragua and Mexico while attempting to establish a "good neighbor" policy with the rest of Latin America.

2. Modernism versus Fundamentalism

Because of the fame of the 1925 Scopes trial, many students may erroneously believe that Darwin's theory of evolution was the sole challenger to religious fundamentalism in the 1920s. In fact, a number of scientific theories gained popular currency in that decade. And although most ordinary Americans failed to grasp the complexities of Albert Einstein's theory of relativity, Max Planck's quantum theory, or Werner Heisenberg's uncertainty principle, most understood that previously held conceptions of absolutes no longer made sense. Many people reasoned, and many more feared, that traditional convictions and faiths had to be abandoned in light of new scientific findings.

3. The 1920s Was an Era of . . .

As the textbook chapter makes abundantly clear, the 1920s era has tended to invite and at the same time defy generalization. Take advantage of students' preconceived notions about the period to introduce them to the difficulties of defining an era, much less a decade. Many will be familiar with the 1920s as the Jazz Age, the Roaring Twenties, and so on. Using the discussion of competing myths and legends about the 1920s at the start of "The New Deal" section, plus any relevant illustrations in the textbook, ask students to consider which labels might be most accurate.

Using the Bedford Series in History and Culture and the Historians at Work Series: Suggestions

Consider assigning Gertrude Stein's *Three Lives*, edited by Linda Wagner-Martin, or Charles Chestnutt's *The Marrow of Tradition*, edited by Nancy Bentley and Sandra Gunning, both in the Cultural Editions series from Bedford's literature list, for literature that covers women and African Americans.

Lecture Supplements and Classroom Activities

Using Multimedia Sources in the Classroom

Perhaps because the 1920s has so captured the imagination of generations of Americans, there are a number of good documentaries about the period. When discussing woman suffrage, consider showing the PBS documentary *One Woman, One Vote*. Episode 17 of Bill Moyers's series *A Walk through the Twentieth Century*, entitled "The Twenties," offers a good overview of the period. The PBS documentary *Against the Odds: The Artists of the Harlem Renaissance* combines rare archival footage and oral histories to give viewers a firsthand account of the movement. The first few episodes of Ken Burns's series *Jazz* capture the early appeal the new American art form had on American audiences.

There are a number of Charlie Chaplin movies you can show to demonstrate the popular appeal of silent movies. *Modern Times* offers a provoking critique of the effect on human workers of scientific management and industrialism. To capture the transition in Hollywood from silent movies to "talkies," consider showing *The Jazz Singer* (1927). You might follow it up with the segment from the episode "1927: The Great Escape" from the *People's Century Series*, which covers the golden era of Hollywood and the film industry.

Historical Contingencies

Most students assume that the Great Crash of 1929 caused the Great Depression. To get them to consider the serious structural problems that existed in the American economy prior to Black Thursday, ask, "What if the stock market had not crashed in October 1929? Would the country still have had the Great Depression? Would it have occurred later? Would it have lasted as long?" These questions will also force students to consider the importance of the stock market as a symbol of American wealth — and the serious ramifications of the shattering of symbols.

Classroom Activities

Consider having students recreate courtroom scenes from the Scopes trial. Transcripts may be found at <http://www.law.umkc.edu/faculty/projects/ftrials/scopes/scopes.htm>. Have students explain why supporters of modernism believed the trial repudiated the claims of religious fundamentalism, while defenders of the faith claimed that the trial demonstrated defense attorney Clarence Darrow to be one of the century's most dangerous apostates.

Using the Internet

In addition to the site mentioned above, you may want to direct students to the Library of Congress's American Memory project's home page, <http://memory.loc.gov>. There, students will be able to find sound recordings from the 1920 election as well as WPA interviews on Americans' experiences in the Great Depression. (Direct students to click on "Collection Finder" from the home page.)

ASSESSING RESULTS
Multiple-Choice Questions

1. The Harding administration increasingly came under attack because of
   a. its inability to stem the tide of immigration and its acceptance of unprecedented numbers of foreigners into the United States.
   b. the wholesale corruption of several of its members.
   c. its refusal to champion the cause of American business through the establishment of protective tariffs.
   d. its propensity to become entangled in foreign alliances and international affairs.

2. Which of the following statements was true of the National Woman's Party in the 1920s?
   a. It was a moderate group opposed to the passage of the Equal Rights Amendment.
   b. It was solely concerned with educating women on political issues.
   c. It was a militant group dedicated to encouraging women to vote as a block and securing the passage of the Equal Rights Amendment.
   d. It was composed of upper-class women who wished to work with men on most issues.

3. According to President Calvin Coolidge, the proper relationship between government and business should
   a. assume the greatest possible independence between the two.
   b. stress mutual cooperation.
   c. allow for government to dictate the terms of commerce, thereby promoting monopolies.
   d. allow for business to influence politics, thereby promoting oligarchies.

4. During the early 1920s, many of America's top business leaders embraced
   a. free-market economics, which ensured the noninterference of the Supreme Court and federal government in business affairs.
   b. a revival of the piecework system of production, because it kept laborers from organizing.
   c. welfare capitalism, which allowed management to ease class tensions by increasing labor satisfaction.
   d. some form of socialism, as a way to alleviate intense labor union activity.

5. The writers of the Lost Generation
   a. found encouragement in the outcome of World War I and cheerily endorsed the U.S. position in the new world order.
   b. championed the values of rural, small-town life.
   c. found the vulgarity and crass materialism of the New Era appalling.
   d. tackled the social, political, economic, and theological issues that confronted modern American society.

6. The revived Ku Klux Klan of the 1920s
   a. never extended beyond the South.
   b. terrorized Jews, Catholics, and immigrants as well as blacks.
   c. attracted fewer than one million members over the course of the decade.
   d. limited its activities to rural areas.

7. Indicators of the U.S. economy's fundamental instability in the mid- to late 1920s included
   a. continued overconsumption of consumer goods by the majority of Americans.
   b. continued overproduction by the nation's leading manufacturers.
   c. an expanding agricultural sector, with skyrocketing crop prices.
   d. an unregulated stock market that encouraged buying on margin.

8. In response to the Great Crash of 1929 and the ensuing economic depression, President Herbert Hoover
   a. believed only massive infusions of foreign capital would pull the U.S. economy out of its downward cycle.
   b. advocated massive federal grants, or "doles," to ease suffering.
   c. remained wedded to the notion that voluntary relief efforts would end the depression.
   d. urged business leaders to curtail investment, cut production, and lay off workers.

9. The *Historical Question* feature on prohibition suggests that
   a. despite the eventual repeal of the Eighteenth Amendment, the "noble experiment" succeeded in encouraging a steady decline in alcohol consumption in the United States.
   b. the dismal failure of the "noble experiment" has discouraged American politicians from prohibiting the sale or use of any mind-altering substance in the United States
   c. getting high is a uniquely American phenomenon.
   d. the ghost of the "noble experiment" has made it difficult for American politicians to develop a coherent, consistent policy on alcohol and drug use.

10. According to Map 23.2, "Auto Manufacturing," which of the following regions was the center of the new automobile industry?
    a. the Pacific Northwest
    b. the South
    c. the Midwest
    d. the Northeast

11. According to the document covering Marcus Garvey's Universal Negro Improvement Association (in the documents reader), the UNIA
    a. stressed accommodation with the white race to improve social conditions for African Americans.
    b. suggested that working-class African Americans and whites should form business cooperatives to shift economic power from the wealthy to the laboring class.
    c. helped African Americans gain economic and political independence entirely outside of white society.
    d. bemoaned the lack of cultural achievements in the African American community.

12. Identify the correct sequence of historical events and figures.
    a. Black Thursday, Scopes trial, prohibition goes into effect, immigration quotas
    b. Nineteenth Amendment ratified, Harding elected president, Sacco and Vanzetti executed, Coolidge elected president
    c. Harding elected president, Coolidge elected president, Scopes trial, Black Thursday
    d. prohibition goes into effect, Hoover elected president, Sacco and Vanzetti executed, Marcus Garvey organizes the UNIA

PROPOSING MORE: Additional Readings

H. M. Gitelman, "Welfare Capitalism Reconsidered," *Labor History* 33, no. 1 (1992): 5–31.

M. Honey, "Survival and Song: Women Poets of the Harlem Renaissance," *Women's Studies: An Interdisciplinary Journal* 16, nos. 3–4 (1989): 293–315.

P. Ling, "Sex and the Automobile in the Jazz Age," *History Today* 39 (1989): 18–24.

G. H. Nash, "An American Epic: Herbert Hoover and Belgian Relief in World War I," *Prologue: Quarterly of the National Archives* 21, no. 1 (1989): 75–86.

C. F. Williams, "William M. Jardine and the Foundations for Republican Farm Policy, 1925–1929," *Agricultural History* 70, no. 2 (1996): 216–32.

Answer Key to Multiple-Choice Questions: 1-b, 2-c, 3-a, 4-a, 5-c, 6-b, 7-d, 8-c, 9-d, 10-c, 11-c, 12-c

THE NEW DEAL EXPERIMENT 24

1932–1939

*O*utlining Chapters: Thematic Questions

I. Why has Franklin Delano Roosevelt been termed "a patrician in government"?
 A. What factors influenced Roosevelt's early political career? What role did Roosevelt believe the government should play in domestic economic affairs? What issues shaped Roosevelt's tenure as governor of New York? How did Roosevelt react to the stock market crash? What were his prescriptions for the Great Depression?
 B. What issues shaped the presidential campaign of 1932? How did Roosevelt's campaign strategy differ from that of Hoover? What did the election results signal?

II. What specific New Deal measures were taken during Roosevelt's first one hundred days in office?
 A. Who were the New Dealers?
 B. What specific measures dealt with banking and finance reform?
 C. What specific measures dealt with relief and conservation reform?
 D. What agricultural initiatives passed the New Deal Congress?
 E. What efforts were taken to hasten industrial recovery?

III. What challenges did supporters of the New Deal face?
 A. Who led the resistance to business reform, and why?
 B. Who led the reaction against the New Deal farm program, and why?
 C. What attacks of the New Deal came from the political fringes? How successful were these critiques in capturing the imagination of the American public?

IV. Why has the Second New Deal been linked to the rise of the welfare state in the United States?
 A. What measures were taken to provide relief to the unemployed?
 B. How did the Second New Deal empower labor?
 C. What measures were taken to provide for the elderly? How did Roosevelt reform the tax structure?
 D. In what ways did Roosevelt broaden the New Deal coalition?

V. When did the New Deal enter its final phase? Why did it ultimately reach a deadlock?
 A. What issues shaped the election of 1936? How did the Democratic Party fare?

B. Why did Roosevelt wish to alter the composition of the Supreme Court? Why has this court-packing scheme been considered a tactical blunder?

C. Why did the economy enter a recession during Roosevelt's second term? What did he do to correct the economic downturn? What was the reaction of the Republican opposition?

D. What initiatives comprised the last of the New Deal reforms? What ultimately signaled the end of the New Deal?

Teaching with The American Promise, *Second Compact Edition: Lecture Strategies*

LECTURE 1
FDR and the First New Deal

In this lecture, impress on your students the optimism Franklin Delano Roosevelt conveyed to the American people during the Great Depression. When FDR entered the White House in 1932, he was already committed to the belief that the government's prime role was to respond to the social needs of the country and not to defend abstract principles. Here you may wish to point out Map 24.2, "Electoral Shift, 1928–1932," to demonstrate the resonance of Roosevelt's message. Unlike his predecessor, FDR was eager to try new remedies to ease the nation's economic plight. Draw students' attention to the 1932 campaign speech FDR delivered to the San Francisco Commonwealth Club (in the documents reader), which outlines his theory for an activist government. It is important to remind students, however, that FDR was firmly committed to democracy and capitalism, and he harbored no desire to supplant America's traditional institutions with radical ones.

As president, Roosevelt signed into legislation an unprecedented fifteen pieces of major legislation during his first one hundred days in office alone, all designed to counter the most wrenching effects of the depression. To help students who feel overwhelmed by all the legislation, you can categorize the material and then hit the highlights, always stressing that planning and coordination were the unifying elements of this new legislation. Refer them to Table 24.1, "Major Legislation of the New Deal's First Hundred Days." Roosevelt tackled banking and finance reform first, endorsing the Emergency Banking Act and the Securities Act. He then sought to provide relief to those with no means of support, creating the Federal Emergency Relief Administration, the Civil Works Administration, and the Civilian Conservation Corps. To meet the crisis in agriculture, FDR created the Tennessee Valley Authority (TVA) and signed into law the Agricultural Adjustment Act and the Farm Credit Act. (Map 24.3, "The Tennessee Valley Authority," shows the area affected by the TVA.) Finally, he turned his attention to industrial recovery and created the National Recovery Administration (NRA).

FDR definitely met the challenge head-on. To give students a good idea of the hard times Americans faced and the expectations and confidence many placed in the Roosevelt administration, have them take a look at the letters from the working people to FDR and his secretary of labor, Frances Perkins (in the documents reader).

LECTURE 2
Challenges to the New Deal and FDR's Response

This lecture conveys that the president faced a barrage of criticism for his programs. Critics on both the right and left attacked FDR's New Deal for failing to address the country's needs effectively. Demonstrate that many within the business community opposed the TVA and the NRA, for example, because they believed the government had no right to interfere in the economy. They accused New Deal initiatives of ushering in socialism and betraying basic constitutional guarantees of freedom and individualism. Here you will wish to demonstrate that the Supreme Court concurred; in 1935, it ruled that the NRA violated the interstate commerce clause of the Constitution. Many on the left, however, believed that the New Deal did not do enough to ease the plight of average Americans. Be sure to draw students' attention to Herbert Hoover's and Minnie Hardin's criticisms of the New Deal (in the documents reader).

You can then go on to cover three of Roosevelt's most vociferous critics. Father Charles Coughlin, a Detroit priest and radio talk-show host, advocated the confiscation and redistribution of the nation's wealth to ease the lives of the worthy poor. Dr. Francis Townsend, a public health official from California who chastised Roosevelt for not dealing with the problems of the nation's poor, devised an Old Age Revolving Pension plan and started his own movement. FDR received his most serious threat from Louisiana politician Huey Long, who advocated a steeply progressive tax known as the "Share Our Wealth" program. You may wish to have the class discuss the details of Long's plan (in the documents reader). Demonstrate that the threats levied against the New Deal forced the Roosevelt administration to shore up its position. Buoyed by strong results in the 1934 congressional election, the Roosevelt administration moved ahead with its Second New Deal. End your lecture by emphasizing the differences between the first and second agendas, explaining how the Second New Deal moved away from the central economic planning of the First New Deal and, in response to its critics, concentrated instead on meeting the needs of various social groups. The Works Progress Administration (WPA) provided work for the unemployed, the National Labor Relations Act (NLRA) secured decent working conditions for laborers, and the Social Security Act helped alleviate the plight of the hard-hit elderly.

LECTURE 3
The End of the New Deal

Begin this lecture by mentioning that FDR, fortified by a stunning victory in the presidential election of 1936, turned his attention to removing the remaining obstacles to his New Deal reform. Thwarted by the Supreme Court, which had ruled eleven New Deal measures unconstitutional, FDR sought to change the makeup of the bench by appointing sympathetic jurists. A justice's change in opinion and the retirement of four other justices gave FDR a chance to reshape the Supreme Court so that it would never again strike down a piece of New Deal legislation. Mention that although FDR secured the support of the Supreme Court, his scheme riled Republicans and Southern Democrats to such a frenzy that they combined forces to obstruct additional reform. To make matters worse for Roosevelt, he assumed (incorrectly) that the reviving economy had completely recovered and therefore reversed a number of strategies, causing the economy to lose momentum. Make it clear that only the infusion of Keynesian economic theory into New Deal policy could have reinvigorated the national economy. Roosevelt's faith in deficit spending reaffirmed, it looked as if FDR was heading toward the Third New Deal, but opposition grew,

especially from the right. New initiatives, such as the Farm Security Administration, ran up against the opposition of major farm organizations, were starved for funds, and eventually petered out. In 1938, major New Deal reform initiatives ended when Roosevelt signed the Fair Labor Standards Act into law. The administration then shifted its attention to foreign policy and the threat of world war. As the nation readied its defenses, Roosevelt declared that he had ceased to be "Dr. New Deal" and had become "Dr. Win the War." End your lecture with a discussion of the possibilities and limits of New Deal reform. Have students consider the ways in which the New Deal articulated the promise of America and the ways in which it failed to live up to that promise. Students may want to discuss, for example, the New Deal's unwillingness or inability to tackle racism in America effectively.

Anticipating Student Reactions: Common Misconceptions and Difficult Topics

1. What Was the Works Progress Administration?

Students may ask about the specific type of projects undertaken by the WPA, which put unemployed actors, writers, and artists to work. You may wish to bring in examples of the interviews that WPA workers conducted with ex-slaves, immigrants, and people who lived in the rural South. Many of these interviews are available online from the Library of Congress at <http://memory.loc.gov/ammem/wpaintro/wpahome.html>. Show students one of the state, regional, or city guidebooks that celebrated American life, or play a brief passage from Aaron Copland's *Rodeo*, which the composer wrote under WPA sponsorship. Mention the productions of the Federal Theater Project (FTP), an organization sponsored by the WPA that promised "free, adult, uncensored theater." For the four years of its existence, the FTP reached an estimated audience of twenty-five to thirty million people. Show students the poster and photo of the opening night of one of the most successful FTP productions, Shakespeare's *Macbeth*, produced by John Houseman, directed by Orson Welles, and featuring an African American cast. *Swing Mikado*, a jazz rendition of the Gilbert and Sullivan operetta, also proved quite popular with depression-weary audiences. These examples should help not only to clarify the types of projects undertaken by the agency but also to emphasize the ways in which the WPA celebrated American culture and made it more accessible to the average American.

2. Radicalism

Many students may question the degree to which Americans turned to radical ideologies during the depression. You will want to remind them that while the president and members of his administration remained fully convinced of the viability of America's political and economic institutions, many citizens, especially intellectuals, and especially during the early years of the depression, did indeed investigate the possibility of radical change to cure America's ills. For those who seemed particularly disenchanted with traditional paths of American reform, the Soviet Union provided an attractive model against which American ideals and institutions could be measured. The Russian experiment proved particularly appealing to progressives enamored of planning and scientific investigation. But the Soviets' brief flirtation with Hitler's fascist state when the two countries signed a nonaggression pact in 1939 caused many of these intellectuals to reevaluate their own commitment to the Soviet model for the American experience. In any case, most Americans felt that under Roosevelt's New Deal their concerns were at the very least heard and addressed, and so they maintained their faith in traditional American institutions.

Using the Bedford Series in History and Culture and the Historians at Work Series: Suggestions

When discussing challenges to FDR's New Deal, especially after the fallout of the court-packing plan, you may find *Confronting Southern Poverty in the Great Depression: The Report on the Economic Conditions of the South with Related Documents,* edited by David L. Carlton and Peter A. Coclanis, a useful tool. The report details Roosevelt's attempts to oust conservative Democratic opponents to his programs in the 1938 congressional elections. The supplementary oral interviews offer evidence on the wrenching effects of poverty during the depression. Richard Polenberg's *The Era of Franklin D. Roosevelt, 1932–1945: A Brief History with Documents,* offers students a fine overview of the Roosevelt administration.

Lecture Supplements and Classroom Activities

Using Multimedia Sources in the Classroom

There are a number of good documentaries about the Great Depression. *After the Crash,* distributed by Blackside, Inc., covers three protest groups — the bonus army, farmers in Arkansas, and autoworkers in Detroit — during the early years of the depression. *America Lost and Found,* distributed by Direct Cinema Limited, offers a portrait of Americans as they experienced the Great Depression. *Union Maids,* by New Day Films, tells the story of three women labor activists during the 1930s. *The Uprising of 1934,* directed by acclaimed documentarian George Stoney, looks at the 1934 North Carolina mill strikes. Episode 5, "Shadow Ball," of Ken Burns's PBS *Baseball* series covers baseball's desperate attempt to survive during the Great Depression. The seven-part PBS series *The Great Depression* offers a many-faceted look at the nation's worst economic disaster. There are also a number of biographical documentaries that are worth showing: *FDR* and *Father Coughlin: Radio Priest,* produced by PBS; *Huey Long,* available from Direct Cinema Limited; and *Harry Hopkins: At FDR's Side,* distributed through the Educational Film Center.

To convey Hollywood's attempt to bolster sagging spirits during the depression, you might consider showing any of a number of popular films. Marx Brothers comedies; Busby Berkeley's musicals; *The Thin Man* series, starring William Powell and Myrna Loy; and the Preston Sturges comedy *Sullivan's Travels* all offer escapist fare. *Scarface* (1932) and *Public Enemy* (1931) offer insight into America's fascination with outlaws during the early years of the depression. (You might follow segments of either of these films with "The Road to Rock Bottom," the portion of the PBS series on the Great Depression that covers the exploits of Pretty Boy Floyd. If so, then draw your students' attention to Woody Guthrie's "The Ballad of Pretty Boy Floyd," whose lyrics are printed in the textbook in Chapter 23.) *The Grapes of Wrath* (1940) and *Mr. Smith Goes to Washington* (1939) offer examples of popular social commentary films that suggested that the people will triumph. Finally, consider showing scenes from *Gone with the Wind* (1939). Most of your students will be familiar with this classic. Remind them that although the book's story concerns the Civil War, the movie was filmed in the 1930s. Ask them to think about how the burned-over and ravaged landscape of the war-torn South may have had a parallel in the depression landscape.

Historical Contingencies

What if Huey Long had been elected president in 1936? Have students note that many saw Long as the only candidate in the 1936 presidential race who offered radical solutions to the nation's ills. Would his "Share Our Wealth" plan have been enacted had he lived? Would he have truly offered meaningful relief to the nation's underclass? What would America have looked like had Long's vision been realized?

Classroom Activities

Consider playing selections of Woody Guthrie's music, available from the Smithsonian's Folkways Recordings, and have students connect the recordings to the letters written by ordinary Americans to FDR and members of his New Deal cabinet. What sentiments do these documents express?

Using the Internet

As mentioned above (see "Anticipating Student Reactions"), the Library of Congress site contains extensive examples of WPA interviews. For one particular aspect of the New Deal era, direct students to the Social Security Administration's site on Father Charles Coughlin and his National Union for Social Justice. Go to <http://www.ssa.gov/history/cough.html>, which contains a brief overview of Coughlin as well as texts and audioclips from selected broadcasts, 1934–1935.

ASSESSING RESULTS
Multiple-Choice Questions

1. Herbert Hoover's reaction to the Bonus Expeditionary Army in 1932
   a. demonstrated the president's predilection for relying on government handouts to solve the country's economic woes.
   b. reaffirmed his unwillingness to use military force to quell domestic disturbances.
   c. proved that the president was willing to discredit those whom he perceived threatened his chance at reelection.
   d. showed that he was genuinely sympathetic to the plight of the unemployed veterans.

2. Franklin D. Roosevelt's approach to the stock market crash and the ensuing Great Depression during his tenure as governor of New York was characterized by

   a. an abiding belief that the government had much to learn from a socialized economy.
   b. a profound distrust of the basic framework of American society.
   c. a desire to limit government regulation.
   d. a wish to shore up the existing social and economic order, not to subvert it.

3. The term "Roosevelt Revolution" refers to
   a. a fundamental realignment of voter allegiance, comprised of farmers, industrial workers, white-collar workers, African Americans, women, and intellectuals, who voted for FDR and the Democratic Party.
   b. the unprecedented number of socialist candidates who rode FDR's coattails into office following the 1932 election.
   c. the sweeping socialist-inspired reforms FDR initiated during his first one hundred days in office.
   d. the derisive epithet used by Hoover to warn American voters of what lay ahead of them if they elected FDR to the White House in 1932.

4. Which of the following initiatives was implemented by FDR during his first one hundred days in office?
   a. finance reform and emergency relief
   b. the WPA and equal opportunity laws
   c. procedural changes to Supreme Court appointee and presidential election processes
   d. Social Security and tax reform

5. The "Share Our Wealth" plan, designed in opposition to New Deal relief plans, was devised by
   a. Father Charles Coughlin.
   b. Francis Townsend.
   c. Huey Long.
   d. Harry Hopkins.

6. African Americans in the Great Depression
   a. made tremendous economic, social, and political gains because of FDR's willingness to risk opposition from white, conservative segregationists in the South.
   b. experienced more symbolic victories than actual ones.
   c. finally won a federal antilynching law.
   d. saw their infant mortality and life expectancy rates finally approach the rates for whites.

7. FDR's Second New Deal was marked by
   a. unchanging opposition by the Supreme Court.

b. friendlier relations with business.

c. a slowdown in the initiation and passage of New Deal legislation.

d. a gridlock between the federal government and a Republican-dominated Congress.

8. The economic theory that bolstered New Deal policies by stating that only government intervention could pump enough money into the system to revive production, boost consumption, and restore prosperity was devised by
   a. Adam Smith.
   b. Huey Long.
   c. John Maynard Keynes.
   d. Alan Greenspan.

9. The chapter-opening artifact, a souvenir needle book from FDR's 1932 campaign,
   a. depicts the changes Roosevelt claimed his New Deal would achieve once he was elected.
   b. illustrates FDR's campaign pledge that he would move workers from hazardous and unproductive factory labor to more economically viable and healthful agricultural labor.
   c. illustrates FDR's belief that economic recovery was possible only with more women working outside the home.
   d. celebrates the nation's ongoing economic recovery in many sectors.

10. Identify the correct sequence of historical events and figures.

   a. Bonus Expeditionary Army, Huey Long assassinated, FDR reelected, Dr. Francis Townsend devises pension scheme

   b. New Deal's first one hundred days, Wagner Act passed, Fair Labor Standards Act passed, court-packing scheme

   c. Bonus Expeditionary Army, Indian Reorganization Act adopted, Huey Long assassinated, FDR reelected

   d. Fair Labor Standards Act passed, Wagner Act passed, FDR reelected, CIO founded

Proposing More: Additional Readings

Alan Brinkley, "The Antimonopoly Ideal and the Liberal State: The Case of Thurman Arnold," *Journal of American History* 80, no. 2 (1993): 557–79.

B. Q. Cannon, "'Keep on a Goin': Life and Social Interaction in a New Deal Farm Labor Camp," *Agricultural History* 70, no. 1 (1996): 1–32.

Alan Draper, "The New Southern Labor History Revisited: The Success of the Mine, Mill, and Smelter Workers Union in Birmingham, 1934–1938," *Journal of Southern History* 62, no. 1 (1996): 87–108.

F. Jeansonne, "The Apotheosis of Huey Long," *Biography: An Interdisciplinary Quarterly* 12, no. 4 (1989): 283–301.

David Montgomery, "Labor and the Political Leadership of New Deal America," *International Review of Social History* 39, no. 3 (1994): 335–60.

Answer Key to Multiple-Choice Questions: 1-c, 2-d, 3-a, 4-a, 5-c, 6-b, 7-a, 8-c, 9-d, 10-c

THE SECOND WORLD WAR 25

1939–1945

Outlining Chapters: Thematic Questions

I. What foreign policy dilemmas confronted the United States during the interwar years?
   A. Why has FDR been termed a "reluctant isolationist"?
   B. What was the Good Neighbor Policy, and how did the United States use it?
   C. What price did the United States pay for its noninvolvement in world affairs? What events convinced FDR that America needed to play a stronger role than it had in stemming aggression in Europe and Asia?

II. What events led to the onset of war?
   A. In what ways did Nazi aggression lead to war in Europe?
   B. When did America abandon its neutral policy in favor of becoming the "arsenal of democracy"? How did the election of 1940 suggest to FDR that he had a mandate to continue his pro-British policies?
   C. When did war come to America, and why?

III. What were the crucial military and diplomatic events during 1941–1943?
   A. How was the United States able to turn the tide of the war in the Pacific?
   B. What were the prime military and diplomatic objectives in the European campaign?

IV. What influence did the war have on American society?
   A. How did the war aid the U.S. economy?
   B. How did Roosevelt's Republican opponents use the war years to turn back New Deal reform? Why was Roosevelt able to triumph in the election of 1944, despite growing opposition to his domestic reform policies?
   C. What role did U.S. women play in the war effort? What role did children play? How did the war alter the structure of the American family?
   D. In what ways did prejudice creep into the U.S. war effort? How did racial tensions lead to a riot between U.S. servicemen and Chicanos in Los Angeles? What role did African Americans play in the war effort? What was the "Double V" campaign? In what ways did Japanese Americans suffer during World War II? What role did gays and lesbians have in the military?

E. What was the U.S. policy regarding refugees from the Holocaust?

V. What military and diplomatic events contributed to Allied military victory during 1943–1945?

    A. What were the key events that transpired from the Allied invasion of Normandy to eventual German surrender?

    B. What factors contributed to U.S. victory over Japan?

    C. Why was the atomic bomb developed? Why did Harry S. Truman decide to drop the bomb on Japan?

Teaching with The American Promise, *Second Compact Edition: Lecture Strategies*

LECTURE 1

U.S. Foreign Policy during the Interwar Years

Start this lecture by conveying Roosevelt's reluctance to abandon America's course of isolationism. Make the point that although FDR entered the White House just as a rising tide of violent nationalism was sweeping across Asia and Europe, he continued the course of isolationism that the country had pursued since the 1920s. Three main factors contributed to FDR's commitment to isolationism. First, the economic exigencies of the depression made the cries of isolationists seem plausible. Second, the findings of the Nye Senate Committee — which concluded that bankers, financiers, and munitions manufacturers goaded the United States into World War I — convinced most Americans of the virtues of isolationism. Third, to ensure the support of the isolationists in Congress for New Deal initiatives, FDR abandoned his inclination to help the League of Nations check the fascist aggression of Japan, Italy, Spain, and Germany. Make clear to your students that, as early as 1934, FDR and American policymakers were well aware of the dangers the Nazis posed and of their plans to dominate Europe, if not the entire world. In any case, the United States signed a series of neutrality acts between 1935 and 1937. You might also refer students to the opening vignette on America Firster Charles Lindbergh to reinforce the point that, even as late as the early 1940s, millions of Americans shared Lindbergh's belief that America should stay out of the war.

Next, explain that FDR's commitment to neutrality ended as German troops marched into Poland and France, and England declared war. FDR immediately set out to persuade Congress to repeal the arms embargo. Congress abandoned neutrality only gradually, first granting selected belligerents the right to buy U.S. weapons on a cash-and-carry basis, and later granting lend-lease privileges to Great Britain, and later still to the Soviet Union.

You may wish to close this lecture by demonstrating that although the United States teetered on the brink of war in Europe, it clashed first with Japan. As the United States increasingly placed pressure on Japan's economic and territorial ambitions, a military clique tightened its control in Japan and developed a plan to launch a devastating attack on U.S. bases in the Pacific, hoping that the United States would sign a peace treaty and leave Japan alone to pursue its goals. Although the United States was aware that a threat loomed, it was completely unprepared for the December 7, 1941, bombing of Pearl Harbor. You might have your students turn to the photograph of the battleship *West Virginia* on fire after the bombing to give them a sense of the devastation inflicted. You might also discuss FDR's war message to Congress, along with Japanese American Monica Sone's reminiscences of Pearl Harbor and the subsequent crackdown she and her Seattle community experienced prior to internment (in the documents reader). Congress declared war on December 8, and three days later, fulfilling their obligations under the Tripartite Pact, Germany and Italy declared war on the United States.

LECTURE 2

The Front Line, 1941–1945

This lecture falls into two parts and will work especially well if you orient your students visually by referring frequently to Map 25.3, "The European Theater of World War II, 1942–1945, and Map 25.4, "The Pacific Theater of World War II, 1941–1945." The first part of your lecture should cover the initial phase of the war, 1941–1943, during which the United States focused on stemming the tide of Japanese aggression in the Pacific and on saving Great Britain and the Soviet Union from Nazi defeat in Europe. The United States turned its attention first to Japan, which had already captured Guam, Wake Island, Singapore, and the Philippines by the summer of

1942. By April of that year, the United States was ready to strike back, choosing first to display its military might by launching a bombing raid on Tokyo, and then launching a two-pronged attack designed to recapture the Philippines and lesser islands in the mid-Pacific. American forces scored tremendous victories on land and sea and turned their attention to defeating Japanese forces in their homeland. In Europe, U.S. forces first had to contend with the German attempt to starve Great Britain into submission. The United States shipped massive amounts of supplies to the besieged country, and by 1943 the Allies could focus on stopping Nazi aggression on the European continent. By 1943, then, the defensive phase of the war was over.

The second part of your lecture should cover the final phase of the war, 1943–1945, during which the United States and its allies went on the offensive, facing the daunting task of battling Germany and Japan on their own territory. Germany remained the top priority. In an effort to divert the Nazi troops that threatened to overtake the Soviet Union, Allied troops struck at North Africa, Sicily, and finally Italy. By June of 1944, the Allies were prepared to launch a "true" second front; they landed on the beaches of Normandy, liberated France, and began their final assault on Hitler's Germany. In the Pacific, Allied troops moved slowly, island by island, toward Japan, and by June of 1945, the United States had all but secured its victory. While meeting with the Soviets in the summer of 1945, Truman learned that the United States had successfully tested an atomic weapon. Eager to end the war in the Pacific, Truman ordered bombs dropped on Hiroshima and Nagasaki. Tokyo surrendered on September 2, 1945. Have the class discuss the letters from soldiers stationed overseas (in the documents reader) to convey the experience of the combatants.

LECTURE 3
The Home Front

Although no battles were fought on American soil, the transformation of a peaceful society to one at war changed the nation. Total war meant the total mobilization of the home front to serve the needs of those fighting overseas. Start by concentrating on the ways in which the conversion to war production lifted the nation out of the depression. Explain that not only did the factories, military bases, power plants, and transportation facilities thrive but agriculture prospered as well. The booming economy and the labor shortages engendered by the more than fifteen million adults who served in the military resulted in new levels of prosperity for American workers. Moreover, new workers entered the labor force, as African Americans and women filled positions vacated by the men who served. Here you will want to discuss the tremendously powerful icon of "Rosie the Riveter" and you may wish to draw your students' attention to the photograph of the female defense worker (tell them not to look at the caption, and see if anyone can figure out that the woman is Marilyn Monroe). Other segments of society were mobilized as well, as the government enforced rationing and price and wage restrictions, and encouraged folks to buy savings bonds, grow victory gardens, and collect scrap metal — all to aid the war effort. Here you may wish to point out the "We're Scrappers Too" poster as an example of clever and interesting propaganda exhorting citizens to support the war effort.

You will also need to demonstrate that the war against Nazism brought America's racial prejudices to the forefront. Although most Americans repudiated Hitler's plans for the "master race," few were in favor of lifting the bar against Jewish immigration into the United States. African Americans waged the "Double V" campaign (whose motto was "Democracy: Victory at Home, Victory Abroad"), though not always successfully. Japanese Americans suffered a wholesale attack on their civil liberties, as tens of thousands were imprisoned in remote internment camps. Here you may wish to have your students discuss the documents on Japanese internment presented in the *Documenting the American Promise* feature of the chapter. In the end, you will want to emphasize that no segment of society escaped the impact of World War II.

Anticipating Student Reactions: Common Misconceptions and Difficult Topics

1. Americans and the Holocaust

Be prepared to answer questions about U.S. policy toward European Jews and the Holocaust. Certainly Hitler's hatred of the Jews was well known in the United States by the late 1930s. In 1938, Roosevelt called a conference of thirty-two nations at Evian-les-Bains, France, in response to

Hitler's burning of Munich's Great Synagogue and subsequent deportation of fifteen thousand Jews to the Buchenwald concentration camp, wishing to discuss what countries could accept Jews as émigrés. Roosevelt maintained that the depression and immigration quotas prohibited the United States from taking more than a token number. Only Holland, already densely populated, agreed to take Jews in large numbers. Capitalizing on the world's reluctance to harbor refugees, the Nazis in late 1938 launched *Kristallnacht* (a night of attacks against Jews throughout Germany) and Hitler devised the "final solution" in 1941. The Germans tried to hide reports of their plan, but news stories leaked to the United States as early as 1942, and the Roosevelt administration confirmed that two million Jews had already been exterminated. U.S. newspapers continued to bury stories of the atrocities in back pages, and the United States did little to bomb the railways running to the concentration camps' gas chambers or to allow more Jews into the United States.

Historians have suggested a number of reasons for U.S. reluctance to act. First, Americans were hostile to any immigration into the United States during the depression, fearing competition on the already drained economy. Anti-Semitism fueled efforts to keep Jews out of the United States. Second, the stories of the Holocaust seemed too horrible to be true. Finally, the Jewish community itself was divided on the issue, as Zionists wished to give priority to the creation of a Jewish state in Palestine and others feared alienating the already anti-Semitic State Department. Be sure to refer students to Varian Fry's article on the Holocaust (in the documents reader).

2. The Decision to Drop the Atomic Bomb

Also be prepared to answer questions on Harry S. Truman's decision to drop the atomic bomb in Japan. U.S. efforts to develop an atomic weapon began in 1939 when two refugees, Albert Einstein and Leo Szilard, told Roosevelt that it would be possible to develop such a weapon. By the time the Japanese bombed Pearl Harbor, American, British, and Canadian scientists had already begun work on the project. Information suggested that German scientists were working on a similar project, and American scientists assumed from the beginning that the bomb had to be built and ready to use. Germany surrendered before it finished its bomb and before the United States had successfully tested its own. But while meeting at Potsdam, Germany, to discuss the shape of the postwar world, Truman learned of the ex-plosion at the Alamogordo Air Force Base in New Mexico. Truman's secret Interim Committee of scientists and government officials had originally considered how the bomb could be used to manage the Soviet Union. If the bomb were dropped on Japan, certainly the Soviet Union would not be needed to fulfill its promise of joining the United States in the war against Japan and would thus be prevented from gaining a foothold in Korea and Manchuria. Truman also wanted to save American lives. Intelligence reports suggested that the invasion of Japan scheduled for the fall of 1945 would be a bloodbath. Truman favored using the bomb if it would mean saving American lives. Finally, calling forth memories of the Japanese attack on Pearl Harbor, Truman allayed any moral qualms U.S. officials may have harbored about dropping the bomb.

Using the Bedford Series in History and Culture and the Historians at Work Series: Suggestions

Because students will undoubtedly question America's policy toward Jewish refugees from the Holocaust, consider assigning *America Views the Holocaust, 1933–1945: A Brief Documentary History*, edited by Robert H. Abzug, which chronicles America's reaction to reports concerning the persecution of Jews during the 1930s and 1940s. This volume reinforces the point made in the text and the documents reader that FDR's administration was aware of Hitler's "final solution" well before Allied troops liberated the death camps.

To give students more background on the war in the Pacific, you might consider assigning *Pearl Harbor and the Coming of the Pacific War: A Brief History with Documents and Essays*, edited by Akira Iriye, which offers both the immediate and a larger global context for the attack.

Lecture Supplements and Classroom Activities

Using Multimedia Sources in the Classroom

There are a number of good documentaries about the interwar years and World War II. Episode 4 of *The People's Century*, "1919: The Lost Peace," gives a good overview of the failure of the Treaty of Versailles to end all wars and the rise of fascism in Europe. *The Good Fight: The Abraham Lin-*

coln Brigade, distributed by First Run/Icarus Films, demonstrates that although FDR maintained a position of neutrality during the 1930s, many Americans considered the rise of fascism under Franco in Spain intolerable and volunteered to fight for the Spanish republicans. You might also consider showing one of the episodes from Frank Capra's series for the U.S. army, *Why We Fight,* which was designed to give American servicemen a crash course in the virtues of American democracy and the evils of German, Italian, and Japanese fascism and militarism. You might follow this with the episode from *A Walk through the Twentieth Century with Bill Moyers,* titled "World War II: The Propaganda Battle," in which Moyers interviews Capra and his German counterpart Fritz Hippler. PBS has produced a number of documentaries on strategic battles: *Pearl Harbor: Surprise and Remembrance, D-Day,* and *The Battle of the Bulge* are especially noteworthy. You could show portions from PBS's biography *FDR* or *George Marshall and the American Century,* distributed by Direct Cinema Limited.

There a number of good documentaries about the home front as well. *We Were So Beloved: The German Jews of Washington Heights,* distributed by First Run/Icarus Films, chronicles the lives of German Jews who fled Nazi Germany in the 1930s and resettled in New York City's Washington Heights neighborhood, and would fit in well with a class discussion on America's response to Jewish refugees. *The Homefront,* distributed by Churchill Films, Inc., emphasizes the changes America underwent during World War II, especially regarding agriculture, industry, labor, and the status of minorities. *The Life and Times of Rosie the Riveter,* distributed by Direct Cinema Limited, covers the government's propaganda campaign to draw women into wartime industries and details the experiences of these "Rosies." Consider showing the segment from the PBS video *Lindbergh,* which covers his involvement with the America First Committee and fits in very well with the chapter's opening vignette. Or you might show the segment from California Newsreel's documentary *A. Philip Randolph,* which covers Randolph's proposed march on Washington, D.C., and Roosevelt's signing of Executive Order 8802.

You might also consider showing Hollywood films so students can see what those who remained on the home front were watching. Remind your students that World War II was the most profitable period in Hollywood's history. *Casablanca* remains a classic. *Stage Door Canteen* offers a campy romance story between an officer and a hostess of New York's famed nightspot. *Mission to Moscow* (1943) gives Hollywood's take on the U.S.-Soviet alliance during the war. *Thirty Seconds over Tokyo* (1944) allowed those at home to experience the action of the war. Alfred Hitchcock's thriller *Lifeboat* (1944) is the story of shipwrecked survivors, including one Nazi, set adrift on a lifeboat during World War II. You might also want to show segments from other World War II–era favorites, such as *Citizen Kane* (1941) or *Mrs. Miniver* (1942).

Historical Contingencies

Ask your students if the United States would have entered World War II had the Japanese not bombed Pearl Harbor. If they say yes, ask when they believe America would have entered. Ask how the war would have progressed had the United States not entered when it did, or if the United States had entered the war earlier. How would the nature of the battles, and the war, have changed?

Classroom Activities

After reviewing Office of War Information posters, and perhaps viewing an episode from Capra's series *Why We Fight,* have your students debate the role of propaganda in a democracy.

Using the Internet

Students can find information on U.S. wartime diplomacy at the Avalon Project, sponsored by Yale University Law School. Direct students to <http://www.yale.edu/lawweb/avalon/20th.htm>.

The Web site "Executive Order 9066: The Internment of 110,000 Japanese," sponsored by the UCLA Asian American Studies Center, makes available photographs and other materials pertaining to Japanese internment. Direct students to <http://www.sscnet.ucla.edu/aasc/ex9066>.

ASSESSING RESULTS
Multiple-Choice Questions

1. The Nye Senate committee concluded that
   a. the United States should sell nonmilitary goods to belligerents if the foreign nations paid cash (thus avoiding American loans) and shipped goods in their own vessels (thus avoiding the use of American ships in war zones).
   b. the United States should officially join the Spanish Loyalists in their fight against the fascist dictator Francisco Franco.

   c. the greed of American munitions makers, bankers, and financiers was responsible for U.S. entry into World War I.
   d. the United States must defend Ethiopia from Italian aggression.

2. Which of the following statements does not account for American isolationist sentiment in the 1930s?
   a. Most Americans wished to protect the U.S. economy from foreign competition and disruption.
   b. Americans remained disillusioned over their failed crusade in World War I.
   c. Americans wished to concentrate their efforts on domestic ills, not on remote, minor foreign events.
   d. Socialists, who had protested U.S. involvement in World War I, gained popular acceptance.

3. Which of the following events "provoked" Japan to bomb Pearl Harbor in December 1941?
   a. Roosevelt's trade embargo against Japan, which denied it access to essential oil and scrap iron
   b. the stationing of U.S. troops in Manchuria
   c. the U.S. capture of Japanese controlled Philippines and Guam
   d. evidence that the American fleet stationed at Pearl Harbor was mobilizing for action with the Japanese

4. The majority of women who entered the workforce during World War II
   a. were single and under twenty-one years of age.
   b. earned higher wages than the men who remained on the home front.
   c. earned more than ever before.
   d. earned comparable wages to their male counterparts.

5. African Americans scored a victory when FDR signed Executive Order 8802, which
   a. ended bans on black membership in unions.
   b. desegregated the armed forces.
   c. directed employers to hire blacks and whites on an equal basis and established the Committee on Fair Employment Practices to investigate violations of the order.
   d. directed employers to pay blacks and whites on an equal basis and established the committee on Fair Employment Practices to investigate violations of the order.

6. Topics discussed at the Yalta conference included all of the following, except

   a. rearranging the political map.
   b. creating an international organization (the United Nations).
   c. defeating Japan.
   d. launching a cross-channel invasion of France, known as D Day.

7. Harry S. Truman's decision to drop the atomic bomb on Japan was motivated by all of the following, except
   a. his wish to keep Russia out of the war with Japan so that Russia could not gain control in Korea and Manchuria.
   b. his hope that the bomb's devastation would convince the Soviets that they could not safely challenge America's leadership after the war.
   c. his wish to save American lives by ensuring a hasty end to the war.
   d. his abiding racial hatred of the Japanese.

8. In the *Documenting the American Promise* feature, what did internee Charles Kikuchi identify as the one beneficial result of his forced evacuation?
   a. He was able to finish his Berkeley degree in a camp university that he and other Japanese Americans set up.
   b. He felt the experience enabled him to identify with what Jews and other concentration camp prisoners were going through.
   c. The experience revealed to him that American democracy was a hypocritical and morally bankrupt system, and he resolved to emigrate to Japan once the war ended.
   d. The experience gave him the opportunity to get to know his family well.

9. According to Map 25.4, "The Pacific Theater of World War II, 1941–1945," which of the following areas in Asia did Japan not control during World War II?
   a. Manchuria
   b. Burma
   c. Mongolia
   d. Korea

10. The photo of the female defense worker
   a. suggested that wartime women workers could maintain their femininity while aiding the war effort by working in traditionally male occupations.
   b. demonstrated that women were incapable of handling the demands of industrialized labor.
   c. showed that industrial work was dirty and grimy, suggesting that women would

have to make a great deal of sacrifices in the workplace.

    d. conveyed the sense that women would have to put up with a great deal of sexual harassment on the job.

11. Identify the correct sequence of historical events and figures.

    a. the Lend-Lease Act, D Day landing at Normandy, nonaggression pact between Germany and the Soviet Union signed, atomic bomb dropped on Hiroshima

    b. Pearl Harbor, Japan surrenders, FDR elected for third time, Germany surrenders, atomic bomb dropped on Hiroshima

    c. Adolph Hitler becomes chancellor of Germany, nonaggression pact between Germany and the Soviet Union signed, Pearl Harbor, UN charter approved

    d. Hitler annexes Austria, Spanish Civil War, Roosevelt authorizes internment of Japanese Americans, the Lend-Lease Act

PROPOSING MORE: Additional Readings

Stephen E. Ambrose, "D-Day: June 4, 1944," *Prologue: Quarterly of the National Archives* 27, no. 2 (1994): 94–109.

John H. Bracey and August Meier, "Allies or Adversaries?: The NAACP, A. Philip Randolph, and the 1941 March on Washington," *Georgia Historical Quarterly* 75, no. 1 (1991): 1–17.

R. H. Kohn, "History and Culture Wars: The Case of the Smithsonian Institution *Enola Gay* Exhibition," *Journal of American History* 82, no. 3 (1995): 1036–63.

Elaine Tyler May, "Rosie the Riveter Gets Married," *Mid-America: A Historical Review* 75, no. 3 (1993): 269–82.

Scott D. Sagan, "The Origins of the Pacific War," *Journal of Interdisciplinary History* (1988): 893–922.

D. C. Watt, "Britain and the Historiography of the Yalta Conference and the Cold War," *Diplomatic History* 13, no. 1 (1989): 67–98.

Answer Key to Multiple-Choice Questions: 1-c, 2-d, 3-a, 4-c, 5-c, 6-d, 7-d, 8-d, 9-c, 10-a, 11-c

Essay Questions, Chapters 21–25

1. Progressive reformers called on the federal government to be an active partner in reforming American society. They demanded the government become involved in areas traditionally left to state or local governments, or private charities and philanthropic societies. In many respects, the progressives' approach to government involvement set the tone for Americans' increased expectations of the federal government. In what way did the federal government expand its powers from 1890 to 1945, and how did this growth affect American society? Ultimately, did this expansion benefit the country? Explain your answer.

2. Many historians cite the 1920s as the decade in which America entered the "modern era." What new issues did Americans face in the 1920s? In what ways did Americans respond to modernism? Why did some embrace modernism and others reject it?

3. Reform movements and impulses had had a long, albeit sometimes checkered, history in the United States by the time Franklin Delano Roosevelt promised Americans a "new deal" during the 1932 election campaign. Did his New Deal truly represent a dramatic departure from the progressive movement, or did it represent a continuation of that earlier movement? Be sure to consider aims, results, motivations, and the reformers themselves.

4. During the first half of the twentieth century, two major global conflicts shattered the country's notions of peace and stability, prompting the United States to send money, munitions, and troops overseas. Consider the ways in which Woodrow Wilson and Franklin Delano Roosevelt approached foreign war. What were their public stances before the United States entered the fray? Why did they eventually commit to U.S. involvement? In what ways did they attempt to mobilize domestic support, and how successful were these efforts? Ultimately, who was the more successful wartime leader?

26 COLD WAR POLITICS IN THE TRUMAN YEARS

1945–1953

Outlining Chapters: Thematic Questions

I. How did U.S. foreign policy shift from the grand alliance to containment?
   A. What conflicts existed in the wartime coalition? What steps did the global community take as it moved toward the cold war? What was the policy of containment?
   B. What was the Truman Doctrine? What was the Marshall Plan, and what was it designed to do?
   C. In what ways did the United States become a national security state?
   D. In what ways did the rivalry between the superpowers play itself out globally? How and why did the Communists triumph in China? What was the U.S. reaction? In what ways did the United States reverse its foreign policy course in Japan? What course did the United States take in the Middle East?

II. What was President Truman's Fair Deal program?
   A. How did Truman plan for the conversion of the wartime economy to a peacetime economy, and what factors contributed to the economic boom of the postwar era? In what ways did labor become more militant? What was Truman's response?
   B. What were the political demands of African Americans, and how responsive was Truman to the burgeoning civil rights movement?
   C. In what ways did Truman's Fair Deal flounder?

III. What factors contributed to the second Red scare?
   A. What were the politics of anticommunism?
   B. In what ways were Richard Nixon and Joseph McCarthy able to capture the American public with their anticommunism rhetoric?
   C. In what ways did Truman participate in the official purge of Communists?
   D. In what ways did the repression of Communists pervade American society?

IV. How did the events in Korea contribute to the heating up of the cold war?
   A. How did the United States become involved in Korea? How did the United States implement containment militarily in Korea?

B. How did American military action move from containment to rollback to containment?

C. What role did Korea and the fear of communism play in the 1952 election?

D. How was the war settled, and what were the final costs?

Teaching with The American Promise, *Second Compact Edition: Lecture Strategies*

LECTURE 1
The Policy of Containment

This lecture on the cold war introduces the policy of containment. You might begin by having students discuss Secretary of State George C. Marshall's warning on the need for postwar military preparedness (in the documents reader). Remind students that the United States, fortified by a successful wartime alliance with the Soviet Union, had agreed to a Soviet sphere of influence in Eastern Europe at the Yalta conference. (It might be helpful to have students look at Map 26.1, "The Division of Europe after World War II.") The Soviets' brutal method of installing Communist governments in Poland and Bulgaria and their occupation of eastern Germany immediately following the war forced the United States to reevaluate its policy toward the Soviet Union, however. Here, perhaps, bring in George F. Kennan's "The Long Telegram" (in the documents reader), later published as an article, which outlines the policy of containment and provides a framework for using U.S. power to check the spread of Soviet influence. Have students look at the *Documenting the American Promise* feature "The Emerging Cold War" to impress on them the swiftness with which the cold war began.

Next, cover the ways in which Truman sought to implement the policy, first by offering military and economic aid to politically unstable Greece and Turkey, warning the American public that if those countries "fell" to communism, "confusion" would spread throughout the Middle East and Europe. Truman's warning carried sufficient weight, and Congress passed an appropriations bill. Your lecture should then demonstrate that advocates of containment turned their attention to securing the passage of the Marshall Plan, a massive infusion of economic aid to war-torn Europe. The Soviet takeover of Czechoslovakia and blockade of

Berlin seemed to confirm the fears of U.S. policymakers, and the United States hunkered down to create a national security state. Be sure to cover the five-pronged defense strategy, which advocated the development of atomic weapons, conventional military power, military alliances, programs of economic and military aid to friendly nations, and extensive espionage networks to subvert Communist expansion. Demonstrate that the United States tested its new foreign policy in the Middle East, Africa, and Latin America as national liberation movements swept across the third world.

You should end your lecture with a discussion of the reasons why proponents of containment experienced their greatest challenge in China, where the Communists, led by Mao Zedong, waged war against the corrupt Nationalist government, headed by Chiang Kai-shek. The United States supported the tremendously unpopular Nationalists, but even the massive amounts of aid might not have been sufficient to provide a realistic chance of defeating the Communists. In December 1949, Mao established the People's Republic of China, prompting Republicans to charge the Democrats with "losing China." Truman's assurance that the United States had the power to check Communist aggression suddenly rang false with the American public.

LECTURE 2
Truman at Home

This lecture covers Truman's domestic policy. Begin by making the point that Truman, besieged by problems overseas, received no respite on the home front. Truman had to oversee the conversion of the economy from military to peacetime production and he had to cope with an increasingly militant labor movement. Present Truman's efforts to deal with an increasingly vocal African American civil rights movement. The president created the Committee on Civil Rights and charged it with investigating incidents of racial discrimination. The committee's final report recommended measures to protect voting rights and eliminate segregation. Republicans and Southern Democrats continually thwarted Truman-sponsored civil rights legislation, but a more sympathetic Supreme Court was able to effect change in the areas of housing and higher education. Truman faced an uphill battle in the election of 1948, with both the Republicans and the Dixiecrats threatening the Democrats. Although Truman won a surprising victory and the Democrats regained Congress, he failed to get Congress to support most of his Fair Deal. Congress continued to vote down measures in education, health care, and civil rights.

Finally, discuss the Red scare of the late 1940s and early 1950s. Truman's domestic program faced its biggest threat from a wave of anti-Communist hysteria that swept the nation. Many Americans seemed unwilling to believe that the United States could suffer setbacks abroad without the help of internal subversives, so the attacks made by Senator Joseph McCarthy and others against domestic Communists seemed reasonable to some. Here you will wish to discuss McCarthy's famous 1950 Wheeling, West Virginia, speech (in the documents reader). It is important to stress that anticommunism infiltrated nearly every aspect of American society, as members of the entertainment industry, academia, the State Department, civil rights organizations, and average citizens found themselves ostracized and discredited by the Communist witch-hunt. To give students a sense of the pervasiveness of anticommunism in popular culture and the media, have them examine the cold war comic book that opens the chapter. Ask them to consider what impact this image might have had on viewers.

soft on communism, confronted by a wave of anti-communism at home, and sensitive to charges that he had "lost" China, Truman abandoned containment and sought the elimination of the Communists from the Korean peninsula.

Despite assurances by General Douglas MacArthur that neither the Chinese nor the Soviets would intervene, the Chinese did in fact join the war. And by the end of 1950, Chinese–North Korean forces had pushed UN forces below the thirty-eighth parallel and had recaptured Seoul. Here it might be helpful to refer students to Map 26.3, "The Korean War, 1950–1953." You might also have the class discuss the testimony of the American POW (in the documents reader). The United States had to revert to seeking containment. You may wish to close your lecture by suggesting that Truman's inability to end the war, coupled with MacArthur's denunciation of containment, gave the Republicans the advantage in the 1952 election. Indeed, the Republicans, headed by Dwight D. Eisenhower, sailed into office by associating the Democrats unfavorably with "Korea, communism, and corruption." Shortly after the election, Eisenhower flew to Korea and negotiated an armistice that left Korea divided — as it had been three years earlier.

LECTURE 3
Korea

Although the United States had tested its policy of containment by offering economic aid to those European countries battling Communist incursions during the immediate postwar years, it actually went to war to implement the policy for the first time in 1950 in Korea. Begin by discussing the reasons behind Truman's decision to implement containment in Korea. The United States decided to send ground troops to protect the conservative government of South Korea after forces of Communist North Korea crossed over the artificial divide at the thirty-eighth parallel. Moreover, it convinced the United Nations to sponsor a collective effort to repel the North Korean attack. By mid-October 1950, UN forces were able to push North Korea back to the thirty-eighth parallel. Explain that Truman now faced the decision of whether to settle for the status quo — a divided Korea — or to launch an invasion into North Korea. Several factors influenced Truman's decision. Vulnerable to attacks of being

Anticipating Student Reactions: Common Misconceptions and Difficult Topics

1. The Marshall Plan

Students may ask how leaders expected that economic aid to foreign countries would help our economy. The lessons of the depression had taught American policymakers that a healthy economy depended on the export of American goods. Foreign trade, however, was hampered by the war-torn economies of Western Europe, which were too weak and lacked the resources to purchase American products. They also seemed vulnerable to communism, especially in Italy and France, where Communist parties were strong. By 1947, the United States had granted or loaned out about $9 billion to Europe but still failed to secure peace and prosperity overseas. Moreover, Europe's multibillion-dollar deficit meant that it could not afford to buy American goods. Secretary of State George C. Marshall proposed a massive infusion of capital — about $13 billion from 1948 to 1952 — to European nations, requiring that some of the aid be spent in America and on American goods, thus maintaining the U.S. flow of exports to the European continent.

2. How Could the Red Scare Happen in the United States, and Why Didn't People Stand Up to McCarthy?

Some students will invariably ask how the Red scare could happen in America. Remind them that the 1950s Communist witch-hunt was not the first episode of Red-baiting in the country's history, prodding them (if necessary) to recall the suppression of civil liberties during World War I and the subsequent Palmer raids and purges. Explain that most Americans felt a heady sense of optimism after World War II. The "setbacks" the United States experienced with regard to the Soviet Union in Eastern Europe, the "fall" of China, and Truman's inability to win the war in Korea shattered this notion of American superiority. It was much easier to believe that internal subversion was responsible for American setbacks than to believe that the United States was not all-powerful. In addition, Joseph McCarthy was a master dissembler. He told so many lies, with so many different parts, and told them so rapidly that no one could keep track of the allegations. In his Wheeling, West Virginia, speech, McCarthy charged that there were 205 known Communists in the State Department. When pushed for evidence, he changed the figure to 81, then to 57, and finally to "a lot." Only when he attacked the U.S. army, an institution most Americans believed above infiltration, did the public tire of his accusations and allow the purges to die down. You should debunk any existing notions that somehow McCarthy alone was responsible for the anti-Communist furor during this period, noting that Truman established his own loyalty-security program. Point out that the violations of civil liberties and repressions of this era could not have taken place without the collaboration of the country's political and social elites, especially Republicans who benefited from McCarthy's attacks on the Democrats. However, mention that not all Republicans supported McCarthy. Margaret Chase Smith, a Republican senator from Maine, and six other moderate Republicans bravely stood up to McCarthy on the Senate floor by circulating the "Republican declaration of conscience," which stated that Americans have the right to criticize ideas, hold unpopular beliefs, protest, and engage in independent thought.

Using the Bedford Series in History and Culture and the Historians at Work Series: Suggestions

Consider assigning *The Age of McCarthyism: A Brief History with Documents*, Second Edition, edited by Ellen Schrecker, to help explain the rise of anticommunism in the 1950s. When discussing foreign policy and containment, you might assign *American Cold War Strategy: Interpreting NSC 68*, edited by Ernest R. May.

Lecture Supplements and Classroom Activities

Using Multimedia Sources in the Classroom

Consider showing part of the PBS biography *Truman*, especially the segments that cover the president's attempts to deal with the expanding Soviet threat. You might also consider showing *Hollywood on Trial*, a 1970s documentary that covers the House Un-American Activities Committee's investigation of Hollywood. Episode 12 of Bill Moyers's series *A Walk through the Twentieth Century*, "Postwar Hopes, Cold War Fears," gives students a good overview of the origins of the cold war. You might also consider showing "The Race for the Superbomb," part of the PBS series *American Experience*, to offer a more in-depth look at the origins of the cold war.

There are a number of Hollywood films that examine anticommunism. Consider showing an example of Hollywood's overt response to the HUAC investigations, such as *I Was a Communist for the FBI* (1951) or *Walk East on Beacon Street* (1952), both of which suggest a Hollywood that was sympathetic to and compliant with federal investigations of communism. *High Noon* (1952), a classic Western starring Gary Cooper, and the science fiction classic *The Day the Earth Stood Still* (1951) also reflect American values and fears during the cold war. When discussing the difficult transition that returning American soldiers faced, consider showing *The Best Years of Our Lives* (1946). Remind students that Hollywood did produce films that countered the image of World War II as "The Good War" before *Saving Private Ryan* (1998).

Historical Contingencies

Have students consider what the postwar political world would have looked like if FDR did not replace Henry Wallace with Harry S. Truman as his vice president in 1944. Remind students that Wallace advocated greater cooperation with the Soviets, including sharing controlled information on atomic energy. Refer students to Wallace's speech featured in *Documenting the American Promise*, "The Emerging Cold War." Mention that Wallace was eventually dismissed as secretary of commerce because of his controversial views. What would have happened if he were vice president when FDR died?

Classroom Activities

Have students debate the guilt or innocence of Julius and Ethel Rosenberg. A number of documents pertaining to the Rosenberg case appear in *The Age of McCarthyism: A Brief History with Documents*, Second Edition, edited by Ellen Schrecker.

Using the Internet

You might direct students' attention to the following site on the Rosenberg trial: <http://www.law.umkc.edu/faculty/projects/ftrials/rosenb/rosenb.htm>.

The Avalon Project at Yale University makes available a host of documents relevant to the study of cold war America. Direct students to <http://www.yale.edu/lawweb/avalon/20th.htm>. Here they will find the text to the Truman Doctrine; defense treaties of the United States, 1950 to the present; and selected papers of Harry S. Truman.

ASSESSING RESULTS
Multiple-Choice Questions

1. The policy of containment was articulated by
   a. Harry S. Truman.
   b. Winston Churchill.
   c. Dean Acheson.
   d. George Kennan.

2. U.S. defense strategy during the Truman administration included
   a. programs of economic aid to friendly nations.
   b. a return to isolationism.
   c. increasing the standing army to combat-ready numbers.
   d. the development of atomic weapons at the expense of conventional weapons.

3. The most severe economic problem to plague the United States during the immediate post-war years was
   a. inflation.
   b. unemployment.
   c. stagflation.
   d. overproduction.

4. The Employment Act of 1946
   a. enraged business because it raised taxes on manufacturing.
   b. was partly a plan to increase consumer spending.
   c. increased the federal government's trust-busting ability.
   d. posited in the federal government the responsibility to keep the economy healthy.

5. The Taft-Hartley Act of 1947
   a. desegregated the armed forces.
   b. prohibited housing discrimination.
   c. limited the rights of workers to strike and organize.
   d. made it illegal to advocate the overthrow and destruction of the U.S. government by force or violence.

6. The Dixiecrat Party was comprised of
   a. Southern Democrats who opposed Truman's growing support for African American civil rights.
   b. Southern Democrats who supported Truman's growing support for African American civil rights.
   c. left-leaning Democrats who supported Henry Wallace's foreign policy initiatives.
   d. Southern Republicans who voted for Truman in the 1948 election.

7. The United States went into battle to implement the policy of containment for the first time in
   a. Czechoslovakia.
   b. Korea.
   c. Israel.
   d. Poland.

8. The most serious threat to Eisenhower's 1952 bid for the presidency came from
   a. allegations that he was soft on communism.
   b. a backlash against Ike's denunciation of General Douglas MacArthur.
   c. accusations that linked his vice presidential running mate, Richard Nixon, to illegal campaign funds.

d. increasing demands for total war against the North Koreans and the Chinese on the Korean peninsula.

9. According to Map 26.1, "The Division of Europe after World War II." which of the following countries did not belong to NATO?
   a. France
   b. Portugal
   c. Austria
   d. West Germany

10. Of what crime did Joseph McCarthy accuse Alger Hiss in his Wheeling, West Virginia, speech (in the documents reader)?
    a. masterminding a plot to sell research from the Manhattan Project to the Soviets
    b. influencing the disposition of the postwar world at the Yalta conference in favor of Soviet interests
    c. colluding with spy Whittaker Chambers to infiltrate the FBI
    d. undermining Secretary of State Dean Acheson's position at the State Department with a spurious claim that Acheson had been a member of the Communist Party

11. Identify the correct sequence of historical events and figures.
    a. Truman assumes presidency after the death of FDR, Marshall Plan approved, Berlin airlift, Eisenhower elected president

b. Kennan articulates his containment theory, NATO organized, Marshall Plan approved, McCarthy begins anti-Communist campaign
c. Truman defeats Dewey, Truman creates Committee on Civil Rights, Korean War, Communists take over China
d. Berlin airlift, Korean War, Eisenhower elected president, Marshall Plan approved

Proposing More: Additional Readings

Nancy E. Bernhard, "Clearer Than Truth: Public Affairs, Television, and the State Department's Domestic Information Campaigns, 1947–1952," *Diplomatic History* 21, no. 4 (1997): 545–67.

Barton J. Bernstein, "New Light on the Korean War," *International History Review* 3, no. 2 (1981): 256–77.

D. W. Davis, "A Tale of Two Movies: Charlie Chaplin, United Artists, and the Red Scare," *Cinema Journal* 27, no. 1 (1987): 47–62.

Daniel F. Harrington, "The Berlin Blockade Revisited," *International History Review* 6, no. 1 (1984): 88–112.

H. Jones and R. B. Woods, "Origins of the Cold War in Europe and the Near East: Recent Historiography and the National Security Imperative," *Diplomatic History* 17, no. 2 (1993): 251–76.

Answer Key to Multiple-Choice Questions: 1-d, 2-a, 3-a, 4-d, 5-c, 6-a, 7-b, 8-c, 9-c, 10-b, 11-a

27 THE POLITICS AND CULTURE OF ABUNDANCE

1952–1960

*O*utlining Chapters: Thematic Questions

I. How did the Eisenhower administration represent the politics of the "Middle Way"?
- A. What was Eisenhower's personal and public stand on McCarthyism?
- B. Why was Eisenhower considered a moderate Republican? What domestic policy initiatives did he oversee? In what ways was his administration shaped by a Democratic majority that maintained the course charted by the New Deal and the Fair Deal?
- C. What were the dominant issues of the 1956 election, and what did Eisenhower promise for his second term?

II. What was the rhetoric of liberation, and in what ways did the Eisenhower administration continue the policies of containment?
- A. What was the "New Look" in foreign policy?
- B. In what ways did containment guide U.S. foreign policy in Vietnam?
- C. How and why did the United States intervene in Latin American and Middle Eastern countries?
- D. What effect did the escalating nuclear arms race have on U.S. foreign policy?

III. Who were the winners and losers in the economy of abundance?
- A. In what ways was American agriculture transformed in the postwar years? What factors spurred the growth of an economy of abundance? How did technology transform American industry in the postwar years? How did labor benefit during this period of economic growth?
- B. How and why did suburbs grow and the cities decline in the 1950s?
- C. In what ways was higher education democratized?
- D. What were the regional variations in the economy of abundance? Why did the variations exist?

IV. How did the economy of abundance affect American society and culture?
- A. What was the great domestic revival? Why did Americans increasingly turn to houses of worship? Why did critics attack these trends?
- B. In what ways did television transform American culture and politics?
- C. What were the countercurrents to mainstream culture?

V. How and why did the civil rights movement emerge?
   A. How did the Supreme Court show its sympathy to the growing grassroots civil rights movement? Why was the president reluctant to support the new movement?
   B. In what ways did the events in Montgomery, Alabama, signal the beginnings of a mass protest?

Teaching with The American Promise, *Second Compact Edition: Lecture Strategies*

LECTURE 1
The Politics of the Middle Way

This lecture introduces Dwight D. Eisenhower's tactics of leadership. First suggest that Eisenhower entered the White House presenting himself as a leader who stood above partisan politics and selfish interest. He surrounded himself with formal and informal advisers but remained firmly in charge, prompting some historians to refer to him as the "hidden-hand" president. Although he championed himself as a moderate Republican, his Middle Way was shaped as much by the Democratic Congress that fought to maintain the course charted by the New Deal and Fair Deal as by his dedication to moderation. Cover Eisenhower's domestic policies on McCarthyism, the economy, and civil rights. The president refused to censure Senator Joseph McCarthy publicly, confident that the tide of anticommunism would eventually roll back. He also refused to reverse the growing federal involvement in economic development, attempting instead to rein in the growth. Finally, Eisenhower reluctantly supported the Supreme Court decisions in the area of civil rights, sending federal troops to Little Rock, Arkansas, to enforce school desegregation only after events gave him no choice.

Next, turn your attention to Eisenhower's foreign policy. His administration pursued containment but modified it and devised the New Look in foreign policy. Rather than spending huge amounts of money on a standing army, Eisenhower gave weapons to friendly nations and backed those gifts with a nuclear arsenal. Eisenhower tested this New Look in Latin America and the Middle East, where his administration tried to oust unfriendly regimes covertly, but the New Look especially guided policy in Viet-nam, where the United States sought to aid the French against the Vietminh but refused to commit ground troops. Eisenhower also concentrated his efforts on reducing tension between the United States and the Soviet Union. You can close the lecture with a discussion of Eisenhower's farewell address (in the documents reader), in which he warns the nation of a growing military-industrial complex. Use the images of school-age children ducking for a bomb drill and the *Protection from the Atomic Bomb* pamphlet as you discuss Eisenhower's address.

LECTURE 2
The Economy of Abundance

Use this lecture to emphasize that economic productivity increased dramatically in the 1940s and 1950s. American prosperity was on the rise because of increased government spending, especially in the defense industry; a population explosion that expanded demand for consumer goods; and consumer borrowing. Here you will need to stress that prosperity did not affect all regions of the economy equally, with the West and Southwest experiencing the greatest economic boom. In agriculture, increased crop specialization, better fertilizers, and greater mechanization led to the decline of the family farm and the creation of the agribusiness.

A rapidly growing economy meant higher rates of employment, and women and African Americans entered the workplace in unprecedented numbers. Emphasize that, above all, the economy was shifting away from one based on production to one based on service industries, an area in which labor unions traditionally had a hard time organizing. The rise of the suburb and the decline of the city perhaps best symbolize America's growing prosperity, and here you will wish to introduce the rise of a middle-class, suburban culture. You might close this lecture by having students look at the chapter-opening artifact — a Cadillac convertible, which symbolized both corporate and personal prosperity of the 1950s.

LECTURE 3
The Culture of Abundance

This lecture allows you to discuss how dominant values of the 1950s — family, religion, consumption, and conformity — went hand in hand with the economy of prosperity and Eisenhower's politics of consensus and moderation. The entrance of women into the workforce in unprecedented numbers was matched by a heightened celebration of women's traditional roles within the home and family — what Betty Friedan called "the feminine mystique." Here you might have students discuss Edith Stern's essay on the oppressions of housewifery (in the documents reader). Your lecture should also convey that concomitant with the renewed emphasis on family life was a religious revival, as membership in churches and synagogues soared, although critics charged that attendance at religious services stemmed more from a desire to conform than from a profound belief in God.

Discuss the role of television and popular culture in disseminating and reinforcing traditional American values. Have students look at the image of *Father Knows Best* when discussing television's cultural influence in the 1950s. By the end of the decade, television dominated Americans' leisure time, influenced their consumption patterns, and shaped their formulations about the nation's leaders and the nature of government. You can end by mentioning the critics of the culture of abundance, citing both the intellectuals who found that it rang hollow and the African Americans who charged that it did not include them. Allen Ginsberg's poem "America" and excerpts from Rosa Parks's memoir on segregation (both in the documents reader) should provide students with a better understanding of the culture's critics.

Anticipating Student Reactions: Common Misconceptions and Difficult Topics

1. Eisenhower and the CIA

Students may question why and whether Eisenhower abused presidential power to defeat unfriendly leaders in Latin America and the Middle East. You can use this opportunity to make it clear to students how and why the Central Intelligence Agency got involved in the covert operations business to begin with. The CIA began in wartime as the Office of Strategic Services, an intelligence-gathering organization; but during the Eisenhower administration, it outgrew its original mandate. Eisenhower reasoned that covert operations handled by the CIA had numerous advantages. They were less expensive than traditional forms of deterrence, they were secret

(and therefore not subject to public backlash or threats by Congress), and they were fast. Policymakers believed that the ends — defeating communism — justified the means. Eisenhower, along with Allen Dulles, brother of Secretary of State John Foster Dulles, directly supervised the operations of the CIA. Under Eisenhower and Dulles's leadership, the CIA ousted several foreign leaders, including Mohammed Mossadegh in Iran and Jacobo Arbenz in Guatemala. The *New York Times* reported in early 1997 that recently uncovered CIA files indicated that before the coup against Arbenz in 1954, the agency had created a list of fifty prominent figures to be assassinated by CIA-trained Guatemalans. Students should understand, then, that this kind of extralegal covert activity in the name of national security did not begin with Oliver North and the Iran-Contra affair but represents a consistent pattern throughout the postwar period from Eisenhower through Kennedy and the Bay of Pigs, Nixon and Watergate, Reagan and Nicaragua, and so on.

2. The 1950s Was an Age of Prosperity and Contentment

You might start a discussion by asking students what ideas or symbols they associate with the 1950s. As you did with regard to the 1920s, point out the difficulties inherent in generalizing about any decade, and explain how we often superimpose our own interpretations on the past. Many students' impressions of the 1950s may have been shaped by television shows such as *Happy Days* or movie musicals such as *Grease*. Others may have read Arthur Miller's *Death of a Salesman*, J. D. Salinger's *Catcher in the Rye*, or Ralph Ellison's *Invisible Man*, or seen the movie *Rebel without a Cause*, starring James Dean, and may wonder how these works fit into the dominant culture of the 1950s. Use this opportunity to discuss the social alienation many Americans felt and to debunk the myth of nationwide prosperity during this period. The central theme in many plays and novels of the postwar years is the overriding loneliness the individual experiences amid the oppressive, suffocating mass culture. Some critics lambasted authors who offered a bleak portrayal of American life, but most championed them for exposing the ugly underside of the crass commercialism of the culture of abundance. The artists themselves believed their works to be more reflective of society than the more celebratory and optimistic works of the period. Here you may wish to introduce the Beat poets, who also rejected the dominant culture but were much more defiant than even the authors mentioned above. Have students look again at Allen Ginsberg's poem (in the documents reader). You might also want to counter the myth of security represented by television sitcoms of this era that portrayed family ideals. This fictionalized domestic contentment allayed the public's fears as the government amassed a huge nuclear arsenal, as the CIA engaged in efforts to destabilize foreign governments, and as cold war tensions grew. Ask your students if the decade of the 1950s was in fact a time of security.

Using the Bedford Series in History and Culture and the Historians at Work Series: Suggestions

When discussing the social composition of American society in the 1950s, you may wish to assign *Postwar Immigrant America: A Social History*, edited by Reed Ueda. Similarly, you may find *American Social Classes in the 1950s: Selections from Vance Packard's* The Status Seekers, edited by Daniel Horowitz, useful when reviewing the culture of abundance. To have students explore more fully the history and impact of the *Brown* decision, consider assigning *Brown v. Board of Education of Topeka: A Brief History with Documents*, edited by Waldo E. Martin. You might also consider assigning *Women's Magazines, 1940–1960*, edited by Nancy A. Walker, when discussing images and societal roles of women during the 1950s.

Lecture Supplements and Classroom Activities

Using Multimedia Sources in the Classroom

When discussing the culture of television, consider showing the PBS documentary *Big Dream, Small Screen*. "The Age of Anxiety," Episode 8 of PBS's *American Vision* series, chronicles the works of avant-garde artists and will complement a discussion of countercultural currents in the 1950s. "Awakenings," Episode 1 of *Eyes on the Prize*, the highly acclaimed PBS series on the civil rights movement, covers the *Brown* decision, the lynching of Emmett Till, and the Montgomery, Alabama, bus boycott. The first part of Episode 2, "Fighting Back," details the desegregation struggle in Little Rock, Arkansas. These documentaries are quite useful when conveying the ways in

which civil rights activists used the burgeoning medium of television to their advantage. You will want to emphasize, however, that television did not "create" the movement. As the textbook notes, African Americans were committed to fighting racism from the time they were brought to America's shores. The first episode of the PBS series *Vietnam: A Television War*, "Roots of a Conflict, 1945–1954," gives students a good overview of U.S. involvement in the region from Ho Chi Minh's declaration of an independent Vietnam to the fall of French forces at Dien Bien Phu. PBS's biography *Eisenhower* allows students to explore the "hidden-hand" presidency.

There are a number of good Hollywood films that relate to the politics and culture of abundance. *The Man in the Gray Flannel Suit* (1956) brilliantly depicts the frustrations of the middle-class work world and the cult of domesticity in the 1950s. *The Apartment* (1960) offers a cynical look at corporate culture in the age of prosperity. *On the Waterfront* (1954) is a vehicle that allowed Elia Kazan, the famed Hollywood director who cooperated with HUAC's investigations of the film industry, to defend his actions. *Invasion of the Body Snatchers* (1956) also sheds light on the anti-Communist hysteria of the 1950s, linking the dangers of communism with an invasion of alien pod-people. *Rebel without a Cause* (1955), *The Defiant Ones* (1958), and *The Man with the Golden Arm* (1955) stand as examples of Hollywood's treatment of countercultural trends in the 1950s. Finally, a segment from *Around the World in Eighty Days* may exemplify Hollywood excess in the 1950s (lavish scenery, a lush musical score, and a "cast of thousands") as the film industry tried to combat the growing popularity and influence of television.

Historical Contingencies

Ask your students how the modern civil rights movement might have fared without the growth of television. Would activists have been able to "reach the conscience of America" had TV news not brought compelling images into the living rooms of millions of Americans? What strategies might the activists have employed to gain widespread support?

Classroom Activities

Consider playing music for your students. Refer students to the passage in the text defining rock-and-roll music as a combination of black rhythm and blues, country twang, and Western swing. Point to the statement about "race music" on page 714 and the rise of Elvis Presley, and then play the original Big Mama Thorton version of "Hound Dog" followed by Elvis's version. Ask if the two performers are singing about the same thing. Play Joe Turner's rock anthem "Shake, Rattle, and Roll" followed by Bill Haley and the Comets' cleaned-up version. See if your students can notice the differences in the recordings. To tie this music in with a lecture on civil rights, explain white parents' fear of race-mixing at the time, citing the opposition to the *Brown* decision, and the fear of "race music," citing the opposition to the rise of rock and roll. Both fears stemmed from the underlying fear of miscegenation. Ask if these fears seem legitimate and if parents still fear rock music.

Using the Internet

The "Trinity Atomic" Web site makes available primary documents, photos, and videos tracing the history of nuclear weapons. Direct students to <http://nuketesting.enviroweb.org>.

The University of Illinois at Chicago sponsors the Web site "Levittown: Documents of an Ideal American Suburb." Direct students to <http://tigger.uic.edu/~pbhales/Levittown.html>.

ASSESSING RESULTS
Multiple-Choice Questions

1. The "kitchen debate" of 1959 was
   a. a public debate between a leading feminist and Vice President Richard Nixon about the place of women in American society.
   b. an informal but spirited exchange between Soviet Premier Nikita Khrushchev and Vice President Nixon about the merits of their societies.
   c. a spontaneous debate about foreign policy that took place between Dwight Eisenhower and Nikita Khrushchev in the White House kitchen.
   d. the title of an article that appeared in the *Ladies' Home Journal* discussing the pros and cons of working versus being a stay-at-home mother.

2. Eisenhower's politics of the Middle Way
   a. included a harsh and angry denunciation of McCarthyism.
   b. completely reversed the trend of the growing welfare state created by the New Deal.
   c. applied the brakes but did not reverse the growing federal responsibility for eco-

nomic development and for the welfare of Americans unable to survive in the free market.
   d. endorsed McCarthy's anti-Communist attacks against the U.S. army.

3. Which of the following statements best characterizes the foreign policy of the Eisenhower administration?
   a. It deplored containment as "negative, futile, and immoral" (because the policy accepted existing Soviet spheres of influence) but pursued it nonetheless.
   b. It directed anti-Communist efforts at the margins of Communist power in Asia, Latin America, and the Middle East.
   c. It let Europe direct relations with Russia.
   d. It moved the United States toward a return to isolationism.

4. Which of the following statements about the 1954 Geneva accords is false?
   a. France conceded to sign only after Eisenhower agreed to committing American ground troops in Vietnam.
   b. They drew a temporary line across the seventeenth parallel of Vietnam.
   c. They prohibited the Vietminh and the government in South Vietnam from entering into military alliances or permitting foreign bases on their soil.
   d. They mandated free elections to be held within two years for the Vietnamese to choose a unified government.

5. Which of the following forces did not contribute to the tremendous boom in the U.S. economy during the 1950s?
   a. increased government spending, which stimulated the creation of jobs and research and development
   b. a population explosion, which expanded the demand for products
   c. consumer borrowing, which allowed people to purchase large-ticket items on the installment plan
   d. conservative government fiscal policies, which kept inflation in check

6. Labor unions in the 1950s
   a. helped elect liberals to Congress and exercised considerable political clout.
   b. became increasingly militant.
   c. made strong headway in organizing workers in light industry and in the clerical and service sectors.
   d. saw improvements in wages and benefits.

7. The term "feminine mystique," coined by Betty Friedan,
   a. meant that advertisers, social scientists, educators, women's magazines, and public officials all encouraged women to seek their ultimate fulfillment in serving others through marriage and child rearing.
   b. referred to the feminization of the workplace, as an unprecedented number of married women entered the workforce during the 1950s.
   c. meant that biological differences between men and women were of no consequence.
   d. referred to the tendency women displayed to marry at a later age and to bear fewer children than women of previous generations.

8. Which of the following developments did not lie behind the rise of the black protest movement during the 1950s?
   a. the exodus of more than three million African Americans out of the South into areas where they could vote and exercise pressure on white politicians
   b. the worry of white leaders that America's dismal record on race relations put the nation at a disadvantage in cold war competition
   c. the growth of black institutions that provided a mass base and an organizational network
   d. President Eisenhower's willingness to risk the loss of support of white southerners and actively champion the rights of African Americans

9. According to Map 27.1, "The Rise of the Sun Belt, 1940–1980," which three states had the greatest population growth?
   a. California, Arizona, and New Mexico
   b. California, Florida, and Arizona
   c. Arizona, New Mexico, and Oklahoma
   d. Florida, Arizona, and Nevada

10. The Norman Rockwell painting *The Problem We All Live With*
    a. is critical of school desegregation.
    b. appears largely sympathetic to the cause of school desegregation.
    c. is typical of the painter's whimsical and lighthearted approach to even the most serious subjects.
    d. illustrates the lack of protection afforded to black students attempting to integrate public schools.

11. Identify the correct sequence of historical events and figures.
    a. *Brown v. Board of Education,* Geneva accords, Eisenhower reelected, Montgomery bus boycott begins
    b. Eisenhower elected, Ginsberg's *Howl, Sputnik,* CIA stages coup in Guatemala
    c. CIA engineers coup in Iran, Operation Wetback, Montgomery bus boycott begins, Eisenhower elected president
    d. Eisenhower elected president, Operation Wetback, Interstate Highway Act, Soviets shoot down U-2 spy plane

PROPOSING MORE: Additional Readings

Henry W. Brands Jr., "The Dwight D. Eisenhower Administration, Syngman Rhee, and the 'Other' Geneva Conference of 1954," *Pacific Historical Review* 56, no. 2 (1987): 59–85.

Clifford E. Clark, "Ranch-House Suburbia: Ideals and Realities," in *Recasting America: Culture and Politics in the Age of Cold War,* ed. Larry May (Chicago: University of Chicago Press, 1988): 171–91.

Robert Griffith, "The Selling of America: The Advertising Council and American Politics, 1942–1960," *Business History Review* 57, no. 3 (1983): 388–412.

George Lipsitz, "The Meaning of Memory: Family, Class and Ethnicity in Early Network Television Programs," *Cultural Anthropology* 1, no. 4 (1986): 355–87.

Joanne Meyerowitz, "Beyond the Feminine Mystique: A Reassessment of Post-War Mass Culture, 1946–1958," *Journal of American History* 79, no. 4 (1993): 1455–82.

Answer Key to Multiple-Choice Questions: 1-b, 2-c, 3-b, 4-a, 5-d, 6-d, 7-a, 8-d, 9-d, 10-b, 11-d

28 A DECADE OF REBELLION AND REFORM

1960–1968

*O*utlining Chapters: Thematic Questions

I. What was President John F. Kennedy's New Frontier?
  A. What was the style of the New Frontier, and what did the platform promise?
  B. How successful was the New Frontier in securing its domestic agenda?
  C. What circumstances surrounded Kennedy's assassination?

II. What was President Lyndon Baines Johnson's Great Society?
  A. In what ways did Johnson fulfill the Kennedy promise?
  B. In what ways did Johnson complete the agenda of the Great Society? Why did the flood of Great Society legislation trickle after 1966?
  C. What are the assessments of the War on Poverty?

III. Why is the civil rights movement of the 1960s called the "second Reconstruction"?
  A. In what ways did the struggle for black freedom flower during the 1960s?
  B. What was the response of the Kennedy and Johnson administrations to the civil rights movement?
  C. What was black nationalism? What caused the dissolution of the civil rights coalition?

IV. What groups demanded power to the people?
  A. What elements characterized the Native American protest?
  B. In what ways did Hispanic Americans struggle for justice?
  C. What were the concerns of student activists, and what was the New Left?
  D. What was the counterculture? What did it stand for? What did it stand against?
  E. What events prompted the beginnings of the feminist movement?

V. What was the "judicial revolution"?
  A. How did the Supreme Court rule on the issues of civil and voting rights? What was the stand of the Supreme Court on issues of criminal justice?
  B. How did the Supreme Court rule on religious issues and issues of dissent?

Teaching with The American Promise, *Second Compact Edition: Lecture Strategies*

LECTURE 1
The Kennedy and Johnson Administrations

This lecture covers the domestic policies of the Kennedy and Johnson administrations. First, remind students that John F. Kennedy entered the White House with the slimmest of victories; from the very beginning he was acutely aware of the balancing act he would have to perform to maintain his coalition. Although Kennedy's administration—the "best and the brightest"—portrayed a youthful dynamism, many of his advisers were not especially well versed in the matters of practical politics. Suggest that there existed a large gap between what Kennedy proclaimed he stood for and what he accomplished in office. Although the president scored minor victories, he failed to push through key parts of the Democratic platform—health care for the elderly and federal aid for education. By the summer of 1963, he promised major legislation in domestic reform, but he was assassinated before he saw any of his plans come to fruition.

Next, you should mention that within six months of assuming office, Lyndon Baines Johnson had announced the goal of his administration—the Great Society—which rested on abundance and liberty for all citizens. Bring in Johnson's proposal for the Great Society, outlined in a speech he delivered at the University of Michigan (in the documents reader). Ask students what Johnson believed the promise of America to be. The president scored major victories in the areas of antipoverty legislation and civil rights. You will want to cover the programs under his Office of Economic Opportunity, the 1964 tax cut, the Economic Opportunity Act, Medicare and Medicaid, federal aid to education, the Immigrant and Nationality Act, and the Civil Rights and Voting Acts.

Ultimately, however, Johnson abandoned his domestic program to fight a war abroad. Note that Democratic losses in the 1966 election stemmed the tide of Great Society legislation. Ask students whether the Great Society fulfilled the promise of America.

LECTURE 2
The Civil Rights Movement

When discussing the civil rights movement, you might emphasize that it was a grassroots movement. By the late 1950s, it had blossomed into a national movement that had garnered a considerable amount of public support. Begin with a brief review of some of the victories African Americans scored during the Truman and Eisenhower administrations, reminding students of Truman's executive order desegregating the armed services, the success of the Montgomery bus boycott, and the major precedent set by the 1954 *Brown v. Board of Education* decision. Divide the rest of your lecture into three phases of the movement.

First, you should address the civil disobedience phase, discussing the importance of Dr. Martin Luther King's philosophy of nonviolence. Here you might include King's "Letter from Birmingham Jail" (in the documents reader)—demonstrating the ways in which this philosophy influenced the sit-ins, the Freedom Rides, the boycotts and marches, and voter registration efforts. Here would be a good time for pointing out the picture of the lunch counter sit-in. Second, consider the legislative victories of the civil rights movement, reviewing the Civil Rights and Voting Rights Acts passed during Johnson's administration. Here, you may wish to have your class discuss the *Historical Question* feature "What Difference Did Black Voting Rights Make?" Finally, discuss the failings of nonviolence and legislation—as perceived by some African Americans—and the rise of the black power movement in the mid-1960s. Call your students' attention to the Student Nonviolent Coordinating Committee leaflet (in the documents reader). Emphasize the resistance African Americans received from hostile whites, especially but not exclusively in the South. Ask students whether King and his followers and SNCC members shared the same vision of what the American promise was. Stress the importance of television in bringing the struggles and victories of the civil rights movement into the homes of millions of Americans, but do not overemphasize the case. Many students may wrongly assign too much credit to the media for the success of the civil rights movement. Remind them that savvy leaders were able to manipulate the media to its advantage but that television cameras were largely absent from the daily struggles activists waged for a just society.

LECTURE 3
Power to the People

In this lecture, you can demonstrate how the black power movement of the mid-1960s inspired other minorities to vocalize their discontent with the established culture. You can discuss first the Native American and Chicano rights movements, explaining how both groups were able to secure greater attention and respect from the public; initiate some federal antidiscrimination legislation; and, maybe more important, instill in their members a sense of cultural pride. Next, discuss student and women activists, who although generally members of the white middle and upper-middle classes, believed that they were nonetheless oppressed by the dominant culture. Here, you might have students read the National Organization for Women's 1966 "Statement of Purpose" (in the documents reader). In what ways did these activists take their cues from the civil rights movement? You should also review the Warren Court's support of the rights of the marginal and powerless in American society — minorities, the poor and uneducated, and political dissenters — especially in guaranteeing the rights of the accused, civil and voting rights, and the rights of religious and political freedom.

Anticipating Student Reactions: Common Misconceptions and Difficult Topics

1. The Kennedy Assassination

Be prepared to answer the inevitable questions on the Kennedy assassination. Many of your students have probably seen the Oliver Stone film *JFK* and may believe that it offers an accurate interpretation of the historical evidence. You will want to emphasize that although conspiracy theories have abounded since the event, there is no direct evidence linking Lee Harvey Oswald with a second shooter or with a larger plot, orchestrated by either ultraconservative Texans or Communists. President Johnson appointed a commission headed by Chief Justice Earl Warren to investigate the assassination; and although it came under a barrage of criticism for its inaccuracies and omissions, it found no evidence to support a conspiracy theory. Later investigations have proved inconclusive. You may wish to take this opportunity to discuss the reasons why Kennedy's assassination has

generated such a flurry of speculation, suggesting the transformative nature of the event on the consciousness of the nation.

2. Malcolm X

Students may have questions about the role of Malcolm X in the civil rights movement, especially if they have seen Spike Lee's movie *Malcolm X* or read *The Autobiography of Malcolm X*. Lee's film clearly implicates the Nation of Islam in the assassination of Malcolm X. You may first wish to cover the reasons for Malcolm's split with Elijah Muhammad and the Nation of Islam and then discuss the assassination itself. Three members of the Nation of Islam were convicted of the murder of Malcolm X, but because Malcolm was such a controversial figure and incurred the wrath of so many, debate has surrounded the conviction. You may wish to broaden your discussion to include Malcolm X's criticisms of the traditional civil rights movement as well as the reformulations he made near the end of his life.

3. The Media Created the Modern Civil Rights Movement

Many students may wrongly assume that the media — especially television — created the modern civil rights movement. Some sources perpetuate this view. PBS's documentary series *Eyes on the Prize*, for example, although excellent in many respects perhaps places too much influence on television's role in the movement. Moreover, students tend to get most of their information from television and may therefore assign it too much credit. Still, you can consider ways in which civil rights activists used the media to their advantage — in other words, demonstrate that activists also had control. You might mention some of the daily struggles that African Americans and their supporters experienced out of view of the television cameras.

Using the Bedford Series in History and Culture and the Historians at Work Series: Suggestions

Lyndon B. Johnson and American Liberalism: A Brief Biography with Documents, by Bruce Schulman, should prove instructive when covering the Johnson administration, especially when dealing with the ways Johnson's vision of America differed from that of Kennedy.

Lecture Supplements and Classroom Activities

Using Multimedia Sources in the Classroom

There are a number of good documentaries on the civil rights movement. Spike Lee's film *Four Little Girls* offers a sensitive treatment of the four girls who died in the bombing of Birmingham's Sixteenth Street Baptist Church, the work of white supremacist "Dynamite Bob" Chambliss in 1963. *Malcolm X: Make It Plain* offers an in-depth treatment of the famed civil rights leader. A number of episodes of the PBS series *Eyes on the Prize* work well in the classroom: "Ain't Scared of Your Jails, 1960–1961" covers the sit-in and Freedom Ride movements; "No Easy Walk, 1961–1963" covers Martin Luther King Jr.'s and the SCLC's Project Campaign in Birmingham and the 1963 March on Washington; "Mississippi: Is This America? 1962–1964" treats the Mississippi Freedom Democratic Party's bid to be recognized as the legitimate representative of Mississippians at the 1964 Democratic Convention and Bob Moses's 1964 Freedom Summer Project; and "Bridge to Freedom, 1965" covers the 1965 march from Selma to Montgomery and LBJ's signing into law the 1965 Voting Rights Act, which many believe to be the pinnacle of success for the civil rights movement. You might also want to show the segments from "JFK" and "LBJ" (both part of PBS's *American Experience* series) that deal with the presidents' domestic policies.

Some Hollywood films have captured the mood of America during the "turbulent decade." When covering the civil rights movement, consider screening the five-Oscar winner *In the Heat of the Night* (1967), which deals with a racist Mississippi sheriff who must accept help from a big-city black detective to solve a murder. You might also want to show scenes from the 1964 film *Nothing But a Man*, the first major Hollywood film with an all-black cast and crew. When discussing America's continuing struggle with communism, consider showing *The Manchurian Candidate* (1962). When discussing rebellion and angst, consider showing *Bonnie and Clyde* (1967) or *The Graduate* (1967). You might also consider showing *Planet of the Apes* (1968) or *2001: A Space Odyssey* (1968).

Historical Contingencies

Ask students what directions the civil rights movement might have taken had Malcolm X and Martin Luther King Jr. not been assassinated. The question will allow students to explore potential changes in the two men's outlooks. After his pilgrimage to Mecca, Malcolm X seemed more willing to work with mainstream civil rights organizations than he had been during the early phase of his career. Martin Luther King Jr. began to speak out on issues of economic justice during the later phase of his career. Remind students that King was in Memphis to support a strike by sanitation workers when he was assassinated. The question will also allow students to explore the nature of leadership. How critical were these two men to the people they led? You might want to remind students of the grassroots nature of the movement.

Classroom Activities

Ask students to identify the social or political issues for which they would fight. Impress on them that students of the mid- to late 1960s were impassioned about the causes in which they believed. Would your students be willing to go to jail for their convictions? Do they identify with any cause as Tom Hayden, Julian Bond, John Lewis, and the thousands of other students did over thirty years ago? Do they believe their generation is as apathetic as critics charge? If they are not as impassioned about causes now as students of the 1960s were, ask them to explain why not. How is American society different now from what it was then? Or *is* it different?

Using the Internet

Stanford University's Black Panther Research Project makes available online primary and secondary sources as well as links to other sites relevant to the study of the Black Panther Party for Self-Defense. Tell students to go to <http://www.stanford.edu/group/blackpanthers>.

Cornell University's Law School makes available online the decisions of major Supreme Court cases. Students interested in learning more about the Warren Court should go to <http://supct.law.cornell.edu/supct/>.

ASSESSING RESULTS
Multiple-Choice Questions

1. During Johnson's first year as president, he secured all of the following, except
   a. voting rights legislation.
   b. the strongest civil rights act since Reconstruction.
   c. a tax cut.
   d. antipoverty legislation.

2. Martin Luther King Jr. first came to national prominence during
   a. the Montgomery bus boycott of 1955.
   b. the Greensboro Woolworth's lunch counter sit-in.
   c. the 1961 Freedom Rides.
   d. Freedom Summer.

3. Which of the following statements best describes the Civil Rights Act of 1964?
   a. It passed despite growing public support for civil rights.
   b. It guaranteed all Americans access to public accommodation, public education, and voting.
   c. It empowered the federal government to act directly and immediately to enable African Americans to register and to vote.
   d. It failed to address sex discrimination in employment.

4. Who coined the term "black power" to express the growing militancy of the civil rights movement in the mid-1960s?
   a. Stokely Carmichael
   b. Martin Luther King Jr.
   c. Malcolm X
   d. Medgar Evers

5. Which of the following statements is untrue of the Native American and Chicano power movements of the late 1960s?
   a. They drew their inspiration from the black power movement.
   b. They rejected the traditional politics practiced by their elders in favor of more militant strategies.
   c. By the 1970s, their members were no longer overrepresented among the nation's poor.
   d. Their members gained a sense of their potential power and respect for their cultures.

6. The Warren Court
   a. reflected the values of a conservative, white, middle-class America as it continually overturned civil rights legislation and struck down older precedents in the area of personal liberty.
   b. refused to hear any cases relating to electoral redistricting, claiming that the power to draw election districts resided with the states alone.
   c. consistently restricted the rights of the accused.

   d. protected the constitutional rights of marginalized and powerless Americans — minorities, the poor and uneducated, and political dissenters.

7. Figure 28.1, "Poverty in the United States, 1960–1974," demonstrates
   a. that the elderly experienced the sharpest decline in poverty during Johnson's War on Poverty.
   b. that African Americans actually experienced an increase in poverty during Johnson's War on Poverty.
   c. that African Americans experienced the sharpest decline in poverty during Johnson's War on Poverty.
   d. that whites had a higher percentage of people living in poverty during the 1960s and early 1970s than any other group for the same years.

8. The photograph of President Lyndon Johnson and his adviser Abe Fortas shows
   a. Fortas's forceful and domineering personality.
   b. how Johnson used tact and charm when dealing with his staff.
   c. how Johnson used his looming physical presence and forceful personality to get his way.
   d. Johnson's notorious standoffishness even with close aides.

9. According to the SNCC leaflet (in the documents reader), who will lead the black power movement?
   a. black men in the ghetto
   b. middle-class blacks
   c. Martin Luther King Jr.
   d. all of the above

10. Identify the correct sequence of historical events and figures.
    a. Greensboro lunch counter sit-in, *The Feminine Mystique*, Malcolm X assassinated, AIM founded
    b. SNCC established, Kennedy assassinated, NOW founded, *The Feminine Mystique*
    c. Malcolm X assassinated, CORE sponsors Freedom Rides, *Miranda v. Arizona*, LBJ elected president
    d. JFK elected president, Voting Rights Act, SDS founded, Kennedy assassinated

Proposing More: Additional Readings

"Becoming Martin Luther King, Jr. — Plagiarism and Originality: A Roundtable," *Journal of American History* 78, no. 1 (1991): 111–23.

James C. Cobb, "'Somebody Done Nailed Us on the Cross': Federal Farm and Welfare Policy and the Civil Rights Movement in the Mississippi Delta," *Journal of American History* 77, no. 3 (1990): 912–36.

D. Cochran, "I. F. Stone and the New Left: Protesting U.S. Policy in Vietnam," *Historian* 53, no. 3 (1991): 505–20.

C. E. Harrison, "A New Frontier for Women: The Public Policy of the Kennedy Administration," *Journal of American History* 67, no. 3 (1980): 630–46.

N. A. Kerr, "Drafted into the War on Poverty: USDA Food and Nutrition Programs," *Agricultural History* 64, no. 2 (1990): 154–66.

Answer Key to Multiple-Choice Questions: 1-a, 2-a, 3-b, 4-a, 5-c, 6-d, 7-a, 8-c, 9-a, 10-a

29 VIETNAM AND THE LIMITS OF POWER

1961–1975

*O*utlining Chapters: Thematic Questions

I. What was John F. Kennedy's New Frontier in American foreign policy?
   A. In what ways was Kennedy's administration prepared to meet the "maximum hour of danger"? How successfully did the Kennedy administration meet the threat to national security?
   B. What were Kennedy's new approaches to the third world?
   C. Why did the nuclear arms race escalate, and what incident placed the United States and the Soviet Union on the nuclear brink?
   D. Why did Kennedy lead the United States into the "quagmire" in Vietnam?

II. How did Lyndon B. Johnson fight the war against communism?
   A. In what ways did Johnson shore up the U.S. commitment in Vietnam?
   B. How did Johnson prevent "another Castro" in Latin America?
   C. How did Johnson "Americanize" the Vietnam War? Was this strategy useful?

III. In what ways was the nation polarized by the war?
   A. How did the gap in opinion on the war widen at home? What effect did the antiwar movement have on American society?
   B. What was the Tet Offensive, and why did Johnson decide to de-escalate after Tet? In what ways did 1968 live up to its reputation as the year of upheaval, both at home and abroad?

IV. In what ways did Nixon's search for "peace with honor" fail?
   A. What was Nixon's policy of Vietnamization, and why did his administration enter into negotiations with the North Vietnamese and the Soviets?
   B. How did Nixon's actions in Cambodia make Vietnam Nixon's war?
   C. What was achieved at the peace accords and when? Why did Saigon fall?
   D. What were the legacies of defeat?

Teaching with The American Promise, *Second Compact Edition: Lecture Strategies*

LECTURE 1
Kennedy and Vietnam

In this lecture on the Vietnam War, explain first that when Kennedy entered the White House in 1960, he inherited the U.S. involvement in Vietnam. Because of the U.S. commitment to fend off any Communist gain, the United States had been supporting French colonial efforts in Indochina during the 1940s and 1950s (despite Ho Chi Minh's numerous requests to Washington to support Vietnamese independence). Here you can review Ho Chi Minh's push for Vietnamese independence, the fall of Dien Bien Phu, the failed Geneva accords, the assassination of Bao Dai, and the installation of Ngo Dinh Diem as leader in South Vietnam. Upon learning that Ho's Communists had made important gains in South Vietnam with the National Liberation Front (NLF), Kennedy increased the number of military advisers sent to Vietnam. He also sent Vice President Johnson to investigate the crisis; Johnson reported back that Diem refused the U.S. government's request that U.S. troops be sent in to help fight the war. Reports filtered back to the president suggesting that only increased U.S. involvement could stop Ho and the Communists, but Kennedy feared the repercussions. At this point, suggest that despite Kennedy's approval for increased military aid to South Vietnam, Diem's unpopular regime continued to suffer, especially after Buddhist monks staged self-immolation protests, all of which were captured by American television cameras. Kennedy did nothing when he learned that South Vietnamese generals were about to stage a coup to oust Diem. Three weeks later, Kennedy was assassinated and Lyndon Johnson inherited the Vietnamese crisis.

LECTURE 2
Johnson and Vietnam

This lecture demonstrates how President Johnson escalated U.S. involvement in the war. Upon assuming the presidency, he proclaimed that he was not going to be the president who lost Vietnam, a "raggedy-ass little fourth-rate country." Events in Vietnam did not break his resolve. You

will need to point out that the assassination of Diem did not bring stability to South Vietnam, as regime after regime fell. When Johnson learned that North Vietnamese torpedo boats attacked a U.S. warship in the Gulf of Tonkin, he asked Congress to pass a resolution authorizing him to repel the aggression and to take any action needed to prevent further attack. Here you should explain the controversy surrounding the passage of the resolution. You will also wish to mention that the Gulf of Tonkin Resolution was the only formal sanction granted by Congress for U.S. involvement in the war. At this point turn your attention to the ways in which Johnson escalated U.S. involvement in the war following the resolution. Promising the American people that he would not send American soldiers off to fight in an Asian war, Johnson nevertheless expanded secret raids on North Vietnam, boosted military and economic aid to South Vietnam, and increased the number of American advisers. In the beginning of 1965, he initiated Operation Rolling Thunder and sent the first combat troops to South Vietnam. This shift to the Americanization of the war marked a critical turning point. Here you can describe the conditions of guerrilla warfare, the tenacity of the North Vietnamese and the National Liberation Front, and the massive protests back home, which began with Operation Rolling Thunder. It will be helpful to refer to Map 29.2, "The Vietnam War, 1964–1975." You might have your class discuss the *Historical Question* feature "Why Couldn't the United States Bomb Its Way to Victory in Vietnam?" You might also bring in the recommendations made by Secretary of Defense Robert McNamara in his 1966 secret memorandum to Johnson (in the documents reader). Close this lecture with Johnson's reversal of his policy after the 1968 Tet Offensive, his announcement that the United States would begin to curtail its bombing of North Vietnam, and his decision to not seek reelection.

LECTURE 3
Nixon and Vietnam

This lecture demonstrates how President Nixon de-escalated U.S. involvement in the Vietnam War. In an effort designed both to "Vietnamize" the war and to quiet domestic opposition, Nixon began a gradual withdrawal of U.S. ground troops from Vietnam. At this point you may wish to have your class discuss the effects of the growing antiwar movement on American soldiers fighting in Vietnam. Again, you can discuss the role images played in the first televised war. Robert D. Heinl's report on the state of military discipline and Arthur E. Woodley's recollections of his war experience (both in the documents reader) should help students focus their attention on this issue. Convey that, concomitant with the withdrawal of troops, the United States sought to strengthen the South Vietnamese military and government, and it negotiated with the Soviet Union and North Vietnam. Failing to reach his objectives, Nixon intensified the bombing of Cambodia and Laos, which served only to inflame the antiwar passions at home and impel Congress to try to rein in the president. Explain that antiwar sentiment continued as the public learned of the My Lai massacre and the administration's attempts to suppress the publication of the *Pentagon Papers*. In one final burst of power, Nixon ordered the "Christmas bombings" of North Vietnam in 1972. In January 1973 representatives from the United States, North Vietnam, South Vietnam, and the People's Revolutionary Government signed a formal accord. The United States began its military withdrawal, and Congress — by passing the War Powers Act — finally curbed the president's ability to fight a war without the consent of Congress. You can end this lecture with a summation of the legacies of the war.

Anticipating Student Reactions: Common Misconceptions and Difficult Topics

1. Americanization

With foreknowledge of the disastrous outcome, students always ask why Johnson chose to escalate U.S. involvement in the Vietnam War. You can explain that there were at least five reasons behind this choice. First, Johnson believed that because every president since Franklin Delano Roosevelt had made a commitment to Vietnam, U.S. credibility was at stake. Second, he also believed that China posed a legitimate threat to the region. Third, he feared that "appeasement" would lead to disastrous results, as it had in the 1930s. Fourth, he feared a domestic backlash if he pulled out of Vietnam. He was not interested in being labeled "soft on communism." Finally, Johnson genuinely believed the United States had the power to win the war.

2. Nixon's Secret War

Many students may question Nixon's secret bombing of Cambodia, wondering what prompted his action in the first place. Here you should explain that the North Vietnamese were able to use trails through Cambodia and Laos to supply troops in the South. The bombing threatened the stability of Cambodia, and in March 1970, Prince Norodom Sihanouk was overthrown by his prime minister, General Lon Nol, who was sympathetic to the Americans' efforts to rid Southeast Asia of Communists. The following month, Nixon launched an invasion of eastern Cambodia in an effort to destroy Communist camps. The effort failed, and by the end of the year, the Communists controlled over a third of the country. Undeterred by failure, however, Nixon attacked neighboring Laos in 1971 for similar reasons. Once again the Communists continued to gain ground, and once again Nixon's policy failed miserably.

Using the Bedford Series in History and Culture and the Historians at Work Series: Suggestions

For a compelling, in-depth treatment of one of the most horrendous incidents of the Vietnam War, have students read *My Lai: A Brief History with Documents*, edited by Randy Roberts and James Olsen.

Lecture Supplements and Classroom Activities

Using Multimedia Sources in the Classroom

The PBS series *Vietnam: A Television History* makes wonderful use of archival sources and news footage to provide a fascinating account of the ways in which that war changed America. You might want to screen scenes from a number of Hollywood films to convey the ways in which popular culture portrayed the conflict. Consider showing *M*A*S*H* (1970), a film purportedly about the Korean War but one that surely offered a commentary on U.S. policy in Vietnam. When discussing JFK's counterinsurgency tactics, you might want to show a clip from *Green Berets* (1968), starring John Wayne — a mediocre film, but the only one made about the Vietnam War during the conflict. When discussing the difficulties Vietnam veterans encountered when they came back to the United States, consider showing *The Deer Hunter* (1978) or *Coming Home* (1976). Finally, to offer revisionist perspectives, consider showing scenes from *Apocalypse Now* (1979), *Platoon* (1986), *Full Metal Jacket* (1987), or *Casualties of War* (1989).

Historical Contingencies

Have students speculate on what would have happened had the United States supported Ho Chi Minh during his Anti-French War of Resistance. Would U.S. security interests have been compromised by a nationalist presence in Southeast Asia from the 1940s to the 1970s? Would U.S. administrations have been doomed for being "soft on communism"? Would communism have spread throughout the region, undermining the stability the United States sought? Remind students that the U.S. policymakers feared that Ho Chi Minh was bent on territorial conquest. Was Ho Chi Minh another Adolf Hitler?

Classroom Activities

Have students debate where the guilt lay for the My Lai massacre. Olsen and Robert's work *My Lai: A Brief History with Documents* (cited above) will prove helpful on this score. How much responsibility rested with the soldiers? How much responsibility rested with William Calley and his staff? How much responsibility rested with the U.S. army for failing to train soldiers properly? How much responsibility rested with the nature of war itself?

Using the Internet

Students interested in learning more about U.S. policy in Vietnam should go to <http://www.yale.edu/lawweb/avalon/20th.htm> and enter "Vietnam" in the search field.

ASSESSING RESULTS
Multiple-Choice Questions

1. Kennedy's approach to foreign policy, which constituted a change from the Eisenhower administration, can best be described as
   a. containment.
   b. brinksmanship.
   c. flexible response.
   d. mutual deterrence.

2. Kennedy's credibility as a strong leader in the area of foreign policy rose dramatically after the
   a. Bay of Pigs invasion.
   b. Cuban missile crisis.
   c. East Berlin crisis.
   d. execution of Diem.

3. The Kennedy administration's desire to score a quick victory in Vietnam was thwarted by all of the following, except
   a. the South Vietnamese insurgents (Vietcong), a genuine indigenous force, whose initiatives came from within and not from the Soviet Union or China.
   b. the South Vietnamese government and army, which were ineffective vehicles for the American goal of suppressing rebellion.
   c. growing intervention by North Vietnam after 1959 and the creation of the NLF.
   d. Kennedy's refusal to escalate American commitment to South Vietnam and his pull-back of American military advisers stationed in South Vietnam.

4. The first president who committed combat troops to fighting in Vietnam was
   a. Harry S. Truman.
   b. Dwight D. Eisenhower.
   c. John F. Kennedy.
   d. Lyndon B. Johnson.

5. Mass protest at home against U.S. involvement in the war in Vietnam was prompted by
   a. the Gulf of Tonkin Resolution.
   b. Operation Rolling Thunder.
   c. the Tet Offensive.
   d. the My Lai massacre.

6. Which of the following statements is untrue of the Tet Offensive?
   a. It violated a truce that both sides had generally observed during the Asian holiday.
   b. It displayed the enemy's vitality and refusal to let the presence of 500,000 American soldiers deter it from launching its most daring offensive.
   c. It was a military success for the United States but a devastating psychological blow.
   d. Johnson escalated the U.S. bombing of North Vietnam in its aftermath.

7. Who ran for president in 1968 on the ticket of the American Independent Party?
   a. George C. Wallace
   b. Eugene McCarthy
   c. Barry Goldwater
   d. Hubert Humphrey

8. From 1969 to 1972, Nixon and Kissinger pursued a four-prong attack to ensure a non-Communist South Vietnam and to maintain American credibility, which included all of the following measures, except
   a. strengthening the South Vietnamese military and government.
   b. negotiating with the North Vietnamese and the Soviets.
   c. escalating the number of U.S. combat troops.
   d. attempting to force Hanoi to U.S. terms at the bargaining table.

9. Students gathered at a rally at Kent State University on May 4, 1970, to protest Nixon's secret bombing of
   a. Cambodia.
   b. Laos.
   c. North Vietnam.
   d. Thailand.

10. The legacy of the U.S. defeat in Vietnam included
    a. a backlash against the Republican Party for its escalation of the war, while the Democratic Party escaped rebuke.
    b. the fall of all Southeast Asian countries into the Communist camp.
    c. the continued friendly relations between China and Vietnam, supporting the U.S. contention that a monolithic Communist power would overrun Asia.
    d. the denial of a traditional homecoming to the American veterans because of the war's unpopularity at home, its characterization as a guerrilla war, and its ultimate failure.

11. According to the *Historical Question* feature, all of the following concerns caused President Johnson to limit bombing at various times in Vietnam, except
    a. concern about provoking the Chinese into intervening.
    b. concern about inflaming antiwar sentiment at home.
    c. worry about criticism from the world community.
    d. concern about provoking a war with neighboring Cambodia.

12. What was Vietnam veteran Arthur E. Woodley Jr.'s reaction to encountering a Vietnamese proprietor of a grocery store who recognized him (according to the document in the documents reader)?
    a. He felt pleased that he could meet and interact humanely with someone who had previously been the enemy.
    b. He resented the fact that the proprietor seemed to be thriving in the United States while he was still struggling.
    c. His old combat reflexes kicked in, and he came close to killing the man.
    d. He apologized to the proprietor on behalf of the U.S. army for the destruction and loss of life he and his fellow soldiers had caused during the Vietnam War.

13. Identify the correct sequence of historical events and figures.
    a. Cuban missile crisis, Operation Rolling Thunder, publication of *Pentagon Papers*, Gulf of Tonkin Resolution
    b. Bay of Pigs, Operation Rolling Thunder, secret bombing of Cambodia, Cuban missile crisis
    c. Tet Offensive, Cuban missile crisis, Bay of Pigs, publication of *Pentagon Papers*
    d. Cuban missile crisis, Operation Rolling Thunder, Tet Offensive, Nixon elected president

Proposing More: Additional Readings

L. M. Cromwell, "Thinking about the Vietnam War: A Review Essay," *Journal of Military History* 60, no. 2 (1996): 339–57.

Robert A. Divine, "Vietnam Reconsidered," *Diplomatic History* 12, no. 1 (1988): 79–93.

G. R. Hess, "The Unending Debate: Historians and the Vietnam War," *Diplomatic History* 18, no. 2 (1994): 239–64.

B. I. Kaufman, "John F. Kennedy as a World Leader: A Perspective on the Literature," *Diplomatic History* 17, no. 3 (1993): 447–69.

J. Lule, "Enduring Image of War: Myth and Ideology in a *Newsweek* Cover," *Journal of Popular Culture* 29, no. 1 (1995): 199–211.

Answer Key to Multiple-Choice Questions: 1-c, 2-b, 3-d, 4-d, 5-b, 6-d, 7-a, 8-c, 9-a, 10-d, 11-d, 12-b, 13-d

RETREAT FROM LIBERALISM

30

1968–2000

Outlining Chapters: Thematic Questions

I. In what ways did the reform movements of the 1960s persist into the 1970s?
   A. What was Richard M. Nixon's "southern strategy," and what effect did it have on race relations? In what ways did the Burger Court resemble the Warren Court? In what ways did it differ?
   B. What was the new feminism? What were the goals of the feminist movement in the 1970s? Why was there a conservative backlash against the movement?
   C. What elements characterized the environmental movement of the 1970s? What victories did it secure?
   D. In what ways did the Nixon administration extend the welfare state? How did it expand the role of the federal government in dealing with energy shortages, inflation, and unemployment?

II. What constitutional crisis confronted the United States during the 1970s, and how did the nation recover?
   A. Why was the election of 1972 a landslide? What events surrounded the break-in at Watergate? What crisis ensued?
   B. In what ways did the administration of President Gerald Ford represent an interregnum? What issues dominated the election of 1976?
   C. Why was Jimmy Carter seen as the "outsider president"? In what ways was the Carter administration unsuccessful in achieving progress on issues traditionally central to the Democratic Party?

III. What factors led to the rising tide of conservatism in America?
   A. What were the dominant issues in the election of 1980? What were the major conservative factions in 1980? In what ways did Ronald Reagan represent the wide spectrum of conservatism?
   B. What is "supply-side economics," and why did Reagan favor it? What role did Reagan believe free enterprise should play in the American economy? How did Reagan's economic policies affect the budget deficit, inflation, and unemployment?
   C. How did the administration of President George H. W. Bush seek to maintain the Reagan legacy?

IV. How did the Reagan administration seek to reverse federal protections of minorities and the disadvantaged?
   A. How and why did a conservative shift occur in the federal courts?

B. What setbacks did the women's movement face during the 1980s? What victories did it secure?

C. What was the agenda of the gay and lesbian rights movement?

D. In what ways did minorities continue to struggle during the Reagan-Bush years? What successes did minorities achieve?

V. What economic shocks rocked the nation during the 1980s?

A. What was the "money culture," and who benefited from it? How was much of the new wealth of the 1980s generated?

B. What factors contributed to the debt-based economy?

C. What was the "other side" of prosperity? What groups did not benefit from Reagan's economic and social policies?

VI. In what ways did President Bill Clinton's administration battle Republicans for center ground?

A. What reforms did Clinton promise Americans during the campaign of 1992?

B. What domestic policies did Clinton implement during his first administration, and what were the politics of incrementalism?

C. In what ways did the Clinton administration represent a move to the right for the Democratic Party?

D. Why did congressional Republicans move to impeach President Clinton during his second term in office? What charges of impeachment were levied against him? Why did the Senate refuse to remove Clinton from office?

E. What factors contributed to the economic boom of the 1990s?

F. What issues of controversy surrounded the election of 2000?

Teaching with **The American Promise,** *Second Compact Edition: Lecture Strategies*

LECTURE 1

The Nixon Administration and After

When covering Nixon's domestic agenda, emphasize the ways in which he sought to curb the government's role in protecting individual liberties and to capitalize on growing public dissatisfaction with social reform. To demonstrate Nixon's

attempts to counter the effects of Johnson's Great Society, you might wish to cover Nixon's relations with conservative southern white Democrats; the reasons he appointed Warren E. Burger, Lewis Powell, and William H. Rehnquist to the Supreme Court; his frequent clashes with feminists and environmentalists; and his initiative of a New Federalism, signaling the president's dislike of an expanding federal bureaucracy. Nevertheless, certain problems proved too threatening to abandon to the state. Here you can discuss the administration's response to three key economic problems — energy shortages, inflation, and unemployment — and explain the federal government's interventions in the economy.

The Watergate scandal fascinates most students, and you will want to take the time to go over the events that led to one of the worst constitutional crises in the nation's history. Explain the break-in at the Democratic National Headquarters, the cover-up, and all the attendant abuses such as the dirty tricks and illegal campaign contributions. When you cover the hearings, be sure to emphasize the role of television, especially in discussing John Dean's testimony that White House officials "harassed" their enemies and Alexander Butterfield's testimony that revealed a secret voice-activated taping system in the White House. Here you can go over the transcripts (in the documents reader), mentioning Nixon's steadfast refusal to hand over the tapes, despite Judge John J. Sirica's court order. Finally, discuss the House's vote to begin impeachment proceedings (explaining to students precisely what "impeachment" means); the Supreme Court's unanimous demand for the unedited, unexpurgated tapes; and Nixon's resignation. Emphasize that Nixon's departure from office did not end the crisis. One month later, President Gerald Ford granted Nixon a full pardon, ensuring that the former president would never stand trial and would never have to disclose his part in the scandal. End this lecture by covering the legacies of Watergate, demonstrating that the crisis precipitated a number of government reforms, such as the War Powers Act and the Federal Election Campaign Act of 1974. Perhaps the most significant legacies of Watergate were the criticism of government and the decline in confidence it engendered.

Include in your lecture the lingering legacies of Watergate that propelled Jimmy Carter to the White House in 1976, pointing to Carter's campaign promise, "I will never tell a lie," which carried a degree of cultural resonance that would have rung false before Watergate. Demonstrate to students that, once in office, Carter proved unable to win the confidence of the people. Be sure to highlight Carter's failings on the domestic front. First you will need to show that Carter worked poorly with Congress — even though the Democrats were in control, he was unable to push through key pieces of legislation. Second, he presided over severe economic and energy crises, which he seemed unable to manage. During the worst of the energy crisis, he appealed to Americans to lower their thermostats, conveying an image of a weak president who could not take charge of the situation. He lost his bid for a second term.

LECTURE 2
The Conservative Resurgence

This lecture conveys how Ronald Reagan's successful run for the presidency in 1980 marked a conservative shift in American politics and society. You might want to begin by having the class discuss "Lee Atwater Spins on the Reagan Campaign" (in the documents reader). Note the continued backlash against the upheavals associated with the 1960s, as well as the increasing political involvement of fundamentalist and evangelical Christianity, the rhetoric of militant anticommunism, and the veneration of the free-market economy. Emphasize the ways in which Reagan represented a wide spectrum of conservative ideology. Once in office, Reagan fulfilled his promise to enact a conservative political and economic agenda. Mention, for example, Reagan's supply-side economics and his support for deregulation. Move on to suggest that although Reagan failed to translate into concrete policy his beliefs in conservative moral and social goals, his rhetoric nonetheless captured the support of many Americans. Remind students of Reagan's ability to maintain popular support, despite his gaffes and his administration's errors, and his landslide victory in the 1984 election.

Move on to cover Reagan's successes and failures during his second administration. First, you might suggest that Reagan's conservative agenda successfully put liberals on the defensive in the 1980s. African Americans, other racial and ethnic minorities, women, and homosexuals scrambled to protect the gains that they had won in the past and secure new rights. Focus on the ways in which pressure groups, realizing that the federal administration and judiciary would stand against them, pursued their agenda at the local

level. Here have your students discuss the *Documenting the American Promise* feature, which presents material on civil rights actions to ban discrimination against homosexuals. Have them also look at the spot map that shows states with antidiscrimination laws for gays and lesbians. Also mention that although Reagan scored important victories in his first term, it became clear by his second term that his economic policies carried a heavy cost, as the U.S. trade deficit soared, investment declined, and the annual deficit and overall debt of the federal government reached astronomical levels. You will need to point out that gridlock in Congress, scandal in the administration, and a temperament that prevented Reagan from launching an all-out effort to secure the most controversial planks of his platform all ensured that the president would fall short of delivering an end to the welfare state.

LECTURE 3
The Culture of the 1980s and the Return of Centrist Politics in the 1990s

This lecture emphasizes the role of money and material possessions in defining American culture in the 1980s. The economy and society led some observers to talk about the "money culture" and to call the 1980s the "decade of greed." Americans clearly venerated free enterprise and entrepreneurship in the 1980s, as books by businesspeople climbed to the top of best-seller lists and television shows such as *Lifestyles of the Rich and Famous* captured millions of viewers. You might also wish to mention *Family Ties* whose character Alex P. Keaton epitomized the worship of money in the 1980s. On the darker side, you may want to mention two of the "brat-pack" authors, Jay McInerney and Bret Easton Ellis, whose respective novels *Bright Lights, Big City* and *Less than Zero* capture the hollowness of the money culture.

Counter your discussion of the money culture with a discussion of those whom the economic boom passed by. Here you will wish to cover the rise of homelessness and the poverty rate. Have your students take a look at Figure 30.1, "The growth of Inequality: Changes in Family Income, 1969–1998," which shows that after 1979, income of the poorest families declined while income for the wealthiest 5 percent of the population rose substantially. You will also want to discuss how the working poor had to struggle not to lose ground during the Reagan administration.

End your lecture by briefly covering the two Clinton administrations, emphasizing Clinton's wish to refashion the Democratic Party, shunning its past associations with liberal politics in favor of a more centrist image. Begin by pointing out that Clinton and his running mate Al Gore billed themselves as the "new Democrats" in the election of 1992, in an effort to distance themselves from the Democratic Party of old. Here suggest that Clinton recognized that the electorate, weary of the economic woes under the administration of George Bush, hungered for change but formed no majority around a particular direction that change could take. By projecting himself as a moderate, Clinton could capitalize on the desire for change without alienating voters. Next, turn to Clinton's record in office. Explore his domestic policy and the degree to which he fulfilled his campaign promises. Cover the threat from the conservative right that Clinton's administration encountered in the elections of 1994 and the degree to which the Republicans delivered on their "Contract with America." You then will want to cover the ways in which Clinton translated his first term in office into an election victory in 1996. End with congressional Republicans' attempt to remove Clinton from office and the reasons why that attempt failed.

Anticipating Student Reactions: Common Misconceptions and Difficult Topics

1. Rating Carter

Many students are familiar with Jimmy Carter's post-presidential activities with Habitat for Humanity, the Carter Center, and other human rights organizations and see him as an elder statesman. It is hard for them to recognize, therefore, that many consider his presidency unsuccessful. Ask them to assess Carter's inability to push through key pieces of his legislation; the weaknesses in his foreign policy; and, most important, his failure to appear presidential. His tactic of appearing as a Washington outsider may have worked to his advantage while campaigning for the White House, but it left him bereft of associates and connections once in office. Although his post-presidential activities seem to have conferred on him the stature of world leader, most historians believe he did not earn such status while in office.

2. The Teflon President

Students may wonder about Ronald Reagan's ability to shake off criticisms of his administration. Certainly Reagan seemed immune from the charges of incompetence levied against him by his critics and the media. He even managed to escape the Iran-Contra scandal — the most serious abuse of power in the executive branch since Watergate — relatively intact. Impart to your students the degree to which loyal members of the Reagan administration orchestrated the president's public appearances to eliminate the possibility of his appearing out of touch with reality. More important, perhaps, was Reagan's genuine affability. Point out the president's ability to laugh at himself (unlike Nixon) and his ability to put even his enemies at ease. Most people seemed to like the man even if they disagreed with his politics. Finally, you could suggest that his continued optimism and boasts of a strong America appealed to many citizens weary from American loss of credibility during the 1960s and 1970s.

3. Why Didn't Clinton Carry Congressional Democrats to Victory in the Election of 1996?

Students may ask why the electorate returned Bill Clinton to the White House in 1996 while at the same time electing a Republican Congress. Point out that this occurrence is not unprecedented. Democrat Grover Cleveland, for example, had a Democratic Congress in 1893–1895 only. More recently, Democrat Harry Truman had a Republican Congress after the elections of 1946, and Republican Ronald Reagan had a Democratic Congress after the 1986 elections. In Clinton's case, explain that voters did not trust Clinton's centrist position, fearing what he might attempt without the check of a Republican Congress. You might also point out that election returns suggest that Bob Dole, the Republican candidate, did not fare well with women voters and that Dole seemed unable to articulate his vision of what his presidency would bring.

Lecture Supplements and Classroom Activities

Using Multimedia Sources in the Classroom

There are a number of interesting Hollywood films that offer insight on America in the 1970s. The legacy of Watergate left a large imprint on American film. In addition to the obvious *All the*

President's Men (1976), which offers *Washington Post* reporters Bob Woodward and Carl Bernstein's account of the breaking of the story, consider showing the Robert Redford film *The Candidate* (1972), which tells the story of a seemingly forthright politician who proved to be susceptible to corruption. You might also want to show Warren Beatty's *The Parallax View* (1972), or Gene Hackman's *The Conversation* (1974), both of which demonstrate the popularity of conspiracy-theory films. When discussing working-class and youth culture, consider showing the cult classic *Saturday Night Fever* (1977). Clips from *The China Syndrome* (1979) can usefully illustrate the fear many Americans experienced over nuclear energy and serve as an indictment of television news. Perhaps the most scathing indictment of television, however, was the 1976 film *Network*, which works well in the classroom.

There are also a number of Hollywood films that capture the mood of the "go-go eighties." Bring up the 1987 film *Wall Street*, starring Michael Douglas, which chronicles the machinations of a Wall Street broker who compromises himself in order to rise to the top. The film adaptations of *Less than Zero* (1987) and *Bright Lights, Big City* (1988) offer the seamy underside of the money culture. Spike Lee's 1989 film *Do the Right Thing* delivers a fine commentary on the state of race relations in the late 1980s.

"Back to the Movement, 1979–1980s," part of the *Eyes on the Prize II* series, looks at the responses and strategies of the civil rights activists who faced a conservative backlash during the Reagan-Bush years. You might also consider showing the PBS biographical documentary *Reagan*.

Once Upon a Time in Arkansas, distributed by PBS Video, details Bill and Hillary Clinton's rise to power in Arkansas and untangles the web of Whitewater. *Frontline*'s "The Choice '96" profiles the 1996 presidential candidates. *Talking with David Frost: Ross Perot* offers Perot's views of the 1996 campaign and his expectations for the Reform Party. Episode 6, "God's Armies: 1989–1994," of the series *With God on Our Side: The Rise of the Religious Right in America* covers the relationship between religious fundamentalism and political activism during the early 1990s.

Historical Contingencies

Ask students what course American history might have taken if Ford had not pardoned Nixon. How would Nixon's almost-certain trial have shaped American political culture? Would Americans have remained so distrustful of their public officials and cynical of politics in general had Nixon stood trial for his crimes? These questions will allow students to explore the profound impact of the Watergate scandal on the political landscape. Would Ford have been able to hang on to the White House had he not pardoned Nixon? Would Ford have been any more successful than Carter in handling the crises of the late 1970s?

Classroom Activities

Have students discuss whether the malaise of the 1970s still affects their generation. Many students remain contemptuous of politicians and politics and no longer believe in politicians' ability to solve many of the problems the country now faces. Find out if your students fit this profile, and why. Does the legacy of Watergate still linger? You might ask them if Clinton's impeachment compounds the Watergate legacy.

Using the Internet

Students interested in Clinton's impeachment trial may want to check out the report by the U.S. House Committee on the Judiciary at <http://www.house.gov/judiciary/icreport.htm>.

ASSESSING RESULTS
Multiple-Choice Questions

1. Nixon's "southern strategy" referred to his attempt to
   a. woo conservative white southerners away from the Democratic Party to the Republican Party.
   b. court African American voters by championing a continuation of civil rights reform begun in the 1960s.
   c. appoint key southern politicians to his cabinet.
   d. persuade the Supreme Court to strike down civil rights legislation passed under the Johnson administration.

2. The National Organization for Women's three central demands included all of the following, except
   a. equality for women in employment and education.
   b. child care centers throughout the nation.
   c. women's control over reproduction, including the right to an abortion.
   d. an end to the judicial sanction of the institution of marriage.

3. The environmentalists differed from the conservationists because the environmentalists
   a. were concerned foremost with preserving portions of the natural world for aesthetic and recreational purposes.
   b. were concerned foremost with protecting human beings from the devastating side effects of industrial development and economic growth.
   c. were much less militant than the conservationists.
   d. failed to secure any legislative victories during the 1970s.

4. Which of the following factors led directly to Richard Nixon's resignation as president?
   a. His secretary of state informed him that remaining in office would seriously impair the conduct of the nation's foreign policy.
   b. His former chief aides testified that he had personally ordered the Watergate break-in.
   c. He began experiencing ulcers and heart palpitations.
   d. The Supreme Court unanimously ordered him to comply with Federal Judge Sirica's request for the release of the unedited, unexpurgated Watergate tapes.

5. Ronald Reagan's successful bid for the presidency in 1980 was aided by all of the following, except
   a. his party's unswerving support of the Equal Rights Amendment.
   b. the poor state of the economy.
   c. the country's declining international stature.
   d. his ability to represent a wide spectrum of conservative ideology.

6. Which of the following was a result of Reagan's economic policies?
   a. Inflation skyrocketed.
   b. The Sherman Antitrust Act was enforced with new vigor.
   c. The tax structure became more regressive.
   d. The federal budget deficit leveled off.

7. The campaign and election of 1988
   a. garnered the largest voter turnout in a presidential election since 1932.
   b. was particularly issueless and vitriolic.
   c. voted a Republican majority into both House and the Senate.
   d. saw the Republican candidate, George Bush, repudiating the legacy of Ronald Reagan, promising Americans to pursue a new course in domestic and foreign policy initiatives.

8. Bill Clinton and Al Gore billed themselves as the "new Democrats" during the 1992 presidential election in an effort to
   a. rid the Democratic Party of its liberal image.
   b. rid the Democratic Party of its conservative image.
   c. embrace the message of Jesse Jackson and his Rainbow Coalition.
   d. affirm their party's label as the "tax and spend" party.

9. Who was "Jane Roe" of the *Roe v. Wade* decision (in the documents reader)?
   a. a single female lawyer who was unable to get a legal abortion in Texas and decided to bring suit in federal court to overturn the Texas antiabortion law
   b. a woman whose true identity has (to protect her privacy) never been revealed
   c. Marilyn Jacobs, a mother of three living in Texas, who, unable to get a legal abortion in Texas, had a lawyer sue on her behalf
   d. Norma McCorvey, a young unmarried woman who was unable to get a legal abortion in Texas and had a lawyer bring suit on her behalf

10. Identify the correct sequence of historical events and figures.
    a. Nixon elected, *Roe v. Wade,* collapse of the savings and loans, Clinton impeachment trials
    b. Clarence Thomas nominated to the Supreme Court, Watergate hearings, Carter elected, collapse of the savings and loans
    c. Watergate hearings, Nixon reelected, *Silent Spring* published, Ford pardons Nixon
    d. *Roe v. Wade,* Nixon elected, Ford pardons Nixon, Kenneth Starr begins investigation of Clinton White House

Proposing More: Additional Readings

D. Brinkley, "The Rising Stock of Jimmy Carter: The Hands-On Legacy of Our Thirty-Ninth President," *Diplomatic History* 20, no. 4 (1996): 505–29.

L. S. Gelman and J. S. Todd, "Clarence Thomas, Black Pluralism, and Civil Rights Policy," *Political Science Quarterly* 107, no. 2 (1992): 231–48.

L. Horowitz, "From the New Deal to New Federalism: Presidential Ideology in the U.S. from 1932–1982," *American Journal of Economics and Sociology* 42, no. 2 (1983): 129–48.

Michael Rogin, "Ronald Reagan — the Movie," *Radical History Review* 38 (1987): 88–113.

David Thelen and Alexander P. Butterfield, "Conversations between Alexander P. Butterfield and David Thelen about the Discovery of the Watergate Tapes," *Journal of American History* 75, no. 4 (1989): 1245–62.

Answer Key to Multiple-Choice Questions: 1-a, 2-d, 3-b, 4-d, 5-a, 6-c, 7-b, 8-a, 9-d, 10-a

31 THE END OF THE COLD WAR AND THE CHALLENGES OF GLOBALIZATION

1975–2003

Outlining Chapters: Thematic Questions

I. What new opportunities and dangers confronted the United States in a multipolar world?
   A. In what ways did the United States move toward détente with the Soviet Union and China during Richard Nixon's administration?
   B. How did the Nixon administration support anti-Communist regimes in the third world?
   C. How did the Nixon administration respond to growing tensions in the Middle East?
   D. In what ways did idealism and concern for human rights influence Jimmy Carter's foreign policy?
   E. Why did the cold war intensify during the Carter administration? What events threw Carter's foreign policy into disarray?

II. How did Ronald Reagan respond to the threats posed to the United States by an "evil empire"?
   A. Why did Reagan favor an increase in military buildup? Why did he favor U.S. intervention abroad?
   B. What was the Iran-Contra scandal? What repercussions did the Reagan administration suffer because of it?
   C. How and why did a thaw in Soviet-American relations occur?

III. How did the post–cold war world create new foreign-policy objectives for the Bush and Clinton administrations?
   A. Why did the cold war end?
   B. Why did the United States become involved in the Gulf War?
   C. Where, and under what circumstances, did Clinton deploy U.S. power abroad? How did America and the international community view his decisions?

IV. How did the United States attempt to shape globalization?
   A. What issues surrounded the debate on globalization?
   B. How did the Clinton administration attempt to liberalize foreign trade?
   C. In what ways has the United States become internationalized?

Teaching with The American Promise, *Second Compact Edition:* Lecture Strategies

LECTURE 1
The Lingering Cold War

Begin this lecture on the lingering cold war by emphasizing how Richard Nixon and Henry Kissinger played China and the Soviet Union against each other under the assumption that "the enemy of my enemy is my friend." To defuse the tension between the Soviet Union and China, Nixon and Kissinger pursued a new approach to foreign policy, judging countries (including ones with Communist regimes) on the basis of their actions toward the world community and the United States rather than their political ideologies. Explain that the Nixon administration exploited three common areas of interest between the United States and the Soviet Union — arms control, trade, and stability in Europe — in an effort to reach détente with the other superpower. The tension between the United States and other Communist and Marxist governments, however, did not ease, and you might finish here by reviewing Nixon's traditional style of American foreign policy with Chile, Vietnam, and the Middle East.

Introduce Carter's foreign policy by suggesting to students that in this arena, as U.S.-Soviet relations deteriorated, Carter seemed weak. His abandonment of his own human rights principles when dealing with South Korea, China, and the Philippines alienated his liberal supporters, and his signing of the Panama Canal Treaty received condemnation from those who believed the United States should retain rights to the vital waterway. He did score a coup in foreign policy when he presided over the peace accords between Israel and Egypt, but any gain was eclipsed by the Iranian hostage crisis. Carter's inability to ensure a safe return for the American hostages doomed his bid for reelection. In a bitter twist of irony, Iran released the hostages the day Carter left office.

Remind students that Ronald Reagan capitalized on Carter's seeming inability to handle the hostage crisis. Once in office, Reagan fulfilled his promise to enact a conservative agenda. Here you will wish to go over the increases in military spending and U.S.-sponsored incursions in Latin American countries in an effort to depose popularly elected leftists and install friendly right-wing dictators. Close by covering Reagan's ability to maintain popular support, despite his gaffes and his administration's errors, and his landslide victory in the 1984 election.

End this lecture by suggesting that Reagan faced his greatest presidential challenge with the Iran-Contra scandal. Be sure to mention that Reagan managed to survive the scandal, in part because of his affable personality but also because he presided over a relaxation of tensions with the Soviet Union.

LECTURE 2
The End of the Cold War

Begin this lecture by highlighting the dramatic events that led to the end of the cold war. American students may be familiar with Reagan's involvement in the process. Be sure to stress that the "fall of communism" stemmed as much from pressures within the Soviet Union as it did from pressures exerted by the United States. Note that in the late 1980s Eastern Europe witnessed popular uprisings whose participants demanded an end to state repression, official corruption, and economic bureaucracies that failed to deliver an acceptable standard of living. Americans cheered the collapse of the Soviet Union. Remind students that a post–cold war world did not signal a post-nuclear world, however. Constructing foreign policy on nuclear weapons in the post–cold war era has proved to be one of the country's greatest challenges in the past decade.

Next, look at foreign policy under the administration of George Bush. Begin by having students discuss his 1991 State of the Union message (excerpted in the documents reader). Be sure to cover Operation Desert Storm, Bush's greatest triumph. Ask students to consider the reasons for U.S. involvement. Ask students why most Americans supported the Bush administration's efforts on behalf of Kuwait. Bush interpreted U.S. support of the war effort — and quick military victory — to suggest that "we've kicked the Vietnam syndrome once and for all." Ask students to interpret the Gulf War in terms of the legacy of the Vietnam War.

Move on to Clinton's foreign-policy objectives. Begin by asking students to list the imperatives of the post–cold war world. What are the U.S. priorities? Then cover the ways in which Clinton sought to act on those priorities, noting limitations placed on him by Congress, American public opinion, and international realities. Cover U.S. (or joint U.S.-NATO/U.S.-UN) initiatives in Africa, the Middle East, the Caribbean, and Central and Eastern Europe. Pay particular attention to crisis in the former Yugoslavia. Ask students to recall the origins of World War I, the boundaries drawn after the war, and the installation of communism in the region following World War II. You might end this lecture by asking students to evaluate the U.S. government's commitment to aiding refugees from Kosovo. Remind students of U.S. policy toward Jews escaping Nazi Europe or, more recently, public outcry against the influx of refugee Haitians into Florida.

Finally, cover U.S. efforts to shape globalization. Mention that although the debates surrounding globalization are not new, they have particular resonance with Americans in a post–cold war world. Remind students that most of the controversy centered on relationships between the United States and developing nations on the periphery. Have students debate the relative merits of attracting foreign investment at the expense of labor and environmental standards. Be sure students discuss the opening vignette on the 1999 World Trade Organization protests in Seattle. Have them look at the "Top Ten Reasons to Shutter the WTO," included in the documents reader. End this lecture by addressing the ways in which globalization has transformed the American economy and society. Be sure to look at the "internationalization" of American companies as well as the surge in immigration that globalization has engendered.

Anticipating Student Reactions: Common Misconceptions and Difficult Topics

1. Rating Nixon

Students frequently have trouble assessing the Nixon administration and often ask whether he was a good or a bad president. They especially have a hard time reconciling his "opening" of China with his involvement in Watergate and the secret bombing of Cambodia. Some students may have seen Oliver Stone's film *Nixon,* and their perceptions will undoubtedly be colored by it. You may wish to have your students discuss the legacies of détente with China and the Soviet Union, the bombing of Cambodia, and Watergate, emphasizing that the same man was responsible for all of these decisions.

2. The Gulf War

Be prepared to field questions concerning the "real" motives behind the Gulf War. The more cynical students will accuse the United States of fighting solely to protect its oil interests in the Middle East. The more idealistic ones will defend U.S. actions to rid the world of Saddam Hussein's regime and to protect the principle of national self-determination. Ask your students to consider the ways in which the Bush administration was able to translate U.S. concerns into global concerns. Remind your class that by late 1990 the UN Security Council authorized the use of "all means necessary" to rid Kuwait of Iraqi forces and by early 1991 almost all the world — including the Soviet Union — participated in an embargo of Iraqi oil. You might want to discuss the aftermath of the war. Ask your students to evaluate the effectiveness of continued economic sanctions; they crippled the Iraqi infrastructure but did not rid the country of Hussein. Have students speculate on the reasons why the United States continues to support economic sanctions while other nations plan to abandon this weapon of international economic power.

3. NAFTA, GATT, and America's Place in the World Economy

Since students sometimes have difficulty with economic issues, you might want to take some time to discuss the effects and significance of the North American Free Trade Agreement pact and the General Agreement on Tariffs and Trade. Who opposed them, who supported them, and why? When describing the battles regarding NAFTA and GATT, make the point that a politically charged debate over issues of free trade has been going on in this country almost since its founding. Ask students about or remind them of earlier debates in U.S. history over tariffs and protectionism. If appropriate, you can then discuss the future of the American economy, the role of the United States in the post–cold war global economy, and the concerns of American workers as a new century unfolds. You may want to end this discussion by looking at the 1999 protests over the World Trade Organization talks in Seattle.

Lecture Supplements and Classroom Activities

Using Multimedia in the Classroom

Rambo: First Blood Part II, Rambo III, and *Rocky III* (all starring Sylvester Stallone) capture the jingoism of the Reagan years. "The Gulf War," a two-part program that is part of the PBS series *Frontline,* explores the fighting on the battlefield and American and Iraqi headquarters. You might also consider showing the PBS biographical documentary *Reagan*.

Historical Contingencies

Students may assume that the events in Eastern Europe and the Soviet Union mean that communism was an inherently weak system destined to fail. Have students speculate the possible course of American history had Communist regimes remained intact. What would have been the implications of a continuing arms race for the U.S. economy? Would Bush have won the election of 1988 so handily? Would Bush have committed U.S. troops in the Middle East to fight Saddam Hussein?

Classroom Activities

Have students debate the degree to which the promise of America has been fulfilled. Consider making use of the *Historical Question* feature "Still a Promised Land?" and the documents reader to have students explore and discuss different aspects of American society in recent years. What role did immigration play in shaping American society during the 1980s and 1990s? Have students read the brief oral history on the Vietnamese immigrants in the documents reader. What are these immigrants' attitudes toward their lives, work, families, and America? Ask students whether they think these people have achieved the American dream. Do the people themselves think so?

Using the Internet

The Avalon Project, sponsored by Yale University Law School, makes documents relating to America's foreign policy available online. Tell students to go to <http://www.yale.edu/lawweb/avalon/avalon.htm>. From the home page, click on "Twentieth Century Documents." Here students will find texts on the Camp David Accords, the Dayton Accords, UN Resolutions on Kosovo, and a host of other material relevant to this chapter.

ASSESSING RESULTS
Multiple-Choice Questions

1. Nixon and Kissinger's strategy of easing tensions with the Soviets is known as
   a. détente.
   b. entente.
   c. brinksmanship.
   d. mutual deterrence.

2. Jimmy Carter scored his greatest foreign-policy victory in
   a. Latin America.
   b. the Soviet Union.
   c. China.
   d. the Middle East.

3. Iranian fundamentalists seized control of the U.S. embassy in Teheran on November 4, 1979, because of all of the following, except
   a. lingering resentment of the CIA's role in the ousting of the Mohammed Mossadegh's nationalist government in 1953.
   b. anger at persistent U.S. attempts to block Iran's modernization efforts.
   c. disgust at U.S. attempts to Westernize Iran.
   d. U.S. support of the shah's pro-Western government.

4. Which of the following statements best describes Ronald Reagan's foreign-policy goals?
   a. Reagan sought to cut back on conventional armed forces.
   b. Reagan scaled back on U.S. interventions in Latin America in an effort to shore up friendly relations with democratically elected leftist governments.
   c. Reagan rejected plans to research a "Strategic Defense Initiative" for fear that it would suggest to Soviets that the United States could launch a first strike without fear of retaliation.
   d. Reagan used economic pressure to destabilize unfriendly Latin American governments and provided weapons and training to "freedom fighters."

5. Which of the following statements best characterized the thaw in U.S.-Soviet relations during the 1980s?
   a. The thaw depended heavily on Reagan's friendly approach to the Soviet Union.
   b. Reagan, facing increased congressional resistance to funding the arms race, responded to Mikhail Gorbachev's arms reductions initiatives.
   c. Reagan refused to ease up on his anti-Communist rhetoric, despite his negotiations with the Soviets.
   d. Despite the easing of tensions, the Soviet Union and the United States never matched the level of détente reached by Nixon and Kissinger in the late 1960s and early 1970s.

6. The Persian Gulf War
   a. cost the United States relatively little in terms of military expenditures or lives lost.
   b. was waged without the consent of Congress.

   c. led most Americans to protest U.S. involvement.
   d. led to increased stability in the Middle East.

7. Which of the following was not a major foreign-policy goal during Clinton's administrations?
   a. promoting stability in the Middle East
   b. tightening restrictions on international trade
   c. checking the proliferation of governments in possession of nuclear weapons
   d. hammering out a workable peace for the troubled states of Serbia, Croatia, and Bosnia

8. The spot map of the breakup of Yugoslavia demonstrates that
   a. the country increased its territorial base in 1991, when Macedonia and Croatia joined its boundaries.
   b. as of 1991 it consisted of three republics: Serbia, Montenegro, and Macedonia.
   c. four breakaway republics were successful in their bids for independence.
   d. the country merged with Austria in 1991.

9. Identify the correct sequence of historical events and figures.
   a. WTO protests, NAFTA signed, invasion of Grenada, communism collapses in Eastern Europe
   b. the United States invades Panama, Iran hostage crisis, Nixon visits China, WTO protest
   c. Gulf War, communism collapses in Eastern Europe, invasion of Grenada, Camp David accords
   d. the United States invades Grenada, Iran-Contra scandal, Gulf War, WTO protests

PROPOSING MORE: Additional Readings

R. L. Beisner, "History and Henry Kissinger," *Diplomatic History* 14, no. 4 (1990): 511–27.

K. Breazeale, "Bringing the War Home: Consuming Operation Desert Storm," *Journal of American Culture* 17, no. 1 (1994): 31–37.

Walter Laqueur, "Gorbachev and Epimetheus: The Origins of the Russian Crisis," *Journal of Contemporary History* 28, no. 3 (1993): 387–419.

G. T. Leonard, "A Loose Cannon: Oliver North and Weberian Charisma," *Journal of Popular Culture* 21, no. 4 (1988): 129–39.

Leo Ribuffo, "Is Poland a Soviet Satellite? Gerald Ford, the Sonnenfeldt Doctrine, and the Election of 1976," *Diplomatic History* 14, no. 3 (1990): 385–403.

Eugene Victor Rostow and Patrick Glynn, "Bosnia: Is It Too Late?" *Commentary* 99 (1995): 31–36.

Answer Key to Multiple-Choice Questions: 1-a, 2-d, 3-b, 4-d, 5-b, 6-a, 7-b, 8-c, 9-d

Essay Questions, Chapters 26–31

1. The events at the 1968 Democratic National Convention in Chicago suggested to many that the nation was disintegrating. But, as the authors of the textbook have noted, the tensions that seemed so palpable that summer had been long in developing and had "revealed deep cracks" in the postwar liberal consensus. How real was the postwar consensus? What caused such a seismic breakdown in social harmony? In other words, why did the optimism and idealism that had characterized the 1950s and early 1960s give way to disillusionment and polarization?

2. In a 1969 address, Vice President Spiro T. Agnew discussed the "importance of the television news medium to the American people." He noted that "it must be recognized that the networks have made important contributions to the national knowledge — for news, documentaries, and specials. They have often used their power constructively and creatively to awaken the public consciousness to critical problems. . . . The networks have tackled our most difficult social problems with a directness and an immediacy that's the gift of their medium." But he also suggested that news anchors may "allow their biases to influence the selection and presentation of the news." Indeed, he even charged that the views of the majority of anchors "do not — and I repeat, not — represent the views of America." Evaluate Agnew's contention. In what ways did the medium of television news shape U.S. public opinion from 1945 to 2001? In what ways did various groups use television news to advance their causes? Did television news dictate America's foreign and domestic policy?

Ultimately, was the power of the television news a positive or a negative force in American history?

3. George F. Kennan, a diplomat stationed in Moscow, sent a long, secret telegram to his superiors in February 1946, outlining his plan for dealing with Soviet aggression. Arguing that "there can be no permanent peaceful co-existence" between the United States and the Soviet Union, Kennan warned that the United States must prepare itself to face certain global responsibilities. "We must formulate and put forward for other nations," he told policymakers, "a much more positive and constructive picture of [the] sort of world we would like to see." Kennan's proposal hardened into the theory of containment, which guided U.S. foreign policy through the end of the cold war. Some have argued that Kennan's policy forced the United States to be a global watchdog, compelling it to intervene in areas in which it had no legitimate claim. Others, however, have argued that this hard-line position was necessary to fend off Soviet encroachment and, indeed, led to the fall of the Soviet Union. In what cases did America follow Kennan's containment policy from 1946 to 1989? Did it unduly restrict possible courses of action? How successful was America in combating Soviet aggression during this period? Were there any shortcomings of this policy?

4. FDR had hoped that the wartime alliance between the United States and the Soviet Union would continue in the postwar world. Yet the two nations soon became locked in a global conflict that came to dominate international relations for the next forty years. This cold war also had profound implications for U.S. domestic policy and culture. Discuss the ways in which heightened tension with the Soviets influenced America's national scene from 1945 to 1989. What were the benefits and losses of this "great fear" in American culture?

5. Some pundits have advanced the "wag the dog" theory of domestic scandal and foreign policy. American presidents, they argue, commit the United States to overseas conflicts to divert public attention from national unrest or outcry. Evaluate this contention from 1945 to 2001. Have U.S. presidents unnecessarily involved troops and economic resources in dubious overseas efforts, thereby masking or stifling discussion on legitimate and pressing domestic concerns? Or have presidents reluctantly become involved overseas for legitimate reasons even though they realize that domestic social reform might suffer?

DISCUSSING *THE AMERICAN PROMISE*

A SURVIVAL GUIDE FOR FIRST-TIME TEACHING ASSISTANTS

by MICHAEL A. BELLESILES
Emory University

Contents

Introduction

> All education is a continuous dialogue —
> questions and answers that pursue every
> problem to the horizon. that is the essence of
> academic freedom.
>
> — *William O. Douglas*

The Role of a Teaching Assistant

Reflect for a moment on the best teachers you have encountered in your educational career. Like most great teachers, they were probably fired by some seldom-expressed idealism, a conviction that teaching is the ultimate form of subversion, capable of touching the lives of the young and permanently undermining complacency. The most effective teaching often appears effortless, but it is in fact the product of a lifetime's commitment to helping others and years of practice and preparation. It is probable that one of these great teachers inspired you to want to teach also, and you may hope to emulate your mentor's example, but you also have to write a dissertation. This handbook seeks to diminish stress, save you time, and increase your self-confidence as a teacher. Taken together, these three goals should make your job a lot easier while making space for your own research. I hope what follows makes clear that the opportunity to teach undergraduates will actually promote the development and clarification of your scholarship.

Teaching and Scholarship

As teaching assistantship is for most graduate students the introduction to teaching, it is a wonderful opportunity to develop skills you will use later in your career. Your TAship raises a justifiable fear: Will it interfere with the completion of your thesis or dissertation? the answer is no, for the opposite should be the case. There are many reasons why being a teaching assistant should enhance the development of your scholarship, especially if you look to your colleagues, your fellow TAs, and professor for help and guidance. this survival guide intends to promote this idea, making a difficult task simpler and saving you from having to reinvent the wheel.

Getting to Know The American Promise

While *The American Promise*, Second Compact Edition, is written with a unified voice, it is the product of the labor of six outstanding scholars, each with his or her own area of research expertise. These six historians — James L. Roark, Michael P. Johnson, Patricia Cline Cohen, Sarah Stage, Alan Lawson, and Susan M. Hartmann — all have experience teaching large survey courses, and they have endeavored to apply that collective experience in this textbook. What you read in *The American Promise* emerges from their classrooms: an appreciation for what worked and what did not. All of the authors have directly confronted many widely held misapprehensions about American history that have hampered their ability to teach effectively. The very nature of history is generally misunderstood, with most people believing it is little more than the memorization of a few, or too many, key facts. This text attempts to sweep away much of that debris, to provide students not simply a compelling version of one of the great stories of all time, American history, but also to lend insight into the working of history itself. Thus, for instance, the value of the *Historical Questions* features of the text, which remind us that history is detective work and that such inquiry begins by asking the right questions.

Naturally, specific chapters of *The American Promise* relate to the authors' own research, but the book is also an effort by six specialists to recapture the broad sweep of American history. Delineating the general currents of American history has, in turn, aided the authors in placing their scholarship within a larger portrait of U.S. history.

Similarly, serving as TA will provide you with a valuable opportunity to conceptualize your dissertation within the main currents of American history. One of the pitfalls commonly encountered while writing a dissertation is mistaking a few trees for a forest. Most of us have, at one time or another, become so engaged with our own research that we cannot imagine how anyone can fail to perceive its centrality. James Roark's ability to frame his focused study of planters in South Carolina within the national struggle to remake the nation in the aftermath of the Civil War won his dissertation, "Masters without Slaves," the Nevins Award. Alan Lawson, another member of *The American Promise* team, also won the Nevins prize for his dissertation, "The Failure of Independent Liberalism."

Your TAship offers both beneficial teaching experience and an opportunity to step back from your research and ask the larger questions of history. In teaching, you should not hesitate to share your developing ideas with your students, who are often interested in the scholarly process. And you may find that one gratifying surprise of teaching is that the instructor learns a great deal from the students.

1. Working with a Professor

DEFINING YOUR ROLES

Make no mistake, a TAship is not easy. Most likely, you neither designed this class nor selected the readings; and you will not deliver the lectures. Your position is essentially that of an apprentice, learning the craft not simply by being shown the tools and their use but by observing someone who has mastered the skill.

The boundaries between professors and TAs differ with the institution, its size and traditions, and the people involved. At UCLA I taught classes with hundreds of students and eighteen TAs. initially I did not know most of my graduate TAs, and vice versa. I was required, as is the case at most large research institutions, to supervise and inspect the work of these TAs. Such a situation necessitates a formal relationship, especially as the TAs knew that I would be writing a letter for their files. In contrast, at Emory, I have never had more than two TAs in a class, and more informal associations result. But in either context, yours in a slightly anomalous position. Most of the time you are entirely free to conduct your section as you see fit, though within a context set by the professor. The professor selects the readings and topics, but you determine how to address the material. In discussion, the initiative is entirely yours; aiding students with their writing and grading they work will probably also be your responsibility. But you should not forget that the first and the final word always belongs to the professor, who sets the syllabus and signs the gradesheet. I therefore suggest that it is wise to follow the tone he or she sets. The professor will quickly make it obvious whether you are a colleague or an assistant. If the latter, adhere to the formalities; if the former, take advantage of the opportunity to work closely with an experienced instructor to learn the art of teaching.

DISAGREEING: WHAT TO DO

TAs often agonize over occasions when the professor presents views with which they do not agree or that contradict the textbook. Such situations are, in fact, likely to happen, as historical interpretation is full of such disagreements; the lack of uniformity is what gives history its life and excitement. The best tactic is to speak with the professor about such perceived inconsistencies, though not everyone is comfortable with the direct approach. While it would be inappropriate to tell your students that the professor's point of view is wrong, it is legitimate to raise the question of alternative perspectives in your discussion sections and to use it as an exercise in historical method. *The American Promise* will prove helpful in such a situation. The professor has assigned this book and so should have no objection to your making use of its contents.

For example, when I was in high school we were all taught that America was founded by people seeking religious freedom. Since I knew that was not true of my ancestors, this version of history always bothered me. Imagine my pleasure when I read William Bradford's *Of Plymouth Plantation* in college and learned that not even those famous Pilgrims came to America seeking "religious freedom." Yet the very next day in class my professor insisted that "America was founded by people seeking religious freedom." If the professor for whom you are working makes such a statement, you may want to turn to *The American Promise* to address the complexities of this issue. Ask the students to establish the degree of religious influence in the settlement of North America. As the students hunt through Chapters 3 and 4 under your guidance, they will find support for religious freedom as a foundation of American settlement, particularly in the opening pages of Chapter 4. Pursue the issue a little further, and ask why, exactly, the Pilgrims crossed the Atlantic. Did the Pilgrims flee religious persecution or did their desire to "protect their children's piety and preserve their community" (ch. 4, p. 70) reflect intolerance on their part? From there, consider the motivations of the Puritans, as discussed in the section "The Founding of Massachusetts Bay Colony," and then move back to Chapter 3 and examine the settlement of the Chesapeake. Was religion at work in this colony, or do we see an English effort to extend power, or perhaps individual greed? The text notes each in turn, from the Virginia Company's boast that they sought the conversion of the Indians to Christianity to the ruthless exploitation of the powerless — Indian, white, and black. As is appropriate in examining the religious, social, and political turmoil of the seventeenth century, no one explanation suffices. Because history lacks a single correct interpretation you must aid the students in developing their own analytical skills.

Highlighting various interpretations does not contradict statements by the instructor. Rather it allows the students to come to terms with the difficulty of the historian's task, while helping them to construct their own informed judgment. The text is your anchor, which you can rely on in any classroom situation.

You can take further advantage of working with a professor by observing his or her teaching style. Decide for yourself what are valuable methods in the classroom. If it is not part of your TA program to have the professor speak with you about pedagogical issues, join with your fellow TAs to invite him or her to do so. Most professors welcome the opportunity to talk about teaching itself, and you may find that the invitation opens a number of doors. For there are other ways to learn and acquire teaching skills. For instance, if your professor invites you to deliver a guest lecture to the class, leap at the opportunity, as it is great practice and can figure prominently in a future letter of recommendation from that professor. Likewise, consider asking your professor or graduate adviser to sit in on one of your sections. When the time comes to enter the job market, you will benefit enormously by having letters of recommendation that speak knowledgeably about your teaching experience. In short, the TAship is your route to ensuring that you get to teach even more after you have finished your dissertation.

2. Working with Students

CLASSROOM ATMOSPHERE

TAs naturally want to work with their students in the friendliest possible fashion. Students, in turn, generally respect TAs and respond well to a relaxed atmosphere. Nonetheless, students also know that the TA is not a professor, and some will occasionally try to exploit the situation. Over the years, instructors have heard every imaginable excuse and plea for special consideration, as well as some that defy the imagination. Your best defense can be a stern offense, clarifying both your accessibility and your professionalism. There are no hard-and-fast rules on how to achieve this balance in the classroom, and every class has its own dynamic. What follows are a number of suggestions on how to establish a professional distance while retaining a sense of camaraderie.

AVOIDING PITFALLS

Some aspects of teaching can only be learned the hard way. It may seem unlikely, but some students feel betrayed if they think of you as a close friend and get less than an excellent grade. Other students may turn to you as a personal confessor and share their most private confidences, leading to embarrassment and the lessening of your professional standing with both the other students and your professor. Most dangerous of all, a student may misunderstand your friendliness as an invitation to intimacy. An accusation of sexual harassment can have dire consequences for your professional and personal life.

How you respond to, shall we say, an excess of friendliness depends on your personality. I tell all the teaching assistants I train here at Emory that there are three rules:

1. No overloads (that is, never increase the size of your class, it is already too large)

2. No sarcasm (students hate it!)

3. No private meetings with students behind closed doors

Always leave your door open when a student is in your office. One of my TAs this year will only meet students in the middle of the quad; two others hold their office hours together. I have no trouble saying to a student intent on telling me stories that are far too personal, "I'm sorry, that is none of my business." Some will turn the conversation back to the textbook. But sometimes there is no way of avoiding the student who tearfully tells you some desperate family trauma and begs for your understanding. Always keep at hand the phone number of the counseling center and make sure you know where the center is located. When I was a TA, one of my students told me that he could not turn in his paper because he had thrown up on his typewriter (yes, we used typewriters in the early 1980s) and that he had a terminal illness. Having ascertained that he was unclear on the meaning of "terminal illness" and did not have such, I learned more than I cared to about this young man's crisis of confidence. Convincing him that others could be of greater assistance to him, I called the counseling center and immediately set up an appointment. In this case, by the way, the student took a semester off, took a job, and returned to college the following year, much better prepared for the task before him. You can only hope that none of your students will throw up on a computer — or claim to — but you may want to be ready for the unexpected.

From experience then, most professors discover the need to maintain a friendly but critical distance. The challenge is to remember that working as a TA is part of the process of becoming a professional and therefore requires an appreciation for the trust placed in any teacher. When a student tells you of a personal crisis, it is best to take it seriously and offer sympathy; it is also best to let those better qualified than you deal with the problem.

Finally, there is a tendency among many professors and graduate student instructors to treat their students with disdain, to make fun of their ignorance and belittle their writing skills. While it certainly can relieve tension to get together with other TAs to compare classroom confusions, making fun of your students will quickly take the joy out of teaching and make you question your commitment. Also, undergraduates usually notice a negative attitude. Try to recall your own undergraduate experiences. At the beginning of every academic year I read one of my own papers from my freshman year. It is a sobering experience, and one that makes me appreciate even more how much I gained from a college education.

3. Leading Discussions

For most TAs, the majority of class time is spent conducting discussions based on the lectures, the readings, or both. In terms of effective teaching, discussions are preferable to lectures. It is easier to keep students' attention when they are part of the discussion. Their involvement helps to ensure that they are absorbing information and alerts the instructor to what is working and sinking in and what is not. As John Stuart Mill noted, a diversity of opinions leads to the discovery of new truths. And a highly interactive class is just more fun.

The key to a great discussion is preparation — not the sort of intricate organization that force-marches the students through the material but a thorough understanding of the topic and a conception of the key issues that need to be addressed. Advance preparation will make it all look easy to the students while allowing you the confidence to respond with flexibility to the flow of the discussion.

This guide is directed at aiding the TA in getting started. Examples are therefore drawn from the first chapters of *The American Promise* that you are likely to use in the first month of classes. While these particular examples are just suggestions, their logic should be transferable to other chapters and other periods in U.S. history.

THE FIRST DAY OF CLASS

Your first task is to ease your students' tension and anxieties. They are generally nervous about taking a history class that requires them to synthesize both lectures and readings at the college level. Often they do not know anyone else in the section and are scared to voice opinions in front of peers. Even though this is an introductory U.S. history course, you may be surprised to learn how many of your students disliked high school history and learned little of what we understand history to be. Many students think of history as the memorization of dates. You therefore need to reassure your students that there is a lot more to history than dates and that it will be worth their time to give it a second chance. As discussed below, you can turn directly to the opening pages of the textbook for a quick introduction to the workings of history. However, if you are comfortable doing so, you may want to introduce both yourself and the subject by talking a bit about the origins of your own fascination with history and what sustains that interest. Nothing — heavy emphasis — makes an introductory course more successful than the enthusiasm of the instructor for the material.

ICEBREAKERS

Before addressing the subject matter, turn to your students. If you can establish even the loosest sense of community on the first day, you will find the days ahead far more pleasant as your students will be a little less hesitant to share their judgments and far more receptive to your leadership. So get acquainted quickly, indicating that they are among friends and that what they have to say will be heard and respected. It is usually not sufficient to go around the room and ask the students to give their names. You must instead try to get a sense of their identities. One way is to ask each student to relay the standard information — name, academic year, major, where he or she is from — and then add something unique, such as a favorite record or the last book he or she read for pleasure. You may even want to write this information down on index cards as a way of helping yourself to learn each student's name over the first few weeks. Alternatively, try some version of the "name game." I pair off my students and ask them not simply to tell one another their names but to say something about the history of that name; what it means, where it came from, if it originally belonged to someone else, like a grandparent. After a few minutes of letting the students talk and relax, I go around the room and ask each student to tell all of us about his or her neighbor. By the end of this exercise, I can be fairly confident that my students will not refer to one another as "that guy" and that they will get a sense of the personal power of history.

After spending some time getting to know one another, you may want to share with your students your goals for the semester. Even here, though, I like to keep the tone light. When students first hear about an essay assignment, they often start worrying almost immediately about what they are going to do it on. I prefer to frame my discussion of the paper assignment within the context of questions or doubts they may have about U.S. history. For instance, ask your students what one fact from American history bugs them most. Write those events on the board — and they will probably run the gamut from slavery to the invention of the shopping mall. Then ask them which single fact makes them most proud to be in the United States. The events you write on the board form a range of possible research and discussion topics.

Before the students leave the classroom, make certain that they know how to reach you, and vice versa. With e-mail, this task has become easier. Circulate a list and ask them to record their electronic addresses. If you have the time, make up a list of e-mail addresses so you can send reminders to your students of upcoming assignments. They will certainly appreciate the extra effort on your part. I usually send out a message the day after the first class, just reminding everyone of my office hours and our first readings together. After sixteen years of teaching, I am still surprised how much students welcome any indication that their teachers care.

Whatever you do on the first day, it is appropriate and advisable to keep it light and informal; a friendly atmosphere pays long-term dividends in the classroom. It is for that reason that I prefer students to use my first name. They know I'm a professor. Likewise, I do not believe that calling an instructor by his or her first name diminishes respect. But if you want to be called Mr. or Ms. TA, it is best to make that clear up front by introducing yourself that way.

PREPARING TO TEACH A SECTION

Traditionally, American history TAs lead sections in introductory U.S. history survey courses, with the first of two parts concluding with the end of Reconstruction. Usually you are asked to TA in that part of the survey into which your own dissertation falls. This perfectly logical approach does not necessarily mean that you are prepared to enter the classroom. You may have read everything written on the nineteenth-century South and yet never taken a class on either colonial or twentieth-century America. To repeat some sound advice from another venue: Don't Panic. Just think of *The American Promise* as your *Hitchhiker's Guide*. You will quickly find that there are a number of ways to get yourself ready for the classroom.

In the twelve years I have been training graduate student TAs, the most common initial response is despair over the seeming ignorance of the majority of the undergraduates. Graduate TAs enter their first classes with high expectations of the stimulating conversations before them, only to discover that, as every study in the last twenty years has found, college students have retained very little of their high school U.S. history. While it is therefore safe — and helpful — to assume that you know a great deal more American history than most of your students, it is a grievous error to treat those students with contempt. You can have confidence that your greater knowledge allows you to avoid the hurdles of overpreparation for a fifty-minute discussion. Remember also that is it a mistake to denigrate students for their lack of preparation; it will only make your job harder. Effective teachers, like all great craftsmen, work with the materials at hand. Your task is to teach *your* students, not some idealized version of what a student should be. And you can feel rather comfortable that you will not be boring your students with well-known material; it is most likely new to them.

There is no rule on how much time to devote to preparing for your class. If you are discussing a theme with which you are personally very familiar, you may find yourself simply walking in to lead the discussion. On the other hand, if you have never studied the initial settlement of the Chesapeake, you may find yourself spending about four hours preparing for a single hour of class time. Half that preparation time may be devoted to rereading the text and any supplemental works assigned, while it will probably take you about an hour to outline the direction in which you would like the conversation to go, with all the main points and page references arranged in a logical order.

The Instructor's Resource Manual can provide assistance in the preparation of class plans. Each chapter of the textbook is outlined in the manual; and while you may not want to proceed simply, point by point, through the textbook, you can certainly pull out a section of the outline for ideas on organizing your own class. For instance, look at the outline for Chapter 3. Parts 2 and 3 form a cohesive frame for a discussion of the relationship of tobacco and colonial development, which would certainly suffice for a day's discussion. Similarly, a single day's discussion could easily be devoted to the theme of urbanization, outlined in parts 4 and 5 of Chapter 17. From this point you can move forward to issues in Chapter 17 on urban politics and Chapter 19 on industrial workers. How you use the Instructor's Resource Manual depends on additional assigned reading. If the class is reading source documents or secondary work on the economy of Colonial Chesapeake or on the growth of cities in the late nineteenth century, then the above suggestions would work very well, and you could easily plug this additional reading into the Instructor's Resource Manual outline.

You should, however, avoid overdoing it. I had one TA at UCLA who had never read a word on industrialization until the weekend before her Monday-morning section. She read a half dozen key works on the subject in that weekend and entered class Monday exhausted but with twenty-five pages of tightly written, quotation-packed notes. It was, by her own admission, the worst day of the year.

Again, there is no rule you can follow on how much preparation is enough. If you don't feel comfortable talking with the other TAs about a subject *after* you have read the textbook, ask the professor for a recommendation of an article or book that might deepen your understanding of the theme under discussion. If you have read the textbook and just one other book on the subject, you are way ahead of your students. By the way, should you feel the need to read a supplementary text, bring it to class with you. Not only will you find its presence comforting but most students will be impressed with your diligence when you tell them you were reading the book the night before and found a great passage.

But you are not really prepared for a class just because you have read and outlined the chapter and stuck some bookmarks into the textbook. Class discussions rarely follow logical schematics of discourse, and your job is not just to summarize what the students read. You need to devote at least another hour before class imagining the types of questions you are likely to receive and considering how you will demonstrate the larger issues under consideration. It is very helpful in this context to get together with at least one other TA and compare notes. You will probably notice that you have outlined the material in very different ways. Of course this divergence is the very nature of history. Historians do not select the same facts or events for their interpretations of the past, nor do they structure their arguments similarly. But just as we learn from reading scholars with whom we disagree, so you can enhance your scholarship and develop your scholarly voice in the classroom by getting a sense of how other educated people address the same subject. In that regard, your premier source for intellectual comparison should be your professor. Listen closely to the lectures and talk to him or her about your understanding of the subject under discussion.

Getting Started

At first thought, nothing is more difficult than starting a lively conversation with twenty or thirty students — many of whom may not want to talk — about a historic topic of little apparent relevance to modern life. But teachers have developed a number of very effective techniques over the years that you are free to steal — a few of which follow. Observe good teachers and note their techniques, appropriating whatever works for you.

An effective discussion should not only clarify the meaning of the lectures and texts but also provide a network of ideas with which the students can connect the material together to form a cohesive whole. You want students to see the big picture. The key is to get your students' attention early on and maintain it. An energetic beginning will make a strong impression on your students, allowing you to keep their interest and provide the framework for the entire discussion.

You will quickly notice that many of your students have not yet learned the necessary analytical skills to make connections between the lecture and the assigned reading or to formulate independent interpretations. It would be wise for you to get in the habit of discussing the texts from the start and explaining to students the importance of substantiating their comments with evidence from the textbook or lectures. At the very first meeting, turn to the first page of the textbook. Even if you have reason to believe that no one has done the reading, or rather precisely because you think no one has done the reading, draw everyone's attention to the opening passages of the book. Why does a history of the United States begin its first chapter on "Ancient America" with the twentieth-century cowboy George McJunkin? Stories are often an effective way of unpacking a whole range of larger issues. In Chapter 1 students are introduced not only to the fact that for "roughly 97 percent of the time *Home sapiens* existed, no one set foot in the Western Hemisphere" (p. 5) but also to the recent vintage of that knowledge, the continuing limitations of scholarship on pre-Columbian America, as well as alternative ways of uncovering history — in this case, literally.

In a similar fashion, the opening pages of Chapter 17 (if you are doing the second part of the survey) inspire some of the same questions. Why did the authors choose to begin a discussion of the formation of modern America with a series of memories? What do these different reminiscences demonstrate? What were the dominant social forces determining the direction of American society in the last forty years of the nineteenth century? By this point the students should be drawing on information gleaned from the lectures and textbook to construct their own understanding of historical development; your role will be more that of a moderator that an instigator.

Effective Methods

There are of course a number of different methods for getting off to a quick and successful start. Try diving into the middle of the chapter to lift out a single fact that allows the students to explore the specifics of an argument. For instance, there were "more than three hundred major tribes and hundreds of lesser groups" in North America at the time of Columbus's first journey (p. 16). What does that tell us about pre-Columbian America? How does that piece of information link up with other points made in this chapter? This technique of finding a "key fact" is most effective when the fact is particularly dramatic. Drawing attention to the number of Native Americans who died in the first years after European contact will shock anyone and certainly inspire a fruitful conversation about the unintended consequences of "the Columbian exchange" (ch. 2, pp. 28–31). Likewise, the graph on American immigration (ch. 17, p. 432) evokes many questions. What accounts for the shift of migration to southern and eastern Europe? Why did half a million Europeans come to the United States

in 1888, 75 percent of those to New York City? What were the consequences of the United States absorbing five million immigrants, one million passing through Ellis Island alone, in 1907? Do the words etched on the Statue of Liberty, as quoted in Chapter 17 on page 431, take on a new meaning in light of these statistics? Can you understand why some Americans may have seen those "huddled masses" as a serious threat? Obviously, some questions convey a certain contemporary resonance for students, an attribute to be encouraged as it will carry your class conversation beyond the classroom.

Similarly, stories and quotations that outrage students' modern sensibilities are very useful. For example, Colonel John Chivington, an American hero who massacred Indians without remorse and justified the murder of Indian children with the statement "Nits make lice," is bound to have an impact on the students (ch. 17, p. 426). To begin the discussion, direct the students to the historical understanding such stories make available. One way to sustain such a conversation is to ask leading questions drawn from the text: Why were Indians seen as "an obstacle to civilization" (ch. 17, p. 425)? How could the railroad pose a greater threat to the Indians' way of life than the U.S. army (ch. 17, p. 427)? What exactly did the U.S. government seek in its policy toward the Indians? What, in the end, drove Chief Joseph to declare, "I will fight no more forever" (ch. 17, p. 427)? by marking up your own copy of the textbook, you can guide the students through a thoughtful consideration of what might otherwise be too easily dismissed as a tragedy — an easy categorization that precludes an appreciation for the historical forces at work.

EXPLAINING HISTORIOGRAPHY

One of the most difficult yet exciting lessons of history for undergraduates is the discovery that the discipline of history changes constantly. The facts of a given event can be altered to suit some later purpose, only to be "discovered" decades later. For instance, in Chapter 17, p. 429 describes a self-conscious and deliberate imagining of the West by such creative entrepreneurs as Buffalo Bill Cody. Even in the lifetimes of participants, historians and popularizers transformed the history of the American West into a story called "the Wild West." Why, you can ask your students, did so many people who knew better accept this "thrilling but harmless entertainment" (ch. 17,

p. 429) as an accurate version of national history? What purpose was served by making Deadwood Dick a white man (ch. 17, p. 424)? In what ways did Cody and Turner alter the story of the westward expansion of the United States? Why did most historians prior to the 1970s unquestionably accept Turner's thesis and the details of Cody's Wild West Show as accurate? When did Deadwood Dick become African American again? More simply, imagine the shock of many students when they read that Magellan's voyage "made clear that Columbus was dead wrong about the identity of what he had discovered" (ch. 2, p. 28). In high school they likely learned a more straightforward account of Columbus's achievements.

For me, the real excitement of history is found in its mutability. I therefore begin each class by reading from an old history text, usually Samuel Eliot Morison and Henry Steele Commager, *The Growth of the American Republic,* which I used in an advanced placement class in U.S. history back in the late 1960s (I can't quite remember how this book came into my possession). Mind you, Morison and Commager were two of the most prominent scholars of their day, so their take on history fairly represents what was considered "objective reality" in those years. Let me provide just one example. To begin a class on the southern slave system, turn to page 537 of *The Growth of the American Republic:*

> As for Sambo, whose wrongs moved the abolitionists to wrath and tears, there is some reason to believe that he suffered less than any other class in the South from its "peculiar institution." The majority of slaves were adequately fed, well cared for, and apparently happy. Competent observers reported that they performed less labor than the hired man of the Northern states. Their physical wants were better supplied than those of thousands of Northern laborers, English operatives, and Irish peasants; their liberty was not much less than that enjoyed by the North of England "hinds" or the Finnish *torpare.* Although brought to America by force, the incurably optimistic Negro soon became attached to the country, and devoted to his "white folks." Slave insurrections were planned — usually by the free Negroes — but invariably betrayed by some faithful black; and trained obedience kept most slaves faithful throughout the Civil War.

The text goes on to describe slaves as "childlike, improvident, humorous, prevaricating, and superstitious" and to praise slave masters for treating their "pickaninnies" so well that the slaves were able to make the "transition from a primitive to a more mature culture."

There are many reasons for beginning with such a text, not the least of which is to get the students' attention immediately. But a major part of what I hope to accomplish in my survey course is to show the students how historians work and how much we have learned in just the past few decades. The students gain a noticeable confidence in formulating their own historical perspectives through an appreciation of history as a work in progress.

Based on their own scholarship, most graduate students can testify to the agnosticism of history. The feature of *The American Promise* called *Historical Question* speaks to this point, as does the *Anticipating Student Reactions* section of the Instructor's Resource Manual. These sections demonstrate that history is always open to new questions and interpretations: historians and students alike continue to seek out answers to questions such as "Why did Cortés win?" and "Why did the Allies refuse to bomb the death camps?" — issues that will undoubtedly pique your students' interest. the *Historical Question* feature allows the authors to pause and provide a broad range of possible answers to problems that usually receive only a paragraph or two of explanation in the narrative of the textbook and serve as points of departure for active classroom discussion. Enabling students to make their own informed judgments of the past, the *Historical Question* feature invites them to consider afresh a number of plausible reasons for the information other books present simply as standard knowledge to memorize. As a historian you may be surprised how out-of-date historical knowledge in high school courses can be sometimes. Students — and their parents — will take it as fact that Columbus discovered America, that all Europeans came to America seeking religious freedom, that the Revolution came in response to the tyranny of George III, and that the abolitionists caused the Civil War. It is our job to show students that there is much more to each of these complicated stories.

SUSTAINING FOCUS

The easiest way to sustain a focused discussion is to require the students to do most of the work. There are a number of short assignments that can help you attain this end. For example, have students select a single passage in the reading that most captures their attention, have them bring a single question to class, or have them write a hypothesis on a single theme covered in the lecture with one piece of supportive evidence drawn from the text. These assignments will lay the basis for deeper discussion and the innovative exercises described below.

Role-Playing Exercises

One of the most successful routes to a lively conversation is that of having the students take sides in a debate. For instance, building on the material in the second chapter, have your students draw on sixteenth-century documents to construct positions for and against further European expansion in the Western Hemisphere (such documents are available in many collections). You can ask students to play the parts of real historical figures — such as King Ferdinand, Juan Gines de Sepulveda, or Bartolomé de Las Casas — or fictional figures, from a native Indian prince to a common Spanish soldier to a Franciscan monk.

Alternatively, Chapter 19 describes the many different kinds of workers — including those in management — who lend themselves well to a role-playing debate. Go through the chapter and assign students different personas: industrial workers — immigrant and native born, male and female, adult and child; common laborers — Asian, white, and black; miners; skilled workers; sweatshop workers; and management. Provide a topic for debate, such as the question posed by President Rutherford B. Hayes: Can't something be done by education of the strikers, by judicious control of the capitalists, by wise general policy to end or diminish the evil [of general strikes]?" (ch. 19, p. 467). Then send students to the library to research their roles. This assignment introduces students to both the library and the way historians conduct research. Given the pleasure that most people find in discovering what was previously unknown, you may find your students quickly getting into the spirit of the historian's work and even of historiographical arguments.

Making Connections

Students will undoubtedly find some issues more difficult than others and will need help making sense of what seems to them a very complicated connection. For instance, Chapter 2 has a section titled "Mediterranean Trade and European Expansion." If your students appear baffled by the relation between the two, ask first for an explanation from them, as perhaps a few have read

closely and grasped this ideal. A student may have spotted a note in the text that states "The vitality of the Mediterranean trade in the fourteenth and fifteenth centuries gave established merchants and governments few reasons to look for alternatives" (ch. 2, p. 25), and it was actually Portugal, a country located "on the fringes of the thriving Mediterranean trade" that led the expansion (ch. 2, p. 26). Students should understand the connection between trade and expansion and that Portugal, a country that had been forced to use monopolized Mediterranean trade, *fostered* European expansion by exploring alternative routes along the coast of Africa and eventually to the Far East. To further this discussion, move on to the statement that "Some [European] aristocrats . . . had reasons to engage in exploration" (ch. 2, p. 26), given Portugal's success in breaking "the monopoly of the old Mediterranean trade with the East" (ch. 2, p. 26) and the establishment of Portuguese trading posts in Africa, China, and India. Again, careful preparation in highlighting the textbook's argument will save you a great deal of time and forestall any mounting confusion that may derail discussion.

It is vital to remain aware of gaps in your students' understanding. If your class does not grasp the foundation of a specific historical sequence, students will not be able to follow its development. Thus, without an understanding of what drove Europeans to the Americas, the discussion of the impact of that conquest on Europe and the Americas will become completely muddled. This is not to say that you should move at a stately pace, page by page, through the text. Rather, touch on the key passages to ensure that vital concepts are grasped and that your students are constructing the historical causality. For example, in the instance of the European conquest of America, you can help your students move from statement to statement. Start with "Columbus's arrival . . . ended the age-old separation of the hemispheres and initiated . . . a transatlantic exchange of goods, people, and ideas that has continued ever since" (ch. 2, p. 28). Then you can jump to how the "destruction of the Indian population was a catastrophe unequaled in human history" (ch. 2, p. 36). Following should be a consideration of the wealth brought from America to Spain (ch. 2, pp. 31–39), to the final irony (or dialectic, if you prefer) of Spain's success at evoking jealousy and more conquest (ch. 2, pp. 40–43). Here you have offered students an understanding of the causality connecting all of these statements. It is obviously not possible to discuss everything, but you can rely on the students to come up with some of the more interesting details of the landscape lying between the peaks.

Attention-Getting Devices

Occasionally you will get the sense that the student's collective attention is lagging. There are a variety of effective attention-getting devises available — voicing an outrageous assertion or quotation, calling on students by name, or even the old classic, "This will be on the final." (The latter can induce a bit of anxiety, which some say reduces attention, so it may best be used as an obvious joke.) One can also be less dramatic and play on the desire of students to generalize about American history by culling examples, metaphors, and analogies from the textbook and then asking students to expand on their representative value. You can ask the students if they find any relevance in the late-nineteenth-century "fear that America had become a plutocracy," since "the wealthiest one percent of the population owned more than half the real and personal property in the country" (ch. 17, p. 435). Or does any part of the debates over the connection between politics and religion covered in Chapter 4 sound familiar? And if none of these approaches works, you may just want to try a complete change of pace, telling the students that you will return to these questions later (be sure to do so), and attack the issue from a completely different direction. If you resort to the latter tactic, it is useful to flip back a page or two and get a running start. Try asking about something that you are sure the students must know as a way of building momentum and getting opinions out in the open. Often the students themselves will then return to your earlier question with a loud "I get it!" (For further ideas, see "Dealing with Problems" on manual p. 216.)

The purpose of using these exercises in discussion-building is to link the knowledge available in the textbook and lectures with the individual students' reasoning powers. Students often read through textbooks and sit through lectures without pausing to consider the broader implications of statements. Until you ask what is meant by "The Geographic Revolution" (ch. 2, p. 28), a student might not comprehend the powerful impact of Columbus's voyages on European culture and society. Put another way, nomenclature has meaning that is not always self-evident: Is it the "Battle of Wounded Knee" or the "Massacre at Wounded Knee"?

4. Testing

STANDARDS

Generally TAs work with the materials the professor prepares. You may therefore encounter many different types of tests. Objective midterms and finals have the advantage of being straightforward; an answer is either correct or incorrect and you just have to mark it as such. Short essays and even short identifications are a different matter, and the standards of grading are generally the same as those that apply to papers, as discussed below. But it is important to note that, since you will be reading responses to questions you did not write, and as those answers are often based more on the lectures than the text, it would be wise to spend some time getting a sense of the professor's expectations. Most professors will hold a meeting for this purpose on their own initiative. If such a discussion is not forthcoming, you should request it. Ask the professor to outline what she or he considers the essential material to be covered in an exam essay. Determine if the professor expects the exam to be based largely on the texts, the lectures, or both. Are students to be judged on the quality of their writing or solely on their ability to touch on several key facts and arguments? Is there a specific scale for grading (for example, is an "A" 90 and above or 95 and higher)? What should you do if a student misses a test and then shows up in your office demanding to take the exam at that time? (The answer from the professor should be "Send that student to see me.") And perhaps most important, what does the professor expect of you in assisting the students to prepare for the exam? Are study sessions with your participation encouraged, tolerated, or forbidden? You must be clear on these standards before you devote time to helping your students and evaluating their work.

PREPARING STUDENTS

Given the enormous stress that most students feel over finals, they will appreciate any help you can offer them. But keep in mind that you will also be making your job easier in preparing the students for the exam, if only because it will prevent complaints later. You can meet with individual students or groups of students during your office hours, though you will quickly find yourself repeating the same advice. The most efficient way to help is to moderate a study session. Note my choice of the word *moderate*.

You are doing your students an enormous favor in holding a study session, but you should not get carried away and essentially do their work for them.

The best approach, once you have gotten the approval of your professor, is to hand out at your last discussion meeting before the exam a number of sample identifications or essay topics (and note, many professors routinely make such lists available anyway). At this point, divide up the list among those interested in attending a study session and make each student responsible for outlining — and only outlining — a useful answer or identification. If you have prepared well, you have already reserved a classroom and a time for the review session. At that meeting, you want to begin with a few general rules to follow during the exam — essentially a summary of the expectations of the professor. For instance, you may tell students to avoid rhetorical flourishes and padding. It is not the length of the answer that matters but the precision. Add that they must write neatly; if you cannot read what is written, you will assume that it is incorrect. (One of the oldest tricks of test-taking, dating back to classical Greece, is to deliberately obscure one's writing in the hope that the grader will assume the answer is correct.)

Now comes the heart of the review session. Ask the student or students who tackled the first problem to write their outline(s) on the board and to explain the logic of their structure. Your task at this point is simply to question the comparative worth of details. By this time in the semester, the students should be talking fairly freely with one another, and you can count on the other students to point out errors or failures of logic. For example, if Abraham Lincoln is to be identified, and the student has made point 3 his marriage to Mary Todd, you can be fairly certain that someone will question the significance of this fact. Someone will surely notice if the student has placed Lincoln's election in 1880. More substantively, students may debate the relative merit of focusing on Lincoln's career as an attorney and politician or his suspension of *habeas corpus*. At this point you can intervene and suggest that the particulars the students select depend on the larger argument they are trying to make. If Lincoln's character is considered to be at the core of his handling of the secession crisis, then his previous experience is essential; if one's argument focuses on Lincoln as a powerful president, then his willingness to suspend fundamental constitutional liberties should be at the center of the essay. A larger point you are making here is that even the shortest, most hastily written essays have a thesis.

Once you have moved through all the problems in turn and covered the chalkboards with sample outlines, you may want to repeat the basic expectations for the exam. Specifically, you can remind students what is considered an excellent answer and what constitutes a barely acceptable one. If students are convinced that they understand the nature of the exam, they will be much more comfortable taking it and produce better work. It is vital that you remember how important it is for students to do well on the final. With a review session you have not only allowed the students to provide one another with sample outlines but have also encouraged them to think about the problems before them. When you come to grade your exams, you will certainly find some recapitulations from your review; but you will also be surprised by the multiplicity of responses you receive to the same question.

5. Paper Assignments

HELPING STUDENTS GENERATE TOPICS

Most professors supply paper assignments. As you already know, these assignments take many forms. Some draw entirely on the assigned reading, which reduces your responsibilities substantially. Other require the students to go to the library. At this point many students will need your help. Your first task is often to clarify the difference between primary and secondary sources. Explain that primary sources are the building blocks of history, that each historian is capable of reading these sources differently, often in dramatically distinctive ways. This would be a good time to hand out the "Guidelines for Writing a Good History Essay" and "The Use of Sources in Writing Research Papers" found on pages 212 and 213, should you be using them. Unless your library has an especially good tour of its resources, it is well worth your time to take your section to the library yourself and show them how you use the resources. After all, you are a historian, and, at least for this paper, your students are as well.

Should you have the chance to craft your own essay assignment, you may want to use your professor's previous assignments as models. You will probably note that many professors operate on the assumption that, at least in introductory courses, there is a difference between first and later assignments. With the first essay — often the student's first college paper — it is best to offer

GUIDELINES FOR WRITING A GOOD HISTORY ESSAY

1. *Preparation.* Good history papers begin with effective reading. Your work will be based on your understanding of primary and secondary literature. If you cannot summarize the point of either sort of document in a sentence or two, go back and read the document again.

2. *Thesis.* Your essay should be driven by a clear, comprehensible, and sustained thesis. Your first paragraph should state that thesis and indicate how you plan to substantiate it.

3. *Organization.* Every paragraph should clarify, demonstrate, expand, or build on your thesis. An outline is a handy tool for ensuring the coherence of your essay.

4. *Evidence.* Every generalization should be supported with specific evidence.

5. *Chronology.* Historians like dates; we use them to organize information and demonstrate intellectual and social developments over time. Be clear in your chronology, using dates to structure your arguments.

6. *Conclusion.* A good essay goes somewhere; it does not simply circle back to repeat the opening statement. Your conclusion should indicate the direction of your thoughts, briefly summarizing your argument, for instance, while indicating its wider historical significance.

7. *Editing.* All good writers rewrite, often. Proofread your essay. Do not hesitate to rewrite if you find flaws in its content, logic, or style. With spell check, there is no longer any excuse for spelling errors. Having a friend read your work aloud is a good way to catch errors of grammar and reasoning.

8. *Style.* The key to effective nonfiction writing is clarity. Therefore, avoid the passive voice like the plague. "Poland was invaded" avoids the unpleasant fact that Germany invaded Poland. Passive voice obscures, which is why bureaucrats love it. Similarly, "this" and "these" should always be followed by a noun so that your reader knows what you are talking about.

9. *References.* All quotations must bear some form of citation, such as footnotes or endnotes. These citations should allow your reader to find your sources easily. Be aware that a writer's facts, ideas, and phraseology are the property of that individual. Anyone using a writer's ideas or phraseology without due credit is guilty of plagiarism.

topics with precise alternatives, such as, "Did racism precede the introduction of slavery in North America?" or "Was the United States justified in declaring war on Germany in 1917?" In each of these instances you can draw attention to very specific parts of the textbook as starting points for discussion. While such categorical assignments posed as questions (rather than the deadly "explain" or "describe") do not determine the individual student's essay, they do provide a clear sense of alternatives on which the student can build his or her analysis. And students will proceed more logically in their research if they perceive the need to answer a historical question and take a definite position on a scholarly question. By the time they receive the final paper assignment students should be able to construct an independent thesis without needing such blatant directional markers.

THE WRITING PROCESS

Most of your work as a TA outside the classroom will be devoted to guiding and grading essay assignments. It is advisable to offer extra office hours during the week before a paper is due. In these consultations, many students will essentially ask you for their thesis. Avoid the impulse to provide one. You will need to ask many leading questions ("Was racism a prerequisite for the institution of slavery?" or "Do you think that U.S. security was threatened by Germany in 1917?"), and you may think the student's thesis lacks depth, but you do not want to be accountable for the paper when it comes time to grade it. And remember, many students try to distance themselves from responsibility for the final product. Don't let them say *"your* paper"; it's *"my* paper."

THE USE OF SOURCES IN WRITING RESEARCH PAPERS

A writer's facts, ideas, and phraseology should be regarded as his or her property. *Any person who uses a writer's ideas or phraseology without giving due credit is guilty of plagiarism.*

Information may be put into a paper without a footnote or some kind of documentation only if it meets the following conditions: it may be found in several books on the subject; it is written entirely in the words of the student; it is not paraphrased from any particular source; it therefore belongs to common knowledge.

Generally, if you write while looking at a source or while looking at notes taken from a source, a footnote should be given. Instructors encourage students to explore, appreciate, and use the ideas of others; but we expect proper attribution for those ideas. Even when written entirely in your own words, the opinions of others must be credited. We do not require students to invent original theories of human conduct; referencing the ideas of Freud is often appropriate.

All direct quotations should be cited. Brief phrases and even key words that are used as they appear in a source should be in quotation marks (see next paragraph for an example).

Paraphrasing is the expression of another writer's words and ideas. As noted in the *Practical English Handbook,* 11th edition (Boston: Houghton Mifflin), a paraphrase "preserves the sense" but not the form of the source. A paraphrase does not merely replace a few words with synonyms or change the sentence pattern; it briefly restates the original document's core meaning in the paraphraser's own words. In *The Bedford Handbook,* 6th edition (Boston: Bedford Books, 2002), Diana Hacker suggests how to avoid plagiarism while paraphrasing: "Close the book, write from memory, and then open the book to check for accuracy."

A primary source is a document or artifact written or created during the period you wish to study. Secondary works are books or articles written after the fact. For example, the Declaration of Independence is a primary source, while Carl Becker's study of that document, *The Declaration of Independence,* is a secondary source.

Some Examples

In reading Linda Kerber, *Women of the Republic* (published by University of North Carolina Press in New York, 1980), you come across the following sentences on page 23:

> Rousseau is well known for his sharp criticism of contemporary society and his vision of radical social change. His statements about women, however, usually reinforced the existing order. . . . Rousseau's conservatism about women may well have served to make his radical comments about men's behavior more palatable.

Quotation:
Kerber questions Rousseau's reputation as a social critic, noting that his "statements about women . . . usually reinforced the existing order" (23).

Paraphrase:
Kerber questions Rousseau's reputation as a social critic, noting that he always endorsed conventional views of women's roles (23).

No need to cite:
Rousseau was a prominent Enlightenment philosopher.

Plagiarism:
Rousseau was a prominent Enlightenment philosopher whose statements about women usually reinforced the existing order.

or

Rousseau is generally perceived to have been a radical social thinker. Yet his conservatism about women may well have served to make his radical comments about men's behavior more palatable.

Note that rearranging a sentence or using a thesaurus search is still plagiarism, as is the failure to use quotation marks.

The single most common gripe about history classes is this: "It was not an English class, and yet I was graded on my grammar." You therefore need to explain, in the strongest possible terms, that writing clearly is an absolute necessity. A history course requires the same level of writing as that required in any composition class. History papers are not the regurgitation of facts but the expression of a mode of analysis. It does not matter how good an idea is if no one can understand it.

To avoid confusion on this point, you may want to establish certain recommendations for the preparation of a superior essay. Generally it is wise to keep such guidelines brief, so that students will actually read them. The particulars are going to reflect your own sense of good writing; what follows is simply an example, which you are free to use.

The very last point in the writing guidelines handout, on plagiarism, may require further guidelines. I have sat on honor council hearings for six years and have repeatedly heard these three defenses: (1) "The teacher did not explain plagiarism," (2) "My culture/former school/ other professors permit copying directly from the book," and (3) "I printed the wrong file from my computer." None of these is a good excuse, which does not prevent students' repeated attempts to use them. Many of us therefore hand out precise explanations of plagiarism in a hopeful effort to prevent problems. My statement appears in the handout on manual page 213, and you are free to plagiarize it.

Plagiarism is usually fairly easy to discern, as you will note the complete absence of grammatical errors or the use of obscure archival sources. Proving plagiarism is a very difficult and time-consuming task, unless the miscreant plagiarizes from the textbook (a great deal more common than you might think). If you suspect plagiarism, inform your professor immediately.

Being proactive with your students' essays is time-efficient, as it takes less time to read and grade a good essay than a bad one. So do not hesitate to welcome, or demand, outlines and rough drafts. You know from your own experience that good writing is the product of several drafts; demand the same of your students. The fifteen minutes required to go over an outline or rough draft with a student can save hours of explanation and defense based on an easily avoided misunderstanding.

6. Grading Tests and Papers

AVOIDING UNCERTAINTY

Grading is a form of communication. The greatest complaint of students is the uncertainty of grading. You will almost always see more students in your office hours after the first grade has been awarded than at any other time during the semester; and what they will most want explained to them is why they received the exact grade they did — why a C+ and not an A. If you cannot explain the distinction, students will very often move on to the professor with bitter criticisms of incompetence on the part of the graduate TA. The more you can make the subjective process of grading appear objective, the more useful and congenial the conversation will be with your students.

Choosing a Grading System

With grading, it is best to provide the answer before the question is even framed. One approach is to define the structure of your grading system in the professor's course syllabus. Some instructors supply general rules of grading, emphasizing the characteristics they expect in a good paper. Others attempt to break down the exact parameters of grading, as much as that is possible, assigning definitions to each aspect of the grading process. Others try "blind grading," having students use numbers instead of names on their papers. Personally, I find this approach an abdication of the teacher's responsibility. Each student is different, each has specific needs and backgrounds, convictions and problems, all of which should be considered when grading a paper. Blind grading allows no opportunity to note improvement, let alone praise and reward it. Think very carefully about your understanding of the process of teaching before adopting such a procedure.

There is simply no way that anyone can provide hard standards for grading. On manual page 215 is an example of such a grading chart, which you are free to use if you like. This chart attempts to clarify the component parts of an essay and define the grade equivalent. Such a chart not only gives students a sense of the seriousness of your approach to grading but also provides the basis for any discussions about grading — if it does not forestall such conversations entirely. Obviously, this chart works on the assumption of an absolute standard rather than on some sort of modified bell curve, as is still used in a few colleges.

Grade	Thesis	Analysis	Development and Support	Structure	Grammar
A	Essay based on a clear, precise, well-defined, and original thesis that goes beyond ideas discussed in class or the assigned readings.	Essay contains cogent analysis that demonstrates a command of interpretive and conceptual tasks required by assignment and course material.	The essay includes well-chosen examples, persuasive reasoning consistently applied, and solid evidence directly applicable to the thesis.	Essay moves easily from one point to the next with clear, smooth, and appropriate transitions, coherent organization, and fully developed paragraphs.	The author employs sophisticated sentences effectively, chooses words aptly, and observes all the conventions of English grammar to craft an eloquent essay.
B	A clear, specific thesis, central to the essay.	Demonstrates a solid understanding of the texts, ideas, and methods of the assignment.	Pursues thesis consistently, clearly developing a core argument with clear component points and appropriate supportive detail.	Clear transitions, the development of coherent, connected ideas in unified paragraphs.	A good command of English, though with occasional stylistic or grammatical problems (most commonly awkward syntax or excessive use of the passive voice).
C	A general thesis, central to the essay.	Shows an understanding of the basic ideas and information involved in the assignment, though with some errors of fact or confusion of interpretation, and a tendency toward recapitulations or narration of standard chronology.	Incomplete development of core argument; weak organization or shallow analysis, insufficiently articulated ideas, or unsupported generalizations.	Some awkward transitions, weak or undeveloped paragraphs not clearly connected to one another.	A tendency toward wordiness, unclear or awkward sentences, imprecise use of words, grammatical errors, and a vagueness of meaning brought on by the passive voice.
D	Vague or irrelevant thesis.	Inadequate command of course material with significant factual or conceptual errors. Fails to respond directly to the assignment.	Discursive and undeveloped, a mere narration that digresses from one topic to another.	Simplistic and discursive, tending to vague summations and digressions from one topic to another.	Major grammatical problems such as subject-verb disagreement, obscure pronouns, and sentence fragments. Language marred by clichés, colloquialisms, repeated inexact word choices, and gross spelling errors.
F	No discernible thesis.	Failure to understand class materials. Essay is not a response to the assignment.	Little or no development; a listing of the vaguest generalizations or misinformation.	No transitions and incoherent paragraphs.	Unreadable owing to the violation of the basic rules of grammar.

Two obvious points: (1) particulars of this or any other such standard of grading will need some precise explanation and (2) by being very rigorous in your statement on grading you allow yourself room for generosity when appropriate. Nonetheless, if you use a grading chart like this one, stick to it and use it as the basis for all conversations with students about their grades. If, in such a discussion, a student begins to wander to peripheral issues like the type style used, bring him or her back to the chart with the question, "Did I establish that as a necessary quality of your essay?" Similarly, if a student complains that you graded primarily on grammar and not enough on "my ideas" (a very common complaint), point out the importance you attached to language skills and make clear that the best ideas in the world are useless if no one can understand them. Suggest that your students think of the grading chart as the rule book; you don't argue with the umpire to switch to four strikes just this once.

Commenting on Student Papers

All this preparation will be wasted if you cannot convey your judgments of their work to your students. In other words, grading is not just the assignment of a grade but an indication of the reasons for that grade. Do not just append a grade to the end of a student essay; write out a paragraph explaining your understanding of the reasons for that grade. Again, it saves time to be as precise as possible in these comments. It is vital that you leave the student with his or her self-respect intact, but you must also be completely clear as to what problems the paper has. The key here is to treat the final comments as a series of recommendations for improvement. Rather than saying something sarcastic, suggest that the student seek assistance at the college writing center. Rather than saying, "You did not understand this book," recommend that the student look again at the author's thesis as presented in the introduction. In short, work on the assumption that your students will want to go back and correct their errors to improve future essays.

You will no doubt feel the urge to correct every error of grammar, organization, and logic that you perceive while reading the essay. Avoid this impulse. It takes up far too much of your time and quite simply can depress a student to the point where he or she feels there is no hope. Highlight key problems with the essay, or circle examples of common errors. The student can then realistically tackle the major hurdles. An added advantage of this approach is that, should the student complain about his or her grade, you can go back and point out further problems, demonstrating the full level of your prior compassion and the justice of your generous grade.

Finally the day arrives when you must calculate a class grade for each student. Avoid sudden gifts, such as last-minute extra credit or forgiveness for some component of a grade for a specific student. Word will get out, and other students will demand similar treatment, even after grades have been turned in. Set a standard and stick to it. The course syllabus should state precisely the relative values of class assignments (for example, each essay equaling 25 percent of the class grade). The one place where you can allow yourself a little leeway in determining final grades is in class participation. Here is where you can reward those students who made positive contributions to the class over the term and penalize those who slept through your wittiest asides. If you have prepared well, no student will be surprised by his or her final grade. Still, it is wise to attach a clear calculation of the class grade to each student's final, reiterating the percentages assigned to each class assignment and recording every grade received by the student — for instance, "1st essay (25%): C+; 2nd essay (25%): B+; final (40%): B; class participation (10%): B+; final grade: B."

7. Dealing with Problems

Teaching carries with it problems large and small. Keep the distinction clear and avoid making those problems easily solved into complicated situations that drain you of time and energy. An overly aggressive student whose conduct borders on sexual harassment is a large problem. A student who comes to you with tales of woe may become a large problem. Do not — repeat, DO NOT — attempt to deal with these large problems yourself. Every college employs people who are trained to handle these kinds of problems. At the very least, it is your professor who should address any complicated issues or threatening situations. Report any such matters to the professor immediately and let others with more authority or professional preparation cope with them. Careers have been cut short by a TA's conviction that a major confrontation or talk of suicide was a joke. Disengage yourself as quickly as possible from an undergraduate's personal problems and let people with more experience and resources take over.

What is of concern to you are the little problems that arise as you learn any skill. No one is a born teacher any more than anyone is a born bicycle rider. Every teacher makes mistakes and confronts roadblocks; recognize them as part of your training, identify the problem, and work on it. Talk with your fellow TAs and professors about a specific difficulty and learn how they dealt with it. While students are most creative in inventing new crises for teachers, there are a few common difficulties you may encounter that we should consider.

You may not suffer from this trauma, but many students have a deep fear of speaking in public. You may observe a student who is a blabbermouth in the cafeteria yet clams up in your classroom. Usually these students are just afraid of making fools of themselves. There are several ways of getting a shy student, or most of a quiet class, to participate. The first step is to avoid phrasing questions in a manner that implies only one answer (factual questions aside). Having the class write their responses to a specific question and read them out loud in class is very effective; even shy people feel safe reading aloud something they have already written. Breaking the class into smaller groups responsible for developing reactions to a historical problem also draws quieter students into the conversation, though you need to be particularly alert to the dynamic of each group.

On the other extreme are those who participate too much. A private conversation during your office hours is the best way to let a student know that, while you appreciate his or her contributions to the class discussion, you would like his or her help in drawing out some of the quieter students. All but the dimmest students will get the hint.

Often in the course of the day, you will find your class getting bogged down. Petty debate over minor details or a frustrating inability to understand the larger issues can prevent your making steady progress. Worse still, you may discover that none of the students has done the assigned reading. It is important on these occasions not to lose your temper. Try, literally, to focus students' attention on something different. Illustrations in the textbook are especially effective for changing direction in a conversation or bringing home a point. For instance, if you are talking about the change from the Gilded Age to the Progressive Era and the discussion is starting to drag, turn to the illustrations in Chapter 21 and ask the students to examine the presentation of children. Is

there evidence in the photos by Jacob Riis or the poster "Making Human Junk" of some shifting sensitivity to children, or are they just being used to make political points? Ask questions about the illustrations that require students to reflect on specific issues raised in the text or lectures. For example, turn to Paul Revere's engraving of the Boston Massacre in Chapter 6 and ask, "What's wrong with this picture?" Once you have established that Revere manipulated the imagery of this event, you can connect the specific back to some larger point, such as the acceleration of anti-British feeling in America.

Illustrations have a way of waking up students and inspiring those who are most disengaged. Even a picture lacking obvious drama can bring forth deep passions and insights. It is easy to glance at an illustration such as "The African Slave Trade" in Chapter 5 and turn the page, but it is hard to remain passive after a close examination. Take the time to decode the seal of the Massachusetts Bay Company in Chapter 4, with its central Indian saying, "Come over and help us," and consider the hypocrisy. Compare the dramatically different images of westward expansion in Chapter 17 and discuss the implications of "Go west, young man." Turn to the enlistment posters in Chapter 22 and imagine yourself in 1917 — how would you respond to this simple, tragic painting of the drowned mother and child? The textbook allows you to bring history to life and ensures that your class discussions reflect that drama.

There may be occasions when none of these methods works or when the problem persists class after class. One approach I don't like is that of outstaring students. Students, like most people, hate extended silences. I prefer to take the silence itself as a point worthy of discussion: "OK, my friends, why doesn't anyone want to talk today?" The few times I have found it necessary to ask such a question, the students have laughed and finally admitted that they just don't get it or that none of them has done the reading. At such a juncture I go back to the book, open it up, and start parsing a passage. But never forget — and this rule applies to all teaching problems — that you have the power of the grade. Sometimes it may just be appropriate to remind a student or the entire class that "F" is an option. A pop quiz can clarify this fact efficiently.

Better still, though, you can avoid such confrontations by careful preparation. It is important to remember that students want to resolve the intellectual problem under consideration. Begin by reaching an agreement on the nature of the topic under discussion, and keep clarifying that issue and where you are in the process — for instance, defining, suggesting hypotheses and evidence, evaluating alternatives — involving the students as much as possible. If you get a sense that many students are overwhelmed by the reading, provide them with questions beforehand to guide them through the material. It is vitally important to make sure students have done the reading, even if you are not confident of their level of understanding. Thus the importance of never denigrating an initial interpretation; rather, build on it, find something positive to say about every comment, rephrase silly comments (and yes, there are dumb questions), write key phrases spoken by students on the board to encourage a sense of responsibility and pride in one's words, and link the comments of one student with those of another to get them to talk to each other and not just to you. Such extra energy early on will convince students that they can master the material and offer something of value. Nourish that confidence, as it is the fundamental foundation of education.

8. Effective Teaching: Polishing Your Skills

Combine your enthusiasm for teaching with a practical appreciation for future employment. A TAship is the first step in building an academic career — every one of your professors was a TA. The point of teaching is to be effective, to impart a body of information and a mode of analysis. The better you teach, the clearer your own perception of the workings of history, an insight that cannot but improve your dissertation. And the accumulation of teaching experience will make any graduate student more attractive on the job market.

There are several ways of improving your teaching while building a supportive portfolio,

which includes recommendations, evaluations, and references that you will show prospective employers. Ask your students for written evaluations and read them carefully. With time you may find these evaluations valuable components of a job application. Be honest with yourself in identifying weaknesses and work to correct flaws. Some methods of self-examination are more attractive than others; videotaping your class is painful but valuable. Just as you encourage your students to show their rough drafts to friends, invite your adviser and any other professors with whom you are comfortable into your classroom so that they can suggest improvements and later attest to your teaching abilities in letters of recommendation.

If much of what is offered in this brief guide appears too self-conscious, please accept that it is offered in a spirit of exploration. Much can be learned from talking with and observing experienced teachers, but that does not mean you should try to become some ideal type of a college professor. You will quickly discover your own voice and style as a teacher, and you should retain your sense of humor in the process. Do not hesitate to experiment — and abandon an idea if it flops. Some approaches work for some teachers and not for others. One of my friends invented a game called "Pin the event on the trend." She posts a time chart citing the major eras in American history — the Colonial and Revolutionary periods, etc. — and then hands out slips of paper with key events written on them, awarding candy to the student who places the event in the correct historical category. I have never replicated her balance of playful mockery of historical categorization and effective focus on the significance of chronology, but maybe you can. Don't be afraid to try something new. It is your classroom, your career — and teaching should be fun. With music, as Duke Ellington said, "If it sounds good, it is good." With teaching, if it works for you, it is good teaching.

SAMPLE SYLLABI

The following sample syllabi suggest ways to structure and pace your American history survey course, using *The American Promise,* Second Compact Edition; *Reading the American Past,* Second Edition; and several supplemental texts from the Historians at Work series and the Bedford Series in History and Culture. The syllabi cover the American history survey as taught in a two-semester sequence, a two-quarter sequence, and in a single semester.

Sample Syllabus 1
American History to 1877
(Semester)

Objectives

This course gives students an overview of the political, economic, social, and cultural history of America from ancient America through Reconstruction. Students will read a major textbook, selected primary documents, and three outside works. Through these readings, lectures, and class discussions, students will explore major themes in American history, such as colonization, the founding of a new nation, the forging of an American culture, the entrenchment of slavery, the coming of the Civil War, and the meaning of Reconstruction. Students will also examine the ways in which the marginalized and disaffected have struggled to ensure that America fulfills its promise.

Required Texts

Be sure that the following assigned texts are on sale in the campus bookstore.

James L. Roark, et al., *The American Promise,* Second Compact Edition, Vol. I (CAP)
Michael P. Johnson, *Reading the American Past,* Second Edition, Vol. I (RAP)

Note: Please note that the chapter numbering in *The American Promise,* Second Compact Edition, is one ahead of the chapter numbering in *Reading the American Past,* Second Edition; for example, documents that relate to the content of Chapter 2 in *The American Promise,* Second Compact Edition, are found in Chapter 1 of *Reading the American Past,* Second Edition.

Neal Salisbury, ed., *The Sovereignty and Goodness of God,* by Mary Rowlandson
Theda Perdue and Michael D. Green, eds., *The Cherokee Removal: A Brief History with Documents*
Paul Finkelman, Dred Scott v. Sandford: *A Brief History*

Grading

Grades are based on student performance on scheduled quizzes and exams, three short essays, and class participation.

Exams — 45% (15% each)
Quizzes — 15% (5% each)
Papers — 30% (10% each)
Class participation — 10%

Week 1: Introduction to Course and Ancient America

Tuesday
Introduction to Course

Thursday
Ancient America
Readings: CAP, Chapter 1

RAP, Prologue

Week 2: European Exploration

Tuesday
Europe in the Sixteenth Century
Readings: CAP, Chapter 2, "Europe in the Age of Exploration" through "A Surprising New World in the Western Atlantic"

RAP, Documents 1.1 and 1.2

Thursday
Conquest
Readings: CAP, Chapter 2, "Spanish Exploration
and Conquest" through "Conclusion"

RAP, Documents 1.3 and 1.4

**Week 3: *The Chesapeake Colonies
in the Seventeenth Century***

Tuesday
The Development of Chesapeake Society
Readings: CAP, Chapter 3, "An English Colony
on the Chesapeake" through "A Tobacco
Society"

RAP, Documents 2.1 and 2.2

Thursday
QUIZ 1
The Evolution of Chesapeake Society
Readings: CAP, Chapter 3, "The Evolution of
Chesapeake Society" through "Con-
clusion"

RAP, Documents 2.3 and 2.4

**Week 4: *The Northern and Middle Colonies in
the Seventeenth Century***

Tuesday
Puritan New England
Readings: CAP, Chapter 4, "Puritan Origins: The
English Reformation" through "The
Evolution of New England Society"

RAP, Documents 3.1, 3.2, 3.3, and 3.4
**Paper on *The Sovereignty and Goodness of God*
due**
Documentary: *Good Wives*

Thursday
The Middle Colonies
Readings: CAP, Chapter 4, "The Founding of the
Middle Colonies" through "Conclusion"

Week 5: *Eighteenth-Century America*

Tuesday
New England and the Middle Colonies
Readings: CAP, Chapter 5, "A Growing Population and Expanding Economy"
through "The Middle Colonies: Immigrants, Wheat, and Work"

RAP, Documents 4.1, 4.2, and 4.3

Thursday
The South
Readings: CAP, Chapter 5, "The Southern
Colonies: Land of Slavery" through
"Conclusion"

RAP, Document 4.4

Week 6: *Exam 1 and the Road to Independence*

Tuesday
EXAM 1

Thursday
The Colonial Crisis
Readings: CAP, Chapter 6, "The French and
Indian War, 1754–1763" through "The
Stamp Act Crisis, 1765"

RAP, Documents 5.1 and 5.2

Week 7: *Independence*

Tuesday
The Colonial Crisis
Readings: CAP, Chapter 6, "The Townshend Acts
and Economic Retaliation, 1767–1770"
through "Conclusion"

RAP, Documents 5.3 and 5.4

Thursday
The Revolution
Readings: CAP, Chapter 7

RAP, Chapter 6

Week 8: *A New Republic*

Tuesday
Confederation America
Readings: CAP, Chapter 8, "The Articles of Confed-
eration" through "The Critical Period"

RAP, Documents 7.1 and 7.2

Thursday
The Federal Constitution
Readings: CAP, Chapter 8, "The United States
Constitution" through "Conclusion"

RAP, Documents 7.3 and 7.4

Week 9: *A New Nation*

Tuesday
Stability and Change

Readings: CAP, Chapter 9, "The Search for Stability" through "Hamilton's Economic Policies"

RAP, Documents 8.1 and 8.2

Thursday
QUIZ 2
Conflicts
Readings: CAP, Chapter 9, " Conflicts West, East, and South" through "Conclusion"

RAP, Documents 8.3 and 8.4

Week 10: Early National America

Tuesday
Jeffersonian America
Readings: CAP, Chapter 10, "Jefferson's Presidency" through "The War of 1812"

RAP, Chapter 9
Documentary: *Thomas Jefferson*

Thursday
Madison and His Successors
Readings: CAP, Chapter 10, "Women's Status in the Early Republic" through "Conclusion"

Week 11: Jacksonian Democracy

Tuesday
Jacksonian Democracy, I
Readings: CAP, Chapter 11, "The Market Revolution" through "Cultural Shifts"

Thursday
Jacksonian Democracy, II
Readings: CAP, Chapter 11, "Democracy and Religion" through "Conclusion"

RAP, Chapter 10
Paper on *The Cherokee Removal* due

Week 12: The Free North and West and Exam 2

Tuesday
The Free North and West
Readings: CAP, Chapter 12

RAP, Chapter 11

Thursday
EXAM 2

Week 13: The Slave South

Tuesday
The Political Economy of the Old South
Readings: CAP, Chapter 13, "The Growing Distinctiveness of the South" through "Slaves and the Quarters"

RAP, Documents 12.1, 12.2, and 12.3

Thursday
On the Margins — Free Blacks and Poor Whites
Readings: CAP, Chapter 13, "Black and Free: On the Middle Ground" through "Conclusion"

RAP, Document 12.4

Week 14: The House Divided

Tuesday
Crisis and Compromise
Readings: CAP, Chapter 14, "Fruits of War" through "Realignment of the Party System"

RAP, Documents 13.1 and 13.2

Thursday
QUIZ 3
The Collapse of the Union
Readings: CAP, Chapter 14, "Freedom under Siege" through "Conclusion"

RAP, Documents 13.3 and 13.4
Paper on *Dred Scott* due
Documentary: *Africans in America*, **Episode 4, "Judgment Day — 1831–1865"**

Week 15: The Civil War

Tuesday
"And the War Came"
Readings: CAP, Chapter 15, "'And the War Came'" through "Union *and* Freedom"

RAP, Documents 14.1 and 14.2

Thursday
Union Victory
Readings: CAP, Chapter 15, "The South at War" through "Conclusion"

RAP, Documents 14.3 and 14.4

Week 16: Reconstruction

Tuesday
Wartime and Presidential Reconstruction
Readings: CAP, Chapter 16, "Wartime Reconstruction" through "Presidential Reconstruction"

RAP, Documents 15.1 and 15.2

Thursday
Congressional Reconstruction
Readings: CAP, Chapter 16, "Congressional Reconstruction" through "Conclusion"

RAP, Documents 15.3 and 15.4

Week 17: Final Exam

Sample Syllabus 2
American History to 1877
(Quarter)

Objectives

This course gives students an overview of the political, economic, social, and cultural history of America from ancient America through Reconstruction. Students will read a major textbook, selected primary documents, and two outside works. Through these readings, lectures, and class discussions, students will explore major themes in American history, such as colonization, the founding of a new nation, the forging of an American culture, the entrenchment of slavery, the coming of the Civil War, and the meaning of Reconstruction. Students will also examine the ways in which the marginalized and disaffected have struggled to ensure that America fulfills its promise.

Required Texts

Be sure that the following assigned texts are on sale in the campus bookstore.

James L. Roark, et al., *The American Promise*, Second Compact Edition, Vol. I (CAP)
Michael P. Johnson, *Reading the American Past*, Second Edition, Vol. I (RAP)

    Note: Please note that the chapter numbering in *The American Promise*, Second Compact Edition, is one ahead of the chapter numbering in *Reading the American Past*, Second Edition; for example, documents that relate to the content of Chapter 2 in *The American Promise*, Second Compact Edition, are found in Chapter 1 of *Reading the American Past*, Second Edition.

Edward Countryman, ed., *How Did American Slavery Begin?*
Harry L. Watson, *Andrew Jackson vs. Henry Clay: Democracy and Development in Antebellum America*

Grading

Grades are based on student performance on scheduled quizzes and exams, two short essays, and class participation.

Exams — 45% (15% each)
Quizzes — 15% (5% each)
Papers — 30% (15% each)
Class participation — 10%

Week 1: Introduction to Course and Ancient America

Wednesday
Introduction to Course

Friday
Ancient America
Readings: CAP, Chapter 1

    RAP, Prologue

Week 2: Exploration, Conquest, and Colonization

Monday
Europe in the Sixteenth Century
Readings: CAP, Chapter 2, "Europe in the Age of Exploration" through "A Surprising New World in the Western Atlantic"

    RAP, Documents 1.1 and 1.2

Wednesday
QUIZ 1
Conquest
Readings: CAP, Chapter 2, "Spanish Exploration and Conquest" through "Conclusion"

    RAP, Documents 1.3 and 1.4

Friday
Colonization in the Chesapeake
Readings: CAP, Chapter 3, "An English Colony on the Chesapeake" through "A Tobacco Society"

    RAP, Documents 2.1 and 2.2

Week 3: Colonization

Monday
Toward a Slave Labor System
Readings: CAP, Chapter 3, "The Evolution of Chesapeake Society" through "Conclusion"

    RAP, Documents 2.3 and 2.4
Paper on *How Did American Slavery Begin?* due

Wednesday
Puritan New England
Readings: CAP, Chapter 4, "Puritan Origins: The English Reformation" through "The Evolution of New England Society"

    RAP, Chapter 3

Friday
The Middle Colonies
Readings: CAP, Chapter 4, "The Founding of the Middle Colonies" through "Conclusion"

Week 4: Colonial America in the Eighteenth Century and Exam 1

Monday
New England and the Middle Colonies
Readings: CAP, Chapter 5, "A Growing Population and Expanding Economy" through "The Middle Colonies: Immigrants, Wheat, and Work"

RAP, Documents 4.1, 4.2, and 4.3

Wednesday
The Southern Colonies
Readings: CAP, Chapter 5, "The Southern Colonies: Land of Slavery" through "Conclusion"

RAP, Document 4.4

Friday
EXAM 1

Week 5: The Road to Independence

Monday
Imperial Crisis, I
Readings: CAP, Chapter 6, "The French and Indian War, 1754–1763" through "The Stamp Act Crisis, 1765"

RAP, Documents 5.1 and 5.2

Wednesday
Imperial Crisis, II
Readings: CAP, Chapter 6, "The Townshend Acts and Economic Retaliation, 1767–1770" through "Conclusion"

RAP, Documents 5.3 and 5.4

Friday
Revolution
Readings: CAP, Chapter 7

RAP, Chapter 6

Week 6: A New Republic: A New Nation

Monday
Confederation America

Readings: CAP, Chapter 8, "The Articles of Confederation" through "The Critical Period"

RAP, Documents 7.1 and 7.2

Wednesday
The Federal Constitution
Readings: CAP, Chapter 8, "The United States Constitution" through "Conclusion"

RAP, Documents 7.3 and 7.4

Friday
The Search for Stability
Readings: CAP, Chapter 9, "The Search for Stability" through "Hamilton's Economic Policies"

RAP, Documents 8.1 and 8.2

Week 7: Early National America

Monday
Conflict
Readings: CAP, Chapter 9, "Conflicts West, East, and South" through "Conclusion"

RAP, Documents 8.3 and 8.4

Wednesday
QUIZ 2
Jeffersonian America
Readings: CAP, Chapter 10, "Jefferson's Presidency" through "The War of 1812"

RAP, Chapter 9
Documentary: *Thomas Jefferson*

Friday
Madison and His Successors
Readings: CAP, Chapter 10, "Women's Status in the Early Republic" through "Conclusion"

Week 8: Jacksonian America and the Entrenchment of Slavery

Monday
Cultural Shifts
Readings: CAP, Chapter 11, "The Market Revolution" through "Cultural Shifts"

Wednesday
Jacksonian Democracy
Readings: CAP, Chapter 11, "Democracy and Religion" through "Conclusion"

RAP, Chapter 10
Paper on *Andrew Jackson v. Henry Clay* due

Friday
The Free North and West
Readings: CAP, Chapter 12

RAP, Chapter 11

Week 9: Exam 2 and the Slave South

Monday
EXAM 2

Wednesday
The Political Economy of the Old South
Readings: CAP, Chapter 13, "The Growing Distinctiveness of the South" through "Slaves and the Quarters"

RAP, Documents 12.1, 12.2, and 12.3

Friday
On the Margins — Free Blacks and Poor Whites
Readings: CAP, Chapter 13, "Black and Free: On the Middle Ground" through "Conclusion"

RAP, Document 12.4

Week 10: The Road to Disunion

Monday
The House Divided
Readings: CAP, Chapter 14, "Fruits of War" through "Realignment of the Party System"

RAP, Documents 13.1 and 13.2

Wednesday
QUIZ 3
Crisis
Readings: CAP, Chapter 14, "Freedom under Siege" through "Conclusion"

RAP, Documents 13.3 and 13.4

Friday
"And the War Came"
Readings: CAP, Chapter 15, "'And the War Came'" through "Union *and* Freedom"

RAP, Documents 14.1 and 14.2

Week 11: War and Reunion

Monday
Union Victory
Readings: CAP, Chapter 15, "The South at War" through "Conclusion"

RAP, Documents 14.3 and 14.4

Wednesday
Wartime and Presidential Reconstruction
Readings: CAP, Chapter 16, "Wartime Reconstruction" through "Presidential Reconstruction"

RAP, Documents 15.1 and 15.2

Friday
Congressional Reconstruction
Readings: CAP, Chapter 16, "Congressional Reconstruction" through "Conclusion"

RAP, Documents 15.3 and 15.4

Week 12: Final Exam

Sample Syllabus 3
American History, 1877
to the Present (Semester)

Objectives

This course gives students an overview of the political, economic, social, and cultural history of the United States from the end of Reconstruction to the present. Students will read a major textbook, selected primary documents, and three outside works. Through these readings, lectures, and class discussions, students will explore major themes in late-nineteenth- and twentieth-century American history, such as urbanization, industrialization, immigration, the expansion of the federal government, and the rise of the United States as a global power. Students will also examine the ways in which the marginalized and disaffected have struggled to ensure that America fulfills its promise.

Required Texts

Be sure that the following assigned texts are on sale in the campus bookstore.

James L. Roark, et al., *The American Promise,* Second Compact Edition, Vol. 2 (CAP)

Michael P. Johnson, *Reading the American Past,* Second Edition, Vol. 2 (RAP)

Note: Please note that the chapter numbering in *The American Promise,* Second Compact Edition, is one ahead of the chapter numbering in *Reading the American Past,* Second Edition; for example, documents that relate to the content of Chapter 18 in *The American Promise,* Second Compact Edition, are found in Chapter 17 of *Reading the American Past,* Second Edition.

Jacqueline Jones Royster, ed., *Southern Horrors and Other Writings: The Anti-Lynching Campaign of Ida B. Wells, 1892–1900*

Robert H. Abzug, ed., *America Views the Holocaust, 1933–1945*

Nancy A. Walker, ed., *Women's Magazines, 1940–1960: Gender Roles and the Popular Press.*

Grading

Grades are based on student performance on scheduled quizzes and exams, three short essays, and class participation.

Exams — 45% (15% each)
Quizzes — 15% (5% each)
Papers — 30% (10% each)
Class participation — 10%

Week 1: Post-Reconstruction America

Wednesday
Introduction to Course; the Promise of Reconstruction

Friday
The New South
Readings: CAP, Chapter 17, "The Changing Face of Rural America"

Week 2: America's New Frontiers

Monday
The New West
Readings: CAP, Chapter 17, "Western Land Fever"

RAP, Documents 16.2 and 16.3

Wednesday
A Clash of Cultures
Readings: CAP, Chapter 17, "The American West: A Clash of Cultures"

RAP, Document 16.1
Documentary: *The West,* **Episode 8, "The Ghost Dance"**

Friday
The Rise of the City
Readings: CAP, Chapter 17, "The Rise of the City" through "Conclusion"

RAP, Documents 16.4 and 16.5

Week 3: Immigration and Industrialization

Monday
Immigration
Documentary: *Journey to America*

Wednesday
A New Industrial Order, I
Readings: CAP, Chapter 18, "Old Industries Transformed, New Industries Born"

Friday
QUIZ 1
A New Industrial Order, II
Readings: CAP, Chapter 18, "From Competition to Consolidation"

RAP, Chapter 17

Week 4: Gilded Age Politics and America's Workers

Monday
Gilded Age Politics, I
Readings: CAP, Chapter 18, "Party Politics in an Age of Enterprise"

Wednesday
Gilded Age Politics, II
Readings: CAP, Chapter 18, "Economic Issues and Party Realignment" through "Conclusion"

Friday
Workers and Managers
Readings: CAP, Chapter 19, "America's New Industrial Workers" through "Managers and White Collars"

RAP, Chapter 18

Week 5: The Age of Discontent

Monday
The Labor Wars
Readings: CAP, Chapter 19, "At Home and at Play" through "Conclusion"; Chapter 20, "The Farmers' Revolt and the Labor Wars"

RAP, Documents 19.2 and 19.3

Wednesday
Growing Discontent: Women's Activism
Readings: CAP, Chapter 20, "Women's Activism"
Paper on *Southern Horrors* due

Friday
Growing Discontent: Militant Farmers
Readings: CAP, Chapter 20, "Depression Politics"

RAP, Document 19.1

Week 6: America at the Century's End and Exam 1

Monday
The Quest for Empire
Readings: CAP, Chapter 20, "The United States Looks Outward" through "War and Empire"

RAP, Document 19.4

Wednesday
EXAM 1

Friday
America and the New Century
Documentary: *America 1900*

Week 7: Progressivism

Monday
Progressive Reform, I
Readings: CAP, Chapter 21, "Grassroots Progressivism" through the start of "Progressivism Finds a President: Theodore Roosevelt"

RAP, Documents 20.1, 20.2, and 20.3

Wednesday
Progressive Reform, II
Readings: CAP, Chapter 21, the rest of "Progressivism Finds a President: Theodore Roosevelt"

Friday
Progressive Reform, III
Readings: CAP, Chapter 21, "Woodrow Wilson and Progressivism at High Tide" through "Conclusion"

RAP, Documents 20.4 and 20.5

Week 8: The Great War

Monday
World War I and the Limits of Neutrality
Readings: CAP, Chapter 22, "Woodrow Wilson and the World"

Wednesday
The Front Line and the Home Front
Readings: CAP, Chapter 22, "The Crusade for Democracy"

RAP, Chapter 21

Friday
Wilson's Postwar Vision
Readings: CAP, Chapter 22, "A Compromised Peace" through "Conclusion"

Week 9: America's Confrontation with Modernism

Monday
Normalcy

Readings: CAP, Chapter 23, "The New Era" and "Rural America and Resistance to Change"

Wednesday
The "New" Americans
Readings: CAP, Chapter 23, "Society and Its Discontents"

RAP, Documents 22.1 and 22.2

Friday
QUIZ 2
The Great Crash
Readings: CAP, Chapter 23, "From the New Era to the Great Crash" through "Conclusion"

RAP, Documents 22.3 and 22.4

Week 10: A New Deal for America

Monday
The First New Deal
Readings: CAP, Chapter 24, "Franklin D. Roosevelt: A Patrician in Government" through "The First New Deal in Action"

RAP, Document 23.1

Wednesday
Challenges to the First New Deal and the Rise of the Welfare State
Readings: CAP, Chapter 24 "Challenges to the New Deal" through "The Second New Deal and the Rise of the Welfare State"

RAP, Documents 23.2, 23.3, and 23.4

Friday
The End of the New Deal
Readings: CAP, Chapter 24, "The New Deal's Final Phase: From Victory to Deadlock" through "Conclusion"

Week 11: World War II

Monday
Interwar Diplomacy and the Coming of World War II
Readings: CAP, Chapter 25, "Peacetime Dilemmas" through "The Onset of War"

RAP, Documents 24.1 and 24.2
Documentary: *1919 — The Lost Peace*
Paper on *America Views the Holocaust* due

Wednesday
World War II: The Frontline

Readings: CAP, Chapter 25, "The Global Challenge," "Military Victory: 1943–1945," and "Conclusion"

Friday
World War II: The Home Front
Readings: CAP, Chapter 25, "The War at Home"

Week 12: Exam 2 and the Cold War

Monday
EXAM 2

Wednesday
Cold War and Containment
Readings: CAP, Chapter 26, "From the Grand Alliance to Containment"

RAP, Document 25.2

Friday
The Fair Deal
Readings: CAP, Chapter 26, "Truman and the Fair Deal at Home"

Week 13: The Cold War Heats Up

Monday
Korea
Readings: CAP, Chapter 26, "The Cold War Becomes Hot: Korea" through "Conclusion"

Wednesday
The Great Fear
Readings: RAP, Documents 25.3, 25.4
Video clips from *Invasion of the Body Snatchers* and *On the Waterfront*

Friday
The Hidden-Hand President
Readings: CAP, Chapter 27, "Eisenhower and the Politics of the 'Middle Way'"

Week 14: America and the 1950s

Monday
Containment to Liberation
Readings: CAP, Chapter 27, "Liberation Rhetoric and the Practice of Containment"

Wednesday
QUIZ 3
The Culture of Abundance
Readings: CAP, Chapter 27, "New Work and Living Patterns in an Economy of Abundance" through "The Culture of Abundance"

RAP, Documents 26.1 and 26.2

Friday
The Emergence of the Modern Civil Rights Movement
Readings: CAP, Chapter 27, "Emergence of a Civil Rights Movement"

RAP, Document 26.3

Week 15: Days of Hope, Days of Rage

Monday
JFK and LBJ
Readings: CAP, Chapter 28, "Kennedy and the New Frontier" through "Liberalism at High Tide: Johnson and the Great Society"

RAP, Document 27.1
Paper on *Women's Magazines, 1845–1960* due

Wednesday
The Civil Rights Movement, II
Readings: CAP, Chapter 28, "The Second Reconstruction"

RAP, Document 27.2

Friday
Power to the People
Readings: CAP, Chapter 28, "A Multitude of Movements" through "Conclusion"

RAP, Documents 27.3 and 27.4

Week 16: The Shattering of the Liberal Consensus

Monday
Vietnam, I
Readings: CAP, Chapter 29, "New Frontiers in Foreign Policy" through "Lyndon Johnson's War against Communism"

Wednesday
Vietnam, II
Readings: CAP, Chapter 29, "A Nation Polarized" through "Conclusion"

Friday
The Conservative Counterrevolution
Readings: CAP, Chapter 30, "Conservative Politics and Liberal Programs in the Nixon Administration" through "Constitutional Crisis and Restoration"

RAP, Document 29.2

Week 17: The Reagan Revolution and Final Exam

Monday
Reagan's Domestic Agenda
Readings: CAP, Chapter 30, "The Conservative Resurgence" through "Winners and Losers in a Flourishing Economy"

RAP, Documents 29.3 and 29.4

Wednesday
Foreign Policy in the 1980s
Readings: CAP, Chapter 31, "Ronald Reagan Confronts an 'Evil Empire'" through "Defining American Interests in a Post–Cold War World"

RAP, Document 30.3

Friday
FINAL EXAM

Sample Syllabus 4
American History, 1877
to the Present (Quarter)

Objectives

This course gives students an overview of the political, economic, social, and cultural history of the United States from the end of Reconstruction to the present. Students will read a major textbook, selected primary documents, and two outside works. Through these readings, lectures, and class discussions, students will explore major themes in late-nineteenth- and twentieth-century American history, such as urbanization, industrialization, immigration, the expansion of the federal government, and the rise of the United States as a global power. Students will also examine the ways in which the marginalized and disaffected have struggled to ensure that America fulfills its promise.

Required Texts

Be sure that the following assigned texts are on sale in the campus bookstore.

James L. Roark, et al., *The American Promise,* Second Compact Edition, Vol. 2 (CAP)
Michael P. Johnson, *Reading the American Past,* Second Edition, Vol. 2 (RAP)

> *Note:* Please note that the chapter numbering in *The American Promise,* Second Compact Edition, is one ahead of the chapter numbering in *Reading the American Past,* Second Edition; for example, documents that relate to the content of Chapter 18 in *The American Promise,* Second Compact Edition, are found in Chapter 17 of *Reading the American Past,* Second Edition.

David W. Blight and Robert Gooding Williams, eds., *The Souls of Black Folk* by W. E. B. Du Bois
Waldo E. Martin Jr., Brown v. Board of Education of Topeka: *A Brief History with Documents*

Grading

Grades are based on student performance on scheduled quizzes and exams, two short essays, and class participation.

Exams — 45% (15% each)
Quizzes — 15% (5% each)
Papers — 30% (15% each)
Class participation — 10%

Week 1: Introduction to Course and Post-Reconstruction America

Wednesday
Introduction to Course; Post-Reconstruction America

Friday
America's New Frontiers: The New South and the New West
Readings: CAP, Chapter 17, "Western Land Fever" through "The American West: A Clash of Cultures"

RAP, Documents 16.1, 16.2, and 16.3

Week 2: Urbanization, Immigration, and Industrialization

Monday
The Rise of the City
Readings: CAP, Chapter 17, "The Rise of the City" through "Conclusion"

Wednesday
Immigration
Documentary: *Journey to America*

Friday
The New Industrial Order
Readings: CAP, Chapter 18, "Old Industries Transformed, New Industries Born" through "From Competition to Consolidation"

RAP, Chapter 17

Week 3: Politics, Workers, and Growing Discontent

Monday
QUIZ 1
Gilded Age Politics
Readings: CAP, Chapter 18, "Party Politics in an Age of Enterprise" through "Conclusion"

Wednesday
America's Workers
Readings: CAP, Chapter 19

RAP, Chapter 18

Friday
The Turbulent Nineties
Readings: CAP, Chapter 20, "Women's Activism" through "Depression Politics"

RAP, Documents 19.1 and 19.2

Week 4: Exam 1 and America at Century's End

Monday
The Quest for Empire
Readings: CAP, Chapter 20, "The United States
Looks Outward" through "Conclusion"

RAP, Document 19.4

Wednesday
EXAM 1

Friday
America and the New Century
Documentary: *America 1900*

*Week 5: Progressive Reform
and the Coming of the War*

Monday
Progressivism, I
Readings: CAP, Chapter 21, "Grassroots Progressivism" through "Progressivism Finds
a President: Theodore Roosevelt"

RAP, Chapter 20

Wednesday
Progressivism, II
Readings: CAP, Chapter 21, "Woodrow Wilson
and Progressivism at High Tide"
through "Conclusion"
Film Clips: *Birth of a Nation*
Paper on *Souls of Black Folk* **due**

Friday
World War I and the Limits of Neutrality
Readings: CAP, Chapter 22, "Woodrow Wilson
and the World"

*Week 6: The Great War
and the Return of Normalcy*

Monday
World War I: The Home Front and the Front Line
Readings: CAP, Chapter 22, "The Crusade for
Democracy"

RAP, Chapter 21

Wednesday
A Compromised Peace and the Return to Normalcy
Readings: CAP, Chapter 22, "A Compromised
Peace" through "Conclusion"; Chapter
23, "The New Era" and "Rural America
and Resistance to Change"

RAP, Documents 22.1 and 22.2

Friday
QUIZ 2
The Roaring Twenties
Readings: CAP, Chapter 23, "Society and Its Dis-
contents"
Documentary: *I'll Make Me a World*, **Episode 1**

Week 7: Depression-Era America

Monday
Crash
Readings: CAP, Chapter 23, "From the New Era to
the Great Crash" through "Conclusion"

RAP, Documents 22.3 and 22.4

Wednesday
The First New Deal and Its Critics
Readings: CAP, Chapter 24, "Franklin D. Roo-
sevelt: A Patrician in Government"
through "Challenges to the New
Deal"

RAP, Chapter 23

Friday
The Rise of the Welfare State and the End of the
New Deal
Readings: CAP, Chapter 24, "The Second New
Deal and the Rise of the Welfare State"
through "Conclusion"

*Week 8: World War II to
Containment and Exam 2*

Monday
World War II
Readings: CAP, Chapter 25, "Peacetime Dilem-
mas" through "The Global Challenge"

RAP, Chapter 24

Wednesday
Victory to Containment
Readings: CAP, Chapter 25, "The War at Home"
through "Conclusion"; Chapter 26,
"From the Grand Alliance to Contain-
ment"

Friday
EXAM 2

*Week 9: The Cold War and
the Culture of Abundance*

Monday
Truman

Readings: CAP, Chapter 26,"Truman and the Fair Deal at Home" through "Conclusion"

RAP, Chapter 25

Wednesday
Eisenhower
Readings: CAP, Chapter 27, "Eisenhower and the Politics of the 'Middle Way,'" through "Liberation Rhetoric and the Practice of Containment"

RAP, Document 26.4

Friday
The Culture of Abundance
Readings: CAP, Chapter 27, "New Work and Living Patterns in an Economy of Abundance" through "Conclusion"

RAP, Documents 26.1, 26.2, and 26.3
Documentary: *Eyes on the Prize*, **Episode 1, "Beginnings"**
Paper on *Brown v. Board of Education* **due**

Week 10: Days of Hope, Years of Rage

Monday
QUIZ 3
The Liberal Consensus
Readings: CAP, Chapter 28, "Kennedy and the New Frontier" through "The Second Reconstruction"

RAP, Documents 27.1 and 27.2

Wednesday
The Shattering of the Liberal Consensus
Readings: CAP, Chapter 28, "A Multitude of Movements" through "Conclusion"

RAP, Documents 27.3 and 27.4

Friday
Vietnam, I
Readings: CAP, Chapter 29, "New Frontiers in Foreign Policy" through "Lyndon Johnson's War against Communism"

Week 11: Vietnam and the Conservative Counterrevolution

Monday
Vietnam, II
Readings: CAP, Chapter 29, "A Nation Polarized" through "Conclusion"

RAP, Chapter 28
Documentary: *Vietnam: A Television War*, **Episode 11**

Wednesday
Nixon
Readings: CAP, Chapter 30, "Conservative Politics and Liberal Programs in the Nixon Administration" through "Constitutional Crisis and Restoration"

RAP, Document 29.2

Friday
The Conservative Counterrevolution
Readings: CAP, Chapter 30, "The Conservative Resurgence" through "Winners and Losers in a Flourishing Economy"; Chapter 31, "Ronald Reagan Confronts an 'Evil Empire'" to "Defining American Interests in a Post–Cold War World"

RAP, Documents 29.3 and 29.4, 30.1 and 30.3

Week 12: Final Exam

Sample Syllabus 5
American History, 1492 to
the Present (One-Semester Course)

Objectives

This course gives students an overview of the political, economic, social, and cultural history of America from the age of European exploration and conquest to the present. Students will read a major textbook, selected primary documents, and three outside works. Through these readings, lectures, and class discussions, students will explore major themes in American history, such as colonization, the founding of a new nation, the forging of an American culture, warfare, the expansion of the nation-state, and the rise of the United States as a global power. Students will also examine the ways in which the marginalized and disaffected have struggled to ensure that America fulfills its promise.

Required Texts

Be sure that the following assigned texts are on sale in the campus bookstore.

James L. Roark, et al., *The American Promise*, Second Compact Edition, Vols. I–II (CAP)
Michael P. Johnson, *Reading the American Past*, Second Edition, Vols. I–II (RAP)

Note: Please note that the chapter numbering in *The American Promise*, Second Compact Edition, is one ahead of the chapter numbering in *Reading the American Past*, Second Edition; for example, documents that relate to the content of Chapter 2 in *The American Promise*, Second Compact Edition, are found in Chapter 1 of *Reading the American Past*, Second Edition.

Jack N. Rakove, *Declaring Rights: A Brief History with Documents*
Terrence J. McDonald, ed., *Plunkitt of Tammany Hall, by William L. Riordon*
James S. Olson and Randy Roberts, *My Lai: A Documentary History*

Grading

Grades are based on student performance on scheduled quizzes and exams, two short essays, and class participation.

Exams — 45% (15% each)
Quizzes — 15% (5% each)
Papers — 30% (15% each)
Class participation — 10%

Week 1: Introduction to Course and European Exploration of America

Tuesday
Introduction to Course

Thursday
European Exploration of America
Readings: CAP, Chapter 2
RAP, Chapter 1

Week 2: American Colonies in the Seventeenth Century

Tuesday
Southern Colonies in the Seventeenth Century
Readings: CAP, Chapter 3
RAP, Chapter 2

Thursday
Northern Colonies in the Seventeenth Century
Readings: CAP, Chapter 4
RAP, Chapter 3

Week 3: Eighteenth-Century America

Tuesday
The Dual Identity of British North America
Readings: CAP, Chapter 5
RAP, Chapter 4

Thursday
QUIZ 1
The Colonial Crisis
Readings: CAP, Chapter 6
RAP, Chapter 5

Week 4: Independence

Tuesday
The Revolution
Readings: CAP, Chapter 7
RAP, Chapter 6

Thursday
A New Republic
Readings: CAP, Chapter 8
RAP, Chapter 7

Week 5: Early Nationalism

Tuesday
The New Nation Take Form

Readings: CAP, Chapter 9

RAP, Chapter 8

Paper on *Declaring Rights* due

Thursday
Republican Ascendancy
Readings: CAP, Chapter 10

RAP, Chapter 9

Week 6: Exam 1 and
the Rise of Jacksonian Democracy

Tuesday
EXAM 1

Thursday
The Rise of Jacksonian Democracy
Readings: CAP, Chapter 11

RAP, Chapter 10

Week 7: "Freedom" in Antebellum America

Tuesday
The Free North and West, 1840–1860
Readings: CAP, Chapter 12

RAP, Chapter 11

Thursday
The Slave South, 1820–1860
Readings: CAP, Chapter 13

RAP, Chapter 12

Week 8: The Road to Disunion

Tuesday
The House Divided
Readings: CAP, Chapter 14

RAP, Chapter 13

Thursday
The Civil War
Readings: CAP, Chapter 15

RAP, Chapter 14

Week 9: America after the War

Tuesday
QUIZ 2
Reconstruction
Readings: CAP, Chapter 16

RAP, Chapter 15

Thursday
America on the Move
Readings: CAP, Chapter 17

RAP, Chapter 16

Week 10: Business, Labor,
and Politics in the Gilded Age

Tuesday
The Gilded Age
Readings: CAP, Chapter 18

RAP, Chapter 17

Paper on *Plunkitt of Tammany Hall* due

Thursday
America's Workers
Readings: CAP, Chapter 19

RAP, Chapter 18

Week 11: America and the Dawn
of a New Century

Tuesday
The Turbulent Nineties
Readings: CAP, Chapter 20

RAP, Chapter 19

Thursday
The Progressive Era
Readings: CAP, Chapter 21

RAP, Chapter 20

Week 12: Exam 2 and World War I

Tuesday
EXAM 2

Thursday
World War I
Readings: CAP, Chapter 22

RAP, Chapter 21

Week 13: From Prosperity to the Depression

Tuesday
The New Era
Readings: CAP, Chapter 23

RAP, Chapter 22

Thursday
The Great Depression
Readings: CAP, Chapter 24

RAP, Chapter 23

Week 14: World War II and Cold War America

Tuesday
World War II
Readings: CAP, Chapter 25

RAP, Chapter 24

Thursday
QUIZ 3
Cold War Politics in the Truman Years
Readings: CAP, Chapter 26

RAP, Chapter 25

Week 15: Conformity and Rebellion

Tuesday
The Politics and Culture of Abundance
Readings: CAP, Chapter 27

RAP, Chapter 26

Thursday
Rebellion and Reform
Readings: CAP, Chapter 28

RAP, Chapter 27

*Week 16: Vietnam and
the Conservative Counterrevolution*

Tuesday
Vietnam
Readings: CAP, Chapter 29

RAP, Chapter 28
Paper on *My Lai* due

Thursday
The Conservative Counterrevolution
Readings: CAP, Chapter 30

RAP, Chapter 29

Week 17: Final Exam